4.50

W9-BXX-923

Love and War

For those who went
and those who waited

ALSO BY ROBERT EASTON

The Happy Man (New York, 1943)
Lord of Beasts: The Saga of Buffalo Jones, with Mackenzie Brown
  (Tucson, 1961)
The Book of the American West, with Jay Monaghan and others (New
  York, 1963)
The Hearing (Santa Barbara, 1964)
California Condor, with Dick Smith (Santa Barbara, 1964)
Max Brand's Best Stories, ed. (New York, 1967)
Bullying the Moqui, ed., with Mackenzie Brown (Prescott, 1968)
Max Brand (Norman, 1970)
Black Tide: The Santa Barbara Oil Spill and Its Consequences (New
  York, 1972)
Guns, Gold and Caravans (Santa Barbara, 1978)
China Caravans (Santa Barbara, 1982)
This Promised Land (Santa Barbara, 1982)
Life and Work, with David Russell (Santa Barbara, 1988)
Power and Glory (Santa Barbara, 1989)

ALSO BY JANE EASTON

*Memories of the '20s and '30s: Growing Up in Florence, New York and
  Los Angeles* (privately printed, 1979)

Love and War

Pearl Harbor
Through V-J Day

by

Robert and Jane Easton

UNIVERSITY OF OKLAHOMA PRESS : NORMAN AND LONDON

Unless otherwise indicated, all photographs are from the collection of Robert and Jane Easton.

Library of Congress Cataloging-in-Publication Data

Easton, Robert Olney.
  Love and war : Pearl Harbor through V-J Day / by Robert and Jane Easton.
    p.cm.
    Includes index.
    ISBN 0-8061-2336-2 (alk. paper)
    1. Easton, Robert Olney—Correspondence. 2. Easton, Jane Faust—Correspondence. 3. World War, 1939–1945—Campaigns—Western. 4. World War, 1939–1945—United States. 5. World War, 1939–1945—Personal narratives, American. 6. Soldiers—United States—Correspondence. 7. United States. Army—Biography. 8. Wives—United States—Correspondence. I. Easton, Jane Faust. II. Title.
    D756.E27A4   1991
    940.54'8173—dc20   90-50686
                                                                        CIP

The paper in this book meets the guidelines for permanence and durability of the Committee on Production Guidelines for Book Longevity of the Council on Library Resources, Inc. ⊚

Contents

Illustrations

Authors to Reader

It's 1983 and we're having lunch with our friend and agent Sandra Dijkstra. "What are you doing these days?" she casually asks Jane.

"Typing our war letters for our children and grandchildren to read."

"Why just your children and grandchildren?" Sandy suggests.

Having lived through World War II separated much of the time by an ocean and a continent, we'd written each other nearly every day. We thought, then and later, of Bob doing a war book, perhaps a novel, perhaps nonfiction, but time and proper format never came together. Now they did.

We'd saved our letters because they meant so much to us when they were written, Jane thinking those she received might be especially precious as last words if she were left a widow and the children fatherless, Bob saving hers as bits of cherished sanity and light in surroundings at times rather dark and mad; and eventually both of us wanting our children to know something about us and the world we lived in when we were young.

What follows, therefore, is a kind of dialog between a young wife and young husband from home front and war front. We've edited the letters slightly for clarity and continuity and to protect other people's privacy. Interspersed here and there are interpolations and footnotes in our today's voice which may help readers understand more fully what was happening in our life and the nation's and the world's as the war progressed.

Love and War

Pearl Harbor Through V-J Day

CHAPTER 1

The Lord is a man of war.
EXODUS, 15:3

Combat

317 BURLINGAME AVE., LOS ANGELES, CALIF., JAN. 31, 1945
The Russians are 70 miles from Berlin. I suppose the Germans will go on fighting after Berlin is taken, but it's a big prize for the Russians. Or will we take it? No mention of your 9th Army in action. Only the 1st and 3rd but I am *sure* you are in it.

Nobody dares be optimistic but the news IS good. Mum talked to Richard Aldington on the phone and he said at least three years more for Japan.

Great burly moving-men came today to dismount the radio-gramophone and take it, along with several other massive things, to Santa Barbara, to our own home at last, yours and mine and our children's, while Mum stays here a few days to close this house. It's strange to be moving again. Seven years ago the move from the villa was very strange and very awful to me. I can well remember those September days of 1938—war in the air, unrest, disaster, seemed to blow in with all the autumn smells and the fireflies even. I was so miserable and lonely at leaving Tuscany that I cared very little *what* the future brought. I'd just broken off with Franz D., and the Italian doctor had pestered me all summer and I was so confused about life that I wandered around the villa getting solace from touching the familiar furniture and the stone walls.

And it was unbearable to say goodbye to old Berti the gardener, aged 84, who had been with us 12 years! The whole agony is so vivid to me! It was a strange despair such as I'd never known in all my life; for, coupled with everything else, I knew about Pop's unfaithfulness to Mum. Suddenly, at 20, I felt as if the life I had loved and the future I had dreamed of, were all impossible, were not the truth, that after all there WAS no such thing as love that lasted. So I used to go and sit in those summer afternoons in the square where the ice cream shop was, at the bottom of our hill at the outskirts of Florence, and derive much pleasure from talking to Giuseppe the waiter and the Paccianis who owned it. I wanted to talk to people about *their* problems and their pasts and their futures, and I wanted none of mine. But that summer is the most vivid of all my life. Why is it sorrow makes such lasting impression?

GERMANY [SCHLEIDEN], 19 FEB. 1945
I write by candlelight from a brick cellar, sumptuously furnished with one rickety wood table and two rickety wood chairs. Tech. Sgt. Branham sits beyond the candle finishing a "sugar report" to the girl he hopes to go home and marry next month—he's next on the rotation plan, after 28 months overseas—and some of our boys are relaxing on their new G.I. sleeping bags on the dirt floor, while singing "Home on the Range," "Birmingham Jail" and other good old American ballads. The center of this domestic scene is our cherished possession, our stove, amply fueled by coal which is plentiful hereabouts, so that we stay cozy and warm despite snow and ice outside—which are beginning to melt at last, I'm happy to report.

Two new recruits today, Texans, a Spanish boy named Machado and a boy from Lubbock named Brinegar, red haired, Scottish, both volunteers from noncombatant 12th Army Group Headquarters at Luxembourg. "Tired of going to Brussels and Paris every weekend!"

When Branham hears this he walks over and beats on the wall comically with both fists, shouting: "Make mine vanilla! You guys stop at the medical detachment and have your heads examined? Volunteers for the infantry! My God!" Their situation was enough like mine to make me sympathize thoroughly.

Now the oldtimers, veterans of D-Day, are discussing things you never hear at home: the superiority of Jerry's weapons—his tanks, his machine pistol or "burp gun,"[1] his flares which I've seen at night light up a landscape bright as day while ours flicker dismally as some old gas lamp, his smokeless powder which doesn't reveal his whereabouts while ours gives us away time and again. In fact you realize it's the overwhelming *quantity* of our material which makes the difference; and if Jerry were here with his whole army instead of facing Russia with most of it, we might be fighting till our hair is gray. They also talk of Jerry's combat methods, none of them very pretty.

"Ever have a woman snipe at you?" I ask.

1. The Schmeisser MP-40 submachine gun.

"Back in France we did. She'd bothered us all day. Hidden up a tree. Of course we didn't know she was a woman. Finally old Whitey he says: 'I'm gonna get that son-of-a-bitch.' Patient, Whitey was. He'd wait all afternoon just to get one shot. While she keeps pecking away, not hitting anybody but coming close, he slips off down a hedgerow. He was near St. Lô then. After a couple of hours we hear an M-1 crack. Just one shot. She's laying there under her tree shot clean as a whistle between the eyes. She'd had on one of them soft gray caps snipers wear and it'd fallen off and showed her long yellow hair."

"French or German?"

"Never found out. We was moving on."

Taking a dare I just did 25 push-ups from my fingertips and therefore don't have to lick any envelopes for a week. You would appreciate the full value of this if you saw the pile of letters the boys contribute to my table nightly and knew how flat the task (and the taste) after the first 30 I read and seal!

Reading and censoring I find no cynicism. These are very unsophisticated people, Janie. No other college graduate beside myself in the entire company, including officers. To these fellows, college graduates are rich men's sons in rear area jobs or the Air Force. Some of their fathers are rumored to be in Berlin having champagne and cigars with the German generals, while deciding which day to bring the war to an end. The rich are mistrusted. The unsophisticated may be naive, yes. But they're seldom cynical. Profoundly and naturally they affirm the goodness of daily life.

Speaking of which, Demasse has prepared our evening's snack of pancakes and canned butter and coffee and I must show my appreciation. We are not in any particular danger at the moment so don't worry.

Enclosed is a first spring bud, perhaps a willow, I do not know. It's a month or so early. Every year we've been apart I've sent a bit of spring and here is the one from Germany. Next spring I hope to deliver it in person.

This is the lull before the storm. Hitler's surprise offensive, known later as the Battle of the Bulge, has pushed deep into Belgium and been pushed back. Now there is quiet along the Western Front while the Allies prepare their counteroffensive. Everyone knows it's coming. Up on the line with K Company of the 116th Infantry Regiment, 29th Division, the chief question I hear is: "When do we jump off?"

For me and my platoon, H-hour is 0300 of a February morning. The ice and snow have mostly melted but it's still very cold. Wearing green woolen mittens and hip-length green field jackets, brown wool caps under steel helmets, heavy packs on our backs, canteens and entrenching tools at our belts, combat boots, rifles slung over shoulders, we form up silently in the road outside the shell-smashed house with the warm cellar.

Our objective is the enemy's strongpoint of Jülich across the Roer River in the lower Rhineland. It consists of an ancient citadel, once considered impregnable, surrounded by a town, with modern fortifications and minefields along the outskirts facing the river and the Americans.

There is a general tendency toward prayer and loose bowels as we move out into the darkness.

For the women waiting at home, the suspense of not knowing is simply something to be borne, as it has been so often before, day after day, night after night.

———————

317 BURLINGAME AVE., LOS ANGELES, CALIF., FEB. 24, 1945
I began breakfast this morning and then opened the paper and read the thundering headlines about the big push of the 9th Army across the Roer River. I confess that I simply lost my appetite and had a bad time while I read about the whole thing.

I can't quite tell you how I feel, knowing that you are in constant danger. My deepest emotions are in my stomach, evidently, for I immediately became a little nauseated and am still trembly.

Anyway, it's all rather unsettling and I have a sensation of being suspended in midair. I can't describe it. It's a form of war nerves, I guess, which I usually manage to control. When I feel anxious about you, more than usual, I immediately think it may mean you are hurt or wanting me to help you or calling for me or something like that. I then begin to think I'm getting brain waves etc. So you see what an emotional twist one sustains staying at home waiting and waiting and hoping and hoping and doing a good deal of fearing also. I am pretty even-keeled, as a rule, but don't worry, I'm not as phlegmatic as I pretend to be.

The description of the crossing of the Roer, the names of the German towns, the planes overhead, the weather, the clear moonlight which we've had here too—it's all like reading about something immersed in water, or the way life looks from a hospital. Next instant it becomes more real to me than my life here. I can *feel* you in your combat suit and see your face and your scowl and your smile and see your nose and mouth and your flat ears and your short hair. Oh, how I love you darling! But love cannot hold you back from war or danger. I *know* that, but I want to protect you. It's no good. The whole thing is completely unununderstandable and I am as lost as a child, just for this morning, just for this day, this moment. It's ten-fifteen a.m. I will go down now and cook some lunch for the children, and think of you and wonder how tired you are or how cold or how lonely or how busy and whether your feet are all right or not. I shall soon be back to my normal plodding self. Why should I feel so uneasy today? And it will be weeks before I know if you are alive. You are in the big show at last. That is your satisfaction and mine too, and you are with men you admire and like. I cannot stand to think of your seeing them hurt or killed. Does this make you feel that death is after all not the end? I am beginning to believe in something beyond death. I cling to it always.

Goodbye for now, for today. Forgive this hysterical note. Deep down I am all right, I'm convinced and I am strong. This passing moment somehow had to be written to you, exactly *why*, I don't know. I am meant to be ironing and cooking and doing a million things, but I do nothing but sit and wait and watch and listen as if some great announcement were to be made to me suddenly, from the sky. Be good, be a little careful, for there are three girls here waiting with all their hearts for your return.

SOMEWHERE IN GERMANY, 3 MARCH 1945

Let me tell about Jülich. You will have read what a platoon of war correspondents said, so I may be permitted a few words. It is named for Julius Caesar. *Castrum Juliacum* was its original label. His legions had a camp there on high ground commanding the river crossing on the main road over the Cologne plain from the Rhine to Holland and the North Sea. They fortified it about 2,000 years ago. Others have added to its defenses. Some three hundred years ago a massive citadel was built at the heart of it

with walls 100 feet thick of stone and earth and more than 100
feet high, overlooking a moat which is now dry. Surrounding the
citadel is a town and, in our direction overlooking the river, are
recent barbed wire, concrete pillboxes, minefields, etc.

We jumped off before dawn. We were lucky. We had two
regiments ahead of us, the 115th and 175th (a division has three
regiments). We, the 116th, were in support. And we were in
support this time because last time this regiment was spearheading
and did most of the bleeding and dying. So it goes. Turnabout.
Fair play.

We moved up through darkness single file on either side of
a road lined with bare trees that ran straight toward the enemy,
straight toward the end of the world, it seemed, straight toward
Jülich.

The whole thing is a sinking feeling at the pit of the stomach
and a numbness in the brain that protectively shuts out all ines-
sentials, and leaves only reactions related to surviving the next
step.

It is called the "soldier's fear," an all-pervading nausea perhaps resembling the morning sickness of a pregnant woman; and
maybe there is some relation between a man experiencing battle
and a woman childbirth.

I think of those who went first, bore the brunt, in our sector
here and in retrospect backward throughout the war—the D-Day
boys; before them the first commandos raiding the European
coasts; and the first green recruits coming up against Rommel's
veterans in North Africa and paying with their lives for their
inexperience—and on and on back to the Pearl Harbor people;
the first Poles and Danes and Norwegians who resisted; the first
Austrians; Czechs; Jews; Chinese. Somebody always took the first
step against the enemy, bore the brunt, paid up in advance for
the safety, however temporary, of all of us who follow.

I feel it very much here, coming late, as I do, to the combat
infantry—the spearheaders now, Janie. You can never know,
perhaps until I sit down and tell you some peaceful day in careful
detail, how much hinges on them.

Incongruously we passed huge guns dug in and hidden under
camouflage nets at either side of the road, blasting away behind
their embankments—so that we could keep moving up without
protection of any kind. Similarly with the tanks waiting like huge
monsters with their motors purring—to support us as we kept

moving up. And similarly too with truck after truck loaded with bridging equipment and other such stuff to keep us moving up. We felt mighty damn naked and alone, let me tell you, the only actors on the stage with all those props waiting in the wings!

I saw other incongruities: a broken-down baby carriage with one wheel missing, a bird sitting on the ground instead of in a tree, expressing the weirdness, the out-of-jointness of that moment. Well, but we were lucky.

As dawn broke ahead—we were marching straight into it— we could see what looked like a dense white fog obscuring the river and Jülich beyond. It was our smoke pots. Our chemical people were smoking the river. Looked great. Made us feel good, as our thunderous artillery barrage did. But, turned out later, the smoke blew back onto our side and blinded people and made them nauseated. And that was only the beginning of the foul-up. Some of our assault boats capsized while crossing the river, dumping guys into the water, or were carried downstream by the current into enemy hands, or were smashed by shellfire and sank or got snagged on underwater barbed wire—and men drowned in the icy water or were shot to death there like ducks.

Some of the Alligators[2] supposed to carry us over never even got to the water because of a minefield. And the combat engineers—who ever hears about them? the guys who go first of all in a situation like this and build the bridges?—came under fire and got wiped out; or, when they did get their pontoon bridge built, it was cut by a mortar shell. And so on and so forth. But somehow the guys got across—the guys, the people, Janie, the combat infantry, the guys who bear the brunt—somehow scrambled and fought and swam and swore and bitched and prayed their way across the river into the town. It was like a miniature D-Day landing. The living came ashore upon the bodies of the dead.

We crossed single file at a run over bodies that lay on the bridge (it had been repaired and was in place at last) hurrying so a shell or bullet wouldn't find us, and deployed into the town. They had left the citadel for us to deal with—the others had. We skirmished up toward its walls, block to block, house to house, often taking cover on our bellies in the gutters below the six-inch-high curbs. Amazing how flat you can make yourself when

2. Amphibian tractors or L.V.T.'s (landing vehicles, tracked).

you have to! Even so a bullet went through my haversack leaving a neat little hole rimmed with gray lead.

We spent that night in a musty cellar close under the citadel's walls. Jerry had slept in it the night before, leaving his distinctive body odor, unpleasantly sour, and we were constantly on the alert lest he counterattack. All night long we listened to our bulldozers clearing rubble and strained to hear the sound of our tanks crossing the vehicles pontoon-bridge that they began to build at dark. What an infantryman dreads is being at the mercy of enemy tanks.

In the morning a plane came over and bombed us and the bridges. It was one of the new "jets" which fly rings around our planes.[3] A swarm of P-47s was giving us air cover but it went through them as though they were standing still. In a doorway not far from ours a dead SS[4] captain lay on his back in a ruin of bricks and dust, his face that strange waxy pallor of death, a potato masher grenade near his outstretched right hand. He had chosen to die in Jülich and held up our boys an hour or more, until they finally set his building on fire and killed him in the doorway as he came out fighting.

Early in the afternoon we stormed the citadel. But first a gutsy youngster volunteered to run under fire across the earthen causeway that spans the moat and lay a satchel charge against the huge double doors of the fortress. Can you imagine the nerve it took? We held our breath as he darted across, laid the charge against the doors, darted back, while our flamethrowing tanks seared the battlements above him with tongues of fire to give him cover and bullets—ours and Jerry's—whizzed everywhere. Then came a tremendous explosion. The doors caved in. The tanks gave them a few rounds for good measure, and we charged across the causeway, yelling at the tops of our lungs with excitement (and fright), and charged through a dark smoke-and-dust-filled passageway, expecting to meet Jerry hand-to-hand, but instead emerged into the bright daylight of a huge courtyard and met no one.

He'd slipped away through corridors in the thick walls, and

---

3. The Messerschmitt Me-262, the world's first jet-propelled combat plane, could fly 540 miles per hour and had just become operational.
4. Literally "Schutzstaffel" or Protection Detachment—elite Nazi troops.

Crossing the Roer. (Photo by George Silk. Life Magazine, © Time Warner, Inc.)

secret tunnels that emerged into distant fields, leaving only a few dead bodies. Three of them lay around a machine gun on a parapet overlooking the town, from where they'd been firing on us. It is strange, eerie, how commonplace, how matter-of-fact death becomes, when you are in the business of dealing in it. In peacetime the sight of dead bodies would horrify and dismay you. Here they become just part of the debris. You feel a moment's pang, a moment's pity mixed with hate, then a feeling of relief and gratitude, and even black humor, that it is not you.

That's all I can write for now. If this gets by the censor,[5] it will give some idea of what's actually happening. I might as well tell it to you frankly as have you see it garbled in news dispatches or, worse, imagine it all out of proportion and context. We are lucky. We are well. That's the main thing. Just keep holding to that, will you? Plus my love?

34 E. PADRE ST., SANTA BARBARA, SUNDAY EVENING,
MARCH 5, 1945

I dare not listen to the radio much, though your division is mentioned countless times. It gets me fidgety and I don't feel there is any way I can help by being anxious. So I plod along but every breath I draw is a breath for you too.

I like being in this house because I imagine you as you were when we stayed in it for a few brief days during your last leave, and I think ahead to the time in a "year or two" (as you put it) when we will be here again together.

In this dream I see you in every room and hear your heavy tread going out to the icebox for a bottle of beer, and I hear the children calling you, while our lunch is cooking in the kitchen and the sun is shining on the terrace and there is music. I think of you at every turn. Your spirit seems close.

Kaffie celebrated this Sabbath by waking at 4 a.m. and so my night was a little short, though I finally got her back to sleep at five and then she woke at six-thirty. However, I don't mind much. I put in a good morning of scrubbing and cleaning and feeding the children and dressing them for Sunday lunch at your parents'. You must have known we were thinking of you very hard when the four of us sat down at the table in the library by the fire, Joan eating nicely and copiously for a change. And Katherine standing up, her head not yet reaching the tabletop, and begging for food like a puppy (I feed her at home first always) and we ate and ate and your father was in heaven because his beloved Tchaikowsky's Fifth was on from New York, and we all sat around and listened and talked and watched the storm brewing on the mountains and the rain coming in patches. The cloud effects were lovely and restless and unsettling and made one want

---

5. Officers were expected to self-censor their letters but higher authority made random checks.

to dash out in search of something. The human soul is never tired of searching, or when it is, it dies, or *should* die.

Your father said grace before lunch and an extra bit about "guide the footsteps of our two boys on the battlefields." I wanted to cry, not because I worry too much, darling, about a husband and a brother, but because of all the accumulated misery which living apart seems suddenly to bring to one's heart in moments like that. I got my eyes dry quickly, however, and we progressed and talked of other things.

Then we heard Cedric Foster give the news in great detail and your division mentioned again. We hear you will not be kept

Jane takes the girls for a buggy ride in front of our house at 34 East Padre Street, Santa Barbara.

up on the front line more than a week or ten days at most and then you get back for 24 hours rest and sleep and perhaps a bath. I suppose there will not be many letters from you now with all this going on and you may not have time to read all these I scribble off each evening propped up in my lonely bed.

GERMANY, 5 MARCH 1945

People who woke this morning with German soldiers in town are sleeping tonight with American soldiers in town. They've quickly learned to make white flags or hang bedsheets from windows and be very subdued—or else over-eager to please us with shelter from the weather in a warm room, plus a cup of coffee, black bread and butter and wine. They laugh excitedly and tell about the "Deutscher soldaten" running away dressed like civilians.

It is difficult to say whether their excitement and gaiety is pleasure at seeing us or relief at not having their houses knocked down and themselves killed, or a combination of both.

The children stare, smile, wave—some of them—and I wonder if they won't always remember the straggly, wet and dirty columns of G.I.'s that passed lightheartedly through the streets of town, some carrying rifles muzzle down, some muzzle up, some wearing this garment, some that, all braced against come-what-may by the old American carefree and don't-give-a-damn.

I wonder what the children will be thinking when they grow up and how long the ruined towns will remain ruined or what our American feet in the rich soil of this Rhine valley mean—slogging, slogging, occupying, bringing the indescribable feeling of home and place with us to a cellar for a few dark hours, and then out again into the attack, the occupation, the slogging on, and again the attack.

After dinner and mail and packages from home we are resting in an upstairs kitchen of a prosperous duplex in a new subdivision at the outskirts of a city, Keating, Labonitch, Demasse, Olander—and Tardo and Sylvester, our bazooka team. We've taken over the premises. They belong to us by right of conquest. It gives you a strange feeling, Janie, rather wild and brutal. We've covered some muddy miles these last days and had our share of combat, shared also whatever comfort and discomfort happened and, at night, even the warmth of our bodies side by side against the cold, for an infantryman does not carry many bedclothes.

We've had good luck, few casualties. Morale is high. We've taken our share of objectives, and I tell you with all my heart this is why we made our commitment, you and I, and I would be nowhere else.

So we push Jerry hard and the sky is full of the beginning of spring, blue, with a bit of hail on a rainy day, over the bottomless black fields where the winter wheat is already an inch of green. It is appalling and magnificent and absurd. You cannot believe in destruction and death, even after it happens—as though tanks and artillery and rifles and airplanes were dangerous toys, with which children are playing and suddenly get hurt.

Yet combat purifies and elevates. It unclogs the perceptions, raises life to where it should be, absolutely first and foremost, and you suddenly see it clearly as never before.

Keating—platoon sergeant now Branham has gone—is pounding out a letter to his wife on a Jerry typewriter. My next may be done likewise.

I wish you were here. You would relish and never be done taking in these days. I'll never consider you just a housewife, Prusse, ever. Beyond that is your integral self, robustly meeting and appreciating everything that happens. Maybe someday American women will be in combat as they are now in Russia and elsewhere. Like to volunteer?

Lying low under fire. (National Archives)

I could say a million things but am weary tonight as only an infantryman can be and will roll into my blanket and be thinking of my love for you as I go to sleep.

34 E. PADRE ST., SANTA BARBARA, MARCH 6, 1945
We hear the Rhine plain swarms with masses of Americans and British. One can only hope and pray that by the end of summer Germany will be done. One simply accepts the business as a bitter burden which MUST eventually end but no one should be fool enough to guess when, after all our disappointments. I sometimes wake at night with the awful dream that you have been switched to the South Pacific and I haven't even been allowed to see you en route!

When you are here I shall NEVER want anyone to drop in on me, but until then nothing ruffles me. Also, your parents are feeling the anxiety that we all have over this big drive on the western front, and so it's a comfort for us to be together. We never mention your danger but it's present in each one of us every minute of the day.

Your mother dropped in this morning and again this evening and spent time reading to the children. When she left at six they both began to cry and I must say they looked very sweet and sad! They always cry at once because there is something contagious about self-pity.

It's heavenly to be here. This house is so right and young and gay. All it needs is you, my darling.

GERMANY [MÜNCHEN-GLADBACH], 7 MARCH 1945
I'm learning more from the radio than I'm supposed to broadcast but I'll repeat: we've captured Jülich and München-Gladbach,[6] if you can believe our news reports and Jerry's.

Co. K is doing fine and so am I. Many miles of hiking with a 40-lb. pack have hardened me. Pack = one blanket; K &

---

6. Population 194,000, the largest German city so far taken by the Allies.

D ration;[7] razor; soap; rifle cleaning set (plastic) in tube form; toothbrush which is used to clean weapons, alas; a candle; several heating units—small cubes of an alcohol compound like Sterno; extra sweater and socks. Added gear is on my belt as follows: entrenching tool which is actually a small collapsible shovel, canteen, binoculars, trench knife, compass, first aid packet, cartridge clip pouch for two extra clips of carbine ammunition. Total counting rifle, two hand grenades, etc.: about 60 lbs.

So we go trudging like loaded mules.

With love!

34 E. PADRE ST., SANTA BARBARA, CALIF., 7 MARCH, 1945
News from the 9th Army is blacked out. We don't know what you are doing. I cannot tell you that I fear for you, and yet I do, and in the next breath I don't. I simply believe you are coming back and nothing else matters and my time of waiting will be as nothing when I see you again.

Mum departed today for a last week of packing in Los Angeles and moving up here. She feels little sentiment about leaving the old home. A year has passed since Pop was killed. It's been a long uphill pull. But now the tie is breaking. I am sure it's for the best.

Thank you for what you said about my going out with R. and S. or whomever. I don't think I care to, really. It so happens that men usually become too attentive and I simply don't want to battle all that chit-chat. I must say that I'm glad men like me, or that some do. R. and S. have said nice things and I am proud they feel that way, but there's always a mysterious danger point in a man or a woman when they are lonely and there's a friendly ear to listen: they get romantic or sentimental or worse. It bores me and makes me angry and I have no heart in it now, with you in the thick of battle. Please don't think I am giving up social life. I am NOT becoming a recluse. I simply don't want parties

---

7. K-ration for one day consisted of three waterproof-waxed cardboard cartons about the size of an ordinary book. One contained canned egg, one a bar of hard cheese, one canned pork or beef. Included were dry biscuits, a candy or fruit bar, instant coffee or powdered fruit juice, sugar, chewing gum and two cigarettes. When ignited, an empty box produced enough heat to warm coffee water in a canteen cup, a godsend to many a fuel-short G.I. D-ration was an "emergency" ration consisting of a bar of very hard, vitamin-fortified chocolate.

à deux. Hope you think I'm right. And please don't say: "Do whatever you wish." I want you to say: "Be for me alone and me only and wait for me!"

The two grandmothers may fairly wreck our privacy by the time they both finish dropping in. When you get back they will not do this but I shall have it to contend with. I love quiet and privacy. Being alone with Joan and Katherine is a deep deep satisfaction and joy.

I was home with Mum for three years last month, you know. And it's three years this month since you went into the Army. I don't suppose I actually believed such a slice of your life would be spent in the war but there it is. How lucky that we can't see ahead so far! What will the next three years bring?

GERMANY [NEAR MÜNCHEN-GLADBACH], 7 MARCH 1945
One late afternoon my platoon led the attack on a small town. We captured it without much opposition but light shell fire, took a dozen or fifteen prisoners including a battalion commander, along with some 200 civilians and Polish and Russian workers who had been slaves there on the land. For the night it was our town. We possessed it. Then I realized the appeal of war to men— the old, old anarchy still rising in the blood for loot and wine and women—and tomorrow we push on.

I find myself imagining you reading the newspaper accounts. I find myself imagining how I shall tell you, some day, about *this* day. Ah, but it cannot be told, Janie! Words never appeared more futile. I cannot read the current American magazines that come in profusion. One must be here, here with the mud of Germany on his boots, having eaten the enemy's food and drunk his wine and slept in his house.

One rainy afternoon our column halted in another town. The "front" had driven through an hour before and we were in support and driving after it. As usual there were hastily improvised white flags, sheets, and tablecloths hanging from doors, windows. People watched us, women, children, old men, some with hostility, some crying, some turning away in utter hate—as I remember a large grotesquely pregnant woman we passed—some with curiosity and a smile.

An order came down from the captain: take shelter and make yourselves comfortable a while. We did, in the first doorway, that of a little seed store behind which a family lived. The seeds—radishes, turnips, flower seeds—were like ours at home. So were the people. They built us a fire. The old man spoke German at us; the old woman too, even louder; the young woman busied herself with the fire and prepared coffee, bread and delicious plum jam. In the room with those three Germans—and two more women who came to observe us and discuss the events of the memorable day in which war came to town—were eight of us: a Russian (Andy Labonitch); a Swede (Hank Olander); two Italians (Adam Demasse and Pat Tardo); a Czech (Jim Holisky); a Pole (Tommy Woleznack); an Irishman (Joe Keating) and I whatever I am. And when I explained in my execrable German that we were all Americans, the conquered people were so extraordinarily amazed there was no mistaking they forgot for the moment they were conquered.

The modernity of Germany, materially, is impressive. In architecture, construction, and machinery what I've seen is superior to anything else over here. There are other tokens of advanced civilization. Books, plenty of them if on the wrong subjects, the glories of Nazism, etc.—yet with Goethe too; and pianos and Bach, Beethoven, Mozart; tasteful etchings and paintings and marvelous photographs.

There is a disciplined, thrifty quality about the neat brick homes, evidence of industry, self-respect, strength . . . but charm? Not much. As in the faces and the cold blue eyes, there is not much charm, warmth, grace.

I do not wonder why I am here. I feel confident I'm here to experience and understand—and maybe help in the peace some day.

Our forward assembly area the day we jumped off and crossed the Roer was a ruined village a mile from the river. We moved up to it before dawn and waited a couple of hours in the shattered rooms and cellars. In one of them I found a copy of *The Secret of Dr. Kildare.* Today, deep in the Rhineland, I picked up *Singing Guns.* These are the Armed Services Editions of the new-style paperback books which are provided us free—by the box-full—and range from Max Brand[8] to Homer. Not only in this way is Pop with me these days, as of course you understand.

---

8. Paperbacks first appeared in quantity in the U.S. just before the war. These were by Jane's father, killed in action in Italy, who wrote under the pen name of Max Brand.

The news keeps saying the 29th Div. is spearheading the attack!
This gives me funny chills up and down, half of fear, of hopes
and a lot of other confused feelings that simply go under the
heading of war! Your letter of Feb. 18th was written on a Sunday
morning when your thoughts were about as gloomy as mine always
are on a Sunday. I am glad you know what I mean when I say I
feel as if I'd lived under water for months. I have moments of
flashes when I see Joan smile or hear Kaffie coo or see them
standing together on our terrace, or when I hear a bird or smell
a plant or listen to the rain or read a Chinese poem, these
moments when I suddenly realize that somewhere life is waiting,
waiting for us to come together and taste all the beauty in every
day and night. And you are fighting and toiling and sweating and
praying on the battlefields, and looking at gray skies and cold and
depression and WAR. How tame my lot is! And yet, let me tell
you that I take little joy in all my blessings. This house is like a
shell, for without you there is no house on earth that would mean
a thing to me. Anything very beautiful strikes me as desperately
sad these days. Why? When the heart has ached a long time I
suppose something snaps in it.

Isn't it strange to feel portions of that loneliness from our
single days, those days before marriage, creeping on again? Never
in the same desperate finality, of course, because once one has
loved there is never again that complete emptiness.

I can remember when I used to think I simply COULD not
live without you. I simply didn't see how it was to be managed.
I asked you, between tears one night in bed, what I should do.
And you were very wise and gentle and somehow made me see
that anything is bearable and everything passes.

GERMANY, 8 MARCH 1945
Remember one Sunday at the B. B. Ranch a "bass derby," when
a number of Chinese came in a bus to go fishing in the Sacramento
River and a number of us gathered at the landing to watch? One
of those Chinese is here in K Company's kitchen. He is T-4[9]
Chow, who cooks up dishes of rice, chicken giblets and onions
and gives me giant helpings.

9. Technician fourth grade.

Chow used to be a rifleman in the 2nd platoon I now command. The captain, chuckling, likes to tell how Chow captured a Jerry with a toy pistol, simply hoaxed him into surrendering, Chow being unarmed at the time and the Jerry very armed.

Chow's father owns a meat and grocery store at 28th and Grove Streets, Oakland, where you and I and the children have been invited to visit him.

Yesterday's *Stars and Stripes*[10] carried a photo of Gens. Eisenhower, Gerhardt and Simpson[11] emerging from the citadel at Jülich. Lacking was a sign: "By courtesy of K Co., ll6th Infantry." Our regiment alone has taken some 800 prisoners since crossing the Roer. We simply overpowered Jerry by force of numbers and equipment and skill, though he fought bravely at times.

We rest easily at the moment. All thanks be given and my love to you.

SANTA BARBARA, MARCH 9, 1945

Thank you for the spring bud from Germany. I remember the one from Camp Roberts too. I remember them all. But I shall never see the spring again without an ache in my heart, for I shall always think back, if only for a moment, to those lost springs when we loved and lived apart.

I have never thought the spring an especially happy time. Isn't it exciting, promising? But is it really happy? It's the promise of what will come. But one knows that evil may come, that the heart may be found untrue or the mind unsteady. But in the summer there is all the ripeness of the year, all the peace and serenity of beauty. I wonder if this means I'm growing old and wanting the middle years of life? Oh yes, of course we'll be fruit tramps and wander the West, pick grapes and peaches and any other fruit you wish, in any hot valley any summer, in old clothes and with car! I will go with you as your "Sweet Pea" anywhere forever and be happy! I give you that guarantee!

Another lovely letter from you today, written Feb. 19th. I wonder if you knew the big attack was coming so soon?

10. The serviceman's (and woman's—there were many W.A.C.'s as well as nurses on overseas duty) daily newspaper, published in Paris, Rome, Honolulu and other parts of the world, and distributed free.

11. Lieutenant General William H. Simpson, Commander of the 9th Army. Major General Charles H. Gerhardt commanded the 29th Division.

Your No. 218 was written Feb. 23rd. You were looking at a full
moon and the crickets and frogs were stirring in the garden with
the small night animals. You had shown Joan the moon and with
the untarnished faith of children she returned its gaze. I was in
Jülich that night, as I've written.

Next night we moved on across the plain, lighted by burning
haystacks and villages and the same full moon you saw, that
occasionally broke through the clouds. As we marched I kept
thinking: this is too pat, too like storybooks: "by the light of
burning villages and the thunder of guns." Nothing could be
quite so melodramatic. But it was. I caught my mind detached,
regarding it so.

Darkness is the soldier's friend. Yet to attack in darkness is
very difficult. Knowing where one is in relation to the next
person, something so commonplace in civil life you seldom think
of it twice, is the very core of any military operation and, at
night, is supremely difficult.

We attacked a town but found it deserted and slept again in
a cellar where Jerry had been the night before. And so the time
went.

I imagined you the morning of the 24th hearing the first
news of the big offensive. It helps that my days are filled with
great and strange experiences; but I never forget your quiet ones,
your patient ones, from which your love comes to me.

The reaction from the past strenuous days has set in and the
boys sleep and sleep and wake to eat, and sleep again.

Watch for me in your heart under the next full moon. I shall
be there.

No letter for four days but it seems an eternity! The papers say
there's a lull in the 9th Army front, and I hope it means you are
resting a little. I can't tell you how I fear and worry and hope.
With all good intentions, one just does.

I saw with a great deal of alarm in the paper today that many
troops will be shifted straight from Europe to the Pacific or Orient,
without coming through this country at all. I suppose that may
mean two or three more years without you. One has to lose all
sense of perspective because if one really were able to understand

the agony of such a long wait, it would be unbearable. We are all
gradually numbed.

Three years ago today you enlisted. It must have seemed
rather exciting and stirring at the moment. I remember being
vaguely moved by it, but mostly too nauseated with Joan to care
whether I lived or died! Three years, what a slice of life! And it
will be another two before you are back, I think. Five precious
years. And you, who have never done any harm, don't deserve
this blow of a war to be fought. I have tried to go with you every
day of the three years and I certainly have thought of you a
thousand times in every day.

Later: No letter for five days. I know there will be a long gap
now, as your last was written just before the attack. I shall try
and wait patiently. We must wait and keep our hearts and heads
firm in the belief that all will end rightly.

I know how strange my little letters about daily life at home
must seem, if they reach you as you say they do, at the end of a
day of combat, and tell you of my life and other women's lives,
and of things their children say and ours say. I wonder if you can
possibly be interested. But you continually speak of the unreality
of war, of moving through the daze. I can see and feel it, I touch
it in your letters. I like your letters better than your stories. I like
them because they are simply YOU and what else can any human
being contribute, except his own little spot of sunlight or shadow?

SANTA BARBARA, MARCH 14, 1945

When THE letter came, I was fixing lunch for the children,
hurried to the mailbox and tore open the envelope to see *when*
it was written, and when I found it was only ten days ago, I ran
down the garden to the fruit trees, shouting for your mother, who
was weeding, and the children were on the terrace, and she
looked up and I said: "Letter from Bob written the 3rd!" And we
embraced and she said: "Now the sun is shining for us!" (It was
a dark, cold and foggy day.)

I flew to the study, forgot about the children's lunch and
devoured your letter. I had to go fast, but then later I came back
to it and read it again and later I read it again and later still, just
now, in bed at 8 p.m. I read it again: your first since the Big Push
began! I was right there in Jülich with you, feeling, experiencing

all you did. I love the way you say things and the way you feel things. Some Frenchman, I forget who, said: "Great thoughts come from the heart." Without heart, what is there on earth? How cold and small we are without heart! Darling, you have heart and gentleness and the will to listen and observe and feel. I would not be able to give you a greater gift, if all the gifts were to be given to you by me.

I gave your parents part of your letter to read and Father immediately wanted to preserve it for posterity by having Miss Parsons type at least two dozen copies of it!!! Oh dear, but you ARE appreciated. However, I have all the last part of the letter which no one on earth will ever share or see or know about. When you speak to me of love and the yearning and the ache in the soul and longing in the body! Oh, my darling, how I know it too. How it pulls! And as you say so beautifully, the ultimate in love is silence. There are no words to speak of love, love cannot be spoken or clasped in any way, it envelops one and lets one see through into some marvelous moment of life when we are completely pure and simple and alive. Everything else is shed.

So we can never feel it wholly again, that moment of pure light, until we are in each other's arms. But I can wait and you can wait because we must and because there are no substitutes now or ever.

Such a wind tonight, and so cozy in this little house with the two girls! Joan spoke of you a million times today and wanted to know if you ate peaches in Germany. She talks to your picture all the time. Your mother takes her for a walk every day, usually down to the market. They enjoy each other immensely. Joan has begun waving at all the old men who sun themselves and they love it. She is so pretty now, just the appealing age. She always asks for "the little prayer" after we have said the Lord's Prayer, and by that she means: "Here a little child I stand . . ." which I now say after the other, each night before bed. Her face as I say them to her is such a picture of eagerness and interest and tenderness and lovely youth that I want to scream with pleasure.

Katherine will give me something she is playing with now, if I hold out my hand to her. She does it with the most wonderful smile and has such fun; it's all a game to her. She lives violently. She either wants *all* her milk, or none; or will play violently and then collapse into dead sleep; no halfway steps for her!

Darling, you often end your letters with a plea for me to be beautiful for you. Heaven knows, I would be anything you wish, if I could. I know that beauty comes from within, so that if I have lines in my face when you see me again, years from now, I can only hope there will be something shining from within which will make up for them.

The radiance of youth lasts only a flash, but something better and more enduring should take its place. I shall work on being better inside, for that reason: to please you when I see you again.

GERMANY, 20 MARCH '45

Back from 48 hours rest-leave in Holland. Officer billets were the Grand Hotel—private rooms, clean sheets, running water, easy chairs in the lobby by the radio, outright sybaritic! After supper a captain and I were strolling in the twilight along the main street (Heerlen is about the size of Santa Barbara) when a well-dressed youngish man came abreast of us and asked pleasantly in broken English if we'd like to spend the evening at his home, he had some beer, he lived four kilometers from town.

A friend was with him. The four of us walked perhaps three blocks when the two suddenly stopped, turned and introduced us to their wives who'd been following discreetly behind! They spoke some English too, so we continued our walk in English, so to speak, out through the suburbs till the homes grew sparse and the fields larger.

Heerlen is a mining town yet you never would dream it. It is immaculate, the brick houses universally trimmed with green or yellow window frames and planted with neat shrubbery and flowers. The well-to-do officials of the mine live at the outskirts in the larger homes. It was to one of these we went. Two children greeted us, a boy 14, a lovely golden-haired girl of 8.

We spent a homey evening of beer, conversation, more beer, more conversation, finally dining on bread and jam and fresh boiled eggs and coffee. The captain and I promised to come again next evening, which we did, and skipped rope with Meisty, the girl, and helped her father plant vegetables. Now we have a home and a standing invitation to stay there and not at the Grand Hotel when we come again.

Briefly, the Dutch are the most up-and-coming people I've met over here. For example, nobody in this family we visited spoke English before the Americans arrived September 1st. Now

they all speak, read, and write it tolerably well and have taught
themselves. The mother continues with one formal lesson a week.

Their interests are unlimited. Wholesomeness and a good
democratic air of independence shine from everyone you meet.
They honor us as liberators.

The modern architecture I saw is a subject by itself which
I'll enlarge on tomorrow.

Oh, so sleepy tonight (4 A.M.) because I got an idea for a
story, another chapter of "The Commander" and, having the
opportunity, got to work and the idea went pretty well.

A. gap in your letters—except for a lovely old one of Dec.
6th which wandered in and told me of a moment in Vienna at
the florist's, when you stole spring in the shape of a plant and
hurried away. A great deal of love is in my heart tonight for you.

SANTA BARBARA, MARCH 21, 1945

I walked up the hill to Mum's house[12] this afternoon while your
mother took the children for two hours. Mum's place is still a
shambles with an incredible number of packing cases and books
and lamps and suitcases and things all over the floors in every
room. But the whole is going to be charming, so MUCH lovelier
than Los Angeles. Now she has it we wonder how we stood the
other. It shows how one's life is divided into stages and what fits
one does not suit the next. Mum says she'll grow old here with
pleasure. I can hardly wait to have you see the house: the view
is lovely, the rooms large, pine trees peep in at the windows and
you look through them to the water, and the islands.

My days pass in a round of dishes and cleaning and sweeping
and scrubbing. I'm developing a great thirst for alcoholic drink!
I hope you will worry! I have an ashtray ready for you in the study
and on the table by the bed, but I have a glass ready for your wife!
I took a bottle of beer (I down a bottle with amazing speed these
days!) last night with F. when he stopped on his way home from
work, and I took one this afternoon after walking up the hot hill
to Mum's. And if I had anyone here all the time I am sure I'd
have sherry while preparing dinner and wine during it. Perhaps
we two will become regular tipsies!

I have a great feeling of self-sufficiency because I see with

---

12. On a hillside near the Old Mission.

amazement that I can take care of this house and the children alone.

Your letters bring you terribly close, and some days, like today, I seem to be able to talk to you easily and intimately. What I would not give for an evening of talk and poetry and story plots and then to sleep in your arms. I shall not really wake up to life again until we have loved in the silent night, in this little house of sun, when the children are breathing quietly in their rooms and all is steady and dark and awaiting the morrow. I shall be recreated then, just as I have been every time I have ever slept with you in the less than two years we had together.

When I start my part-time job at the hospital early in April I shall feel better about this thing, this living during wartime. I'm sorry I haven't extended myself sooner and more devotedly. But I think I was not ready for it physically and there is no time, these days, for anyone to break down from fatigue.

I feel pretty strong now, though the end of the day finds me exhausted, especially when one begins as it did today, at 5 a.m. with Kaffie waking. Her new teeth sometimes make her fussy and restless.

The news continues good. One reporter said the sky was blue and fair over Germany today and various armies were poised for the crossing of the Rhine, including yours, the 9th. It's pretty grim and exciting and maybe by the end of summer Germany will be done for. But then there is Japan; the whole thing seems endless.

Goodnight darling, I wonder if you are asleep or awake. I wonder about a good many things, only I always know you love me, so that doubt does not exist and that is what matters. All my faith is in you now and forever. Remember. Take me with you on your night marches and your battles and your waitings and your actions.

GERMANY [NEAR DORTMUND], 3 APRIL 1945
We are across the Rhine, as you've doubtless read, getting first-hand glimpses of a nation in the throes of defeat and disillusion. People line the roads and watch us curiously and some of the girls blush and smile as my boys call to them and some scowl or turn away.

Many liberated slave workers come streaming towards us—

Poles and Russians mostly—calling out to us as they pass, laughing, exchanging brief phrases with our Polish and Russian boys. They are a motley assortment, wearing a patchwork of ragged clothes, pushing loaded carts of belongings, riding bicycles, walking, sometimes singing—men and women linked arm in arm—and sometimes they run to us and walk alongside, the girls linking arms with a soldier they like.

I saw one, Polish or Ukrainian, walking between two men, full-lipped, full-bosomed, wearing dark slacks and a tailored blouse and no hat, probably just free a few hours, and she was shy and afraid like a creature long caged.

A moment later a pretty German girl came toward us pushing a bicycle, wearing blue slacks and a brown corduroy jacket, a white scarf around her hair. Her face was splattered on one side with mud thrown up by our passing tanks, which were just ahead, and there was no expression but hatred on that face as it regarded us coldly.

We passed carcasses of horses cleanly butchered—every scrap of meat removed, only the fresh entrails remaining.

We met a solitary Frenchman wearing his tattered gray uniform of 1940 and he saluted us with grave dignity.

We came into a town where a man ran out offering a bottle of schnapps and three glasses and when we hesitated to drink demanded: "Do you think it's poison? Look!" And poured himself a glass and drank.

An old woman put her head out a window and said: "Are you Americans?" And when we told her she shouted: "At last we are free!"

In another house we saw the head and carcass of a half eaten dog.

Then two girls came up and one inquired politely: "What do you do with murderers?"

We replied: "That depends, why?"

"People who've killed German people?"

We said we had nothing to do with that, that would probably be all right with us.

"There!" she said to her companion. "You see?"

She told us that the day before when the first Americans approached the town, her boyfriend threw a hand grenade in the burgomaster's window and killed him "because he was a Nazi swine and everybody hated him—he joined the Party and became burgomaster only to put money in his pocket and drink schnapps and sleep with pretty women!" Three other youths gunned down the military commander in the street, hit him once in the leg, once in the belly, once in the arm; and because the people hated the military commander, they hid the three boys until we came.

Next we talked to a woman about 35—very thin, with a hungry pallor and red-tipped nose. She said she received as ration 2 potatoes per day, a few grams of bread, a bit of margarine, baloney on weekends. But the rich officials, the Nazi Party members, had plenty to eat and drink. Her husband is a prisoner in Russia.

She was glad we came, not the Russians, because the Russians (Bolsheviks, she called them) "are so uncivilized, not our kind." We asked if she knew the crimes committed by the German Army against the Russians and she said, yes, they showed them as entertainment at the movies. "At first the people did not believe them. Later some would get up and leave when the brutal scenes showed. So the rule was passed nobody could leave the movie or talk until the end. Finally almost nobody went to movies except members of the Party."

We asked if she realized that the cause of her present misery, and Germany's, was following bad leaders; and she said, "Yes but what can I do? The leaders are too strong!" She said the Nazis in 1932, when Germany had very little, promised much and people believed them—the Nazis got power and then it was too late. Now all she wants is her man to come home, and something to eat, and peace. "Wenn mein mann zu haus kommt," was her constant refrain: "When my husband comes home."

I love every word of your letters. Receiving them where I do is a little unbelievable but also the only firm reality in this convulsion, this death struggle of a monster.

SANTA BARBARA, APR. 9, 1945

Tomorrow I lunch with a bevy of my fellow war-widows. I suppose you played with some of them as a boy and pulled their hair! Would you have pulled mine? I had one long curl that went down my back. I was a funny little girl with a very sentimental face and the desires and habits of a wild Indian. I always looked angelic and really wasn't very nice at all and always got John into trouble by picking at him and quarreling and teasing. He wanted to play or read alone and I wanted him to be father to my dolls!

How MUCH longer? I really now think it will be another two years, at least. What are your guesses? I don't see how they will get you back here before sending you on to the Pacific. I don't even know whether I could stand another goodbye and all the attendant fears and those perfectly HORRIBLE first months apart—they simply tear the heart out of me and letting you go into the war again a second time would be a nightmare to say the least. Why won't you ever even talk about it? Don't you want me to realize how long a separation we have ahead?

CHAPTER 2

December 7, 1941

Sometimes it seemed a lifetime, back to where we started and it started. Sunday, December 7, 1941, is peaceful and sunny. We're lunching at the kitchen table in our employee's cottage on a ranch high in California's Coast Range, enjoying a broadcast by the New York Philharmonic on our Zenith portable, when the familiar voice of John Daly breaks in. "We interrupt this program to bring you a special news bulletin. The Japanese have attacked Pearl Harbor."

Americans bombed, strafed, wounded, dead—ships blown up, barracks and airfields blasted! We feel as if the floor is being pulled out from under us, leaving us at the edge of an abyss. In our lifetime such horrors happen in other countries, to other peoples: Poles, Danes, Norwegians, Dutch, Belgians, British, French, the Greeks, the Chinese, the Russians. Over our suddenly unappetizing tuna and egg salads we stare at each other in stunned silence. Like so many others we'll remember for the rest of our lives exactly where we were, what we were doing, how we felt when we heard the news—and realized we were no longer immune. Bob and millions like him will have to go to war. Jane and millions like her will have to stay home. It seems almost the ultimate disaster, almost like death.

Dazed, strangely mute, we wander through our beloved cottage as if already saying farewell. Piled by the typewriter on the deal table by the fireplace are carbons of stories Bob has sent the *Atlantic Monthly*. Here in the bedroom is the nook by the window where Jane has planned to put the crib when a baby is born. We are going to lose this home which has become a cornerstone of the life we are building. We are going to lose each other. What the future holds nobody knows. Our chief consolation is the thought we'll not be alone there, we'll have plenty of company— a whole nation. We sense it, speak of it, rising invisibly around us, feeling the same anger and outrage we do, the same dismay and loss.

Bob: The shadow of war has hung over our marriage of fourteen months. Ours is, we like to joke, the last in this country "arranged" in old-country style. We'd never met but our mothers had a mutual friend who knew us both and put the idea in their heads that we might hit it off. I'd come home to Santa Barbara, that summer of '39, after a disappointing first year at Stanford Law School. I'd concluded that law as generally practiced consisted less in the pursuit of justice than in arguing about other people's property, and at the same time I was breaking up with someone. So the last thing I felt like was "doing something," as Mother kept putting it, "for that nice girl who's over here from Europe and doesn't know a soul."

I spent most of July and August working on a cattle ranch near Santa Maria, writing stories in spare time, and whenever I went home Mother would tactfully suggest: "What about Jane Faust?" Finally to get her off my back I said: "Okay—Ellis and Connie are coming up next weekend. Go ahead and ask Miss Faust if you want!"

So here I am on the station platform feeling a little nervous, looking for a tall blonde girl without any hat—hats were still the fashion—carrying a tennis racket. Doesn't sound too bad. Evidently she's unconventional. Besides she's grown up abroad and I've never met one of those. Sharp at ten-thirty the Daylight Limited comes steaming in from Los Angeles and I see her get off, complete with tennis racket and all-American look, not the least foreign. I notice a shyness but think I see through it to something I may like very much.

Jane: Bob looks handsome in brown tweed jacket and gray flannels—the Ivy League uniform of those days. He doesn't know I've been as reluctant about our meeting as he. When his mother telephoned from Santa Barbara I felt petrified at the idea of a weekend among strangers and glibly pleaded a previous engagement. Afterward Mum scolded: "You've *got* to get over your shyness, get out and *meet* people!" Like most mothers of unmarried twenty-one-year-olds, she was eager to have me meet some young men. We'd just moved from Florence—had been living in Italy for fourteen years—so Daddy could do the Kildare stories for M.G.M. and I didn't know a soul in Southern California my age. But I knew Mum was right. Though I'd been to a girls' school in New York, I felt backward where boys were concerned, embarrassed by my six-foot altitude, afraid I couldn't hold up my end of the line of chit-chat that seemed expected of American girls. Mum's scolding prompted me to phone Mrs. Easton back and say there'd been a change of plans, I could come.

Now my chief sensation is relief that Bob's height is the same as mine. Most of my dates seem to have been around five-five. I'm impressed by the fact he's gone to Harvard and Stanford while I've never been to college but don't want him to think so and begin teasing about his driving as he takes us up State Street a little too fast, shifting gears of the Ford V-8 four-door a little too masterfully. He replies as solemnly as if revealing a state secret that the car belongs to his parents—as if that explains everything! Consequently I'm not quite sure how I'm doing but gather he doesn't have much money to spend on cars. The house near the Old Mission is big but not grand. Mrs. E., bursting with energy though over sixty, greets me affectionately. Still it isn't till I've beaten Bob at tennis that I begin to relax.

Bob: On the contrary I let her win a set because she looked glamorous in short white skirt with those long brown legs. I guess my downfall began right there. Or perhaps it was afterward on the lawn during our discussion of books and writers. By what seemed remarkable coincidence we'd both been reading Chekov and particularly liked his story "The Darling," about someone who needs a special kind of love. I soon realize I've never met a girl I can talk to this enjoyably and find myself confiding my big secret—I want to write and am not going back to law school but to San Francisco and look for a newspaper job. I feel a twinge of regret when Connie and Ellis arrive and interrupt us.

Jane: Before dinner Connie and I change to evening dresses. The men wear black tie and the white tablecloth gleams beneath silver candelabra while we sit in ghastly uncomfortable Chippendale chairs and prepare to eat with sterling knives and forks. Bob's father startles me by saying grace, something I've never experienced. Like Mrs. E. he's short, wiry, a rancher-businessman in his sixties, and also like Bob's mother so full of vitality he seems much younger. Their formal Victorian manners put me off but I see that at heart they're terribly decent and kind, while regarding their only child as a bit unpredictable.

Then we all go downtown to see Herbert Marshall, a popular British actor, on stage in a frothy little comedy called _Ladies and Gentlemen._ It's dreadfully boring. At intermission we troop outside with most of the audience for a breath of fresh air in the portico. Bob and I begin talking again and become separated from the others. When he suggests we step across the street to the El Paseo Bar for a quick drink, it seems only natural. Half an hour flies by before he looks at his watch. Horrified we hurry back, find the curtain up and Marshall on stage, climb into our third row seats over people's feet to the accompaniment of muttered disapprovals and knowing looks.

Bob: That summer is a turning point for Jane and me as for the rest of the world. A few days later on September 1, Hitler invades Poland. He's been ranting, bullying, breaking treaties, invading the Rhineland, Austria, Czechoslovakia, while England and France back down before him. But we hope it won't lead to war. Of course we want peace. We just think it can be achieved on the cheap, by accommodating a monomaniac. When England and France finally declare war a few days later, that summer of 1939 becomes like the summer of 1914—the summer before World War I—a point from which there will be no return but one to which we and millions of others will long to return— with its unclouded tennis games, its hats, double-breasted suits, unforgettable melodies like "Night and Day" and "Smoke Gets in Your Eyes," movie stars like Fred Astaire and Ginger Rogers, Dietrich, Garbo, Gable, Gary Cooper, its frothy little comedies and grand Broadway musicals, zany crazes like flagpole sitting and dance and roller skating marathons, its innocence, and its ignorance of the scope of human evil.

Jane: At first the war seems unreal, it's so far away. It's something you read about in papers, hear about on the radio, see in newsreels at the movies. Nobody calls it World War II. That comes later. It's just "the war," or "the European war," away off "over there." People begin urging us to stay neutral. "It's Europe's quarrel, not ours!" But I feel we might not be able to. I'd been living with a Jewish family in Vienna when the Nazis took over Austria. For weeks there'd been turmoil, pro- and anti-Nazi mobs opposing each other in the streets. Then German bombers flew back and forth overhead. Then from my upstairs window at No. 3 Brahms-platz I see the goose-stepping invaders march by, hear the welcoming shouts, sense the invisible terror, while Lily Pereira, my landlady, and Iti, her daughter, my age, cower in dread by the radio. When I go out I see "Juden Hier" (Jew Here) scrawled on doors and walls. I feel anger and disgust. I also feel sick at heart for being a member of a humankind that behaves like this. Some of my friends, Jewish and non-Jewish, disappear in the murderous reprisals that follow the Anschluss, while others risk their lives to smuggle Jews and other anti-Nazis to the Italian or Swiss borders. With breathless excitement I listen to Franz and Wilfred tell matter-of-factly of these secret errands of mercy and resistance. Their lives are in danger but they continue to do what they feel they must.

Experiencing a Nazi takeover even from the safety of my American citizenship fills me with horror. But afterward like most of the rest of the world I want to get on with my life and hope such evil will never touch me or mine. Now what's happening in Poland makes me think it will.

I liked Bob but we didn't see each other again that summer and in the fall I went to New York to stay with a former schoolmate, Fanny Myers, who lived with her parents in an apartment on 86th Street. Fanny painted her miniatures in the morning while I wrote my stories. Afternoons and evenings we improved our minds, supposedly, by attending lectures on philosophy by Will Durant or visiting art museums whereas actually, like most singles our age, we were on the lookout for husbands. A prosperous young Yale professor asked me home to meet his mother and offered me a job as his secretary. It was either a proposal or a proposition but I declined on grounds of lack of secretarial talent. Meanwhile Fanny and I went to dinner at the apartment of a schoolmate from Spence days, Honoria Murphy. Her parents were wealthy patrons of the arts—Gerald effeminate and artistic, Sara masculine and assertive. They'd owned a villa in the south of France and were becoming celebrated as the Dick Divers of Fitzgerald's novel *Tender is the Night*. Mum and Pop had known them during our New York days when we'd had an apartment on East End Avenue and Gerald and Pop shared a liking for the poetry of Gerard Manley Hopkins with its unusual rhythms, but Gerald wasn't a published poet like Pop. Now he and Sara were shattered by the recent deaths of two teen-age sons and seemed to have little affection left for their remaining daughter.

As my social whirl continues, my bachelor godfather, "Dixie" Fish, prototype for Dr. Kildare in the magazine and screen stories Daddy is writing, takes me to Roosevelt Hospital to watch him operate, and dinner and the theater afterward and to rub elbows with celebrities at the Stork Club.

It's all very heady. New York at Christmas time. All the

shops aglitter. Everything so glamorous. I fall in love or think I
do. Jack is ten years older, lively, witty, a successful stockbroker.
We get engaged. Then my girlhood dream of a little red farmhouse
on a hilltop—far from the madding crowd with a devoted husband
and six children, all of us wearing blue jeans and doing our own
work—reasserts itself. Bob, too, is continually at the back of my
mind. We're exchanging copies of our stories. His aren't very
good. Neither are mine. But I like his ambition to become a
writer and perhaps subconsciously I know I'm going to marry one
despite Daddy's admonitions to the contrary. Anyway, when I
break off with Jack and head west early in 1940, after that dizzying
New York whirl, something tells me I'll be seeing Bob before
long.

Bob: After trying several San Francisco papers I find a job on *Coast
Magazine,* headquartered on Bush Street just below Montgomery.
Coast's content is largely an imitation of the *New Yorker's* combined with black-and-white photos like those of the new and
highly popular *Life,* and the society gossip of *Town and Country.*
It's staffed mainly by ex-Ivy Leaguers, one of whom I'd known on
the Harvard *Lampoon,* which is partly how I get my job of associate
editor at the glorious salary of fifteen a week. My parents aren't
backing my new career so I must watch every penny. I rent a
room on the roof of an apartment building at 1228 Washington
Street near the top of Nob Hill. It isn't much bigger than a piano
box but has a heart-stopping view: the new Bay Bridge, ships
coming and going, Pan Am flying boats making their runs across
the water, leaving a white wake and taking off for China straight
through Golden Gate; and in the middle of it all, Treasure Island,
constructed especially for the world's fair then in progress—
gleaming out there at night like a veritable jewel.

   To get to work I walk down precipitous California Street to
our office at 130 Bush, next the lofty new—all of fourteen stories
high—Shell Building, and afterwards ride the crowded cable car
back up, clinging among other passengers like bees on a limb,
feeling myself part of the picturesque life of a great city. I do most
of my serious eating at the Hotel de France in the French district
on the north slope of Nob Hill, where a three-course dinner
with wine and plenty of bread, common table, costs 45¢. In
Chinatown, halfway down the east slope, I find equally good
bargains; and for social life there are guys and girls I'd known at
Stanford plus the *Coast* staff, Innis Bromfield, editor, Christopher

Rand our star writer. When we can afford it we go dancing to Jay Whidden's orchestra at the Hotel Mark Hopkins atop Nob Hill, or Ted Fiorito's at the St. Francis down on Union Square. Betty Grable, later a famous pin-up girl, got her start as a vocalist with Whidden and used to perform a sensational scarf dance which would hardly raise an eyebrow today.

I'm settling in, getting satisfaction out of seeing my words in print even if they do no more than advise people what movies to see or where to eat inexpensively, when one of those apparently random events occurs that change our lives. I'm transferred to head *Coast's* Los Angeles office. There isn't much to head. I'm the only one there beside our advertising manager. But on the frosty morning of February 2, 1940, while walking from my three-dollar-a-week pad in a dilapidated Victorian on the 6th Street hill, to my office in the Clark Hotel at the heart of downtown, I get a hunch Jane is home from New York and decide to call her. Reaching the lobby I'm amazed to find a letter in my pigeonhole, forwarded from San Francisco, saying she *is* home. It seems an astonishing case of mental telepathy. I go to the pay phone nearby and get her out of bed—it's only 7:45—and agree to come to lunch on Sunday.

Jane: I keep telling myself I don't want to be in love with anybody. I talk it over with Daddy, sitting as usual on the toilet seat while he shaves. We have our best talks then, just as Mum and I do when she's sitting up in bed recovering from one of her migraines. "Do you want another scalp to add to your collection or are you serious about this guy?" Pop demands while scraping his chin. He takes a dim view of my potential suitors. He has something like a cross between Achilles and Homer in mind for me. "Oh, I'm not serious!" I assure him.

Bob: It was a different Los Angeles in those days. No traffic gridlocks. No freeways. No smog. You could see the mountains and you could get almost anywhere in twenty minutes. Now and then a flight of twin-fuselage Lockheed P-38 fighters comes roaring overhead like something out of science fiction, reminders of what's happening overseas. The L.A. aircraft factories are booming with orders from foreign nations and our own military, and Franklin D. Roosevelt, now in his third term, is talking about the U.S. becoming "the arsenal of democracy." But nobody gets very excited. It's not going to touch us, oh, no! It's the period called "the phony war." France and England are playing it safe on the defensive, and Hitler is pretending to do likewise while planning his next blitzkrieg.

Anyway, my pulse rises as I drive out Sunset Boulevard toward the ocean, turn off at Burlingame Avenue in leafy Brentwood and come to a stop in front of a gracious Mediterranean house, half-hidden behind a hedge of Algerian ivy. I've scraped up $120 to buy a secondhand 1936 Dodge coupe, dark green, with spare tire in a well in the righthand fender and a silvery ram rampant as radiator cap. Not quite in keeping with upscale Brentwood, maybe. But my role is that of poor but honest young fellow striving toward success.

Jane looks better than ever. And now we have that shared feeling fate is bringing us together, there's an unspoken understanding between us. Her mother, Dorothy Schillig Faust, is the most exquisitely feminine older woman I've ever met—soft dark eyes, full figure, gently welcoming manner. Her father Frederick Faust comes on like a giant, massively tall, combative jaw, sternly lined face, talking brilliantly in a rich bass voice. I don't know it but under Max Brand and nineteen other pen names he's published over 600 magazine stories, over 130 books, while dozens of movies have been made from his work including *Destry Rides Again* as well as the smash-hit Kildare series; but he prefers to write poetry on classical themes. Twelve-year-old Judy's suspicion of those who come courting her adored sister is formidable. The house speaks to me almost as much as the people in it: it says welcome, it says home—with its book-lined walls and warmly lived-in atmosphere. It's the kind of house I want someday and makes the people who occupy it now seem like relatives.

Jane: We were married in Berkeley in September as bombs rained down on London. France has surrendered. Hitler is preparing to invade England. The first draft law in U.S. peacetime history has just passed Congress. They aren't drafting married men yet but we guess they will soon and want as much time together as possible. The ceremony takes place at 8:00 P.M. in grand old St. Mark's Episcopal Church across Bancroft Way from the University of California. Bob's grandfather was its pastor back in the 1890's and his parents were married there, so a lot of tradition and religion are involved, but most of it goes over my head because we Fausts have no formalized religion and, besides, I prefer living in the present rather than the past.

We've chosen Berkeley because it's near the ranch where

Bob got a job after *Coast* folded and because our parents attended college there and numerous friends and relations live nearby. I'm grateful for the way Bob's parents have accepted me as the daughter they never had or, rather, as replacement for one they lost in infancy. By strange coincidence her name too was Jane. It gives me a sometimes eerie, sometimes profoundly moving, sense of carrying on and trying to compensate, even now as I prepare to walk down the aisle. I wear an ivory-satin dress with a train that threatens to trip me and flat slippers to keep me under six two. My only attendant is Judy, still scowling about Bob. My brother John has had to go East to school and can't be best man so Bob's boyhood chum, a Stanford medical student, John Merritt, hefty and even taller than I, holds the ring. He and Bob wear white tie and tails. So does Daddy. As I wait at the back of the church with my right hand on Daddy's arm I see beads of sweat on his forehead that aren't there because it's a warm evening. "You don't have to go through with this!" he mutters grimly. He means it. He likes Bob but is ready to turn and walk out of the church, me on his arm, forever to keep him company. But when I look down the aisle and see Bob I know my future is there—there and in our apartment at Rio Vista, Rio Vista looming like a bit of paradise beyond the reception, the thrown rice, the Just Married sign someone is sure to attach to our old Dodge.

Rio Vista is a tiny town on the Sacramento River just before it empties into San Francisco Bay. Our three furnished rooms occupy a ground floor corner opposite the grammar school. Down at the end of the street we can see the Sacramento gliding placidly by. The rent is thirty-five a month. I'm so happy I burn the chops for our first dinner. But Bob says it's all right—we're going to live mainly on love anyway.

Bob: In fact I was worried lest Jane might not like Rio Vista or the B. B. Ranch people, having grown up in Europe and knowing nothing of American smalltown or ranch life.

Jane: On the contrary fate was putting me where I'd long wanted to be, among down-to-earth people. They were part of that girlhood dream of a farmhouse on a hill. Ironically the dream first came to me when I was living in a villa in Florence with plenty of servants to look after me, but the servants interested me more than the sophisticated guests who appeared for dinner or to play tennis or swim in our pool. They seemed so much less inhibited, so much more directly connected to life and able to express it without the barriers of manners and education. When not attending Miss Barry's American School, a Florentine institution of long standing, or taking additional lessons prescribed by Daddy as beneficial to body and mind, including fencing and Greek, I spent much time in pantry or kitchen or up in the sewing room on the second floor or out in the garden listening to their talk. Giulia the maid; Elia the butler, her husband, who arranged fresh flowers in the house every day as well as serving meals wearing white gloves; Griselda the second maid; Olimpio the chauffeur, irascible in traffic like most Italians; dear old Berti, age 80, the head gardener—all seemed inhabitants of another world, one far more interesting than the one I lived in. From servants of neighboring villas they knew what really went on behind all those walls and hedges, and through them I did too. Similarly with the peasants who cultivated the fields adjoining our villa and often sang as they pruned the grapevines or plowed behind white oxen that moved with such dignity under the olive trees and among the grapes. We discussed the crops, the weather, latest births and deaths, and why the oxen wore leather muzzles to prevent their nibbling the vines. "Jane," my mother would reprimand, "you must learn to be more ladylike! The *contadini* and servants are all very well, but you mustn't become too intimate!" Not that Mum and Pop had social pretensions. They just didn't see things my way.

Nor was our villa pretentious. It was a sixteenth-century farmhouse enlarged and remodeled at our own expense. Daddy added three rooms and a tower-study to make it more livable and to accommodate his thousands of books and desire for spaciousness. He wrote every day, poetry in the mornings, prose in the afternoons. We belonged to no clubs, saw few people except those interested in the arts. Arthur and Hortense Acton, our landlord and landlady, who lived in palatial La Pietra across the lane, came for dinners; and Arthur, an Italianized Englishman, painted us all in watercolor, rather badly. Hortense was an American from Chicago. Their oldest son Harold, now Sir Harold thanks to his literary achievements, was away in China but William came to dinner wearing a monocle, which fascinated me. He was to die in the war.

Leonard and Patty Bacon, old friends of Pop's and Mum's from Berkeley days, occupied another of Acton's villas nearby with their three daughters, and John and I and the young Bacons played in the *podere* intervening; and I eavesdropped from the head of the stairs while Pop and Leonard, a Pulitzer poet, discussed writers and poetry late into many nights. And one summer we took a house near the Bacons and Aldous Huxleys on the beach at Forte dei Marmi near Viareggio. Leonard, Pop and Aldous would sit by bonfires on the sand and talk about everything under the sun, and moon, while we children played nearby, sometimes listening, sometimes oblivious as we eyed the distant Carrara Mountains, ghostly white in the moonlight, where Michelangelo got the marble for his statues. Even so I identified less with those talking and writing about life than with the common people who seemed to live it so much more directly and colorfully. Maybe like Tolstoy I saw virtue in peasants because I wasn't one and had a villa to go home to at night. Nevertheless my interest was genuine.

Bob: Again my feelings matched Jane's but with different background. I'd grown up in Santa Maria, a small town north of Santa Barbara, where we kids went barefoot as Tom Sawyer along unpaved streets and alleys, swiped watermelons from neighbors' yards, engaged in bloody fistfights to see who was boss, admired the American Legion when it marched up Broadway in uniform, guns at right shoulder, in the Memorial Day Parade, fresh home from World War I. War was over, war was a thing of the past. The Legionnaires had put it away for good, finished off old Kaiser Bill. The last thing any of us expected was to be involved in a war when we grew up. My mother read aloud to my father and me almost every evening, something out of the *Atlantic* or *World's Work*, plenty of Kipling, Sir Walter Scott, Dickens. On Sundays we attended tiny St. Peter's Episcopal Church which accommodated all of the dozen or fifteen Episcopalians in town. It was so small it had no Sunday school. I didn't care much for church but the words of the Bible and Book of Common Prayer sank in deeply, then or when read aloud by Father at home on Sunday evenings when for some reason we hadn't attended services.

At school I harassed girls much as Tom did Becky, with spitwads of paper propelled by thumb and forefinger, to show mute adoration. My friends included Japanese, Portugese, Mexican, Italian and Jewish kids. I brought them to our comfortable house at 730 South Broadway and they took me to theirs, more or less comfortable, without altering our basic relationships. There were feelings of prejudice among some of our elders, true, but little of this rubbed off onto us. We regarded ourselves mainly as Santa Marians and dreamed of playing on the high school football team and becoming millionaires.

Most of us grew up with the work ethic. I earned my first big money, took my first step toward millionaire status, salvaging heads of lettuce and bunches of carrots discarded by local packing sheds and peddling them to housewives for five cents each. Growing older I worked on outlying farms and ranches. What I liked best were vacation trips into the back country with vaqueros of the Sisquoc Ranch, which Father managed, to hunt wild cattle, fish, observe condors and explore Indian caves. Later he and I helped National Audubon Society and Forest Service establish the first refuge for the California condor. The great birds soared into my life and remained there, soaring out from time to time in books and magazine articles. The backcountry became a spiritual heartland I took with me wherever I went. And about this time, too, I developed a youthful dream remarkably like Jane's—a ranch house on a hilltop shared with a loving wife and numerous progeny. Are there psychic connections? I think so.

Jane: At Rio Vista I spent most of the day with Flora, my neighbor across the hall, wife of an alcoholic oil worker. She taught me how to wash and iron, and when we went to the market explained that string beans were purchased by the pound, not by the bean! Though only my age, Flora had two adorable young children, Billy and Susan, who called me Aunt Jane. Like her I wanted to be a hands-on mother. My parents were so busy when I was young—and Pop so ill with heart trouble and Mum so weak from nervous breakdowns—that they hired a governess for John and me. I loved young children and admired the way Flora managed hers in a realistic manner that didn't spoil them. I'd get everything ready for dinner and wait for Bob to come home. He'd stop in front of the apartment and honk—dirty and smelly from all day at the ranch but looking glamorous in blue jeans and cowboy boots—and I'd run out and we'd drive together to our garage, down by the river, then walk back arm in arm in a blissful moment of reunion, I carrying his black tin lunch pail. After he bathed and shaved, me sitting on the toilet seat to keep him company and talk, we'd eat. Then I'd read aloud—from *Don Quixote* or *Look Homeward, Angel*—until he fell asleep in his chair, having been up since about 4:30, and then it was bedtime.

Whenever we read the war news in the paper or heard it

over our Zenith portable, we realized how fortunate we were, and how bad it was becoming, with England standing alone against what seemed an invincible Germany.

Bob: The B. B. Ranch and Feed Yard where I worked occupied ten thousand acres on the west bank of the Sacramento where it joins the San Joaquin to form the headwaters of San Francisco Bay. The rich delta soil produced tons of hay which was baled and stored in massive stacks as long as city blocks. Twelve thousand cattle were accommodated in pens, separated by alleyways wide enough for feed trucks, in what amounted to a factory in the field, a beef factory. There was a pit the size of a small stadium that contained sugar-beet pulp brought down on barges from a refinery up the Sacramento, and a huge corrugated iron mill that ground up the hay, along with cottonseed cake and molasses and vitamins, into a special formula that was fed the cattle along with the beet pulp.

My job was to ride a dependable sorrel named Barb through the alleyways in company with Dynamite Carter, head cowboy, a colorful character who'd run away from home in Illinois at fourteen on a freight train and knocked around all over the West. Day by day while Dynamite told vivid stories of his experiences, I mounted the bottom rungs of the cattle-business ladder toward, I fondly imagined, an executive position, if the war permitted. I looked forward to a future that might combine writing and ranching. Meanwhile we watched to see the cattle weren't stuck with their heads between fence rails or out of water because of a leaky trough; and when new stock arrived we helped the drivers unload their trucks or the train crew their trains, because the Sacramento Short Line connecting Oakland with Sacramento and the Southern Pacific system ran through the ranch. For reasons best known to those who schedule trucks and trains, these unloadings usually occurred late at night. We got overtime pay at our regular daily rate of 30¢ an hour, and were expected to be at work next morning, seven days a week, no matter how late we'd been up the night before—because cattle must be fed and looked after daily while they gain valuable weight. We shipped the fat ones off to San Francisco and Los Angeles, steers selling at 9¢ a pound, heifers at 8.

Jane: I worried lest Bob's new friends might not accept me. "Just be yourself," he advises as we drive to our first dance along the dirt road that bordered Montezuma Slough and thousands of acres of delta marsh beyond it. We pass several deserted farmhouses abandoned when their owners sold out to the B. B. They make me think of solitary gravestones. Finally we come to one that's also been deserted but is lit up for this special evening. It stands in a grove of gloomy cypresses. A dozen or two jalopies of various makes are drawn up around it like the horses and buggies of an earlier era. Though it exudes light and music, this lonely old house which has once been a home seems ghostly and unreal. The wind moans through the cypresses, adding to the eerie atmosphere. Inside I find the most remarkable sight I've ever seen.

Bob's friend Dynamite, small, vibrant, dressed to kill in a purple sateen shirt, red neckerchief and new Levi's, sits on a box in a corner playing a guitar and at the same time a harmonica held to his mouth by a wire frame. With one cowboy-booted foot he's stamping out the rhythm of "Turkey in the Straw." Beside him sits a gaunt mournful-faced man in blue bib overalls sawing a fiddle as if his life depends on it. And shuffling to and fro over the bare board floor under the pale light of a kerosene lantern that hangs from the ceiling are the dancers—all so gaunt and wild looking. The women wear everyday cotton prints. Later I learn their dresses are often pieced together from patterned bags that contain feed for their chickens. The men wear khaki or denim. These are the Okies, Arkies, Texans driven west by drought, dust storm and hard times—John Steinbeck's people as depicted in his *Grapes of Wrath* published the year before. They move with a strange solemnity as if this is a trance, not a dance. Watchers stand as solemnly around the walls. "They're just warming up," Bob whispers. "Come on!" Soon we're partners in a square dance being called—squealed, actually—by Fritts, the rawboned cattle foreman:

> Grab your partner, give her a whirl,
> And don't disturb that pretty little curl!
> Around and around and around we go,
> With a little more swingin' and a do-si-do!

We've never square-danced before but somehow it comes naturally. After half an hour we stop for breath, perspiring and laughing with partners in similar condition, and I feel I'm being accepted. A few minutes later in the kitchen a young woman wearing a formal black afternoon dress and high heels asks politely: "Would you like a little gin, dear?" and pours me half a glass full as a token of sisterhood. The high point for everyone comes toward midnight when delectable "eats"—delicious sandwiches, scrumptious cookies, fabulous cakes, all homemade—are served, and I see Rod Krug, the farm foreman with whom I've recently been dancing, standing in front of me, offering a mug of pitch black coffee, and hear his friendly declaration: "Mrs. Easton, this'll put hair on your chest!" Later Rod gave us an adorable gray female kitten we named Montezuma after the slough we danced beside, that unforgettable night in the ghostly old house.

As I got to know the women of the B. B., helping with their children, accompanying them on shopping trips to Fairfield or Napa where they made pennies count in highly efficient ways, I began to identify with them as with those backstairs or in the fields at Florence. These too were direct, unsophisticated, loving, hating, suffering, enjoying, surviving with courage and cheerfulness. Dynamite's wife, Bernice, for example, lived with their five small children in a house like the one we danced in which the company let them use rent-free. Dynamite made $3.10 a day. With overtime he brought home around a hundred a month. There was nothing left for extras such as doctors and dentists. When the children got sick they simply got well eventually. When Bernice got a toothache she soaked the tooth with whiskey and deferred the inevitable trip to Napa to have it extracted. Dynamite had a roving eye but she put up with it, proud he was the most dynamic male for miles around and sparked the ranch's social life. Sometimes he slapped her, as when she inadvertently let a pregnant sow out of its pen into the hills where it hid its valuable piglets. But she loved her man, her children, life, in a somber gritty way that was enduring as rock. I admired her as I admired Flora and felt my protective cocoon of privilege disappearing as I shared some of their ordeals—and mingled mine with theirs.

Early in November I miscarried. Bob and I had decided against birth control. We wanted children, especially one that might keep me company if he went off to war. It was Flora who explained what might be the matter when I missed my period and then passed a lot of coagulated blood one night in bed. But there were complications and I went to a hospital in Berkeley for treatment. Bob drove down every night to see me. Sometimes when alone I cried for the lost baby we'd wanted so badly. When at last I went home I was weak but our little apartment seemed more precious than ever, our marriage stronger because of shared sorrow, and we decorated our first Christmas tree with joy and hope.

Bob: That winter of '40–'41 was the wettest in California history. Day after day Dynamite and I rode the alleyways in yellow slickers and rain hats. The river rose and broke the levee protecting our lower pens and we had to evacuate cattle to high ground in a hurry. Strange things happened as if triggered by strange weather. Anthrax had been unknown on the delta for so long it had been forgotten. So when a steer dropped as if hit over the head and a trickle of blood ran from its nose, we couldn't imagine what was wrong. Nor could the veterinary. Soon they were dropping like flies. The fact that anthrax could be fatal to humans added suspense when we learned the truth.

Since *Coast* days I'd carried a notebook and jotted down ideas and bits of overheard conversations. Now I began a series of sketches about life on the B. B., getting up an hour earlier to write at our kitchen table. I felt these were better than any writing I'd done because they were more solidly based on actual experience: the ranch life and married life I was living. When Jane's father encouraged me, I decided to make my sketches into stories. Meanwhile world events were catching up with us.

On the scorching hot afternoon of June 22, 1941, while waiting at the railroad station in Lodi for Jane, who'd hurried to Los Angeles after her father suffered a severe heart attack, I saw the headlines announcing Hitler's invasion of Russia. All that spring he'd been extending his conquests—into Yugoslavia, Roumania, Bulgaria, Greece, even the island of Crete from where he might launch an attack on Egypt to support the sensational advance of General Erwin Rommel across North Africa to the Egyptian border. Now it would be global war with a vengeance: Germany, Italy, Japan and their allies against England and the Soviet Union, with China holding out as best she could against the Japanese who'd seized most of her territory.

We talk it over as we drive toward Rio Vista, stopping for dinner at Giusti's Italian restaurant on the riverbank where the Lodi road joins the Sacramento levee road. Will Hitler pull it off, or will he meet the fate of Napoleon, bogged down in Russia's vast expanse and snowy winter? Over veal parmigiana I remember those fearless young Russians, male and female, I'd seen as a tourist in Moscow in '37 jumping from a hundred-fifty-foot-high parachute tower at the Park of Culture and Rest.[1] They might be hard to beat. I also recall the Germany I'd seen that summer. Aside from the park which was full of gaiety and enjoyment, Moscow seemed like a prison—grim, torpid, oppressed by Stalin's bloody purges then at their height. Once as we were walking across Red Square, a procession of three black limousines, curtains drawn, shot out of the Kremlin gates and zipped away down a side street like gangster getaway cars—carrying VIP's or dead bodies? We could only guess. Passersby scarcely turned their heads. Probably they were afraid to.

Berlin, by contrast, seemed alight with energy and purpose— of a sinister kind. Swastikas everywhere—on flags, banners, arm-bands. Uniforms everywhere. Young people marching and sing-ing. And in the dining room of our hotel, middle-aged men in business suits raising right arms in the Nazi salute and muttering "Heil Hitler!" as they entered. Yet on the boat floating down the Rhine, drinking the new September wine with my college mates and me, young non-Nazi Germans—all of us students, all of us full of the optimism of youth—proclaimed that war was absurd and only wine and friendship mattered.

I also remember Italy. There'd been a comic-opera touch, for sure, about black-shirted fascists marching to music in their shiny brass helmets and plumes. But Mussolini evidently had strong support and the country was alive with a spirit of militant vigor. In Rome I stood in the crowd at the curb watching the funeral of Marconi, the great Italian inventor of the wireless, and saw a jut-jawed uniformed "Il Duce" pass within a few yards of me as he walked behind the coffin. Mussolini looked tough if pompous. He would later deride our "decadent democracies" as afraid to fight and boast of no breadlines in Italy or Germany, and indeed there were none, the otherwise unemployed being busy on state projects or military service. By contrast France and England seemed listless and defeatist-minded, accepting war as inevitable but unable to muster energy to do much about it. The "Moose" might be pompous but he was also dangerous.

Just recently during the fall of France, he'd jumped her from behind while she reeled under Hitler's onslaught and grabbed a piece of territory along the Riviera; then tried much the same thing in North Africa against the hard-pressed British but got his

1. Now called Gorky Park.

nose bloodied until Rommel turned things around. And this past spring the gallant little Greek Army had been kicking the dew out of the Italians until, again, the Germans came along. Yet one by one the democracies *had* gone under: Austria, Czechoslovakia, Belgium, Holland, France, Denmark, Norway, leaving England standing alone against Hitler—England and now Russia. Jane and I agreed the U.S. probably couldn't sit on the sidelines much longer.

On the other hand she brought good news. While in Los Angeles she'd met an attractive woman in her early forties, Josephine McCreery, who with her husband, an Englishman, owned a cattle ranch near Hollister, two hours drive south of San Francisco. Selby was a captain in the British Army reserve and was being called to duty and Josephine needed congenial company as well as working help on the ranch. So when she wrote inviting us to come take a look we did. The place was perfectly beautiful, golden mountains and a secluded valley three thousand feet high in the Coast Range—Royal Ranch of the Eagles, its original Spanish owners christened it. Josephine's modern one-story H-shaped house, stucco with tile roof, surrounded a bricked patio where honeysuckle and plumbago bloomed. We would have the rustic frame cottage dating back to the mid–1800s. Near it was an almost equally ancient and charming cookhouse where two young Chinese-Americans, Thomas and Roger, presided; and beyond was the bunkhouse, home for three or four bachelors; and then a large barn and adjoining corrals—all set in that high valley dotted with huge oaks, surrounded by peaks of golden grass. It was truly a Shangri-la and we fell in love with it at first sight.

Josephine offered us the magnificent sum of $90 a month cash plus the cottage, our milk and meat free and the possibility of Sundays off now and then. It seemed almost too good to be true. With the war situation what it was, the B. B. job looked increasingly temporary. And at the McCreery we would have improved pay and working conditions and conceivably a home where Jane might stay should I take up soldiering. Furthermore it brought our dream of a hilltop house a step closer.

Jane: We moved in September as Hitler's armored divisions were penetrating deep into Russia and the Japanese were extending their conquests in China and Southeast Asia. There seemed no stopping the Axis Powers, as they called themselves. I rose in the dark each morning at 5:00 o'clock when the alarm went off, lit the big black kitchen stove which burned chunks of fragrant oak and prepared breakfast while Bob went to the barn to water and feed his horses and saddle the one he would use. During the day I worked at my diary or, accompanied by our beloved Montezuma, who like most cats was developing a remarkable personality, I gossiped with Josephine or with the two boys at the cookhouse. Smiling with ancient Chinese wisdom, Thomas and Roger showed me how to soak pink beans overnight in cold water before cooking, then let them simmer until blowing gently on one—held up in a spoon—peeled away its skin and it was properly done.

Little Joe Correia, the choreman, surreptitiously brought me "extra" eggs he'd found in the mangers of the barn where the hens liked to lay, and we kept up this conspiratorial relationship with her approval after I told Josephine all about it. Joe told me about his life. He was especially proud of having worked on a ranch near Carmel for Mrs. Herbert Hoover whom he greatly admired—just as proud as he was of his honorable discharge from World War I. I loved Joe and all the simplicity and good faith he stood for.

Toothpick-thin Weldon Lynch, the foreman, who'd home-steaded on the Mexican border of New Mexico until forced out by drought and bandidos, showed Bob how to break horses without letting them buck, a departure from Wild West ways; and in the evenings Bob worked on his stories or we read aloud Katherine Mansfield's stories or some of D. H. Lawrence's letters. Lights went out at 9:00 when Josephine turned off the Delco system that generated our electricity. Afterward we could read by kerosene lamp if we wanted but seldom did.

Because the ranch was sometimes isolated for weeks during winter storms, we drove to Hollister, twenty-six miles by lovely if undependable road, and purchased cases of canned food—tomatoes, apricots, peaches, corned beef—and Bob bought two pairs of Levi's for $2.10 each, up from $1.85 because of wartime demand for denim. And thus we began a new life, making friends with our surroundings and its people and feeling accepted as we had at the B. B.—grateful for every day, with the Damocles sword of war hanging over us. Even so, when the sword fell, that peaceful Sunday noontime of December 7, it took us by surprise.

Bob: A few weeks later come the first goodbyes. The men, Little Joe, Weldon, "Hoot" Gibson, Thomas, Roger, shake our hands gravely with inarticulate understatement of what we all feel: this is the end, we'll probably never see each other again. Jane and I decided months ago that if the U.S. enters the war, I'll enlist and she'll live with her parents. Josephine has tears in her eyes as she hugs us. "And you," glaring at me almost angrily with a toss of her red head, "you come back, you understand?"

We live with Jane's parents in Los Angeles while I try to enlist in the cavalry, which seems a good place for ex-cowboys, and with better luck—horses are being replaced by armored vehicles—add to those stories of ranch life I've been working on. As the war comes closer.

At 7:05 P.M. on February 23, 1942, as the President is telling us over the radio that the oceans no longer protect us from attack, a Japanese submarine begins shelling onshore oil installations twelve miles north of Santa Barbara. During the twenty-five minutes while F.D.R. talks, twenty-five shells from its deck gun hit U.S. soil, doing only slight damage. Fortunately all men at work escape injury. An earlier submarine attack had left a Union Oil tanker sinking off Cambria, near today's Hearst Castle, while people watched helplessly from shore as lifeboats carrying its crewmen reached the beach. The sub slipped up on the *Montebello* in the early morning darkness, hit her with a torpedo, then shelled her with its deck gun and subjected the crew to a small-arms fire after they took to their lifeboats. Local authorities didn't know where to turn so they phoned Earl Warren, the state's attorney general, in Sacramento. Warren, later Chief Justice of the U.S. Supreme Court, phoned the military who replied there were only four military planes operational on the entire Pacific Coast and none was capable of bombing a submarine! Santa Barbara was similarly helpless.

These attacks plus others—a number of ships were attacked or sunk off the coast in the months immediately following Pearl Harbor—make us realize how unprepared and vulnerable we are. With most of our fleet and much of our air power out of action in Hawaii, there's little between us and the enemy but space and time. Today's experts say Japan's big mistake was not following quickly with a second strike at Pearl Harbor, destroying its oil storage and other facilities as well as remaining ships, and thus perhaps extending the Pacific war for years, perhaps even to a negotiated peace. By similar reasoning the experts of 1942—and the general public—thought that if an attack on the Pacific Coast were coming, it would come soon, while our defenses were so weak. We were given repeated warnings, including the President's. Therefore Jane and I weren't greatly surprised next day when news came of the Santa Barbara shelling. Perhaps it was a feeler for more to follow. I telephone my parents and find them calm.

But that night the big attack *did* seem to be coming, aimed right at Los Angeles, right at us. Around three in the morning a sound like fireworks on the 4th of July wakes us. It's the anti-aircraft batteries guarding the city opening up. Air-raid sirens begin wailing. As we grope toward our blacked-out bedroom window—there was mandatory blackout every night and windows were covered with heavy curtains or blankets—we think: "This is it! They're bombing us as they did Pearl Harbor!"

Drawing the curtains we see the sky, our sky, red with bursting shells and streaked yellow with the fingers of searchlights. It's incredible, frightening. As the explosions continue we huddle with Jane's mother and Judy downstairs by the radio. Jane's father, a volunteer air-raid warden, is out patrolling the neighborhood to see that no lights make targets for enemy planes. He returns knowing not much more about what's happening than we. All of us huddle by the radio in the front room, joking to keep spirits up, listening to conflicting reports, until local stations go off the air so as not to be targets or navigational guides. Not till morning do we hear the all-clear.

The event was never fully explained. Some observers reported seeing from 1 to 200 planes, others absolutely none. Washington contradicted itself. Secretary of the Navy Frank Knox called it a false alarm. Secretary of War Henry L. Stimson said that as many as fifteen unidentified planes were over Los Angeles and were fired at by guns of the 37th Coast Artillery Brigade. One civilian was hit by a falling shell fragment. Several houses were similarly damaged. One man died of a heart attack while driving an ammunition truck. False alarm or not, for those of us present it was real indeed. The atmosphere was very tense and the fact that our troops were being bottled up and besieged in the Philippines added to it. The Japanese seemed invincible.

Against this background thousands of residents of Japanese ancestry, some alien, some native born, were removed from

McCreery Ranch, 1941. Jane sits with the boys on the bunkhouse steps, Weldon Lynch at right.

coastal areas to detention camps inland. Deplorable though it was, under the circumstances it was approved by most public opinion as by officials up to and including F.D.R. who signed the removal order. The authorities had what they believed reliable evidence of disloyalty among some West Coast Japanese, and they feared these and others might aid an enemy attack. There was some racial prejudice involved, some war hysteria, but the main element in public feeling about the deportation was fear— fear of an attack such as Pearl Harbor had sustained, fear and animosity toward all things Japanese.

Some Japanese I'd known in Santa Maria were summarily deprived of homes, land, and liberty, forced to sell on short notice at much less than fair value, denied recourse to law or any other remedy, and sent off to camps. Recently Congress voted to pay indemnities to those who survive and to apologize for injustice suffered. But for many the compensation and apology came too

Bob on Cinderella.

Feeding calves on Sunday. The best thing about weekend work was sharing it.

At 7:05 P.M., February 23, 1942, while F.D.R. was telling us over the radio that the oceans no longer protected us from attack, a Japanese submarine began shelling the coast near Santa Barbara. (Wide World Photos)

A number of U.S. ships were attacked or sunk off the Pacific Coast by Japanese submarines in the months immediately following Pearl Harbor. Here the tanker *Camden* goes down after being torpedoed. (From: *Silent Siege-II: Japanese Attacks on North America in World War II* by Bert Webber, WEBB RESEARCH GROUP © 1988)

late. And before the war ended, thousands of young Japanese-Americans would demonstrate their loyalty in unmistakable terms by becoming voluntary members of our armed forces and distinguishing themselves in combat. One teenager, Toru Miyoshi, too young for military service, returned to Santa Maria where he became a respected city councilman and today is a county supervisor. He has deep feelings about wartime days but prefers not to express them unless asked.

Finally on March 11, 1942, we stopped being spectators and became participants. I went to the Army recruiting office in downtown Los Angeles, stood in line and enlisted. Many others were feeling as we did. Emperor Hirohito, Hitler, Mussolini, and all they stood for must be defeated or life as we knew it might perish. Besides, it was rumored that if you volunteered you could choose your branch of the Army, a rumor which proved unfounded in my case. I think the whole country realized there was a long fight ahead against heavy odds. Certainly an exhilarating sense that we were part of a nationwide and worldwide commitment to freedom ran through Jane and me. On the down side was

"The Great Air Raid on Los Angeles" turned out to be a false alarm but for many of us there at the time it was real enough. (From: *Silent Siege-II: Japanese Attacks on North America in World War II* by Bert Webber, WEBB RESEARCH GROUP © 1988)

the knowledge that war was like a giant lottery in which some survived and some didn't.

After being inducted into the Army at Fort MacArthur in nearby San Pedro, I was sent, to my pleasant surprise—most recruits were apparently being sent as far away from home as possible—to Camp Roberts near Paso Robles only three hours north of Santa Barbara. From there and from 317 Burlingame Avenue in Los Angeles we began a new life. Our experience was to be unique yet representative, typical but different. Heightening it at the beginning was Jane's precarious pregnancy which again threatened to end in miscarriage.

CHAPTER 3

"See here, Private Hargrove," the sergeant sighed, "can't you try just once to do something right?"

MARION HARGROVE

Basic Training on Two Fronts

BATTERY B, 52ND FIELD ARTILLERY, CAMP ROBERTS, CALIF.,
MAR. 22, 1942

These barracks are so new you can smell the sawdust. Mine is located on a point of land between the Salinas and Nacimiento Rivers at the north edge of camp. The view is breathtaking. Up the Nacimiento your eye follows glimpses of running water westward among cottonwoods and green meadows that wind away into high blue hills between us and the sea. The first Spanish conquistadors and padres wandered around back there and founded Mission San Antonio de Padua, and as usual they chose a beautiful site.

I thought this morning I might try a story about this place from the present moment backward until it first fell under the eye of mankind, telling what happened here, right down to my arrival.

At the moment I'm in a room full of soldier boys trying to get a buzz on by drinking non-intoxicating 3.2 beer, all that the Army allows, while they jabber, play ping-pong, play the jukebox, bang the piano in what is called a "recreation hall." It seems more like a madhouse. I wish I could convey the weirdness, the unreality, of this metropolis of 30,000 young American warriors and all their military machinery imposed on a tranquil spring landscape.

However—efforts toward our welfare appear limitless. We're blessed with live comedians like Harpo Marx, classical pianists, college lecturers, movies everywhere. Each battalion has its mess hall and there are post exchanges (called P.X.'s) well-stocked with everyday items and recreation halls within easy walking distance. Also churches, medical dispensaries, etc. Everyone is friendly. I see many faces I like.

Coming up on the bus I passed the new artillery emplacements along the coast north of Santa Barbara. They bring the war close to home—sandbags, camouflage nets, gun barrels in our peaceful lima bean fields and pasture grass—installed since the Jap attack last month.

Be sure to get plenty of rest. And tell Mum and Pop staying with them was a great pleasure, of the very greatest. I'm going to miss my corner of his study and my Royal portable. Perhaps I can have the typewriter here later. Anyway there will be time for reading and note taking.

317 BURLINGAME AVE., LOS ANGELES, CALIFORNIA,
MAR. 26, 1942

Your first letter came yesterday and I've worn it out reading it. I felt half as if it was the engaged, not the married, Bob who wrote it because I connect our letters with that first spring and summer when we ached for each other.

And such good news about your stories has made our baby very emotional and me a bit more nauseated than usual but I *hate* your not being here to discuss our miraculous luck! Evidently it's wonderful for you to publish first in the *Atlantic*. I believe I'm the happiest wife in the world and certainly it's all excellent for our baby. Camp Roberts isn't far and I'll be able to come whenever you get a few hours off, just let me know when you want me. Please share your life with me always.

Mine here is quiet which suits me beautifully. I do feel like a lazy bum just lying around and trying to eat but evidently it's best for "my condition." I wish you were here to give me a kiss and let me lie quietly in your arms so I can feel your rough chin against my forehead.

Montezuma is very sweet. I saw her yesterday at the vet's and she put her paws through the bars and tried to get out to me, while meowing so piteously! I told her about your stories selling and she said she always knew they would. Her kittens look exactly like her, some a little lighter gray, more like papa, who has been around today, by the way. My dream is a glimpse of the McCreery Ranch in May with you. The colts would be divine and I have a longing to see that lovely land. I'm terribly pleased they named a filly "Janey," so Josephine wrote. The next is to be called "Bob." My thoughts are with you constantly.

BATTERY B, 52ND FIELD ARTILLERY, CAMP ROBERTS, CALIF.,
MARCH 29, 1942

As we put in 9-hour days on a regular program with good food, we begin to think seriously about this new world we live in. A day begins with reveille at 7:00, breakfast at 7:30. Fall in at 8:15 for calisthenics followed by marching, lectures, training films, hour by hour, these punctuated by additional vaccinations, dental and eye clinics (tomorrow I go to be examined for glasses). Lunch is from 12:30 until 1:45, then training again until 5:30. Supper at 6. Then we are free until lights out at 10 and taps at 11.

Next week we begin at 6 A.M. and get *strenuous*. Overnight hikes. No leaves for six weeks. But visitors are permitted during daylight hours on Sunday. Also there is a guest house where you can stay. So when you're able to travel, you can come for a night. Yet one-night stands aren't altogether successful, to my notion. I would almost prefer to wait till I get a 3-day pass, wouldn't you?

Unfortunately the noncoms of our resident cadre aren't good teachers. They have sinecure jobs and hence don't really care. But there are six or eight rawboned recruits among us—lumberjacks, ex-cooks, C.C.C.[1] boys—men best described as "guys," sunburned, brassy, profane—who've become our natural leaders. They possess that priceless quality called initiative and get up early and get us moving so we can have the cleanest damned barracks in the regiment. On marches they break out with our rollicking theme song:

> You're in the Army now,
> You're not behind a plow!
> You'll never get rich,
> You son-of-a-bitch,
> You're in the Army now!

Chanting in unison, accenting the "in" and the "Ar" of Army and the "now" in the first line, and similar alternate syllables in the other lines, we get a nice one-two cadence which our feet keep time to. Wish you could hear us.

I'll write every day. Keep $30 of this check toward the doctor bill and send me back $20 please. I say this with a bit of sheepish feeling, asking my old lady for a handout.

---

1. Civilian Conservation Corps.

I've been thinking how we dashed off on spring afternoons, when you got home to Rio Vista early by some good fortune, up to where the blue mountains began and how all the world seemed enchanted. And invariably one of our tummies acted up. But it was so marvelous just to be together. And at the McCreery Ranch I remember evenings in front of our fire, with Puss Cat asleep in your chair and all the coals so bright—and outside the cold hills fast asleep and the lonely men of the bunkhouse and poor tortured Josephine. Yet you and I an oasis of joy, in our own home!

I think perhaps our joy did help others. They saw it and warmed their hearts at it. But there were private moments all our own that nobody but we understood, and how gently we loved each other in those evenings!

Excuse this feeble letter. I just don't have much energy.

CAMP ROBERTS, APRIL 4, 1942
Today I made a formal call on Lt. Wilson who commands our training battery, got permission from the first sergeant in approved fashion, then knocked on the flap of headquarters tent. "Come in," says a businesslike voice.

Cap in hand I advance to within two paces of the desk where Wilson, a dark-haired competent-looking fellow not much older than I is sitting, salute, and declare that I have permission from the first sergeant to speak to the battery commander.

Wilson sits erect and looks me over with a cool eye. It isn't a professional military eye but the eye of an American civilian obliged by necessity to play a military role. He asks what I want. I profess a desire to go to officer candidate school. After some questions, he obligingly calls regimental headquarters and makes an appointment for me with the personnel officer.

To tell you the truth, I have no great desire to become an officer but a private's pay of $21 a month less $4 for insurance and laundry is hardly enough to support the two of us, let alone baby.

This evening a lad from Texas and I walked along the bluff above the river. He sleeps in the next bed. For two days I thought he would perish of homesickness. Then three letters came from his girl and one from his mother. "Dad didn't write," he explained with woeful frankness. "He must be drunk." He showed me a picture of his girl standing in front of a Woolworth window full of kitchenware. Nice girl.

His eyes fill with tears when he speaks of her. They've been going together four years but he was making only 50¢ an hour until recently, and when he got his good job the war broke out. He thought it over and one day took a deep breath and enlisted. Said he wouldn't have been happy otherwise.

Last night after getting the three letters he telephoned Irene. I asked what she said. "Desert and come home!" He was literally crying for joy.

We discuss life, love, marriage, the church. Don is a devout Baptist. Of 30 members of his young people's group, all the boys but two married secretly before or after the attack on Pearl Harbor. Only he and his brother refused, though engaged, feeling it dishonorable since married men were not subject to immediate draft.

He asks when I think the war will end. "Oh, a year," I say. "Maybe two!"

Thank you for being 24 years old. I love you and Puss Cat and our baby. No one else.

LOS ANGELES, APRIL 5, 1942

Sorry I spoiled our phone talk. Forgive me. As you guessed, I've been using the ice-pack to help control the uterine bleeding. And it has stopped, *so don't worry.* Just pray God we can have this baby! I'm much better today.

A sweet birthday letter came from John.[2] I wish you could talk with him. He needs a sensible outlook on the war which you could help develop. Anyway I feel sure he'll come out all right. It's a difficult time to be in college.

This afternoon Pop and Judy and I had a wonderful discussion which started with trying to define a great man. In the end we disagreed violently as to where "brain" ends and "heart" begins. We agreed heart matters more. Without much heart you can be a great scientist or philosopher but never a Shakespeare. It was a novelty, after months of nausea, to be able to use my mind again and not feel sick.

You were in church today and I thought of you there. We

2. At Harvard.

must discuss whether our child is to be christened, etc. I hope devoutly *not*, but we'll talk it over. Can't we give our offspring a certain amount of religion without those dreadful ceremonies? Somehow, it's all so *untruthful* in my mind. I'm afraid I can't agree with you about the church. I've been dwelling on the subject in my thoughts lately and always have to tell you what goes on inside me.

CAMP ROBERTS, APRIL 8, 1942

Today on the rifle range I scored 15 out of a possible 25, not very good, but my rifle (a 1917 Enfield, tell Pop) is not sighted properly and my glasses though ordered have not arrived.

Our equipment is hodgepodge. My haversack was made in October of 1917. On my shelter tent are names of men who've used it ever since World War I, I guess. We wear World War I helmets.

New equipment is coming, including 105-mm. howitzers just off the assembly line (confidential information, this). MacArthur probably has some in the Philippines. Our old 75-mm. guns are going out of production. The entire field artillery will use howitzers. Look up the difference between a howitzer and a gun!

So Aidan[3] has gone to war at last, well well! I wonder what Helen[4] will do? What a dearth of good company there seems to be in Los Angeles. Someday we shall all live together on a ranch and make our own.

Lights are due to go out. I love you, my sweet, and look forward to that 3-day pass.

———————

General Douglas MacArthur, commanding U.S. and Filipino resistance to the Japanese invasion of the Philippines, had left the islands secretly by motor torpedo boat nearly a month earlier, under orders from F.D.R., and was now in Australia, leaving General Jonathan Wainwright in his place. On April 9, after bitter fighting against heavy odds, nearly 100,000 Americans and Filipinos on Bataan Peninsula surrendered to the Japanese, while

3. Aidan Roark, movie studio executive.
4. Mrs. Roark, the former Helen Wills Moody.

Wainwright retired with a small force to Corregidor Island in
Manila Bay. Those who surrendered were marched off to prison
camps in such brutal fashion that thousands died. It was our
biggest and most humiliating defeat since Pearl Harbor. Renewed
anger and hatred toward the Japanese swept the country, along
with a sense of continued impotence and fear.

Sometimes we asked ourselves the big question: will we lose
this war? And the answer was always no. Deep down, we felt we
must ultimately prevail because, whatever its faults, our cause
was more just than our enemies'! The truth seemed as simple—
and as profound—as that.

In our personal sectors, Jane was finding it increasingly difficult to live with her parents again, having had a home of her
own.

I was bitterly homesick for that home, as for her, but rarely
said so, feeling it would serve no useful purpose.

———————

LOS ANGELES, APRIL 9, 1942

This morning the war seems terribly near. The immense *pressure*
and somehow *rush* of the whole upheaved world translates itself
into our daily lives.

Your letter deals with camp life, the Viking Press sends its
contract to be signed, a letter from a little paralyzed girl I used to
tell tales to in Vienna comes from Switzerland. It's *all* so bound
up with the war. Everyone is pushed about crazily. I hope we can
keep ourselves sane.

Daddy is mailing you a letter regarding the Viking contract.
Remember there's no hurry. Good writing cannot be turned out
at the rate *they* wish. It must come from the quiet peaceful inside
of Bob. Viking or probably Harper's will want your book no matter
how long it takes to get ready, so don't worry about that. Also,
between us all we can get a much better title than "Wind." It's
been used too often, as: "Wind, Sand and Stars," "Listen, the
Wind," etc. Don't you agree?

Well, our baby's papa is giving his mama plenty of excitement these days!

A letter also from Dyke Brown's wife Kate. She's at her
family's awaiting the arrival of a baby daily, Dyke is taking a
Naval supply training course at Harvard Business School. His

best friend from Berkeley, a young doctor, is off to Africa. Kate says another boy I know is in Alaska! It all makes us excited and slightly scared: the youth of the nation scattered far and wide and being sacrificed.

Thank God we have in mind exactly *what* we are fighting for. It is worth any sacrifice. The miracle is that we go on having babies galore and clinging to as normal a life as possible.

Next Morning:

Can't write much as I had no sleep last night with Pop on a bender. He is intolerable when drunk and I'd forgot how mean and abusive he is towards Mum at such times. I can stand a good deal but do not intend to with baby on its way when I need a lot of rest. Unless Pop behaves—and I can probably persuade him to—I'll go to your parents in Santa Barbara if you think it would be convenient.

Anyway, it's all rather stupid and I can't get used to this weakness of Pop's. All of us are under the strain of his drinking every night and he just doesn't control it as he should. I realize that he longs to be in some war assignment—but that is almost impossible for a man of his age with his dependents and bad heart.

It now transpires that Betty and Bonnie[5] will be fully on his hands as her husband is slightly cracked. Well, everyone has worries of some kind and I don't think life is particularly easy for *anyone* these days. Also a blackout last night added to the general confusion. After serving his midnight hitch, Pop picked up a few other air raid wardens and brought them back here where they all caroused until 5:00 a.m. The *noise* men can make is fantastic. Enough of this vile subject. Drinking is a nightmare to me and I have thanked heaven many a time for your sobriety.

CAMP ROBERTS, APRIL 11, 1942

Spent all afternoon in the gas chambers receiving training whiffs of mustard, Lewisite, chlorpicrin, and phosgene. Sounds dreadful doesn't it? The first sight of a gas mask is apt to make you shudder. (I'm in the rec. hall and a boy at the piano is playing a lovely Mozart concerto!) But actually gas is no longer fearful. All known types are readily made harmless by our masks and protective

---

5. Jane's aunt and cousin.

clothing. Only 20% of World War I gas casualties were deaths, some 14,000 out of 90,000—I believe the figure was—contrary to popular opinion.

I do hope Pop is managing himself better. It is hard for you, I know, and if ever you feel he's interfering seriously with your rest and best possible physical condition I'm sure he would be glad if you told him. I would feel better too. This is not the time to be other than self-considering.

All our problems are really nothing, I feel, when I see these poor lads unmarried, or in love or wishing they were. My Texas buddy's girl has written asking him to ask me (as a married man) what I think of their being married now. I undertook to advise against it—with some misgiving. Yet I feel I was right. I would not have married you under these circumstances. Or would I? At any rate I tried to present all possibilities. If he didn't come back there would be a young widow waiting, living on a memory of a day or two, perhaps with a child. Wouldn't it mar her life? Or would she rather be his widow with his child?

I did say something with which he agreed: if I should not come back from this war I would indeed die unhappy if I thought you, my wife, were then going to spend your life alone. When the right man came along I should want you to marry again. If he never came, all right. If you never loved him as much as me, all right. But never let a sense of respect or sentiment keep you from doing the strong and natural thing which is to live while we are young among our kind, and not by ourselves; only then are we fully productive. I think this a true statement. I do feel strongly that life and the qualities we love most in one another are far larger than we, and are carried by others beside ourselves. Perhaps we meet these special people in the course of our lifetimes, perhaps not. But if we do let's recognize them.

My sweet Janie, this is a pretty serious subject to tag on the end of a letter. Do you feel heavy after reading it? Believe me it was not written heavily. This sort of thing must be said once and for all and now we are done. I love you, my darling. Don't think me lugubrious please.

I can't tell you how happy your letter made me this morning. You feared it might be "heavy" but I loved every word for I had been thinking of the very things you spoke of. I don't agree with the advice you gave Don about marrying. I think you and I would have married under *any* circumstances, at least I pray so. Love may come more than once to some people but to others it just *doesn't*. I think as long as one is sure of it being real love, time has little to do with it and I believe how *long* one is married is unimportant.

I would have forced you to marry me even if you were in the Army—perhaps you forget how essential and compelling that instinct is. It makes me furious to think you would not have taken the step in time of war! For war is only a transient thing and love lasts forever. So surely it can take its place ahead of war.

I think Don would be a much better man and soldier if married. If he is killed or you are killed it is still alright—love cannot stop with death. His girl may never have the love for anyone else that she has for him. She might find companionship, etc., yes. But, darling, the really purest love is not given out like that. I wonder if I'm wrong? I *feel* I am right and if we talked about it we would come to a conclusion that would satisfy us both.

It is so damnable not to talk these things out. I suppose I should thank you for saying you would not mind my marrying again—given your death (ah, cheerful!). But I cannot understand marrying twice. I certainly could never fall in love again the way I did with you, and love that is only companionship seems to me very strange and almost fake. So you may have to give up the idea of my second marriage and go into battle without any such thought.

I cannot be so magnanimous as to think of marriage on *any* terms but the highest and the highest doesn't come more than once in a lifetime. If you are killed, my darling, I shall not marry again because it would shut me off from you and our love, your love, and I could not bear the seed of another man. Don't try to alter this conviction but admit I'm right.

I cannot feel that our love ends in death and so I can never be really alone again in my life. Please answer this argument and tell me how you feel about it. My love, our love could only really die if one of us were to marry again. Don't you see? I have thought of this for a long time, long before I met you, and it's become a firm belief. It's a great comfort to me and your statement on the subject is to me very dead and depressing. Perhaps you were just being altruistic! Anyway, let's list all subjects we want to discuss when we see each other again. And be sure to tell Don this argument of mine! My advice would be: marry. Try and remember how *you* felt in the summer of 1940—you who wouldn't even wait an extra month!

I can hardly wait for your answer on the above. After that we can drop the subject though to me it's not gruesome or sad or tragic.

Am going to the hospital today for minor surgery (removal of the cyst from my chest) tomorrow. An excellent doctor is doing it and there is no danger for the baby. I look forward to your letters.

By the way, if I die *do* feel you could marry again! How does that sound? I put it up to YOU, not ME! I don't see how one could do it but I am not going to bind your heart in fetters! Only, I am going to arise from the grave and give you a few nightmares!

I adore you and love you and need you. That's all this letter wants to say.

CAMP ROBERTS, APRIL 16, 1942

This is being written in the latrine, the only place there's a light at this hour, while two guys from Minnesota take a shower. When I phoned, Mum said you were all right, and not to worry. I wish I'd been there to see you coming out of the anesthetic all sweet and fuzzy. I know life in the hospital will drag, but hope you have an intelligent nurse who can read to you. Wish so dreadfully it were I.

We've had our first experience of guard duty, 24 hours "guarding" our section of camp in true military style. My shift as sentinel was from three A.M. to six, walking the edge of a road alone in the dark, bored to death and chilled to the bone. Then I began thinking of all the sentinels of all the armies since time began and to feel myself one with them—in a momentous, even noble, responsibility for the safety of comrades, generals, "the cause," etc.! Just as dawn broke I halted a milk truck. "Dismount, Golden State Milk," I ordered in firm fashion, "and stand in front of your headlights to be identified!" He complied with alacrity, perhaps thinking my rifle loaded and uncertain what a green recruit might do with it.

HOSPITAL OF THE GOOD SAMARITAN, LOS ANGELES,
APRIL 16, 1942

There is a good hand guiding us because the cyst, located just above my breasts, was only a cyst and the baby hasn't suffered. I worried a little about the whole matter as surgery is always a shock to the system. In my innocence cancer never entered my head. My only concern was for our baby and the fear something might upset my pregnancy again.

Mother's face was full of anxiety. But everyone tried to be calm and reassuring, while I lay there in bed waiting and feeling nauseated and miserable. In the early evening a young intern breezed in. He was brusque and I disliked him at once. He began feeling around for the lump and asked me blunt questions. I suddenly burst into tears. "Oh, now, what's the matter?" he demanded in an exasperated tone. "What are you crying about?"

"I don't want anything to happen to my baby!" I sobbed.

"Are you sure you're pregnant?" he snapped, as if I were some kind of animal. "You don't look pregnant to me!" And without ceremony he yanked up my hospital gown and began poking around in my stomach while the tears rolled down my face. I was terrified he was going to start me bleeding again and I'd lose the baby. Finally he announced: "After they get you ready for surgery, just go to sleep!" and departed. Oh, how I hated him!

The night was one long nightmare. I was operated on early next day. When I waked in my room after the anesthesia wore off, I saw Mum and Pop leaning over me and heard them saying: "It was benign, dearest. Thank God!"

There are sweet peas in my room and other flowers. I don't do much but lie and dream of you and our next home. I have such a stream of things I want to talk to you about. And I hate your not being present at this episode in our life.

No strength for long letters yet but my love flies out to you every day and I hope you are well and cheerful. With a thousand gentle kisses!

CAMP ROBERTS, APRIL 17, 1942

Don's father has been drunk 14 days. I've loaned him $5 to send his mother who has no money. Poor kid, he is distracted! Irene didn't want to marry when the war broke out; now she does. His mother is trying to get him out of the Army. Talking to me relieves him. I suppose you're right that we could have got married on a 10-day leave and been very happy, but I cannot agree with your attitude on remarriage. My God in Heaven, let us conclude the subject soon! The years are long—life comes again and again, following spring over the green hills. I do not believe love is peculiar to individuals but is universal—as widespread as beauty among flowers. I grant you certain flowers are more beautiful than others. But these can be recognized, can't they?

I adore you, sweet wife, and pray your lovely body may be whole and you restored to me. I also pray that out of this war music will come, that out of misery and death a song—because we as yet are journeymen, marchers without music. I mean nationally. I think we can look at this war as the expiation of the collective shortcomings of mankind, paid in blood because we could not—or would not—live peacefully together. Chiang Kai-shek[6] says so much when he says: "If we sweat more in time of peace we would bleed less in time of war."

You won't understand why I'm carrying on about this until you've been in the Army and seen the expenditure of effort and money released by war. We must somehow get it through our heads that peace is as important as war, and that if we work harder for peace we may not have to go to war and live in barracks far from our wives.

If anyone asks what I'm "getting" out of the Army I wish you would tell them the foregoing. I feel it with all my heart.

I can't imagine a less comforting letter for one convalescing from an operation as you will be when you receive this—poor Janie, she got expounded at!

317 BURLINGAME AVE., LOS ANGELES, APRIL 19, 1942
Daddy put Bach on the gramophone just now while I was feeling very nauseated, and the blessing of Bach's genius flooded over me. There is no war, no fear, in his beauty and I realize that my thoughts for months have been only of war. Why do I get lost in such absurdity when Mozart and Bach are far *truer* and more enduring? We will have music in our lives in time to come and war will be a strange illusion.

Now I'm watching the prettiest fire opposite the couch and

6. Leader of Nationalist China in its struggle against the invading Japanese.

the trees are dark against the sky but soon there will be nothing but night outside. I'm still a bit weak.

Perhaps our baby is three months old today. I hope so. My darling, my body aches for yours and every night my bed is empty.

CAMP ROBERTS, APRIL 19, 1942

Sometimes on these Sundays I miss you most of all, just in the little moments that should be mine alone to spend with you in quietness. Today at noon we went "on the alert"—one gun squad of us—and will remain so until retreat tomorrow (4:30). It has something to do with enemy submarine activity. Anyway, for nine days we have shifts of this: being on 3-minute call day and night and sleeping in our clothes, ready to repel Japanese invaders!

This morning at the rec. hall I finished what I hope is the final version of "Jim Magee" on my new Royal portable (I have a cozy corner by a bookcase and a little coffee table that is just the right height for a typewriter). One of the fellows asked to read my manuscript so I gave it to him and before I could take it back three or four others read and criticized it, and we got a literary discussion going: Somerset Maugham, Mark Twain, Kipling, came in for their share, also James Hilton; also *Gone With the Wind* and a volume of the best stories of *Collier's* from 1910 to 1916 which was loaned me. "Jim Magee" got consensus approval. The plot is somewhat modified and at last has continuity and pace. I'll let it rest a while before mailing.

We're all much cheered by the foreign news: the bombing of Tokyo and Germany,[7] etc.

317 BURLINGAME AVE., LOS ANGELES, APRIL 26, 1942

We read your story aloud and were delighted, as was Bernice,[8] whose note I enclose. I'll send you a copy to work on if you wish. But perhaps better push out another story and revise later. Bernice loved it this way.

Enclosed also is a letter from Cass Canfield at Harper's who

7. Tokyo by American planes led by Lieutenant Colonel, later Lieutenant General, James H. Doolittle; Germany by the British.
8. Bernice Baumgarten, affiliated with the Brandt & Brandt literary agency.

sounds decent. Pop is quite pleased that Viking is publishing your book so have no qualms on that score. Bernice promoted you so fast that it was all fixed before Harper's had a chance.

Daddy leaves tomorrow for New York on business. It should be a profitable trip if he stays on the wagon.

Judy asked last night what the baby is like now inside my tummy. She is growing interested though used to be revolted by the whole idea. I'm well and strong and I love you.

CAMP ROBERTS, APRIL 28, 1942

Today was a waste and betrayal. At times you want to scream, so many lives are being entrusted to people who don't give a damn, or not enough of a damn—somehow these latter are worse in their carelessness, their pretty-good-enough quality. Our disasters in this war will probably not be from cowardice but because somebody was detailed to put shrapnel in the ammunition carrier and never got around to doing it, or put in smoke shells instead. Really, the sloppiness is maddening. A simple movement of drill is explained one way by our lieutenant, another by our sergeant. Then when the mistake is palpable it's allowed to go uncorrected. Then some well-meaning kid catches hell and humiliation for doing what he thought was right. There is grumbling now. You understand how the French must have felt during the fall of France. Something wrong in high places? And you understand why the British needed Churchill at the helm.

But there are good days too and this is only a training center after all. Do you have plenty of money? I suppose a check will be coming from the *Atlantic*.

Worked three hours of K.P.[9] today, then got excused by naming all the parts of a howitzer from memory. So virtue pays.

Will you send a two-dollar check to the Crocker Bank? On this firm financial note I close, with a great deal of love.

LOS ANGELES, APRIL 28, 1942

Our first check from your writing! Two hundred dollars less commission, less expenses, for a grand net of $163.45. I think we

9. Kitchen police.

should keep it and frame it! How domestic if it should be sunk into a baby carriage, crib and bath!

You will be amazed at my health and strength. I can hardly believe they're true! All my desire to write comes back. I wish my sketches, which Daddy took off to New York today, were bigger and better. I'm too young yet, perhaps, to have much to say. You tell me the proper age is thirty. In the meantime kitchen and babies will keep me busy.

I can see all the boys crowding around and reading your stories. I adore you. My heart is with you every minute.

P.S. I won't *feel* the baby for another six weeks.

CAMP ROBERTS, MAY 15, 1942

This morning the battery commander called me in and sent me to headquarters for an interview with a major, after which I made out application for officer candidate school. Someday soon I will appear before an examining board—not this week probably because we leave tomorrow on a three-day trip to fire our 105- howitzers for the first time.

Must run. You do seem very strong and very well and happy and all good things that make a wife and mother. I love you my darling—all your warm body and heart that lie by mine.

2442 GARDEN ST., SANTA BARBARA, MAY 15, 1942

Think of me here in Santa Barbara in this quiet house, my walks and my sitting in the late afternoon on the bench that looks to the mountains. Think of me as loving your dear parents and think of the happiness I will have when you phone or write. When the baby moves in a few weeks, I'll send a telegram.

I feel reinforced from our good talks and from having your beautiful manly body next to me. When the flesh is happy and strong it is so good and true. When my body was sick I had only visions of your heroic death on some battlefield!! Now, I believe there is an equally good chance of a heroic *life*!!

Will sleep in a lonely bed tonight. I am not brave about that, I hate it, and long for you. Please keep my heart very close to yours or it will die.

If our child is a girl, I will be happy because I want you to love
and touch and cherish a new little female babe when it is warm
and terribly young, the way your sister was. I've often wished
there were something I could do to make up for the loss of that
lovely little sister whom you have loved and remembered all these
years. Perhaps a daughter will be as near to my wish as I can
come.

My whole being wants space and quiet in which to grow and
bear my child in the *best* way. How very thrilling a first baby is.
I've stopped grieving over the miscarriage and realize our good
angel knew best. Please God, make me a mother who is gentle,
strong and tender always. Bob, we will have many fertile years
but this first baby is breathlessly miraculous to me.

Anyway, I hope you don't care if our baby is a girl. I
know most people want boys first. But we are *not* most people.
And you and I have always agreed it was foolish to care which
sex arrived.

Everything you say in your letter today is true: our first real
separation has taught us that *time* is of no consequence, that we
will always have this incredibly simple and pure love, made of
perfection itself. I feel so happy now we have discovered this.

Have thought often of our ideal church too. It may be on
an open slope of country. Perhaps walls are not needed. What do
you think?

What an exciting rumor that you may be sent to officer's
training. Knowing you want to go overseas, I hope you won't
have to wait long. As you say, it must be done the *whole* way—
this Army business. I'm all for it.

I'll type the Dynamite notes first. Just at the moment I don't
want to go indoors, for it's so lovely here on the grass—a thousand
birds, a quiet feeling, and the thought that beyond these mountains is an even lovelier wildness. There's a wonderful healing
quality here too. I hope I'm not being a nuisance to your mother.
She is so good, so patient. Tell her how much this visit means to
me, please. Her approval, and your father's, of your new status
as writer is very touching.

Daddy can't come up tonight but Mum will. He has to be
on hand for the signing of a long-term contract at Columbia
Studios. It seems his script is to be used and he will work on that

picture.[10] It's very satisfying to have his first script liked. Also he wants to keep busy on his Civil War novel.

CAMP ROBERTS, MAY 18, 1942

As the end of basic training nears we suddenly become aware how lucky we've been—how healthy, happy, friendly, how much we hate to leave dear old Camp Roberts we've cursed so many times. As you say, it's in the presence of death that life flourishes. In a crazy, dreadful way old Nazi Joe at the B. B. Ranch was right when he said: "Dere us nudding accomplish but vat dere is destruction first!" Beyond doubt war is a dark blessing.

I wish you could know the comradeship our platoon—particularly my 6th section—has developed. Among us are three whose parents were born in Germany, who could speak almost no English when they began school. There is Chapeno the gentle Mexican bred in Texas, with beautiful eyes like a deer, who has studied and listened and said no word for seven weeks until the sergeant began to realize he knew his job and to select him as gunner. Now he's one of us. We say: "That Chapeno—boy, but he's smart, really smart!"

There is Brun the freckled sunburned Norwegian, formerly a railway postal clerk, now our best marksman, best poker player, best barracks philosopher—"I never bought a woman in my life. Honest, fellers!" Apparently they flocked to him voluntarily. He has an extraordinary I.Q., is waiting for Military Intelligence to finish checking his record and then he'll be off for special assignment.

There is W., the neighborhood gossip, a contact man, something of a jackal and hanger-on, partially bald with glasses. He has been a district manager for United Air Lines.

There is Baskerville, lately with Standard Service Stations, now one of three waiting for officer school. He is truly at home here among trucks and mechanical apparatus and those military matters he had the foresight to study years ago in citizens' military training camp—an institution you likely never heard of that instructed some of us in the art of war back in the 1920s and '30s when anyone with any sense was at a country club or beach!

10. *The Desperadoes* starring Randolph Scott and Claire Trevor.

Basic training, Camp Roberts, April 1942. The old French-design 75-mm. gun dated from the First World War, as did our helmets. I'm second from right, back row.

At Roberts our barracks looked much like thousands of others across the country. For health reasons we slept head to foot. For inspections, as here, barracks bags containing personal belongings were placed at foot of beds and footlockers carefully aligned. (Courtesy San Luis Obispo County Historical Museum)

There is Erickson from Minnesota who plays the drums in a jazz band and Adolf, the Bohemian, whose father is a well-to-do dairyman. Adolf is almost as dumb as the cows he loves. He likes comparing a howitzer to a corn cultivator in price and productivity until we laugh at his honest naiveté.

There is Alan C., the idiot, who always answers "What?" no matter what you say to him, calls a "deflection" a "reflection," and when told to set out the aiming stakes ran away into the woods and hid behind a tree. Ask him how old he is and he replies smiling: "How old are you?" And if you tell him he nods happily: "That's how old I am!"

There is Blackwell, hard-rock miner from the Coeur d'Alenes (Idaho), who once got 60 days for tearing up a town on Saturday night, has been a cowpuncher, farmer, ardent C.I.O. member (mineworkers), can tell you of the dark innards of the earth, the stopes, foot walls, hanging walls, jumbos, single jacks and dry buzzies—of rats that became so tame they would sit on your knee at noon-hour to be fed. Once he saw them all running past him in the shadows, hundreds of them, till the damp ground became alive and moved. Then he ran too, not knowing but taking wisdom from the rats, and moments later a great under-ground river broke the hanging wall and filled the mine with a rush of water which foamed close behind him as he ran.

I've omitted Byrnes, the "old Army," a grizzled veteran at 36, who brings our mops and brooms upstairs every morning and routs us out of bed. He loves horses so much he's begun to look like one. In the cavalry he was a proud member of the honor guard that fired salutes when the bodies of his comrades were laid in the ground. He buried a wife and child at Salinas alone.

Tonight Baylor, the near-sighted lad with glasses who is waiting court martial for breaking quarantine and going to the P.X. for beer, who has been in trouble, A.W.O.L.,[11] or on sick call or something ever since he arrived, whose life consists mostly of lies about the great deeds he has done so that nobody believes a word he says, who is called a "gold brick" and held in contempt, who talks fondly of his girl, his father the colonel, his service with the R.A.F.[12] and Canadian Army. . . . Tonight Baylor the lost child without enough brains or ability of any kind to do a

---

11. Absent without leave.
12. Royal (British) Air Force.

worthwhile thing, is going blind. The eye clinic said in five years
or less he will not be able to see. It's apparently congenital. Since
he's been here his sister has gone blind. Tonight he lies in our
tent, asking me whether he ought to write his girlfriend about his
eyes. I advised against doing so.

Sunday I asked him to go to church but he can't leave the
battery area, pending court martial, even to cross the street to
church. I gave him the pocket edition of the New Testament
furnished gratis on the table in the chapel. Tonight as I left the
tent he was writing his name in the front of it. Later I watched
him reading it. He would make your heart break. Well, maybe
he will live in sickness better than in health. Or maybe he will
be given his moment to die nobly.

There's a mighty spirit brewing here, Janie. Woe to the
tyrants, it seems to say, who trespass too long against ordinary
people. Woe to the Hitlers and Tojos.[13] These boys don't brag
about what they are going to do in combat. And they may not
catch on quickly to abstractions like deflections and firing angles.
They prefer to talk about tangible things. But sometimes in a
quiet moment they'll say: "I want action!"

Well, this has gone around and around, only to end with
what matters most—I love you.

SANTA BARBARA, MAY 21, 1942

I know how you're feeling. One often has a surge of realization
when a certain portion of one's life is ending. I've had it many
times: when leaving my Swiss school, when leaving Spence, when
leaving Vienna, when leaving Italy, when leaving home to be
married. They were moments of extreme lucidity, it seemed,
when I could see clearly that we must love every day of our lives
and never feel an instant is wasted.

The story of Baylor made me cry. I can see him so well. He
has nothing but pain ahead, except perhaps the power to rise, as
you say. I am sure he will do it. His girl will forsake him, of
course. He will go on telling lies. He will take the easy way out.
He will always be in trouble, until one day he will turn up
the other road and become suddenly aware of his power toward

---

13. Hideki Tojo, premier from October 16, 1941, until mid-July 1944, had become
a symbol of Japanese militarism.

goodness—that he CAN be like others, that he need NOT have lived in vain. I feel there is no limit to what the most forsaken person on earth can change into.

When it's hot and summery like this, I always feel as if some wonderful thing were just around the corner. The sense of anticipation is everywhere. It reminds me of nights when I swam in our pool at Florence. There were the shadows of roses from the arbor nearby to swim through and the path of the moon to touch on the water, and in the fields roundabout a thousand million fireflies sparkled in and out of the tall dry grass. And during those moments when there was barely the sound of water moving about me, I had that sense of watching for approaching miracles. I think I was waiting for love. I waited for it from 14 on, was aware of it, of the man-woman love very early, so that I really loved you long before we met. And on those summer nights when I was finally forced to go to bed under the oppressive mosquito net, I lay waiting, sometimes tiptoeing to the window to see how the night had changed since I came in, and there were new stars above and the moon was behind the house and the fireflies fewer.

I lay waiting. But nothing, no one, came to tell me what I was waiting for. And last night as I lay in bed half asleep, feeling that same kind of heavy heat in the air, I was that same child, waiting for something great, marvelous, new.

CAMP COOKE,[14] CALIFORNIA, MAY 28, 1942

We left Roberts at 7:30 a.m. while the band played "Auld Lang Syne" and our buddies waved goodbye. They were our first and dearest. Leaving was hard. At our graduation ceremony the colonel said: "There are two places I hope to meet you men again. One is Tokyo. The other is Berlin."

As I walked toward the trucks a stubby little Minnesota Swede named Buska, who wasn't leaving, ran from behind and jumped on my shoulders, laughing, and threw his arms around my neck. Can I tell you how much that meant?

We left in a convoy of trucks and needed overcoats all the way. What disgust there was among the Texans who thought

---

14. Now Vandenberg Air Force Base, the West Coast's space center, fifty miles northwest of Santa Barbara.

they were going home, and the Minnesotans who thought they were going home, and the Washingtonians and Oregonians and New Yorkers who thought they were going home—to end up here, after three hours.

I must say I found few words to justify my native habitat when we left the Santa Maria Valley behind, crossed the ridges and saw Camp Cooke's barracks squatting on a sandy plateau above the ocean in such a dust cloud you couldn't look with more than half an eye. Really, it was pretty bad.

I've never known it so windy and dusty here. When I first saw this spot it was part of the Jesús y María Rancho, isolated at the water's edge, an old Spanish land grant named for the Prince of Peace and his Mother. Now it's a center for war. The whole 5th Armored Division is here plus several smaller outfits like ours. The way these camps are springing up all over the country makes me wonder if our landscape—internal as well as external—will ever be without these grim reminders.

After we settled into new barracks, were issued new blankets, met our new captain—not a day over 30—heard him say frankly this was for keeps, this was our last stop before the front and we would go there together—we felt better. We are part of the 807th Tank Destroyer Battalion—whatever a tank destroyer is. Nobody seems to know because no such thing exists yet. It is said to be a highly secret weapon, the answer to Hitler's tanks. Of course we're excited at being associated with a secret weapon and a new part of the Army—the Tank Destroyer Command. Our little world consists of our battalion, about 800 men, and one next door of similar size. We share a common post exchange and church—not much else because the camp only opened in February.

Most of our officers are from the infantry and know little about the 75's and 105's and 37-millimeters we will be using—maybe.

The core of the tank destroyer idea is a heavy gun mounted on an armored vehicle that will combine features of a tank and an armored car and be capable of extremely high speeds, say 60 to 70 m.p.h., which will enable it—theoretically, at least—to combat tanks on a hit-and-run basis.

So I begin another home. But for you and me our home is always the same and travels wherever I go.

SANTA BARBARA, MAY 28, 1942

Your mother and I had Helen Roark and her mama up here for tea yesterday and then we were given tickets to see Helen's match today. So I am a gay dog again and we had a fine spree this afternoon—with a tea after the tennis—and are just home now.

I feel very well but don't want to go out nights yet, though some of the uniforms make me feel I'd love to be on a dancing evening with a handsome man clutching my waist (before it disappears entirely)!

You can't imagine how I hate to think of going back to 317 Burlingame. Much as I love my family, ever since I was a child I've hated the storm and confusion in our home. Isn't it funny? I was always the calm one.

I want to tell you that I weigh 160 lbs.—that our baby is completely made and 7 inches long!! This baby is very happy, my darling, and will soon move in my body and be really between us when you love me—making us a family: a mother and father and a new and perfect form to cherish and lead. And so the future stretches but in such a bright pattern—with such work and play to be done—with laughing and music and poetry!

CAMP COOKE, MAY 30, 1942

I write from our day-room: bare bulb overhead, concrete floor below, two amber-colored reading and writing tables and a green billiard table where three sergeants are playing. There is a Victrola opposite me and a sheaf of ten-year-old records ("You're driving me *cray-zee!*" etc.) but the thing is broken, thank God, and its bowels lie strewn where some amateur mechanic left them in disgust. Tonight I waited twenty minutes at our one telephone to get a free line and then had to return to the barracks as we were on special alert and I had permission to be away only thirty minutes. We've just been issued rifles and five rounds of live ammunition—why, no one seems to know but it's part of the alert. Don feels much better since I told him Irene can come and stay with Mother in Santa Barbara, and he and Irene and you and I go to the little church in Montecito and stage a wedding.

I'll try to call tomorrow.

———————————

The mysterious alert occurred because the decisive naval battle of Midway was imminent and Japanese attacks on the West Coast were feared. They held the initiative and the greater power. If they could seize and hold Midway Atoll, about a thousand miles west of Pearl Harbor, they would have a base from which to threaten Hawaii, Alaska and the West Coast while dominating the Pacific.

Fortunately our cryptographers had broken their secret code and we knew their intentions and were able to concentrate our forces most effectively to meet their challenge. Their loss of four large aircraft carriers plus a number of other ships and hundreds of trained aircraft pilots changed the balance of power in the Pacific. But it was a very close thing—how close few of us realized until after the war when records became available.

At the moment all we knew was that we'd "won one" at last. The heavy burden of constant defeat began to lighten. The Japanese no longer seemed invincible. There was light at the end of the tunnel.

---

317 BURLINGAME AVE., LOS ANGELES, JUNE 14, 1942
Don't be concerned about my being back here. The last few days have been good—no guests and Daddy less nervous. We all gather in the kitchen for breakfast and each one cooks a portion of it, and Pop drives off to Columbia and Judy dashes off in a joyous whirl to her precious horseback riding.

Then Mum and I cope with housework—flowers, lunch, planning, etc. It is all very pleasant and quite easy for just the 4 of us—it's only when we have a series of guests that it becomes tiring—dishes mount up, Pop inclines to drink, be noisy, sit up late, etc. But now you need not worry for we are settling into a routine. I will certainly go back to Santa Barbara should things overwhelm me here.

I'm wearing flowers in my hair these days and whenever I put one on, I say: "This is to Bob, my husband." Sometimes Mum says: "It's a pity Bob can't see you now"—followed by some great compliment I am too modest to repeat.

Saw Margie B. the other day. She's a gypsy now—very arty in dress, pathetic in outlook on the war. I find such people hard to take. They don't see anything worthwhile in the war. They try to escape. They complain. They ridicule. She asked me: "Why did Bob enlist, *what* was the point?" I was stunned. She has a beau at UCLA, a medical student hoping to evade the draft.

I've just drunk a huge tumbler of water—just for you, you old tyrant. And I am quite afloat now. I'm going to garden this afternoon. The tummy sometimes gets in my way but I go around it. It's very soul-restoring—to work in the earth.

CAMP COOKE, JUNE 17, 1942

My rise to fame came in a way you won't believe. I won the Indian wrestle—you know, stand sidewise with right foot beside your opponent's, take his right hand and try to pull him off balance without moving your feet? Men and officers formed a ring in the center of which we competed. It was like a scene from *The Call of the Wild*, Buck versus Spitz. I won the company championship probably because some of the bigger fellows happened to be on guard duty.

Immediately afterwards Capt. Rainey sent for me and, after some questioning in the presence of his young officers (he being about 30, as I've mentioned, with red hair, glasses and 6'2" of robust body), asked if I would like to make application for officer's school. I explained I'd done so already. Yes, he knew about the delay in the records. They would be along some day. Until then, stand by.

Partly as consequence of all this I've been promoted to "Acting Corporal"! To further justify my distinction, I can now disassemble the latest model Browning air-cooled, recoil-operated, belt-fed machine gun and reassemble same. The next step is to do it blindfolded since in combat we may have to do it at night.

I got in three pretty good hours on the Death Story this evening despite all radios blaring again.[15] How clean and refreshed you feel after even a partially good session of writing, as though you'd gone for a good swim. The bugler is blowing taps. A lovely sound through the foggy darkness. Tomorrow night we have another field problem. I am thankful for long underwear.

15. Early in June all West Coast radio stations were silenced from dusk to dawn for five days as a precautionary measure against Japanese attack, in connection with the Battle of Midway, June 4–6, and air raids on Dutch Harbor, Alaska, June 3–4.

The hardest thing of all to take about the Army is its spiritual dreariness. It is all aimed at killing and destruction. This has to be, for now, at least, but it is a very great negative. It is anti-life.

While I was reading your letter our baby jumped about so much that I laughed aloud at the little rascal. I'm glad it's an energetic baby. This morning your mother phoned to get Irene's address and will invite her to come to Santa Barbara. Once we get these two married we'll all have peace of mind and I'm sure they'll know what happiness is at last. Your parents are very good to undertake such a project.

I send you these pictures of the commandos because they seem extra good. Notice the fine, if taut, face of the young German prisoner. Some woman's heart is weeping for him surely. I cannot hate these young men. When you are in action I shall remember other women who have suffered more than I ever shall.

When young Frank Rieber's little fiancée said to me: "How will I live when Frankie has to leave me?" I tried to tell her that love is not ultimately or profoundly concerned with the physical separation—distances. One can thank God for having loved and been loved—there is no need to ask for more. How the war makes one ready to sacrifice! I feel how much you and I have learned.

I like to think of you doing a man's job and me doing a woman's—having a baby. This is good and true.

After chow we appeared before Colonel Matthews, our commanding officer, to receive formal appointments as corporals. First you salute, standing before the colonel's desk, Capt. Rainey sitting at your elbow as a sponsor. "Stand at ease," says the colonel. He holds my record card. "You've had considerable military experience, I see?"

"Yes, sir. Four years all together." I'm counting high school R.O.T.C.

"You've also had more education than most men and your I.Q. is unusual."

Now this business of my I.Q. has gone far enough, I'm beginning to feel. Are they pulling my leg? Or am I a genius?

"I see no reason why I shouldn't sign your warrant. I hope I'll have opportunity to sign another before long."

"Thank you, sir!"

Smile.

Smile.

"That's all!"

We exchange salutes. I do a left face and withdraw. And two stripes will appear where none grew before.

LOS ANGELES, JUNE 25, 1942

I am very proud of you, my angel, being a *corporal*! I too am in a daze about your I.Q. I'd like to find out, though, whether you're brilliant or stupid. Anyhow, you're *wonderful*!

Irene comes, as planned, on the 30th. I guess I'd better stay on in Santa Barbara after the weekend with you at Mattei's.[16] I might be able to help her in some ways and, as you say, keep her calm. She will need peace after all this turmoil and indecision.

Yesterday Pop had too much to drink. A lot of the men drink at the studio and he was caught up with the rest and quite soggy by the time he came home. He gave me a long and violent lecture on what a bum wife I was and how no men are understood by women, etc. He ended by throwing the terrifying statement at me that if I'd learn about the various weapons you were using, I might be of more help and interest to you. He really gave me a berating, ending up as usual with the declaration that *he* was the only one to really know Bob and I knew nothing at all about you!

CAMP COOKE, JULY 1, 1942

Have I described our first sergeant, a rough old leather-faced Regular Army top-kick who insists, with suitable profanities, that beds be made so tightly that a dime dropped on the middle of your blanket will bounce? He keeps a bottle of whiskey in his room for friends and favorites, such as me, but mostly for himself and as consequence is slightly pickled most of the time.

This morning he handed me—from personnel—a reply to their letter of inquiry to Camp Roberts. All record of my previous

16. Mattei's Tavern in the Santa Ynez Valley.

application to officer school is lost. However, Capt. Wilson
kindly wrote a good recommendation and Capt. Rainey says I'm
to take it to personnel tomorrow and begin the whole process
over.

Saw Don a minute this afternoon. He says you were wonderful and Irene more beautiful than ever.

I love thinking of you alone in the garden watching the
night come down. That's when our baby grows, I'm sure, and
begins to be a man wiser than his father, or a woman as beautiful
as her mother. Think of it: our pulse never stops beating, our
blood flows on, perhaps forever.

In *The Pot of Earth*, Archibald MacLeish writes: ". . . the
generations/ Of man are a ripple of thin fire burning/ Over a
meadow, breeding out of itself/ Itself . . ." If you have seen a grass
fire you will know how good that is.

Don't be concerned by these lapses of Pop's or by thinking
I want you to be a lady militarist. Of course I do not. The
mechanics of war are pervading enough as it is. As the reports
from Libya say, Rommel's army is a machine for killing; the
British soldier wants to do as little killing as necessary. There you
have the difference in modern war. The soul plays second to the
machine and courage to technique. But you be well and unworried
about anything at all.

LOS ANGELES, JULY 2, 1942

Irene will impress you. I really liked her. She was very tired when
I left S.B.[17] yesterday because she and Don naturally sat up late
and she was worn out from strain and emotion.

Your mother put her to bed and she slept like an infant. She
is shockingly thin but gives the impression of grit and knows her
own mind. She'll make out.

I talked to her about birth control. She is as much in a fog
as I was and I hated to introduce that note into their marriage.
But she is too young and weak to have a child now. The doctor
she went to in Texas was a CATHOLIC, she found out later. Of
course he didn't tell her a thing, except that there is no way to
prevent babies!

I really was cross. She is very much adrift about all this and

17. Santa Barbara.

hasn't even had a pelvic examination. It might prevent her feeling pain when they first have intercourse and she might need to be stretched a little, as I was. She wants me to go to a doctor with her before she's married, as she's afraid to ask questions, etc. I feel old and wise and will gladly go with her.

I said my prayers last night and pretended you were with me. I love you very deeply and want you near me forever and ever.

CAMP COOKE, JULY 9, 1942

My military career proceeds at dizzy speed. I've been made a sergeant, no less, with three stripes! It means I'm responsible for forty-eight men and earn $78 a month. We'll soon be filthy rich.

Life was almost too much for me this week. I couldn't keep a dry eye over those pages about the Kentucky town where the tank company came from, our first to strike the Japs near Manila. Then followed the pages on the South as a source of fighting men—thank God this country has the South, I thought—and when I saw the picture of the house of Thomas Lee, where all the great Virginia Lees were born, I really started swallowing lumps. What names: Francis Lightfoot Lee, Lighthorse Harry Lee. Each one a song. The article speaks of the "singing courage" of the South. How true. If I make officer school it likely will be Ft. Benning, Georgia. I shan't be sorry.

So my 27th birthday passed, somehow my happiest. I want this book of stories to be called *The Happiest Man* because that will be me, then, right on the cover.

Don't forget it's you who makes me happy, so bright and clean inside that I must sing even among machine guns.

LOS ANGELES, JULY 11, 1942

Sometimes I realize in a sudden *burst* how many people and places I've known and how each person, even the abnormal ones, contributes so vastly to one's life. The first summer here I got a letter from a boy still in Florence with a horrible deformity of the neck. He ended like this: "The news that you are not coming to Italy is sad. Maybe another summer, fate will put us in the same piazza, on the same evening. Here, the same trees are outside and the same Tuscan sky. Inside, is the same pensione room. And I have found that all happiness lies in imagination. And that is why, as Leopardi says, the child sees everything in nothing, and man, nothing in everything."

Can you understand why that gave me a terrible nostalgia? I was 21 and very bewildered by this country and its people at times—and then this echo of Florence—of trees and piazzas and the breath of summer which will always mean only Italy to me. And the sad voice of this poor misfit.

Sick though his mind was, I can remember how he once said quietly: "In Paradise I'll be a beautiful man." And oh how useless and weary I felt at those words, for there was nothing I could say or do to comfort him. He had an old guitar too. Once he strummed out a tune of Bing Crosby's (of all things) and in his odd, hoarse voice sang a few lines—silly words—but he poured out all his sorrow in them. The sun was going down behind the cypresses and I felt terribly powerless. Because though I pitied him, I knew that the strong, normal, human turns away from the sick.

Why all this? When we were married I tore up my old letters, not because I wanted to hide things or forget them, but because everything in my former life seemed suddenly a little tainted; perhaps it was just that they represented Europe; and you, my darling, were my New World, so new and strong, and I wanted our life and love together to be pure and fresh.

Coming across this letter which escaped my tearings-up, I saw it far more clearly: the decadence of Europe with all its mellowed beauty and delights. And how much older I feel now! I hope I am wiser and better and gentler! There is so far to go and so much to learn.

Tomorrow I pack and will stay in Santa Barbara through the weekend. For the wedding[18] on Saturday I'm bringing our present to them—something silver because they'll treasure it and it lasts.

How gloriously happy I am when I think I will hold you close to me soon. I am quite large really and won't let you see me naked—it's not too pretty to be so enlarged—even for such a beautiful cause.

CAMP COOKE, JULY 12, 1942

The long summer day is ending in a bank of fog. Such peace comes here when the wind dies that you seem inside another

---

18. Don and Irene were married at Bob's parents' home by the local Baptist minister and departed on leave blissfully happy.

world, waiting, holding your breath. Last evening I walked alone
on the mesa as the sun went down and smelt the odor of evening
on the grass and listened to the distant surf. I could touch the
shadows, almost. Then I came in and wrote my story over again.
It now stands at four pages instead of a dozen and is better. I work
in the day-room with the boys often looking over my shoulder
and the Victrola playing. One learns!

I am repaid for every day here, Janie. I never knew what it
meant to love a fellow human until I came into the Army—not
man-woman love, of course, but that abiding recognition of a
link, a bond, a common source and destiny, the respect that must
exist between all living things and the matchless glory of the life
they embody. This alone, this fact of life, surpasses all others.

The enclosed will get you and Mother through the gate. I've
a hunch I go on guard duty Saturday night but will call you
beforehand.

                                SANTA BARBARA, JULY 18, 1942
I loved especially sitting on the golden hill at the ranch while
the evening noises came slowly. And I loved the sight of you
again in blue jeans, smelling of earth and sage and your face
lighted up with happiness—and I thought of all the evenings you
came home to me dressed just that way—and how happy we were
to be reunited at the end of every day.

May the time come again when you will come to me fresh
from the hills as I always remember you! That is our way of life.
And if we escape the war safely we will return to that life. And
if we are to be denied the long years we want together, we have
at least known the existence we love best and have been happy.
Think of the restless, endless searchings of men and women for
the perfect mate and home! We are very young to have found all
those blessings.

I do not know why I was a bawl-bag last night—perhaps just
fatigue, or the fact of having you so close and knowing you are
to be away so soon. *No matter*, there are no excuses for such an
act of folly.

                                CAMP COOKE, AUGUST 4, 1942
After lunch we traveled by truck to a canyon that runs out to the
Santa Ynez River where the 5th Armored Division built their

obstacle course, and it is a beauty—one mile long, uphill all the way, through barbed wire, over water hazards swinging by ropes, dangling from ladders, crossing pools on narrow logs, tripped by wires hidden in the grass, jumping trenches, climbing high walls made of logs by pulling yourself up with a rope—all while carrying a rifle and full field pack.

Because I love you I came in first among my group and was immediately, while still out of breath and panting heavily, handed a .22 rifle and told to shoot five rounds at 5 tin cans that sat on a board 20 yards away. I hit 5 out of 5.

Then I felt very happy. To feel muscles, nerves, and brain in harmony is a joy. Running alone up the quiet canyon through the grass I know so well, through oaks and tarweed and all familiar smells, something in me was released and I could have run all day. Tonight the company is happy, having sweated, showered, eaten. They say: "We ought to do this every day and get in shape!" I agree.

As you will know by now I leave early Wednesday on the great adventure.

CHAPTER 4

They will be 90-day wonders—
officers and gentlemen by
act of Congress.
ANONYMOUS

Officer Candidate School and a Baby

This was our next big step into war. And it happened so abruptly. No chance to say goodbye. It presaged others similar, until that ultimate one of going overseas and into combat. That one was never far from our minds, as it was never far from ever so many others. How much anxiety and agony was rising all over the world as these months wore on! But at the same time as if to compensate, life never seemed sweeter or people more important. The postman, the garbage man, the clerks in the stores became like members of a united family. More and more service people and workers everywhere were women as men went off to war. Food rationing was stiff at first: red stamps for meat, green for vegetables, blue for sugar, brown for what coffee you could get. Bread wasn't rationed but it was often scarce. Still none of this seemed to matter much. In uniform or out, most of the nation was pulling together as never before.

Overseas the British had halted Rommel at El Alamein in Egypt but in Russia the Germans, though stopped at Moscow and Leningrad, were pouring southward, nearing the Caspian Sea and Caucasus and were consolidating their conquests of Greece and Crete. It looked as if the Suez Canal might yet fall into Nazi hands, one of Hitler's dreams, or that he might reach India through Iran—another once incredible idea now within the realm of possibility.

Again we wondered if we would ever win—and if so how, and after how much sacrifice?

TROOP TRAIN, THURSDAY, AUGUST 6, '42

I woke this morning in Douglas, Arizona. Am now in high country where the earth is red and valleys are a day's travel across. I lean out the window and see that the sky ahead of us descends to earth between mountain buttresses 3000 feet high. We shall climb slowly up between them, nose over the crest and down the next slope and up the next and by then it will be afternoon. People gather beside the tracks to watch us pass. All the little children wave. Their future is in our hands.

I wish you could smell this delicious air. I understand why Arizona cattle and people are strong. I think also of all the glory of our native land, from which war is removing me, and the determination fills me to spend a thousand years if necessary to change this. Sweeping statement number 506. Yet I do feel we, the youth, are paying for the mistakes of generations that begat us. I do feel this very strongly. And if we are not careful, are not like giants in war and in the peace to follow, our children will continue to pay for the mistakes of their parents. I tell you it is ghastly when some kid of 19 asks: "Why are we fighting? I don't want to kill Germans! I got nothing against 'em!" We must change the world, Janie. Otherwise the children pay unto the third and fourth generation if there are any children left. This is the deepest conviction I've received from being in this war.

Now we are over the crest and I can see a hundred miles. Nineteen of us from Camp Cooke are together in this car but the conductor will only make up berths on the ratio of 2 occupants to a lower, 1 to an upper, which causes some discomfort. Luckily I drew an upper.

Later:

As we descended into New Mexico, I began thinking of Weldon[1] and remembered that Hachita, N.M., was the shipping point for his cattle when he homesteaded on the border. So I started writing him a letter. Just as I finished what should we do but pull into Hachita! What a place! Crumbling sunburnt adobes, white wooden schoolhouse where there must have been a teacher Weldon courted, a church, then "The Hachita Eating House," then a bungalow without any paint. And all of it set in a giant trough between two ranges.

I hastily finished my letter and jumped off. It wasn't a scheduled stop but our engine was halting whenever it got the notion. So I took a chance and ran with your letter and Weldon's into

---

1. Weldon Lynch of the McCreery Ranch.

a little yellow station where a gray-haired guy wearing earphones was taking down Morse Code with pencil and pad. In a minute he removed the earphones and said sure he could mail my letters. "Just leave 'em there on the counter."

"Ever hear of Weldon Lynch?" I showed him the address. "Used to live around here."

"Sure, I knew Weldon. Where is he now?"

I explained.

"Sure," says the old boy. "Whadid you say your name was?"

I told him.

"Mine's Skipper." We shook hands. From the corner of my eye I saw the train begin to move.

"Skipper, you put a postscript on the outside of this letter and sign it. Weldon'll be glad to hear from you!" And I beat it out the door and caught the last car.

FRIDAY AFTER BREAKFAST, AUGUST 7, 1942

We've just left Abilene, one of many tidy Texas towns. The men go in shirt-sleeves and straw hats and are very clean. Now we are passing acres of red soil where crows fly over the corn. Sudan grass and cotton seem to be the main crops. Interspersed with them are uncultivated patches where short yellow grass grows and the famous mesquite which is not spiny at all but—at least from a distance—delicate and wavy like our pepper trees. It grows six to twelve feet high and is absolutely the *only* natural tree or shrub.

This is not a great cattle country, I judge, but it is a big country, oceans of earth, dark headlands rising far away. What room there is, what a lift to your spirit! We're still in the car in which we left Camp Cooke but are attached to the crack "Sun-shine Limited" of the Texas & Pacific which will get us to Fort Worth at 2:30 P.M. The train for Temple leaves at 11 so we'll arrive there tomorrow morning, about 24 hours late.

One fine day you and I shall farm out the children, half to one grandma, half to the other, and come away alone into this land. There is something more profoundly American here than you find by the sea.

My next letter will be from Camp Hood. Meanwhile I'm as excited as a little boy about being on a train in new surroundings, and I love you.

317 BURLINGAME AVE., LOS ANGELES, FRIDAY, AUG. 7, 1942
Strange and not nice to be unable to mail a letter to you. I'll add
a few words to this every day and feel as if I'm talking to you till
your new address comes.

My weight is now 180 lbs. That's a gain of 2 lbs. in 3 weeks.
The doctor says it's alright, the baby is probably large. He listened
to our offspring's heart, then said: "Would you like to hear a *good*
heart?" And I actually listened to our sweet baby's heart beating
so strongly and well—just like a metronome, very fast. Babies
always have faster heartbeats than adults.

I do feel amazingly well and I hope you can get back from
your campaigns often enough to give me a baby every two years
or so!

Judy and I are to read Molière's play *Tartuffe* together. Daddy
insists. I imagine my French is pretty rusty. In the evenings all of
us are doing *Henry IV*, Part I, aloud. Marvelous.

Sad to relate, one of the kittens, the plainest, got run over
by a car. But Montezuma and her single child are very happy.

Saturday Morning:
Ecstasy of joy!! *Two* wonderful, long letters from you—one
marked Fort Worth, the other, ah magical name, Hachita, N.M.

I couldn't be more excited! To share your enthusiasm for
Arizona and every village in Texas you passed—it is very thrilling.
And the encounter with the old boy who knew Weldon—why,
it's incredible! How terribly rich every moment of life can be, my
darling! Surely we'll always know the real people of America and
the western lands of Texas and Arizona. As you say, we can board
out our brats to grandmas and take off together. Oh my darling—
I say, as you say in your letters—why must there be a war to
separate us? Why do we all have to be sacrificed? Why are we
paying for sins committed long ago? May we avert these evils so
our children can live in peace!

I know that not even death can part us. We will be given
time, after the war, to live in California hills and travel to Arizona
and Colorado and live in the small, clean towns. Surely, we will
be granted a life together—years in which to love and cherish
each other, grow and mature with grace and wisdom. I believe
we *will* be granted this.

We must have faith in the future, strength in the present,
and accomplish our given tasks with no self-pity. As you say,

when we're tired and lonely, it seems unbearable to be apart, with our unborn child kicking in my tummy. But those must only be the fleeting moments. When we are well and strong and know that our love can never change or be changed, we have no fears!

You are at Camp Hood now—I wonder what your first letter will say. I wonder if I *like* all the many miles of land that come between you and me! And as I finish saying that, I realize the heart knows no distances. That is my comfort now and always. And I hope it will make me strong and brave when I have the birth of our baby to undergo.

Somehow, I have lost fear of anything—as long as you love me. If you stopped loving me I believe I would stop living—not dramatically or suicidally—just gradually fade and disappear.

GATESVILLE, TEXAS, AUGUST 9, 1942

We live in tents on a grassy knoll—what used to be a C.C.C. camp outside Gatesville, Texas—a village I haven't seen because we are restricted to camp. It is hot—drippy hot. We sweat without moving, sleep under mosquito nets at night without blankets.

We are the 4th O.C.S.[2] class. Others will follow at intervals as all move through in stages of 13 weeks each, so some will be graduating and some entering.

There must be 500 or 600 here. And this at last is the *real* Army. Things happen; we *move*—even physically. You can't leave your tent to go to the water buckets in the mess tent without running. You don't go to the latrine without running. When you go downtown to the Gatesville auditorium for classes you double-time all the way (a mile or so).

They say: "You must take a 4-year college course in 13 weeks." Impossible. But there is an urgency here lacking so far.

Candidates come from all corners. In my tent are boys from S. Carolina, N. Carolina, Rhode Island, and Los Angeles.

(There's been no water at the mess tent buckets for three hours and we are getting a faint idea of North Africa and soldiering. Enough of this Hollywood Army.)

Next week we move to new barracks in the nearby camp which aren't yet completed. Meanwhile I sit here wringing wet as the pounds roll off and look out across a meadow where cattle

2. Officer candidate school.

graze, over a parched cornfield to green trees in a valley, then bare plowed fields, then a stony ridge sparsely covered by low growth. Although there has been no rain for a month the country is green. You find more neat little towns here than on our coast. They are green and white like New England. You feel our native land here, limitless, nourishing so many kinds of people.

Time out for lunch. We live and eat under field conditions. Lunch was roast chicken, though. I got a neck. Salt is served in tablets: dosage three per day to make up what you lose in sweat. I sat next to a boy who was on Louisiana maneuvers last year and says this seems much hotter.

Now the katydids are singing in the trees. Their sound rises in the heat like the song of tires on hot pavement. Seven-year-locusts, they are also called.

Did I tell you we must address each other as "Mr."? No more familiarity; no more insignia of rank. For every mistake we receive a demerit—a "skin," as it is called—and being as you know the dirtiest, most wrinkled man in the Army I live in constant terror.

So hasten the extra clothes. Also will you send me: 1) a sheet, 2) a bath towel, 3) any odd prs. of lightweight socks unless you already sent at least four or five pair. And will you telephone Mother and ask her to include in her package to me one khaki field cap size 7-3/8?

In a climate like this you can use a uniform a day, and we've had no chance to buy anything.

This afternoon we'll take mattocks and dig rocks out of our tent. I see faces I'd forgotten. I went to school with them: Eastern, Western, good and bad but all American and at the least vigorous.

After Dynamite and Weldon I don't find them very interesting. They adapt, modify, master information and use it, but for real living they originate so little. Their courtesy is small; their minds far larger than their hearts. Most of them never grew up. If the Germans are a childish people politically we are one psychologically, and this is the great American strength and weakness. It can be either innocence or irresponsibility.

Please send me a red-and-blue pencil, possibly an Eversharp that writes both. And will you find out from somebody—maybe some Army officer Pop knows—what the address of the *Infantry Journal* is in Washington, D.C. and the *Field Artillery Journal* in the same city and subscribe for me?

I hesitate to ask you to do this but nobody here knows

anything or has time to talk and there are no reading facilities or library. I go to mail this on the run.

Please note that my official address is: 4th Company, Officer Candidate School Regt., Tank Destroyer School, Camp Hood,[3] Tex.

317 BURLINGAME AVE., LOS ANGELES, AUG. 13, 1942
Your first letter from O.C.S. seems a voice from a new world. I think of you sweating, dripping, running, and living in tents, of the new men about you—of the hard work ahead. I know it's all to the good but I long to be in Gatesville to see you—and Texas.

Life has suddenly become the old story of husband at war and wife at home to produce progeny. And *your* progeny, darling, has become very active in my tummy and never seems to stop jumping. I enjoy the feeling. I take comfort already from our seed and can be less lonely now you have gone.

TEMPLE, TEXAS, AUGUST 16, 1942, SUNDAY MORNING
For over an hour the operator has tried to get a line through to Los Angeles. This hotel lobby is like 42nd and Broadway; and Temple, our nearest town of consequence, is swollen to twice normal size. During the next few months as recruits arrive for the many new T. D.[4] battalions out at camp, it will swell beyond belief.

This Hotel Doering is my eating and phoning center. Fritz (German refugee background) and I have rented a room with shower in the residential section for use on weekends. It has a small kitchen we share with two other rooms.

Now the first week is over I feel I've lived ten years and can't remember the days that made them. We really soldiered. There was a schedule and we kept it—to actual *minutes*. The whistle governed. "On the double, gentlemen! Come running!" And the gentlemen came.

Back at Camp
Because of the heat, we lie in our underwear on cots—cots, as a wiseacre commented dourly that first dreadful night we arrived

3. Now Fort Hood.
4. Tank destroyer.

dogtired to find no lights, no running water, no barracks—"cots, canvas, folding, Model 1912!" Everything in the Army is a model of sooner or later—tents, machine guns, trucks, ourselves. So we lie in our tent with radios blaring, fellows returning noisily from the weekend, fellows showering, fellows arguing, fellows asleep, fellows studying for the exam tomorrow on .30 caliber machine guns, none of us separated by much more than arm's length.

Please never stop writing and please understand when nothing comes from me it's because no time—not a single five minutes—is given us in which to write.

P.S. The Texans are a lovely, youthful, friendly people, lots of sunshine in them. Their hospitality towards soldiers is beyond belief. And their accent! Yum-yum!

LOS ANGELES, AUGUST 20, 1942

I picture your every move. So you saw Mrs. Miniver[5]—very good I thought. The commando raids on Dieppe[6] are fine news. The photographs of the men involved moved me deeply. Such good faces. And our victories in the Solomons![7] I wonder how long the war will last?

But it's no good wondering. I try to live entirely in the present—it's the only way. Our baby is going to help me no end. Still I will hate your being away and not seeing our little child as it grows day by day. I want "it" to look like you.

Must get lunch now. Have hung out the wash, made beds, baked a cake and will eat *something*. I'm ravenous and quite gigantic but feel *very* well.

CAMP HOOD, TEX., AUGUST 21, 1942

We've moved into the barracks of the new camp. It sprawls like a sleeping giant ready to wake. Eight-five thousand men will be

5. Starring Greer Garson and Walter Pidgeon, about an English family in wartime.
6. The raid on the port of Dieppe on the French coast by Canadian and British Commandos and American Rangers, early the morning of August 19, 1942, was the first Allied ground attack on Hitler's "Atlantic Wall."
7. The successful landings at Guadalcanal, Tulagi, Florida, Gavutu, Tanambogo in the Solomon Islands on August 7, 1942, led to our first victories on land in the Pacific.

here by spring. The buildings spread in endless rows like columns of troops marching westward over a high plateau. Headlands loom roundabout in the clear air. These are the Texas Mountains,[8] a kind of limestone or chalkstone much like Camp Cooke, so we still have white dust.

We sleep 74 to a building which is too many. "Service companies" care for us. By care I mean janitor service in a two-story barracks (mopping and sweeping only), guard and C.Q.[9] duty, which certainly are nice to avoid, and truck driving.

We have a team of Negro boys who operate big 16-passenger GMC 16-wheel-drive trucks. They deliver us on schedule to all parts of the reservation. Today a center seat was added so we ride 27 to a truck, which is crowded. How their sergeant makes them strut and shine and how he shepherds them in his flying jeep up and down the convoy! They are very beautiful physically, these fine black Negroes. In the past, too, they've made good soldiers.

Many tank destroyer battalions are tucked away in tent camps in the recesses of this huge reservation. Some tanks are here too, to make real our games of hide-and-seek. We inspected three today, "General Grants," with the 75-mm. gun in a turret on the side, like those being used by the British in North Africa.

LOS ANGELES, AUGUST 22, 1942

Enclosed is the latest from Bernice Carter. I do hope her Roberta is alright. What a wild, mysterious, gypsy child she was! In a way more attractive than the others. I couldn't help realizing that women like Flora and Bernice have the most amazing *enduring* powers. Bob, they love their men—but they have to endure those men, in a lonely way. They are alone—their husbands are not sharers of their burdens. Those women stand like rocks and endure life and love and rear their children alone. Now Dynamite, seeking to be eternally a boy, wants the thrills still—wants to be off to Dutch Harbor! He is such an odd combination of good and bad. But when he hears his little girl is deathly sick he dashes home to her bedside! And I can see him encouraging the twin boys—aged 3 now—to fight and Bernice—so typically—wanting to prevent it but unable to!

8. The Hill Country near the center of Texas.
9. Charge of quarters.

The radio is giving me Kate Smith singing "God Bless America" and "Praise the Lord and Pass the Ammunition."

I dream of our weekends at Mattei's. I think you are perfect. I live with you in my mind many hours of every day—and I wonder if you find time to think of me? I'm not much to dream of now—large in every direction. Please love me always.

TEMPLE, TEXAS, AUGUST 23, 1942, SUNDAY MORNING

If I have to wait by this accursed telephone all day I will talk to you because I cannot go another week without hearing your voice.

Two Negro boys who work the elevators (here in the hotel) tell me to go into the coffee shop and have breakfast—they will call me if the phone rings. They are lovely, Janie. They laugh easily, look at you directly and speak so musically—friendly, casual people.

My fellow candidates from the South are much like them. One is the grandson of a Confederate general—tall, blond, amateur boxing champion of Georgia, nervous, hell-bent, and declares engagingly: "Anything that's got danger in it is interesting!"

Well, bad news. The operator tells me it will take at least two hours to get through to Santa Barbara so I'll send a telegram and try to place the call later.

From Our Weekend Room

I am learning about Germany from my new friend Fritz who was born there. Having worked his way through the University of Miami in Ohio, he now lives in Detroit. He's a student of sociology, speaks fluent French and German, believes honestly— I think—in the making of a postwar world where violence and oppression will not be tolerated.[10]

As we talk I sense his impassive German strength. He has ideals and ideas but lacks grace. He admires people who are suave and detached, like the English, and though he is far more humanly concerned than most, at times that terrible German disregard comes through like too much brass from the back of a symphony or like a hobnailed boot over a bed of pansies. Yet he means no harm—it is the German way and bearable in his case. Quite

10. Fritz would become a noted professor and author.

rightfully he's proud of his blood and ashamed that tramps like Hitler and Goebbels should lead his people after Goethe, Kant, Schopenhauer and Heine.

I grow daily more attached to him and the other fellows. As we learn together, I realize how shrewd these lads are—adaptable, quick to comprehend and master. Without genteel tradition or manners or any apparently impressive qualities they somehow total an immense competency which is all on the good side of the ledger.

LOS ANGELES, AUG. 28, 1942

I'm glad the readers at Viking were enthusiastic. What do you think about the title, *The Happy Man?* I like it! Does it mean *you*, my love? I hope it will always be so—indeed.

This week has been a blessed one because of your many letters. And when you tell me you love me and think of me and our child, then I'm completely happy. I am consummately proud to be able to say: "My husband enlisted in the Army." This is *the* big struggle and I certainly could not rest easily if you weren't in it. The faces of men, women and children—of Chinese, Russian, Austrian blood, etc.—could never let us rest easily. My happiness is great when I am sure you are doing so much for those tortured people abroad and for our dear, dear country.

So when I tell you I miss you, it is not that I want you living a civilian's life—I want you where you are—working as you are, with your heart and soul in this struggle.

I hope to be able to do my share, also, when the time comes, when the baby is old enough. If we are to be given a few months of life together—the baby, you and I, before you go abroad—I will ask for nothing more. If we are not given that, I will be brave.

And in this faith of mine I feel happy. Those who die in this war leave so much to the living—and the living give so much to the dead. Sometimes I think it's all one: the living and the dead. I know that if you die I will never be alone—death does not take away the life of love. But my heart tells me you are not to die—there will be such a need for men like you in the big task *after* the war. Those will be days harder than these in many ways, don't you think?

CAMP HOOD, TEXAS, AUGUST 28, 1942

Yesterday on the firing range the disaster occurred which looms whenever I face mechanical problems. I took a screwdriver and did wrong things to a machine gun. First this came apart, then that. Somebody asks incredulously: "Whadayer trying to do?" Somebody else walks up and growls: "Whatsamatter, break down?" By now mine is the only gun left on the firing line. Everyone else's is in march order ready to go home. A lieutenant stands over me and demands impatiently: "What's the trouble, Gun 3?"

By now parts are falling onto the ground along with sweat from my anxious brow. A sergeant with mechanical talent takes charge and the trouble is cured in about 1/2 minute.

Saturday Evening

More about my German friend. During the First World War his father served 6 years with the Kaiser's Navy including the North Sea battles. The father emerged an ardent Socialist Democrat to take part in the revolution that overthrew Kaiser Bill and established the Weimar Republic. He worked twenty years for Krupp and was one of the board elected by the great Krupp union of 60,000 to sit with the managers of the plant and run things. Also he served two terms in the Reichstag.

Then one Sunday morning Fritz and his father and mother went to the cathedral in Essen. The minister began spouting hatred against England and France for the "unfairness to Germany of the Treaty of Versailles" and calling for revenge. "My father's hands went out on either side, grasping my mother and me," Fritz says. "We were well down in front. He made the three of us rise together and we walked up the aisle and out of the church with all the congregation staring at us." His father never went to church again. In 1932 they came to America.

Fritz says the Communists and Socialists weakened each other by disagreement and left room for Hitler. He said, as we know now, that the stupidity and greed of the ruling classes and governments of England and France left Democracy to perish in Germany and thus aided Hitler.

Dear fatty, I wish I could see you at 180+ pounds. Tell the personage inside to cut down on the grub a little, ration itself—after all, this is wartime!

Yes, I've seen the moon these nights, or in the mornings

rather as we fall out for reveille and face the morning stars and a faint rim of light eastward. The weeks are going. Ten more, only!

LOS ANGELES, SEPT. 8, 1942

This morning has been something! Judy rushing wildly about getting ready to go riding, Pop taking her picture and then dashing off to the studio before catching a plane to Oakland and the weekend with the Harts in Berkeley. Mother quite frantic packing up Daddy, and Judy asking a million questions about HORSES, of course. I tried to feed them all a decent breakfast starting with figs and cream (no cream for me). Now they're off and I'm quietly writing you in the study which is a great whirlwind of laundry baskets, manuscripts, etc. Mother is taking me to the doctor this afternoon. I'll tell you in tomorrow's letter *where* the baby is now.

Do the Russians haunt you as they do me? I think of their courage and endurance and terrible task as they try to hold Stalingrad. Oh, the ghastly blood on those fields. I can hardly name what I feel. And the German blood mixed in with the Russian and who is to choose the difference?

TEMPLE, TEX., SEPT. 13, 1942, SUNDAY AFTERNOON

Fritz and I hitch-hiked here in an open truck with 20 others. The truck was driven wildly by two Negroes. We happened to be traveling with Mr. Daniels, the only Negro candidate in our company and one of our smartest. Daniels is a good hitch-hiking companion because so many trucks around camp are operated by Negroes and when they see him they stop.

Soon we were transporting nearly a dozen blacks. Once when we stalled on a hill we put out guards and halted traffic (like stopping 5th Ave.!) and let the truck coast back downhill and start against compression.

I discovered a fellow passenger from Merced, Calif., a wild-eyed, half-bald, swarthy guy about 40 named Jack Rose. He showed me his card. He owns a trucking business in Merced and hauls cattle out of Los Banos, Hollister, and many places you and I know. Rose tells me Joe Ramoso who also operates out of Los Banos killed four people in an accident the other day. We agreed

Judy and her father watch the horse races at Santa Anita.

California is the only place to live and Texas just a bit better than hell.

So we whizzed into Temple through green countryside very lovely from recent rain. After a huge steak dinner, Fritz and I returned here to our room for conversation. He speaks with horror of the Junkers like von Bock,[11] ("der Sterber")[12] who backed Hitler and have always sought to crush the Democratic movement. In every oppressed country it seems the same: a small band of power-seekers trick the people by playing upon their prejudices, greed,

---

11. Fedor von Bock, German field marshal.
12. "The one who preaches death."

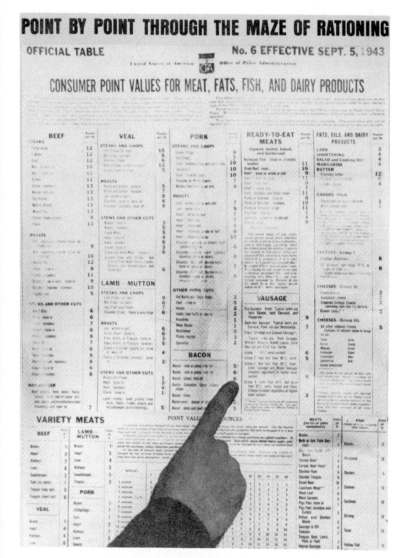

Along with millions of other wartime shoppers, Jane had to deal with ration tables like this. (National Archives)

etc. until in the end the people pay with blood for their foolishness.

Did you see in *Life* the picture of our countrymen imprisoned by Japan? Somehow it left me with an absurd desire to laugh. How really juvenile the whole thing becomes, however horrible. Truly I feel little hatred against the Japs though I should kill a number of them gladly to free the men in that picture. Yet the Japs are so pitiable—we all are so pitiably entangled in each other's prejudices and mistakes.

The grass and earth are all that matter. Fritz tells me the Germans have a proverb to describe a person who does evil: "Where he ranges no grass grows."

LOS ANGELES, SEPT. 13, 1942

When I go to bed I shut my eyes and think of you very hard—but still your arms will not be around me and the empty sheets will be cold. I wonder what it will be like to finally have your lips on my forehead. There can be no *real* peace in my heart until I am close to you.

Do you ever ache for me? Or are you braver than I? I don't often indulge in longings. But sometimes when the evening air is clear and all mates are together it's very lonely in my heart and soul.

Goodnight, my love. Say our prayers always. The baby is in the correct position and everything is excellent, the doctor says.

TEXAS, SEPT. 15, 1942

This evening came the crowning indignity. For two days, returning tired out from classes, we've had to "police" (pick up cigarette butts, gum wrappers, etc.) the area and also pile all carpenters' scraps, sticks, and stones (a million stones) in a huge pile by the road. This for the new colonel. It hurts our pride. Oldtimers were heard to say they've policed in eleven states from the Atlantic to the Pacific and were looking forward to being damn good officers in *that* category if no other. And then tonight, behold, having amassed this huge pile of debris by the road, we are ordered *to move the pile forty feet back and sidewise to the northeast corner of the mess hall*!!

It really was hard to believe. And if you knew the background of pestering, of what seems systematic harassment, you would appreciate it even more—because almost every day there is a new diagram on the bulletin board of how to make your bed and where to place your barracks bags. And this *steadily* for 6 weeks.

I'm not telling you all this just to grouse. There were no hard words—only laughter. We pitched in. We'd show this goddamned colonel, this goddamned army and O.C.S.! We made a perpetual motion bucket-brigade across the forty feet to the new location and passed the rubbish hand to hand. Candidate Watts read aloud scraps of letters he found in the debris. Candidate Milsaps flushed a mouse and a whiskey bottle. Candidate Wood said he sure wouldn't be afraid to fight in Egypt now, 'cause when they wanted the pyramids pulled down and turned around he would know how.

Janie, in combat I suspect it will be the same. As the going gets tougher, so will we. One thing is certain—after O.C.S. there can be no real harassment. They do it deliberately to see how we react. And nobody minds, really.

Formal opening of Camp Hood, Friday, to which will come John Bell Hood, the son of the Confederate general for whom the camp is named.

I am glad our John[13] is soon to be inducted. Tell him to wait till he is permanently assigned and then to move in the directions he prefers.

LOS ANGELES, SEPT. 27, 1942

John and Pop have had some excellent talks and many hours of croquet. Now that John's views on the war are more like his, they get on better and Daddy is much pleased. John said to me: "You know, Janie, it's very hard to find a mate for life."

How lonely one is until married! I cannot forget how unhappy I was, at least in comparison to what I am now!

Judy writes demanding letters,[14] so I must get a note off to her. She is going to be a fine letter writer; she's amusing and laughs at herself.

Sorry I didn't write yesterday. I hate a day to go by without

---

13. Jane's brother.
14. From boarding school near San Francisco.

writing. Sometimes I get swamped and yesterday we had nine people for dinner.

CAMP HOOD, SEPT. 28, 1942
For two days we have fired the 75-mm. gun mounted on a half-track vehicle (armored, open, with 2 wheels in front and 2 caterpillar-type tracks behind) which will probably be our chief tank destroyer weapon. My turn came this morning. The target, a rectangular white cloth towed on a wooden sled, moves across the field 600 yards away. As it starts, the gun commander standing in the front seat of the half-track ahead of the protective shield, right beside the tube of the gun, shouts: "Moving target, left-front, 600, one lead!" and I, the gunner, behind the shield, repeat each element in his command, while "tracking" rapidly with elevating and traversing handwheels to keep the crosshairs of the panoramic sight on the target.

The loader slips a long yellow stick of H.E. (High Explosive) into the bore and rams it home, shouting "Clear!" as he steps back and crouches at the rear of the deck. The assistant gunner slams shut the breechblock and shouts "Set!"

With eye to the sight, steadily tracking, I bring the target where I want it and shout "Ready!" The assistant gunner draws back the lanyard (a short piece of cotton rope attached to the firing hammer), and I shout "Fire!" The assistant gunner releases the lanyard. There is a deafening explosion. For a moment all I see through the sight is dust from the shell ripping the earth beyond the moving target.

I scored at least one hit and was proud of my buddies when the frame was brought in and we counted a dozen holes in a piece of cloth the size of a bed sheet, representing a tank.

Did you see in *Time* that Selby McCreery's brother Richard is chief of the British Army's staff in Egypt?[15] Perhaps Selby is with him. I wonder how Josephine is managing at the ranch with no help. And did you see the picture of the Russian woman sniper, who visited Washington D.C.? And read what she said?

15. Richard McCreery would command the British 8th Army in Italy. Later knighted, he served as the United Kingdom's military representative to the United Nations. He was a Californian in that as a boy he'd spent much time on the ranch there with Selby—Selby being now with the 12th Lancers in Libya. Both were grandsons of a Gold Rush '49er.

Something like: "American women are too interested in lingerie. We in Russia are interested only in wearing our uniforms with honor." She had a lovely serene face and a broad woman's figure.

Our daughters must be strong. Let them hike in the hills and dance and work with their hands. I would like about a half-a-dozen, please.

LOS ANGELES, OCT. 4, 1942

In ten days I have gained only 3/4 lb. and that brings me to the delightful weight of 195—I may not see 200—and that will break my heart! Also I'll lose a five-dollar bet with Pop.

I hope the baby is a boy for our parents' sake—also I think you might like to leave an heir before you go abroad. Everyone surmises that my baby *is* to be a boy—*why* I cannot make out— so I am quite prepared for a girl. But I'm getting very anxious to *see* my baby!

I dreamed of you last night. You were sleeping with me in a large bed, and you woke and said: "Darling, better look at the baby in the crib before you sleep."

CAMP HOOD, OCT. 4, 1942

This week we begin tactics—road marches and field operations instructed by numerous lieutenant colonels.

We are getting out our woolen uniforms so they can hang up and regain shape by October 15, for the change from sun-tans. I cussed your workmanship quietly when I began undoing the sergeant's chevrons you sewed on at Mattei's so thoroughly. What lovely hours we spent there on the lawn under the great palm tree.

I hope you're not depressed. I try to understand what it means to carry a baby night and day and be kicked and dieted and poked by doctors and advised and made uncomfortable generally. A woman accepts such things. I want you to know I understand a small part of them and feel a good deal of awe–and much, much gratitude.

No male can have a true idea of what it means to carry a child. I think of "carry" in all its senses and find it beautiful. Nobody but a woman understands the *important* things like childbirth. Men are like a bunch of cock sparrows. They make a great show. I can tell you all about military law and administration. Yet compared to you and baby this O.C.S. is ridiculous.

LOS ANGELES, OCT. 7, 1942

A check from Brandt[16] for $163.45 arrived this morning. I am terribly proud. I love the idea of you supporting your baby so magnificently and us paying for it at one fell swoop—not by installment. You are a wonderful husband, provider, soldier, author! I don't see how such a combination is possible! Anyway, it has been a marvelous thing to have this extra money while our baby was coming—we can truthfully say we can afford our child— and soon your Army pay will be ample for us to live on. Why does everything work out so well? Our good angel, again!

They say it's wise to go slowly for the first month after the baby and so I've agreed to have a nurse stay with me when I get back from the hospital. Mum couldn't cope with everything herself, anyway, and I will have more free time to be with you when you're on leave. Don't forget that husband is always *first* and children second.

When the baby and I are with you at your next post, you will have time to see me acting as mother and wife all in one. Won't it be thrilling to be a family?

Please don't give me so much credit for our baby. I cannot understand a woman who finds childbearing hard—even these last weeks are really a song. So think of baby and me as perfect and happy and only rather anxious to see each other. And after that to meet our husband and father.

Still, I cannot quite make myself believe you and I have created a whole human being and that soon this new person will pop into the world and draw its first breath. Sometimes the thought comes over me as a complete miracle. Believe me—it's easy to have babies and I want lots of them, darling, all strong and true—and to look like you.

John leaves tomorrow night. He is reluctant to go but anxious to get into the Army. We've had a lovely visit and he is far nicer than ever before.

16. The Brandt & Brandt literary agency.

CAMP HOOD, OCTOBER 12, 1942

Don't hurry the baby on my account. I shan't be along until November 10—maybe I'll not be along at all. But I think there will be furloughs immediately after graduation. So just let baby kick away for a month more if necessary and develop those Achilles tendons so he can be a great runner some day. You say you know this is a boy, that I want a boy, that everybody says this should be a boy? Nonsense! As you know, there will be 94 more and we should be able to hit on all varieties.

This afternoon I rode in a tank. I was lucky enough to ride in the turret, the commander's position, and get rattled around like the poor devils of a regular crew. Really it is a miserable place to be. I rode ten minutes and nearly got car-sick because I didn't have my eyes on a view slit looking at the outdoors. We easily knocked down some good-sized trees, lurched over ditches that would beat your brains out if you didn't wear a helmet and if the steel around you wasn't padded with rubber.

We've watched training films of the Wehrmacht in action across France, Poland, the Netherlands—and believe me you want to crush and destroy those steel bugs as though they were so many snails on your front lawn!

Last evening a Polish boy said: "In Poland the bread always goes first into a new home. The head of a house crosses the threshold with a loaf and lays it on the table. He asks the blessing of God on this new home and that its larder may be well filled."

Their bread is that wholesome dark rye. This silly white bread we Americans eat with 2/3 of its nutrition processed away is a symbol of our counterfeit values. Confound it! Why can't we be simple like Poles and Russians and eat dark bread and not paint our women like Indians and tune our ears to jargon?

Now a cowboy fiddler is scraping on the radio. *There* is the true American music! I tell you I love it!

I have thought all day about Pop's trip to Yugoslavia to write about Mihailovich.[17] I think it would be so good for him. Then perhaps he never would go back to the movies but continue with the writing he has wanted all his life to do.

---

17. The Yugoslavian Government in Exile in London had given tentative approval for Jane's father to be dropped by parachute to join Yugoslav guerrillas fighting Germans.

LOS ANGELES, OCT. 17, 1942

Mother and Daddy are pretty nervous these days—with no job on hand. I can't quite understand their finances but they just *don't* get ahead. Of course, they support Tante, Elizabeth, Judy, John and various others. You cannot guess what it means to me to have us financially self-sufficient.

I hope we never have to touch our $1000 savings. Your officer's uniforms will be quite expensive, won't they? I am scrupulously paying for my expenses here. Sometimes it's a struggle but I manage.

Oh—but your child is kicking away! After all these months of pounding, I may feel queer when my tummy is flat and quiet.

Now it's almost dark—warm but very still. I want my mate at this time of evening. Remember when you came home in Rio Vista and honked outside the apartment? And we put the car away in the garage down the street and walked back arm in arm—you and I, husband and wife—to our home and supper?

Oh, the happy, countless moments of our memories together! I find no pain to look back on, darling. But the ache for life with you and our own home and children—I cannot quench it.

CAMP HOOD, OCTOBER 20, 1942

We had a fine day in the field today. Nine British officers came to observe our tactical problem. Visiting officers often accompany us now, many Negroes among them. The Negroes walk in pairs. The white officers are civil but there's no real mixing. What a national disgrace the whole matter is! I discovered last night that Daniels, our one Negro candidate, lives in a room alone whereas all other "private" rooms (those at the end of a barracks designed for noncoms) contain at least 3 candidates. He was out so I left the package of cigarettes I'd bought for him on his bed and went away downstairs ashamed of my countrymen—and myself.

A test on reconnaissance this morning and on methods of instruction—85% of an officer's time is spent teaching. All day I shall be waiting till five o'clock and your letter.

Our commandant, Colonel D., is a red-necked cavalry colonel like you read about. He shouts criticism and profanity, *demands* everything be right, makes his officers double-time on errands, handed out 20 demerits when he caught a member of our company *not* double-timing in the battalion area, stalks around in shiny riding boots.

A full moon tonight makes me wonder if you see it too. How very pure is that light.

> Queen and huntress chaste and fair,
> Now the sun is laid to sleep . . .

Yes, it is good to make money, isn't it? And pay for our new baby and ourselves as we go, though $250 a month still seems to me the ideal salary—plus several thousand a year from writing to educate our children and take a trip now and then.

                                          LOS ANGELES, OCT. 21, 1942

Nothing conclusive about Pop's trip abroad but eventually it will happen I think. As for his health, he is pretty well, on the wagon, but does get tired easily. He probably would survive but one cannot tell. Of course Mum would worry, we all would, but then every woman worries about her husband, no matter what age, in wartime. Do you think I wouldn't worry about you overseas? Anyway, Mum is not going to dissuade him from anything that will be a vital experience, or a real help in the form of war propaganda, etc., which is what his book would be in a sense.

Pop never felt he contributed anything in the last war and wants a chance in this. Certain risks must be taken and I do think he should be allowed to go if the chance materializes. You and he can talk about it when you come.

Your mother came yesterday and we had a happy but short visit. I was *so* glad to see her looking well. Really she looked beautiful, young, strong and happy. It makes me sing to see her so. She and Father may be down in a week and I pray the baby will be here by then. I go to the doctor tomorrow. Frankly, I don't expect the baby until after the 25th. Will the days ever pass? Do you remember the horrible night in February when we thought I'd lost this baby too? Oh, how wretched I felt at the prospect—and how utterly sweet you were to me with the ice pack! I am terribly thankful God let me keep this baby for I love it so much—even unseen.

Today am packing a little suitcase so everything will be ready to go to the hospital. After you get the telegram about baby, write me at:

The California Hospital
1414 South Hope Street
Los Angeles

Now don't *lose* this—I'll be there for 10 days and it's quicker if you write me there. I'll be able to write you a note two days after the baby comes—if not sooner. Of course your letters will be my main joy—they and the brief glimpses I'll get of the baby. I dread the 10 long days—but I can look forward to seeing you soon after I get home.

CAMP HOOD, OCT. 25, 1942, SUNDAY

Darling, I'll not lose your hospital address. I'll write you every day all my life long. I almost hope the baby is late so I can be with you on November 7 or 8. Think how close that is!

Last night I dreamed we danced together and laughed and played like young people instead of an old married couple with a child living through war. What wonderful stuff dreams are made of!

LOS ANGELES, OCT. 28, 1942

The military books you ordered came. I've enjoyed perusing *The Army Wife*. I will of course study it so as to be a competent military appendage!

I've gained more than 50 pounds and now weigh an even 200, yet the doctor says I needn't worry. He's never said a word about dieting, so I continue to eat and feel ravenous *all* the time! It's such a strange feeling. Since childhood I haven't had much appetite—eating has been my problem, as you well know. But the doctor says my weight will have no effect on the size of our baby.

Thank you for dreaming of me—of us together in laughter and love and the days of peace to come—when all the horror, absurdities and sacrifice of war will have faded into the distance. They *will* fade—but I feel the struggle ahead is long. I am calm but sometimes I weep to see our youth spent in a wasteful war.

CAMP HOOD, NOV. 2, 1942

Did I tell you of my friend Eisenberg who sleeps in the next bed? He was in our original tent at Gatesville. He has an unusual gentleness which led him to say quietly, when several of us were talking about rings: "I've lost three of them, giving them to girls," and somebody said: "You were jilted, were you, Mr. Eisenberg?" And he said smiling a bit sadly: "Three times. You see, I'm Jewish and when a girl finds out . . ."

Tomorrow I go to be fitted for my uniforms and purchase—on credit—more of my officer trousseau to be paid for my last day here with the $150 cash allowance we receive that day in addition to our pay.

I arrive Burbank 11:28 A.M. Saturday Nov. 7 via American Airlines. Don't let anyone try and meet me. There is limousine service right to L.A. and I'll come from there by bus or taxi. Let's save the family tires.[18]

I read that the San Francisco area is blacked out again and the East Coast is having similar alerts, which latter gives me the perverse satisfaction of knowing others are going through what we've experienced.[19]

P.S. Though we'll not be infantry school graduates, we will wear crossed rifle insignia on lapels and shirt collars because the tank destroyers are not yet officially recognized as a branch of the service, so you can be looking for an infantry second-lieutenant with said rifles plus a gold bar on each shoulder.

Resplendent in new uniform, Bob is riding a bus to Fort Worth, and I'm enjoying a mid-morning snack of cinnamon toast in Los Angeles when I feel the first dull pain in my abdomen. Trembling with excitement I call Mother. Daddy is in a conference at Warner Brothers and can't be reached. The pains come more sharply. Mother is an erratic driver at best. As the Buick sedan careens through heavy traffic at high speed, I think we may end in the hospital's accident ward.

Our family doctor, Kenneth Eikenberry, lean, kindly, badly overworked because of wartime shortage of doctors, examines me briefly and tells me not to worry—he'll see me later.

In Fort Worth Bob finds himself "bumped" from his plane.

18. Tires were strictly rationed because of wartime rubber shortage.
19. German radio broadcasts were promising air raids on New York and other East Coast cities, and German submarines were sinking oil tankers off the coast and had landed spies and saboteurs on Long Island and in Florida.

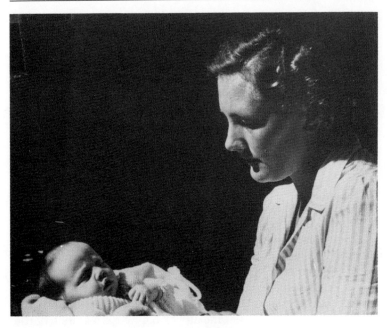

New mother, new baby.

The airline authorities turn a deaf ear to his pleas. Thousands of military personnel are using commercial flights, and higher ranking officers and also civilians on important government business have priority over second lieutenants with or without babies expected. -

My pains become more frequent. After four hours of regular contractions, now two minutes apart, I feel I'm due at any moment. Just then a nurse hurries in, examines me and announces briskly: "Got a long way to go, young lady!" but helps me onto a gurney and wheels me down the hall to a cubicle-size labor room, where she rolls me onto a bed and administers a tranquilizing shot. "Now, have a good sleep!" she orders, raising the sidebars and locking them in place, making me feel like a trapped animal. Then she turns out the light and leaves me alone in the dark. Nurses, too, are in short supply and overworked.

I lie with eyes open, trying to cope with a pain which seems unbearable. As I writhe from side to side gasping for breath, I hear myself groaning: "Oh, God! God!"

The new second lieutenant with his proud parents.

After what seems an eternity another nurse enters carrying a flashlight, peers unceremoniously between my legs, says nothing and departs. I long for Eikenberry to come and explain what's happening. Next time a nurse enters I ask meekly: "Could you call the doctor?"

This one flies at me scornfully: "Young lady, there's a war on! The doctor is trying to get some rest!"

After what seems another eternity two more appear and make what I pray will be the final examination. "Why, there's fifty-cents worth of head showing," one exclaims, "time to go!"

The delivery room is a bustle of white figures wearing masks. Overhead the brightest lights I've ever seen force me to close my eyes. An anesthetic mask is placed over my face and a voice orders: "Breathe deeply!" I feel myself drop off the cliff of pain and, just before I pass out, the sharp sting of the knife making the episiotomy.

When I wake Eikenberry is saying: "It's a beautiful girl, Jane. Nine pounds, six ounces."

Joan was born early November 7 as the first American troops landed at Algiers and Casablanca in North Africa. Next day at noon Bob walks into my hospital room. It's a moment of pure joy. A grouchy nurse is persuaded to bring our baby from forbidden regions and we gaze at her in rapturous wonder, undo her blanket, marvel at tiny pink fingers and toes and perfect little body. We didn't know we were producing a member of what would be called the baby boom generation. It just seemed miraculous that new life could spring into being in the face of so much death. I've been propped up on pillows for the occasion. Afterward I'm required to lie flat again since lying flat is supposed to help the uterus return to normal size. I'm not even allowed to sit up for meals. I prop myself on one elbow and of course grow weak from lack of exercise.

After three days of this modern medical treatment, so outmoded today, I'm permitted to walk around the room several times, followed by more resting. After ten days I go home.

There for forty-eight near-delirious hours of happiness we're together with our baby—before war reasserts itself and Bob leaves for his new assignment.

CHAPTER 5

As a wife you have a most important role in your husband's Army career. . . . In this respect you also have an important part in our national security, and a duty to your country.

NANCY SHEA

Army Family

Again a turning point in our lives parallels one in the war. While we've been producing a baby, the British have decisively beaten Rommel at the second battle of El Alamein and sent him retreating across North Africa. In Russia the Red Army has launched a massive counteroffensive at Stalingrad which will lead eventually to Berlin. And in the South Pacific the American landing at Guadalcanal continues successfully. The tide is turning, we feel. If we can beat the Japanese on land at Guadalcanal as we have beaten them on sea at Midway, it will be truly significant. We two feel very lucky. While others are bearing the brunt, we've been at home with our baby. We sense the all-embracingness, the interconnectedness of this war. It is truly a world war. Nearly every continent, every ocean, every people is involved. It makes us feel very small and insignificant and at the same time very important to be part of such an enormous event.

825TH TANK DESTROYER BN.,[1] CAMP GRUBER, OKLA.,
NOV. 1942

This is a bit of level ground at the foot of rolling hills, partly open, partly wooded, that reach up into Arkansas sixty miles away. I arrived at camp headquarters at ten this morning, signed in, filled out papers for travel allowances, pay vouchers, etc., met other O.C.S. grads doing likewise. No reception could have been friendlier.

Then I came on here to the outskirts where they always seem to put the tank destroyers and talked with Major E., our commanding officer. The major is a Columbia graduate who played squash there, as I did at Harvard, and lived in San Francisco, as I did, and enjoyed football games at Stanford, as I did.

---

1. Battalion.

He's a reserve officer about 45, perhaps more of a gentleman than a soldier but very kind. The rest of us are under 30, mostly second lieutenants fresh from Ft. Sill, the field artillery O.C.S., or from Hood—"90-day wonders—officers and gentlemen by act of Congress!"—because Congress creates officer ranks and regulates promotions.

As for the men, they are apparently green as grass. We have no combat vehicles, no weapons except a few borrowed rifles and machine guns, and will train with broomsticks on jeeps to simulate anti-tank guns. So prospects of going overseas seem distant.

Motoring without you was a dreadful bore though our little blue car[2] is a joy. I floated over the lovely lands of the West, the Painted Desert at dawn, the lonely and forgotten places of Arizona, those great pasty-brown rivers, those solitary ranch houses that haunt me always with a thrill. I saw more California license plates than any other. Half the state must have been Back East and was coming home along Route 66 (the *Grapes of Wrath* route) on their last gas coupons.[3] There were caravanners with all worldly goods strapped atop the sedan, towed trailers, swanky Packards, impoverished Model-T Fords, everything. No wonder Steinbeck calls it the "mother road." And here in Oklahoma where the poor already are without tires you pass many wagons and mule teams even on main highways. People actually traveling by wagon, not just hauling cotton to the gin, although they are doing that too. Western Oklahoma is terribly poor. East of Oklahoma City the country richens and hills appear. Here it is quite pleasant.

At lunch at the mess hall we share with officers of two adjacent T. D. battalions I met two fellows who were at Camp Cooke with me. It made us feel like veterans. Being an officer is better in some ways. But in a fundamental way I don't want to be one—they don't interest me as people half so much as enlisted men. Yet I continue to feel I may be of more use as an officer and there is the matter of money.

This afternoon I moved into my room on the second floor of our officers' barracks. It's as bare as my bunkhouse cubicle at the B. B. before we were married but has a closet, steam heat, etc. I bought a folding canvas chair at the P.X. and shall get a

2. A 1941 convertible Ford coupe had replaced our old Dodge.
3. Like tires, gasoline was strictly rationed.

card table in our nearby metropolis of Muskogee and then my premises will be furnished. Muskogee, by the way, isn't bad, rather like a bit of New England transplanted. The leaves of autumn blow along the streets under bare limbs. Several officers tell me they've found homes for their wives, which promises well for you and baby and me.

LOS ANGELES, NOV. 19, 1942

The first hours are always unbearable—especially the night you left. We seem to be forever kissing goodbye on dark mornings—tearing our hearts apart, living the strange existence of separation. And I still must shed a few tears the night before you leave, for it does seem unbearable to have you go so quickly. Joan is more delectable every day and we've gotten on nicely. With the nurse off for 24 hrs. Mum slept in the nursery and her grandchild behaved beautifully. I long to take over myself.

Weighed last night—168 lbs. which is a big drop from 200—and of course I'm still losing. I'll be all slim next time you see me.

I have enormous pangs of joy when I suddenly think of our daughter. I'm so thankful she is here and all is well. Until they are actually *in* the world there is the vague anxiety lest something go wrong. In a little over a month I'll be with you. I can barely contain myself for joy! Don't suddenly decide that you have no use for a wife at Christmas! I am coming no matter what you say, young lieutenant!

I feel strong today—am allowed to walk to the bathroom by myself now, a great relief to get out of bed for such functions.

Having you for a week changed my very heart into a bundle of happiness. You cannot know how much I love you—for this love increases daily. Never think Army life has changed you—nor the war—none of these temporary and horrible years can change us or our love or our ideals. I feel closer to you as we grow older and have more memories we've made together.

Joan is no longer red at all—her skin is lovely, pink and fresh. I'm so eager to take care of her myself. I can't grasp the fact we have a child, our own creation—the fruit of our love. She is so strong and calm and has such big blue eyes—I do want her always to be calm and happy. I like to say her name over and over to myself—it is pretty and suits her.

The bed next mine is very empty and I keep thinking of how

lovely it was to lie beside you before we slept. Such a peace and joy.

On the drill ground this morning, the lieutenant in charge suddenly asked if I'd like to drill the men. I was taken aback for a moment at the prospect of my first command as an officer. However I accepted and drilled the platoon, instructing them on some of the finer points of the hand salute, right face, count off. Janie, it is deep satisfaction, working with men, hearing your voice carry a meaning to them, watching their faces catch that meaning and their bodies respond. Later we were on the range under bitter gray sky with a north wind blowing straight from the pole. The poor guys trying to fire rifles shook so hard they sometimes missed their targets entirely.

Last evening I went with two officers to Muskogee for a steak and shopping. We investigated the officers' club that has just opened in the Severs Hotel. It reminds me of New York City: indirect lighting, dance floor, tables around, modern art on the walls. We shall investigate it further when you come, slim wife.

Then there's the brigade officers' club near our barracks with a bar and dancing every weekend. Finally we have a little dayroom right here by the barracks where we sit in easy chairs, read, play cards and have beer and cokes. The wives got together and decorated it for us. So you see we're well clubbed. It sickens me a bit, reminding me of college social castes and all the abominable exclusiveness mankind lives by. I thought the cataclysm of war might change human nature but am beginning to wonder.

I've been assigned the two worst possible jobs: supply and officers' mess, and now must study regulations governing company property. They make me mad. In peacetime such duties might be acceptable but not now. There's no reason why qualified civilians shouldn't take over all this dreary detail which ties up a company commander and his junior officers so many hours.

A tomcat is calling for his lady outside my window, reminding me of our most delectable puss. You must be careful not to hurt her feelings now the baby has come. Give her a kiss for me. But give Joan many real kisses. I shall have a large credit owing me when I see that young lady!

I love to hear you say you are strong and walking, and reading Pepys. He is great. There's an elemental curiosity in the human mind, and when you have it you aren't just in business or politics or soldiering or housekeeping but into everything, like Pepys was, the old gossip!

P.S. Proofs of *The Happy Man* came this morning and since we had the afternoon off because it's the day before Thanksgiving, I corrected and sealed them to go back. Can't quite believe it is all done. I've also read this week's excellent *Time* and *Life*. The description of Admiral Halsey and the naval battle[4] makes me very excited. What other country produces men like Captain Mike Moran of the cruiser *Boise* who, when the first Jap ships were sighted, ordered: "Pick out the biggest and fire!"

Love!

CAMP GRUBER, NOV. 29, 1942, SUNDAY EVE.
Yesterday I went to Muskogee and had an extraordinary adventure. Lt. Wilson and I visited the chamber of commerce and got a list of apartments for rent. Wilson has a wife and nine-months-old baby he wants to bring here from South Carolina. So we drove to the address at the top of our list. It was what we both wanted: in a nice part of town, a seven-room house occupied by Mrs. Smith whose husband is away on gov't. work and who decided it was her duty to offer their extra room for rent at $85 a month, all utilities and garbage paid. She would keep one bedroom, you and I would have the other, share the bath, use her nice little kitchen, garden, etc. But Wilson liked all this too. We flipped a coin and he won. On leaving I asked the good lady: "Don't you know someone else who has a room for rent?"

"No . . . but wait a minute. Yes, let me telephone Mrs. Griffiths across the street. She's a dear and . . ." Mrs. G. had just rented hers but she thought Mrs. Phillips, back on *our* side of the street, might have an extra room, so we went next door to the big white two-story frame house with lawn and garden.

Mrs. Phillips was lame. I saw her through the glass in the door get up shakily from her chair by the fire. I introduced myself and Wilson. No, she couldn't take people for a number of reasons, she had arthritis badly, she was old and set in her ways. But she

4. The battle of Guadalcanal, November 12–15, 1942.

kept talking, and I made her laugh, and after fifteen minutes. . . . Well, to be brief, it is one of those extraordinary things. Mrs. Phillips has two sons, one is a petroleum engineer in Tulsa, the other a curator at the Metropolitan Museum of Art in New York City and I know this is true because she showed me an article by him[5] with lovely illustrations. And *now*: he studied in Florence and while there married a girl named Sodi. I was mildly flabbergasted. By this time I'd told Mrs. P. my history. Now I told her yours, including of course your girlhood in Florence.

Somewhere along the line she asked me to run upstairs and see the bedroom. It's an old-fashioned beauty: big closets, vast double bed, family portraits around the walls. The house is like those nice old ones in Berkeley, and Mrs. Phillips is like those fine Berkeley people, really distinguished, graceful, humorous. She loves reading but arthritis has affected her eyes. When I told her we liked reading aloud, she said: "Oh, reading aloud won't bother me!" as though she might listen.

I made no mention of your bringing the baby since the doctor advises against it—and Mrs. Phillips probably would rule against it too.

Gradually her objections subsided. What settled everything was your picture, the one Pop took of you on the back lawn looking right at him. I put it in my wallet, remember? I handed it to her as evidence. She looked at it a while and said: "I should like to meet this girl."

Thus we have a home at 2021 Broadway, Muskogee. I was so pleased that when we came to money I would gladly have paid $100. She had no idea what to charge and asked me. I told her what Mrs. Smith charged Wilson. She said she didn't need the money, really; she lived on a small but adequate income. We finally agreed on $70 a month.

At the end she said: "Well, if I have to go to my son's in Tulsa at Christmas before your wife arrives, I'll leave you the keys." Imagine!

LOS ANGELES, DEC. 3, 1942

I adored the account of your visit to Mrs. Phillips! I have written her a note today expressing my appreciation. Also told her I

5. John Goldsmith Phillips, Jr., was Curator of Renaissance Art at the Metropolitan Museum.

cannot arrive before the 24th. I really don't think I should leave until the 6-weeks examination is over, and Ikey can't examine me earlier. So I'm not going to attempt any change in plans. I know you want me to be well and normal when I come to you this time, after all these months. I'm spending the night of the 23rd in Ft. Worth as the connections are too close to risk. It may be just as well to have the house to ourselves the first days—then we can enjoy Mrs. Phillips more when she returns. I *think* I may know the girl her son married. Wouldn't that be an amazing coincidence?

Goodbye, my angel. We'll sleep in that vast double bed at Mrs. P's. Maybe I will never leave you again.

CAMP GRUBER, DEC. 10, 1942

Today there were 213 pounds of meat for the entire battalion, 860 men. Our mess' share wouldn't make stew for half-a-dozen hungry cowboys. To compensate I must go out and buy, either at retail stores in Muskogee or at the sales commissary here, which is a retail department run by the post quartermaster. Military personnel and wives can buy at the commissary at considerable saving. If we begin housekeeping I can stop there on my way home. Hope you aren't having these shortages.

Starting Saturday I'll be acting intelligence officer, or S-2. The job is the best on the staff, if anyone wants a staff job. I don't. Seems I'm never going to get outdoors again. I really loathe this indoor Army. On the other hand the experience is good, couldn't be better in some ways, and will give me a picture of operations as a whole, the administrative picture.

Our T. D. insignias have come. They are circular shoulder patches worn high on the left coat or shirt sleeve—depicting the face of a fierce black leopard crushing a tank in its jaws against a flaming orange background. Really hideous.

I shall be proud when you're here. Everyone is asking when my wife is coming, the mother of that most extraordinary new baby.

Write me what train you are taking from Ft. Worth and what time you expect to arrive. As you come, keep me informed by telegram, telling me how things go and how late the trains are, because they will be late. Bring warm clothes. I'm excited about your new evening dress. Have applied for additional gasoline rationing, a C book, that will cover the 1000 miles a month I plan to drive between here and Muskogee.[6]

Tonight I walked for forty minutes in the clear frosty air to look at the stars and hear the foxes and coyotes over yonder in the timber. The knowledge that coyotes and foxes continue unchanged by the war is reassuring.

Time out while I show your picture and Joan's to 1st Lt. Blackwell, Commander of A Co., who rooms next to me. He was for three years with Texaco in Venezuela and is now—was before the Army—one of their engineers at Tulsa. We compare our Spanish but I'm saving my French for Corporal More who will lead my S-2 section. He headed the French dept. at Groton School as I think I mentioned.

Bonne nuit, ma chérie. Je vous aime beaucoup.

LOS ANGELES, DEC. 18, 1942

Yes, we have shortages but they don't hurt much. Mum goes to Ralph's, a big chain store branch in Westwood, and usually gets what she needs, though coupons are required for almost everything—red for meat and butter, blue for canned goods. Sugar and coffee are scarce too. But nobody suffers really. We get two pounds of meat a week. Of course nylon stockings and cigarettes are virtually non-existent as are household appliances such as toasters and refrigerators. But really the only hard part is standing in line. Somehow we in America thought *we* would never have to queue up like the British, instead of having a friendly clerk wait on us promptly. And when you *do* get to the clerk, he or she isn't so friendly because of the long lines and red tape.

I'm going to the doctor this afternoon. I feel very well indeed, at least externally, and can't see why there should be anything wrong internally. Anyway, I'll ask Eikenberry all about it and he will tell me frankly. If he says it is too soon for marital relations (I *hate* that phrase) I'll tell him that that is not the main reason for going to you, anyway. But of course if he says to wait, we will. He is very sane about such things. But he believes that

---

6. Non-military commuters received a B book worth varying quantities of gas depending on their distance from work. Pleasure drivers got an A book worth 3 to 5 gallons per week. Meanwhile the national speed limit had been reduced from 45 to 35 m.p.h. as a conservation measure.

two people who are in love should have each other in body and soul, which is true. I'll send you a telegram tonight with his report.

Darling, all I do is run around in circles, thinking of you and my trip and all the marvelous talks and readings and happy times we'll have together. Everything is stirring me deep down inside. In a way, I'm quite dead without you, and suddenly all life becomes beautiful and meaningful when you are close. Think how heavenly it will be! New memories to make and take with us all through the years to come, and we have made so many already. Probably we are the happiest and luckiest of human beings.

I, too, am only just getting used to the idea of parenthood. It's rather a lot to grasp, you know. I didn't tell you about Joan's ills because I thought you'd worry. I was quite frantic for a week and was afraid if I wrote you, all my anxiety would be shifted on your shoulders. So I just was miserable. The first worries of being a parent hit me pretty hard, as I was not very strong yet. Result: I looked rather weak and white the evening the doctor came and that's why he told me I couldn't leave until I had pink cheeks. The terrible sight of seeing little Joan, at three weeks, suffering, was too much for me and reduced me to tears many times in my room. Daddy was a nervous wreck too. The boil was an infection she got in the hospital (the hospitals are so shorthanded that many epidemics have broken out, not enough nurses for all the sterilizing that should be done, etc.). The boil burst and looked horrible. It then had to be medicated with a painful sulfa powder (they've been using it on the wounds of soldiers) and the poor baby really suffered.

I can't describe what it was to see her screaming with pain. By far, ten million times, worse than the pain of giving birth to her, to see her go through that. It made her nervous, you know, and every time anyone went near her she thought it was for another application of that powder and started to tremble. Well, enough! She's fine now, all calm again, sleeps hours and is gaining and eating beautifully and growing prettier every day. The rash on her face (also a manifestation of the infection) is gone. She is normal at last and terribly sweet.

When I get to Muskogee I want to write Giovanna Sodi who married Mrs. Phillips' son. We scarcely knew each other but she was at Miss Barry's school in Florence with me. Very blonde.

Goodbye darling. Oh, I nearly forgot to tell you—Judy arrived last night, MUCH improved. She is sweet, more thoughtful, less nervous, very calm. She has enjoyed school greatly.

I leave Monday unless something unheard of develops. Leaving the baby is going to be hard but she is in good hands and perhaps at your next post we can all be together.

                                        CAMP GRUBER, DEC. 18, 1942
Since Konopka's (my mess sergeant's) wife arrived, he's been winning at dice. He gives her all his money, says she's been the making of him. Before, he gambled it away, got drunk, was content to stay a private. She can't cook, though. He does that.

Konop used to be a "bolt monkey" high on the steel frames of skyscrapers, the guy who catches the red-hot rivets in a bucket as they are tossed up to him. He has seen many a man killed. The best bolt monkey he ever knew was Jerry Gallagher who could have walked a telephone wire and not fallen. But Jerry was scared to death of cats. Once in a beer parlor when he saw a cat he ran and jumped out a window. They had to put up a sign on every construction job where he worked: "NO CATS!" Jerry said it was because his mother had been frightened by a cat while carrying him. Jerry is dead now. "Got shot while bootlegging in western Pennsylvania. But he sure was a guy with the hot bolts!"

I watched Konop make pasta fagioli today. You boil macaroni in one pot, pink beans in another with meat and parsley, tomato sauce in a third. Then you add the sauce to the beans and the macaroni (dipped and strained) and let it all steam and gurgle together with pepper, salt, bay leaves. The result is beyond description.

Yes, I do want you in my arms again. The sense of you near me is such a precious memory, connected so closely with summer in our golden hills, that I cannot think of Mattei's or the ranch, or the dusky evenings creeping down the canyons, or that marvelous smell of fog coming inland from the sea, or the little stream we looked at by the church in Los Olivos, without thinking of you, my love.

You will like the Army. I'm absolutely sure it is *the* central feature of these times and therefore must be participated in and understood, both the training Army and the fighting Army; and when I go overseas, we must recognize the justness of that, too, and how men have been doing it since Odysseus and how wives have waited at home since Penelope. We are eagerly expecting news of the tank destroyers in action against Rommel in Algeria-Tunisia.

Despite good news I see no early end. If we celebrate my 30th birthday on the veranda of some ranch house it will be a *great* good fortune. I think of all the years to come, the thirties and forties still young and active because we shall never grow stiff. The fifties to consolidate in and gain in wisdom. The sixties to see our grandchildren, to advise and modify. I should like it if we both died together when we were 75, right in the same day. That's forty-five years from now and more. We've been married two. I don't think it will be long enough. Shall we make it 85? Then you can count another score grandchildren, because if we have babies up until you are fifty, why, *they* won't stop having babies, at least not all of them, until we are nearly eighty. And I sure do want to see *those* babies, yessir! Now I've got to stop and prepare for tomorrow.

For a month we enjoy the motherly hospitality of Mrs. Phillips while Jane becomes a certified member of the battalion's Army wives—"the camp followers," they call themselves. She's spared much protocol by the fact the colonel and the major have left their spouses elsewhere. All is groupie and relaxed among these consorts of 90-day-wonders. She masters coffee klatches, many personal histories. Most of her new friends are newlyweds, she discovers, among whom she ranks as old married woman. Many are from small towns, never have "been anywhere" before becoming officers' wives and are delighted by their new status. All share the common bond of marriage threatened by war.

We dance in the Severs Hotel, read aloud Sandburg's *Abraham Lincoln* while Mrs. Phillips listens contentedly, take walks in the wooded hills overlooking camp, feel sometimes—when we think of the war—as if we are strolling on the brink of a precipice—at other times blissfully lose ourselves in a midwinter interlude of warmth, joy, hope, and a little selfishness, while Jane's mother assures us the baby is fine.

The order comes without warning. The battalion must move immediately to Texas. The transient nature of military life comes painfully home to us as we prepare to say goodbye to Mrs. Phillips, to familiar if dreary Camp Gruber and friendly Muskogee. It's the first of many such goodbyes. Our life together seems comprised of leave-takings of one kind or another.

This time the wives lead the way. "The commando hens" are determined to establish a beachhead for selves and mates in an Army-camp town almost certainly overcrowded with wives feeling exactly as they do. In freezing weather they sit up all night on the train in an unheated car, taking perverse pride in even this minor discomfort since it unites them more closely with the war effort. Next morning Brownwood seems to their bleary eyes lost in the level expanse of west Texas. Only its hotel, rising five stories, says for sure: "Here's a town!"

Jane and Peg share a bed in that hotel for three nights. During the day they walk surrounding streets ringing doorbells, seeking rooms for rent. Finally they come to 1912 Avenue D and gentle middle-aged Erin Brooks who radiates decency and good will. Her husband is away selling cattle feed. They've just decided to open their home to needy couples.

Peg draws the spare bedroom. Jane settles for the dining room in which a double bed will replace the table. That 9-by-15 dining room with its sideboard, cut-glass chandelier, and incongruous bed becomes our home. We feel fortunate to have it. Many can find no accommodations at all.

As a rule Bob manages to get off two nights a week from nearby Camp Bowie. Jane in company with Peg and other wives makes bandages at Red Cross headquarters downtown. Still others find their new status as officers' consorts elevates them above such menial labor and spend their days over coffee and cigarettes discussing their sex lives and degrees of pregnancy.

Again with what seems cruel suddenness the battalion is ordered to move—this time for combat-readiness training in field quarters at Camp Hood, which has become the national center of the new Tank Destroyer Command. Wives are obliged to leave for home. We part smiling, tears held painfully inside.

———————

TABLE ROCK CAMP NO. 1, CAMP HOOD, TEXAS, 30 MARCH 1943
I am grateful for small favors, as you admonished me to be. Even to sit here in this shed of a battalion headquarters—once a

barracks for a C.C.C. camp—and feel the heat from the stove, smell oak wood burning, sense the presence of the colonel and the major at their rough pine tables a few feet away, each silently writing—while Bob Freeman, officer of the day, reclines on his cot smoking a cigar and reading—all this is worth much, if with it I can talk to you.

I write by candlelight. We're at Antelope Crossing on Table Rock Creek in a remote part of the reservation. The creek is big and muddy like those of California after a rain. In 13 weeks we are qualified for combat or we are not.

Poor old colonel—he's just wandered out to get a drink of water and I'm afraid he'll do himself harm in the process. People will be getting the axe as part of this combat readiness process and he could be next. Though he means well he is *so* ineffective.

Joe B. left today not to return. He didn't even come through headquarters to say goodbye. Poor, poor fellow. Since being relieved of command of his company, he's become morbidly ingrown. My heart aches for Peg, as does yours, I'm sure. Give daughter a kiss. I miss you bitterly yet am quite content to have you gone.

317 BURLINGAME AVE., LOS ANGELES, APRIL 4, 1943

My weekend turned out interestingly. Pinckney McLean, contemporary of Daddy's, flyer in the first world war, and now of the Marine Air Corps, brought two young Guadalcanal heroes (pilots) from the Santa Ana air base where he is press officer. Jack Conger, 22, Iowa, shot down ten Jap planes and told Pop about it in detail as Daddy is going to write the story of their squadron.[7] The other boy was a TEXAN: Bob D'Arcy, 23.

He also shot down numerous Japs. He had the marvelous Texas quality you and I love, natural courtesy, easy to talk to, shy, manly. Judy was in heaven. Both looked very snappy in dark green uniforms with wings and ribbons. Mum did her stuff and charmed everyone and I made them laugh too.

They told calmly of experiences in the Solomons that made our hair curl, of 15- and 16-year-old boys there—pilots, too—

7. The 212th Marine Fighter Squadron, based on Guadalcanal, flying slower but sturdier Grumman Wildcats, were the first U.S. airmen to encounter the faster, more maneuverable Japanese Zeroes in sustained combat and to devise effective tactics against them.

and how absolutely barbaric they became, collected Jap ears, etc. These two feel no youngsters that age should be allowed such horrors—they become completely desensitized and will never make citizens in peacetime.

They also told of the amazing feat of carving Henderson Field[8] out of the jungle, of the mosquitoes, of lack of gas for their planes, of always being outnumbered by the Japanese, of sleeping in foxholes, of dead friends. They spoke quietly and had such straight eyes and such premature maturity. I shudder when I think what they've been through. But yesterday they were happy in the garden in the sun. The Texan and I joked a lot (to make you jealous, though I know you never are).

Joan is a handful. We could never have coped with her in any of those rooms we rented, or in anything less than an apartment of our own. I mean her endless bottles have to be sterilized and her various orange juice and vegetables and cereals, etc., carefully prepared. One is busy all day long with her, and yet she is so sweet and so happy about being alive that it's all a pleasure. I never knew children could be so good and smile so constantly. She has a lovely disposition. I don't know where she picked it up, except perhaps at Mattei's Tavern where you and I were so very happy on three-day passes a long time ago in a beautiful summer.

When you speak of Lincoln and the people, "the listeners," I think back to my childhood in Italy and remember I was always running into the kitchen to talk to the servants, running into the fields to talk to the peasants, and so it was all my young life, I loved and felt for those people more than for my own kind, as it were. I was always happy with them and they had so much to tell me and my parents were often angry about it. "What do you find so interesting with them, Jane?"

How much do you love me? I want positive proof that you love me or I will desert to the Marine Air Corps.

TABLE ROCK CAMP NO. 1, CAMP HOOD, APR. 6, 1943

Spring is suddenly here. Please send my khakis. Tonight after a day of teaching and administration, dashing around, handling

---

8. On Guadalcanal.

papers and talking and talking (though teaching my "Intelligence and Operations Section" is a pleasure) I walked alone after supper westward across hills that are turning green, where old abandoned orchards bloom and the wild brush is white and yellow and a kind of apple or haw is lavender along the gullies. I heard doves call, frogs begin their song. I stepped over a small stream and stood a moment between two rocks, a foot on each one, looking at willows just leafed out and some cottonwoods and the moss and sedge, while I smelled that odor we know so well and heard a faint trickle of water.

It could have been many places we've been. Such is beauty. Usually private. At times I feel my life now is one great public noise which will culminate in the final din of war.

Our tents and these outdoors are worth a thousand barracks. However, Sunday I must report to camp for a two-week course for intelligence officers. I rather look forward to it.

The Viking Press spring catalog has come. They managed to include you and Joan, I'm happy to say.

LOS ANGELES, APRIL 7, 1943

What you say about Lincoln and your father's face seems true—there can be resemblance between men who live by ethical principle. I have never been able to get over the shock of discovering that my own father did not live by principles—he has lived by emotions, intellect—many good things but from childhood I looked for the "good" (in a large sense) man. Suddenly I found you. But my father is not one—and it has grieved me many years. Our relationship has never been the same, not to me at least—from the time I was 18 and discovered he was *not* always just or moral. How strange—this desire of a child for perfection in the parent.

Above all, Bob, let us *never* sell our souls for money. I cannot bear to think of you working as a writer for *money*. Let us not do that. A thousand times I'd rather live scantily from the soil and have you write on the side, or at least write what you *feel*, but not to write for bread. I wonder what course Pop's life would have taken if he'd not been tempted by big sums. This Hollywood is so degrading—it changes Pop and pulls him down to the level of the box office.

Evening (4 P.M.) is coming on and it is gray outside and still.

Mum is resting, Daddy not yet home (he rides in a car pool now to save gas), Joan is still asleep. The days go rapidly. Two weeks ago tonight you came to Brownwood and our lovely, large room for the last time—I can remember how you looked—it was late—11:30—after officiating at the court martial—and you talked to me and ate about 6 grapefruits in rapid succession. And we lay down side by side and you loved me and we fell asleep happily.

CAMP HOOD, APRIL 8, 1943

I'm sitting in the lounge of Building 409 with a typewriter between my knees, while two fellows play ping-pong across the room. Thus ends the first day of intelligence school. I find S-2s are a group earmarked as bright, and you know the American definition of bright. I mean they have developed too far to retain any color and not far enough to be interesting. Still we learn a good deal.

But let me tell what happened Sunday. Remember I said I would walk into the country west of camp which is off the reservation? I did so right after breakfast. Cutting across pasture land to get there faster, I nearly stepped on a big rattlesnake.

He was lying stretched full length absolutely still and was almost the color of the gray limestone. As my foot was coming down my eye made him out and I managed to step over rather than on him. He never moved or made a sound. Perhaps he was lethargic after emerging from hibernation. I usually kill rattlesnakes but left him, rather gratefully, to his own devices, feeling that maybe once again our guiding hand had guided my foot—how's that?

Emerging onto Boundary Road I passed a tumble-down farmhouse where honest-to-God people were living and earning a living. There was no paint on the house but I enjoyed looking at it and the messy barnyard, hearing the gabble of chickens and the music of a windmill, smelling that incomparable odor of straw and manure.

Then I found a deserted side road (all roads hereabouts are unpaved except main highways) and followed it up a little valley. Topping a rise onto rolling tableland I saw, a hundred yards ahead, a flock of turkeys moving across the road, driven by a lanky man in country clothes and battered straw hat. After he eased the flock through a wire gate leading toward a weather-beaten and absolutely paintless house on the crest of a rise nearby, he squatted beside the road to wait for me.

As I got nearer I saw his hat was stained all around the brim with sweat and his faded khaki trousers had been washed and mended many times. His blue shirt had so many patches of different shades that he looked like a clown dressed in motley or a peculiar sort of Blue Boy. His eyes were blue too. He hadn't shaved recently but was absolutely clean. By the touch of gray in his beard I judged him about 50.

When I got close he rose, said good morning, held out his hand. "Stiles is my name!" And by God Almighty he meant it and was glad to see me on that Sunday morning! "Broke down, are ye?" He thought I'd left a car or motorcycle back behind the rise. I said I was out for a walk.

He asked me to repeat my name to be sure he had it. Janie, his voice was the sheerest delight. So musical, gentle, strong, grave, full of air and sunlight and manhood. For a moment I could not believe it was real.

"Well," he said, "where you from?"

I told him.

"Californy, eh? I always wanted to go to Californy. What is that country like?"

His question startled me. It was the first put to me in a spirit of spontaneous interest in a long, long time. I told him about California, drawing a map in the dirt beside the road with a straw. He wanted to know about the Desert Training Center near Palm Springs where the husband of his second girl was; about the climate and the cattle and the rains. He really wanted to know.

He has a boy in the Army in North Carolina. "Sure do miss my boy. Not that I'd prefer him back. But we get along so good together. I like handling stock so I work out for hire and let Edgar take care of the place. Edgar, he likes to plow." I wondered what there was to plow as I glanced around that barren hilltop.

Stiles had been to "town"—Copperas Cove, population about 200—the night before, Saturday, and watched the soldiers having a good time, said it gave him a better idea of what his own boy was doing.

"I'm a poor man," he said with great dignity, "but that don't make no difference around here—we all go to town together, them as has lots along with the rest of us. Saturday night we're all the same as the next feller."

He rents sixty impoverished acres from an elderly "maiden lady" who owns 1200 hereabouts which she "heired from her daddy."

He had a quality about him, Janie, that I find hard to describe. Humility says only part of it. He was also intellectually curious. We discussed the fighting in Tunisia—he'd just heard the news over his radio and pronounced the names right, grasped the entire situation. We discussed Russian Communism and decided we thought better of it now the Russians were fighting so well. I wish you could have heard him. His heart and speech are as profoundly simple as a child's, growing perhaps a shade vindictive when he touches on Hitler but brightening when he predicts what our boys will do. "I ain't frightened of old Hitler. Why, I'd like to get my hands on him!" Not long ago he went to the draft board in Copperas Cove and volunteered but they rejected him as too old—which he finds hard to accept.

A pickup passed and its driver shouted a greeting. Stiles pinned him with a pointing finger and replied with a high squeal of good humor.

Now a towheaded child came out of the house and wandered toward us. "Watch out, Sonny!" he called. "Stay in the path or you'll get onto a snake!"

I asked if it was his grandson. "No, James is my boy. Nearly fifty as I am I got a boy his age."

He said it serenely, as though it were the will of the one who sends the crops.

We talked nearly two hours squatting by the wire gate. When I rose to go he said I must come in and "take dinner." I thought of staying but the recollection of the scarcity of food nowadays stopped me. I said I would take a drink of water.

So we went up to a house that was absolutely made of bare boards. Nothing on the floor but more boards yet not a sign of dirt or disorder. I glimpsed neat bedrooms, every bed made, white sheets, spreads.

We went out back and drew water from a 150-foot well in a 3-foot length of stovepipe closed off at one end to make a cylindrical bucket that just fitted the mouth of the well. The water was sweet and cool. Sometimes it doesn't rain here for seven months.

He showed me his old saddle, blankets, bit and rope lying by the back door. He'd ridden out early that morning to work cattle with a neighbor. He showed me a frayed old lasso rope on the saddle and said he must take it off soon and lay it away, because it was his son's rope and if anything happened to Edgar he would want to have the rope as keepsake.

Mrs. Stiles has borne seven children. She is prematurely aged, stooped from work and childbearing, but her eye is bright. She is painfully shy and oh so decent and kind. They wanted me badly to stay. I'd told them about you and Joan, got your pictures out of my wallet and laid them on the dining-room table beside an open box full of turkey eggs. How delighted they both were.

They took me into their bedroom and showed me their family pictures arranged atop the dresser—you know the kind.

They kept insisting "stay," but I had to go and pack up to come here.

They said I must return and bring you and stay all night or come alone and stay. I said I would. I've never experienced such hospitality.

As we walked out onto the porch Stiles put his hand on my shoulder. "You come back. We'll be lookin' for you."

I waved to them as I went through the gate. Down the road I found myself singing as I walked.

LOS ANGELES, APRIL 10, 1943

I adored your *letter* this morning—all about the Stileses. Oh my, how terribly I wish I'd been with you—they are the people I love and feel for and appreciate, as you do—and I hate to miss such a lovely visit. Will you *please* go back and see them—promise me you will—forgetting you are S-2, etc.? I hope you will always write naturally about such fundamentals. They *are* the earth—and they *are* America.

Darling—I love you. One of the many reasons is because you can see and feel such people.

Last night the Richard Aldingtons came to dinner (he wrote *Death of a Hero*, a novel about the 1914–1918 war—he was in the infantry, emerged a lieutenant like you). He is English[9]—so is his wife—he is 51—she about 30. They seem intelligent—have something to say—and are not too arty or bohemian as far as I can make out. He did know D. H. Lawrence well—also Ezra

9. Aldington was poet, biographer, and editor as well as novelist.

Pound, etc. But he is evidently finding England not the place for him. As D. H. L. felt too, likewise Huxley. They all feel that here is the only freedom left—perhaps they will bring us many things we need.

Mrs. Aldington—quite beautiful—told of staying in New Mexico with Frieda Lawrence who is now married to an Italian— a pure peasant—and they live like peasants on a real farm and the literati of the world drop in and out, and they all sit crosslegged and talk of art—books, etc.—and she, *old* Frieda now—arises and goes to churn the butter—and her husband tills the land and built the house they live in. They are happy.

Evidently artists are forever after the simple life—but why all the tortuous routes to achieve it? Anyway, it was an interesting evening—a desperately far cry from the Army wives of Brownwood. I hope never to fit into a "set" anywhere—let us be free to have all kinds of friends.

                                        CAMP HOOD, TEX., APR. 10, 1943
General Bruce[10] spoke to us impromptu this morning, just dropped into our class. He gives me new respect for those who must bear top responsibility in time of battle. Indeed I have new appreciation of all practical people: those who make the world work. They are too often overlooked by our intellectual friends.

The Happy Man selling at 3,000 in these first weeks seems a miracle. Sometimes the thought of writing words people pay to read is so preposterous I can't grasp it. Next moment I'm impatient with a public who won't buy 5,000 copies and 5,000 more, to read about the real people and the beautiful country we know. I can't do any writing now. I must feel deeply and move slowly into what I say.

Goodnight. Kiss Joan for me in the sun.

Yes, it is pleasant to be reviewed in *N.Y. Times* and *Herald Tribune*, but it's all mere prattle compared to what I want to say to you.

                   LOS ANGELES, APRIL 10, 1943, SATURDAY NIGHT, 9 P.M.
I'm in bed—tired—after feeding the Marine Corps (3 of them)— and dashing about with baby, etc. But the 2 boys (heroes) have

10. Major General Andrew D. Bruce, commanding the Tank Destroyer Center, Camp Hood.

gone to a nightclub show and I declined their invitation. I hate
the idea of going out with any male but you—even the Marines.
Hope you are flattered.

These youths (one is about to receive the Distinguished
Flying Cross *and* the Navy Cross) are very modest, very unedu-
cated, very brave. Wars give such men such fake significance. I
do not believe it is right to go into hysterics over a boy who dived
his plane into a Zero—they are all boys out for the fun of it and
the thrill—they are brave, yes, but they get distorted ideas of
their value. The little home town in the Middle West surely will
seem mighty dull after the war.

They both spoke of the violent praying they do when in
danger in action.

As I was giving Joan her orange juice in the living room,
one of them showed me his snaps of Guadalcanal and it was
interesting. Joan loved it too—wanted to grab the pictures and
destroy them, I suppose. Symbolic? But it all brings the war too
close and depresses me.

Too many of these dark days—too many evenings when Pop
drinks and Mum gets glum. But after 3 months away from it all,
I feel pretty calm and am almost cheerful when the parents start
spatting. I cannot get too perturbed—there are so many bigger
things to ponder.

This is April 10th. Three years ago today you proposed to
me while we were having a picnic. I feel very ancient tonight
thinking back all that way—you have made me a different, a
better person, my darling, but I still have a long way to go to be
worthy of *you*. Excuse this note.

LOS ANGELES, APRIL 12, 1943, MONDAY, 12 NOON
More about the Marines. They have such an awareness of death—
and feel nearly certain they will not come back. Their job—the
fighter pilot's—is about as dangerous as can be. They accept it,
and love it—are absolutely crazy about the air. They are busy
training recruits—but will return to action soon. They are upset
at being here so long (since Xmas). But a new squadron has to
be formed.

Their CO,[11] a young 32-yr.-old col., was killed in the Solo-

---

11. Commanding Officer.

Frederick and Dorothy Faust in the garden at 317 Burlingame Avenue, Los Angeles, 1942.

In the battle-conditioning course at Camp Hood, Texas, we crawled through barbed wire under live machine-gun fire while buried charges simulating shell bursts exploded around us, then "fought" our way through a "Nazi village" with pop-up human-figure targets and booby traps. (National Archives)

mons the day they were to sail for home.[12] These boys absolutely adored him and his death took away much of their joy of home-coming. It is all a most moving heroic tale. Pop is writing it verbatim.

As to Pop and the Merchant Marine, it may or may not come to pass. His idea is to sail via M. Marine convoy to Murmansk! Of course, if torpedoed, his heart could never stand the exposure in an open boat, even if there were one. The decline of Mihailovich has ruled out the Yugoslav thing completely.

A woman who comes to help us in the house in the after-noons has a young daughter with an exceedingly fine voice. Daddy is helping her with singing lessons and everyone feels one day she will be in the Metropolitan. She sang for us yesterday. I cannot remember *ever* hearing such a sympathetic and perfectly glorious voice. It is a God-given gift. Really, thrilling.

As usual, when beauty comes my way, I thought of you and wished for you. And having the Marines and Hargraves here—and young people all about—made me horribly conscious of how lost I am without you. Tell me your plan to have me with you in July—and *if* you get a leave, let me return with you for a while then. You *did* promise, didn't you? I'm already looking forward to our joys. Life is so inexpressibly beautiful with you, Bobbie darling—for you *feel* deep down, all the good and lovely meanings of the earth and the people who move on it.

Also, yesterday, a girl in my class at Spence came in with her husband (engineer for Pratt & Whitney). It was fun to see her after *six* yrs! Her husband is nice—*enormous*—6 ft. 8! He feels conspicuous out of uniform but I guess has been rejected on account of his height and is doing an essential job anyway. It was like pre-war days to have a young couple, united, walk in for Sunday tea—*minus* the ridiculous drama of uniform.

Must stop—Joan is awake—kicking violently, her legs in the sunshine and talking to the trees and flowers. I will hold her soon and play with her. She smiles at her "Gramps" now and he is quite enslaved. She grows prettier every day and will be a lovely little girl when she walks around at 1 1/2 yrs. Her disposition is absolutely miraculous—never a cry—always happy.

12. Joe Bauer was engaging five Japanese Zeroes alone and was posthumously awarded the Congressional Medal of Honor. He was like many who gave their blood and lives against heavy odds, until our war effort could be fully brought to bear.

The war news is good, which helps tremendously. Daddy and I intend to play tennis every evening at 6 when he comes back from the studio. I love you, love you, love you.

CAMP HOOD, TEX., 13 APRIL, 1943

Your description of the Aldingtons reminds me how much I regret missing that lunch with your father and Huxley. Curious, how these talented men leave England in search of greater freedom, a new land, inspiration, not to mention dollars.[13] And speaking of refugees I was immensely interested in what you said about Frieda Lawrence. How eccentric, how circuitous, but how right to get back to basics as she has. We've done the same in our way, and when I sit at supper with Jake Stiles and his wife, as I did last Sunday, I almost believe we have learned how to behave anywhere.

When I got there they were chasing a turkey hen around the yard, a setting hen who'd left her nest. After they caught her and cooped her up, Jake showed me over his 60-acre farm: the corn planter, the stack of broom corn in the loft of the cowshed from which brooms are made (I never before thought what brooms were made of), the black boar, the six lambs and ewes, the Jersey calf and its mother that gives it all the milk it needs plus two gallons daily for the family.

We saw, in the storeroom, the empty jars Mrs. Stiles filled last summer with fruit and vegetables from the garden. He said simply: "This here's how we live."

We saw the long white sack he drags behind him on hands and knees through the cotton rows. It weighs 60 pounds when full and he fills it three times a day during harvest.

Also I saw the traps she sets for coons and possums who raid her chickens and turkeys, and the horseshoeing outfit he shoes his horses with.

Then we entered the house and I was shown—in the spare bedroom—the seeds of his broom corn, maize and hegari and received samples of each in an envelope which I'm sending Father to see if they will grow at the ranch.

Now, miraculously, supper was ready. I removed my green fiber helmet liner with which you are familiar and left it on the

---

13. Both Aldington and Aldous Huxley were Hollywood screenwriters.

trunk in the hall beside Jake's battered hat. He ushered me gravely into the kitchen where there was fresh well water (no running water) in a basin, and a towel. I washed and dried, then he did likewise while Mrs. S. put finishing touches on fried eggs at the heavy, black iron, wood-burning range within a few feet of us. And then with as much ceremony as a king's chamberlain, Jake said: "There's a comb in yonder!" and ushered me into their bedroom and to the comb which lay in state on a white runner on a high chiffonier in front of a mirror. We combed in succession.

Then we passed on into the hall, not back through the kitchen, and so approached the dining room properly. I cannot describe the simple dignity with which all this was done.

The table was covered with a fresh white cloth. On it were ham, eggs, fresh milk, fresh cornbread, home-canned corn, home-canned peas mixed with mayonnaise, pickles and cheese, French-fried potatoes—and banana pudding with wafers for dessert. I said I didn't notice any food shortage in these parts. It was all delicious. I told about California, the ranches, Charlie Tant, the mountain lion hunter who when tired scoops a hole in the earth and sleeps in it with his dogs on top of him. I described your cooking a pheasant on our wood stove at the McCreery Ranch. And finally the wild cattle of the Sisquoc.

"Now tell us about your brothers and sisters," they asked. When I replied I had none, they smiled together: "We thought so."

After supper we all went out onto the porch and sat. The sun had gone down behind a distant blue headland but there was a notch in it still red against the sky. Jake lit his pipe. "See that notch yonder?" pointing with his pipe stem. "That's Lampasas Gap. In early days cattle herds went out through there. This here's the old Chisholm Trail. You maybe heard of it?" I said indeed I had. "Yessir, them big herds went right by here, and when they reached them western countries, they headed north!"

I wanted to stay and talk but was facing a seven-mile walk home, so I said goodbye and promised to bring you when you come, and to come myself meanwhile.

LOS ANGELES, APRIL 16, 1943, FRIDAY
I am mortally ashamed of the horrible note I sent yesterday! Please forgive me a million times. I just got panicky and vengeful and

very mean and I really don't deserve to be forgiven at all. My life is so terribly dependent on your letters, just two words is enough, and I'd had nothing for four horribly long days. None of which justifies my nasty note. Please say you don't feel too angry with me.

This morning your long special delivery came at breakfast and I read it with such tremendous joy. I'm so happy you went to the Stileses'. I was gabbing to a lot of people that afternoon and wondering where you were. May we always spend our Sundays with the Stileses—their kind of people, at least. But there is a place for the Aldingtons and the Marine heroes as well, and all our Army friends too.

Daddy and I have started tennis and to his amazement I was very good, for me, though I haven't touched a racket for two years.

By the way, I've gained 6 pounds. I feel awfully well, darling, and if you were here would probably suddenly weigh 180 out of sheer delight!

I can't tell you what a shock it was when we heard yesterday that Boyd Comstock, Jr.[14] had died of acute arthritis. His life has been one long consummate pain since birth, perhaps death is a blessed release. It is very sad though. Pop may collect the best of his poetry and have Dodd Mead publish a small volume. It would be a loving tribute to a friendless boy and suffering spirit.

Daddy was his greatest joy, you know, and he spent so many hours with him, not easy hours either. Pop has taken the blow very hard, but the future could only have meant more agony, especially with this last ghastly arthritis.

Helen Carver, the girl with the miraculous voice, came the other morning and I helped her with pronunciation of German songs. She's a very lovable, sweet and eager person, my age, willing to work hard to make her voice perfection. Darling, all these words are mere asides from the main issue which is to tell you I love you constantly. Over three weeks have passed since I saw you; perhaps time will go faster and faster. Joan loves you too. Please eat properly.

P.S. Last night I insisted we read the story of Ruth aloud from the Bible. It is a beauty. I thought of you.

14. Son of former University of Southern California and Italian Olympic track and field coach, Boyd Comstock.

CAMP HOOD, APRIL 16, 1943

Today we saw films of the German invasions of Crete, Poland, and Russia. They are German-made, dreadful and wonderful. The accompaniment throughout was Wagner—I recognized "The Valkyrie" and others, and doubt if Wagner will ever be much of a pleasure to me again. You would be surprised how well it fits these scenes of strife and ruin.

The films of Crete are best, made from the parachutists' point of view, from the planes that dropped them. You see the shore line, the villages, the people, the captured Greeks and British, and a number of other maddening scenes, all most flattering to the Nazis.

How heroic the British have proved themselves in their ordeal by fire, and how immature and ineffective our military efforts in Tunisia seem alongside theirs. A number of reasons may qualify this but the underlying fact remains.

We shall both be so glad—you and I—to see the wonderful American cockiness, which is becoming nothing but brassiness in so many, reduced a little, however painfully. Confound our breezy attitude, though it is charming. A bunch of callow boys never *won* anything or *did* anything that lasted a long time. But I'm always going around with a long face and must remind myself that however deeply an American feels or thinks he is not apt to say so. He is apt, rather, to read the funny papers and talk about Lana Turner.

LOS ANGELES, MAY 4, 1943

Each letter of yours I think the loveliest and most perfect. So I keep them all. They are very precious to me and will keep me company all my life if anything should take you from me. Not that I believe anything will, for I feel we are destined for happiness and you have so much to give the world, not only in the written word but in the spoken one and in your way of life.

I quote to you here a few pages, all there are, of a diary one of the Marines gave Daddy. He evidently kept it only a few days. But if you could see the scrawly words in pencil on the battered sheets of paper, it would give you a turn as it does me. Here it is:

May 11, 1942. 0830

Took off the good carrier *Hornet* for New Caledonia. Flew
course 200 thru foul weather and finally sighted island. At 1130
while looking for spot to land, Capt. Quilter ran out of gas and
went down about 2 miles offshore in shark infested waters.

By this time all pilots were low on petrol. A field was sighted
and the squadron sat down. Some with 2 gallons of gas left, some
with only a pint. The field turned out to be at Ton-Touta built by
the French some years ago and about as smooth as Dago Red. The
remainder of an army P-39 Squadron was operating from the field
but equipment and morale were plenty low. They were mighty glad
to see us. We had 20 Grummans left but no mechs or spare
parts. We are still operating, each pilot doing his own repair and
servicing.

I don't know why they want to save this place. There isn't a
pint of rum on the whole island. It is a Free French island and
they have a revolution every other day. The high commissioner
kidnapped the governor and put him out to sea on a French man-
of-war. Next somebody kidnapped the high commissioner. The
native Bolos love to fight and are first on one side and then on the
other. They make certain that no side loses else their revolution
would cease and they could no longer slice noggins from the torso.

They were once all head hunters and most of them still have
a hangover. Deer, wild boars, etc., are plentiful and some of our
boys are out for meat. The natives around the field are quite friendly
and are the source of amusement for everybody. One of the boys
taught one of them to sing 'Clementine' and the fellow is now
chief of his tribe and sings it constantly. We have a mess boy who
was imported by the French from Java to work in the mines. He
was intercollegiate boxing champ of Java and goes around beating
his chest all the time. In Java a boxing match is a cross between
a sword fight and a free-for-all with a blend of homicide. We get
along fine and I kid him (with my gun in his back).

Dorothy Lamour is reported to be somewhere in these parts.
No doubt her lair is hidden in this jungle vastness. As soon as my
Tarzan call improves I go to seek her.

One of the enlisted men (army) went berserk the other night
and started to shoot up the place. He claimed to have received a
wire from the President himself informing him that Hitler was on
the island. He was personally to supervise the execution of said
Hitler, so taking no chances that Hitler might be disguised as an
American he started firing upon everyone. Fortunately nobody
was killed. Even the toughest are apt to crack. Please notice the
steadiness of this hand.

The army's big bombers have commenced to arrive in large

numbers so a major attack must be forthcoming. The *Lexington* was sunk in the Coral Sea and the remainder of her task force put into Noumea harbor. 1500 wounded were to be put ashore. We still get reports that the British are continuing rearguard actions. Don't know how much of a knockout punch this action carries but it certainly gets a lot of publicity.

The T.B.D. Squadron[15] from the *Lexington* is with us now. They have no planes as they were lost with the carrier. All have hopes of returning to the old country soon.

Lt. Art Finucane was killed today, dive-bombing. He dove on a ship and never pulled out. An army chaplain held services for him which amazed but certainly pleased us. They aren't in the habit of taking time off for such triflings. It was a very impressive military service and makes life seem less cheap.

That's all there is of the diary. Isn't it moving in its understatement? Its *American* vein?

Must go darling. I never manage to say all I want to. The very important thing, however, is that I love you.

IN BARRACKS, CAMP HOOD, TEX., 10 MAY 1943

We've been designated a "towed battalion" and have received new long-barreled 3-inch anti-tank guns which will be towed behind half-tracks much as the field artillery tows its howitzers behind trucks.[16] It's disappointing not to get the vaunted new secret weapon that will wipe out Hitler's tanks with a puff of smoke, but to have a weapon of any kind helps a lot—gives us identity and purpose. The men show new interest. And we have 26 field artillery officers who don't know or care much about tank destroyer tactics but do know guns and are now in their element.

The colonel is not much improved, however, or will ever be, I'm afraid. (The kindly man! As one officer puts it: "Every inch a civilian!") But the major is definitely capable and a bear for work.

15. The T.B.D.'s, or Douglas Devastators, were the Navy's first all-metal monoplane carrier aircraft. Outmoded by 1942, they suffered fearfully at the Battle of Midway and elsewhere.

16. Other battalions were receiving more innovative equipment in the form of the new M-10 tank destroyer—a tank-like vehicle with open, rather than closed, turret mounting a powerful 76-mm. gun. These superseded the make-do half-tracks with old French-designed 75-mm. guns which had seen service against Rommel's tanks in North Africa with disastrous results. In final analysis, the best weapon against a tank would prove to be a better tank.

Next week we move to the tank hunting and commando course for combat conditioning. As preparation we are double-timing around camp and climbing ropes. I personally accomplished 30 push-ups, numerous exercises of the body from the prone position, 12 more push-ups, 1/2 mile double time, a rope-climb of 20 feet, and an obstacle course. We'll soon be crawling through barbed wire under live machine gun fire and other harassments.

I'm more than thankful you are not here. Sometimes I wonder if you understand my feelings? To sum them up: if we go overseas without delay I shall be satisfied. I am afraid we won't, though. I'm afraid we shall go on maneuvers or be attached to some larger unit and hang around.

But, whatever, you *must* wish with me for an early sea voyage and an accomplishment of the business at hand.

Later:

As duty officer I sit at battalion headquarters typing with a gasoline lantern on one side and a candle on the other. The clerk on duty with me is Private Provenzano who owns a flower store in Fresno, California. Of course he—the funny, bandy-legged, little man, partly bald—is the first person in a month whom I've heard use the word "beautiful." He meant it quite seriously, speaking of spring in the San Joaquin Valley. He hated not being in his shop at Easter, the busy season. For eleven years he has not missed an Easter. "After that until Christmas I might as well close," he says.

Oddly enough, he raises no flowers but goes to San Francisco and buys them. He pays a dollar there for a dozen roses which he can sell for five. About this he says naively: "Lieutenant, I being here, and you being here, I will tell you that I make that profit."

A lone soldier is playing a horn somewhere. A single melody for a single man, and oh-so-lonely on this spring air.

Now I declare if we can just get our guns on them we will repay the enemy for this lost spring, for all the Jugoslav villages burned, for the Greeks murdered, for the Nazi children brought up in hatred so that their flesh is only animated evil. I think this is worst of all. By this Hitler does become Satan, incarnate evil.

Provenzano has just brought me a candy bar, a Baby Ruth, the kind I used to buy as a child on my way to school. I don't really like candy and this will make me all the thirstier on a hot night, but I would not disappoint Provenzano for the world.

LOS ANGELES, MAY 13, 1943

Last night I thought of the evenings at the McCreery Ranch when you were late and I waited about the house and watched the hills for you and your horse. And then, after hours, the hoofs on the yard—the barn light suddenly on, the dismounting, the gruff goodnights to the men—and you, your arm through mine (me in a white apron) walking back to our home, our food, our cat, our lighted fire—our love—all shining bright.

But it will come again—more mature, more beautiful, more complete.

Four days: no letter from you. I *hope* for one tomorrow. I feel a little distressed though I know you are probably well and just too busy. The woman's heart is forever anxious for her mate.

CAMP HOOD, TEX., 14 MAY 1943

Janie, how would you like to be married to a parachutist? I passed the physical and will forward all papers soon. For weeks I've known this might come. I couldn't tell you because nothing was definite. I am very happy. Now when I see, hear, read of the fighting I feel confident I shall be there. The 825th is in the doldrums and may remain so indefinitely. If I should finish my experience in this war as it has begun, I could not respect myself.

Now I want you here. I promise there will be no more of those tortured indecisive evenings we spent at Brownwood, pondering the future. I regret them. They left you weakened in body and spirit so that you lost weight and caught a dreadful cold. Please forgive me. I only want to be your man, your husband in whom you take pride.

Yes I love and desire you, your long sweet body, your brown limbs, and the lips and the touch that delights me. No face or woman's figure but yours has any meaning at all. Just the instant's thought and the sweet memories—and I'm reminded this is spring, spring-in-summer, May, the lovely time, when the green turns to gold and the magic scents of youth and ripeness mingle.

Then I yearn for you, for our strong youth, and I long to

laugh and lie with you and take joy in our flesh. Please come to me.

Why not fly? Fly to Dallas (1/2 a day!) and perhaps I could meet you and by suppertime we'd be here. I urge you to fly. Make reservations well in advance and see if you can't. Make them by train, too, in case they cancel your flight the last minute or take your seat away. Make them on a streamline train. Come, Janie.

Lampasas is 40 minutes' drive: a nice small town like Brownwood. I will find us a home there.

LOS ANGELES, MAY 16, 1943, SUNDAY 7:30 P.M.
Hearing your voice last night was a joy—most of all to know you really want me with you again! The whole thing has burst upon me and sent floods of happiness through me. I then read your wonderful letter and couldn't fall asleep for hours—the thought of you makes me all excited and ready to jump up and down. And all day I've been busy but so very happy that I smiled vaguely at people and couldn't hear a word they were saying.

Most of all, I am glad *you* are happy. You will be doing something you can forever be proud of—and let me tell you, *I* am proud of you now, as always, my paratrooper. I am sure you have taken the right path and have not stepped hastily. I am happy about it, darling.

Oh please *always* tell me you want me—every bit of me, I can never grow weary of hearing you desire me—my flesh as well as my soul and heart. But do you know—I believe that in our love, the flesh and the soul and the spirit become one? When you kiss me or touch me—I feel much more than your physical presence—something deep and *you* suddenly become so close to me that we are one and I cannot ever feel alone again.

CAMP HOOD, MAY 20, 1943
Just returned from Lampasas, a lovely town, set in a hollow among large oaks and pecans, all so green. Though I feel disloyal in saying so, I rate it more attractive than Brownwood and just as neighborly. After ringing doorbells unsuccessfully I decided to take a room at the Wachen Hotel. I think you will like it. Wachendorfer's father built it decades ago as his home—of native

fieldstone two stories high with walls two feet thick, shaded by two giant pecans. It was only recently converted to a hotel.

Lampasas, population 4000, reminds me of California when I was a boy. Nearly everybody owns a cow which is staked out alongside his house or in the green ditch bordering the unpaved street. Lawns, too, go right to the street, and there are flower and vegetable gardens, fruit trees, and chickens everywhere.

You must think carefully over what I say now: if further treatment is required before you have another baby and if coming to Texas will interrupt such treatment, I don't want you to come. The reason is this: our second baby had best be started before I go to Ft. Benning, Georgia, for paratroop training because I may go overseas soon afterward. I've been faced already with that overseas decision. Quite aside from the 'chutes, somebody comes up to you and says: "Volunteers are needed for overseas duty. What is your decision?" And you leave tomorrow. I find I wasn't qualified, as I think I wrote, because I have not commanded a platoon. I count on my orders for Benning coming in mid-June and a furlough around July 1. Of course this is a *guess*.

But the baby is *the* important consideration—your health relative to the baby. So please clear with Ikey before coming.

Mother and Father seem a little upset about my transfer to the paratroops. My answer is: a call has gone out for volunteers, I'm answering it.

The time is 9:15. During the break (above) I walked with four other officers four miles in 50 minutes and ran another half-mile. This is a punishment prescribed for them, morning and evening for seven days, because they straggled recently when their company went on a road march. I am the umpire to see they complete the course.

Love you most tenderly.

LOS ANGELES, MAY 23, 1943

Seems to me I spend *hours* daily explaining *why* you are transferring to the parachutes. As I guessed, it has been a big shock to your parents. Apparently they thought you were quite happy. People make me mad who can't understand—but I do my best.

The news of Mary Jane P.'s husband being killed has left me

in a stupor. They had one *week* together. Oh, Bob, there cannot be any more wars. I feel very downcast as I think of that poor young girl—only *one* week! I am not sure one can stand such blows—I know that the temptation to lie down and die must be very great. But if anything happens to *you* I cannot afford such an attitude, not with two children. Still, my very heart believes that you will come back, though everyone rushes to assure me that paratroops are suicidal.

At the moment I am terribly sick of *people*, of chit-chat—of dinners where I dash up and down serving guests. I guess I just have an acute need of you. I feel a little bad-tempered and venomous and only Joan makes me happy.

Perhaps this weekend you'll have time to write me a long letter. I am pretty lost just now. I need you to lean on, as I am doing in this letter. I am so rarely in this mood of confusion (inside) but when with you it all straightens out.

Great news—Joan has a tooth. She likes to hear it clink on the spoon as I feed her.

CAMP HOOD (BACK FROM BROWNWOOD)
MAY 23, 1943, SUNDAY EVENING

Hearing your voice last night in Brownwood was pleasure indeed. Roscoe Brooks and I met at the ringing telephone in pajamas (time: 1:14 A.M.) and there was the voice of the old gal herself, just as good as ever. Then I lost a little sleep thinking how much I love you.

The men's Sunday School this morning was one of those rare Texas experiences. It is called "The Line Riders." Its leader is a red-necked cattleman who looks like Will Rogers and talks like him. It was just mighty good, the kind of worship we shall practice one day in the little church at Los Olivos. They ended by singing "The Old Rugged Cross" as if they were at a high school football rally.

Later we all went to the regular service—men, women, children. The simplicity and directness of these people continues to astound me. I heard grown men, leaders in the community, discussing the conduct of the Jews toward the Samaritans, the speech of Peter to John—the actual pith and tissue of the Bible—as if they were current events.

LOS ANGELES, MAY 27, 1943

No words can ever express just how much a long Spec. Deliv. means to me. One came to the side door this morning at 8:00 when I was getting breakfast. I *adored* having a real letter from you—it was like talking to you at last—it made me serene and happy. Yes, if you think it best to start our second baby the end of June or during your leave, I'm all for it. I can think of nothing more wonderful in the relationship of man and woman—a creation—a baby.

I see Ikey tomorrow and he will give me a last treatment if necessary. So it's all fixed. I was pretty shocked to hear you may be overseas so quickly—but I know it's right. I sometimes am sure I cannot bear to have you sail—making a future life with you so very uncertain. But it *must* be, obviously. I will be brave, as you are always. But a part of me will die until you are back again. You must know that and it cannot be otherwise. Two children will keep me busy enough.

I long to see Lampasas. The Wachen Hotel sounds wonderful and the town perfect. I can barely wait to be with you in the summer. What fun it will be to live in a little town again. I miss life and the people you and I understand and like. Can we see the Stiles family? And can we spend hours and hours alone?

If you can get the day off—I mean Wednesday—it could be heavenly. But it doesn't matter. We will have time for happiness.

CAMP HOOD, MAY 27, 1943

Well, my papers started up through channels yesterday, all signed, with so many carbons it will take half a day to read them. If they're approved (and I have no doubt they will be) my orders for the 'chutes should come by the middle of June. I've asked the colonel for troop duty which will help qualify me.

What fine European news. Maybe the war won't last forever, though I see Mayor La Guardia is warning of air attacks on New York City like those on Oregon.[17]

Our room in Lampasas is waiting. Please hurry!

17. The Germans facing the Russians at Stalingrad had surrendered and the Russians were advancing westward on a broad front. North Africa had been cleared of Axis forces. Allied landings in Sicily and on the Italian mainland were expected soon. But Mayor Fiorello La Guardia was warning of possible air attacks on New York City, and military authorities were describing such raids as probable. During the month, there were two Japanese attempts to set forest fires in Oregon by exploding aerial bombs dropped from a plane based on a submarine.

Yesterday at Ikey's all went as it should. He gave me a last treatment and said I was "set." Finally I got up courage and asked about another baby in a month or two—he said "O.K. Jane"— and so it's all fixed and I *am* relieved. We will start trying for a baby after I've been with you for a while, so that your leave will not be spent with me in nausea. We'll plan when I see you Tuesday—and yet it seems *so* far off!

Each new place we live in temporarily, Muskogee, Brownwood, Lampasas, is enhanced by the thought this may be our last stop together.

When Bob is on duty at camp and can't get back to Room 8 in Hotel Wachen, "Uncle" Charlie Wachendorfer, our host, and "Aunt" Verna, his similarly rotund and benign consort, take Jane under their wing, loan her washing machine and ironing board, take her shopping on the nearby square—a classic western square, wood or corrugated iron awnings extending from store-fronts over sidewalks around all four sides, old stone courthouse in its center—the sort of square where you expect to meet Gary Cooper in *High Noon*, though instead of horses tied to hitching rails there are pickups parked at curbs or in the square itself, loaded with bales of hay, hogs, sheep, even a cow for swapping or sale. There Jane meets those beguiling Texans with their melodious: "Hurry bay-ack!" and "Come-see-us!" Never has she encountered such friendliness, such pervading gaiety of spirit. When Bob is exposed to it, he too succumbs.

Again we discover another America. In their calicos and khakis, cheerfulness and courtesy, these people seem the enlisted men and women of life—the ones who fill the ranks in peace and war, who live and die uncelebrated but are like particles holding nation and world together. We delight in their "Yessir, nossir," and "Yes, ma'm; no, ma'm." We rejoice in blue-plate specials at the Bluebonnet Cafe featuring huge T-bones, black-eyed peas and sticks of golden cornbread. The fact that the Lions Club meets every first and third Tuesday seems a dispensation from the gods of normalcy and freedom. We wonder why we never understood in peacetime how precious ordinary life can be, and wonder if these people in their civilian clothes know how lucky they are, what a treasure they hold in their hands. At his tiny switchboard in his parlor-lobby, Uncle Charlie Wachendorfer says it all as he begins his intimate telephone conversations: "Hello, this is me—that you?" He speaks for a world of trust and friendship, a world beyond war, a world to hold to.

One sunny Saturday we drive back from Camp Hood to Lampasas through the rolling Hill Country. Jane has spent the night in the camp's guest house and now we're driving "home." Spring is in full bloom around us, the landscape carpeted with bluebonnets and goldeneyes, and as we dip into a certain green hollow and see an old stone courthouse and surrounding town, we suddenly realize with exclamations of wonder and delight that Lampasas is *our* town—because we've discovered, identified with, loved it.

Excitedly we drive along tree-lined streets choosing houses we'll maybe buy and live in with our children after the war. For six precious weeks our idyll continues. Jane becomes pregnant. Bob becomes a first lieutenant. His application for the parachute troops is turned down for reasons that are never clear. His commanding officer, well-intentioned but ineffective Colonel E., is replaced by abrasive but effective Colonel M. and he's obliged to remain in a staff job he loathes, while Jane prepares to return to California—as the battalion moves on.

CHAPTER 6

To be prepared for war is one of the most effectual measures for preserving peace.

GEORGE WASHINGTON

Final Preparations

ON MANEUVERS, SOMEWHERE IN TENNESSEE, NOV. 11, 1943
We're camped on a wooded knoll between cultivated fields 30 miles from Nashville. Outfits are pouring in around us: armored divisions, infantry divisions, engineers, anti-aircraft. Luckily we arrived early and were able to make what arrangements and purchases we needed. There have been large-scale maneuvers here for several years but never before in winter. Ours is said to be the largest and last before the invasion of Europe. Over 100,000 men are expected.

We are the Blue Forces, the good guys. Our vehicles wear bands of blue paint eighteen inches wide. It is gasoline-solvent and will come off when we change to the Red Force and become the "enemy." Flights of bombers and pursuits go over daily, representing the air support both sides will have.

Outside our C.P.[1] tent the U.S.O. portable movie unit is giving a show for the men. I can hear the dialogue and music. It's *The Pride of the Yankees*, the story of Lou Gehrig.

Now Colonel M. comes storming in half-frozen and made sad by the movie, and begins telling stories and singing ribald ditties he sang with the cavalry in the First World War. And now he has gone off to bed in a flurry saying he wishes he had Lana Turner to keep him warm.

I am living in that kind of limbo without you which only the Army produces.

LOS ANGELES, NOV. 14, 1943
Tomorrow it will be four months since we separated. I hate every day of it. My biggest hope is to see you in February. Now the nausea is over and I no longer stay in bed, I feel well and strong and the days *do* pass more quickly, but there is such a lack in my

---

1. Command post.

life that I'm really unable to *feel* anything deeply but my missing of you.

If I were not in my *eternal* "delicate condition" I'd jump at Betty's invitation and go stay with the Ashfords in Nashville until you leave Tennessee. Isn't it awful to be so completely in the power of the "new Easton" at this early stage? How many more must I propagate?

Pop is in bed feeling very wretched and grumpy and full of self-pity (as all sick men are!) because his injections yesterday for typhoid, tetanus, smallpox, etc. have left him ill. He'll probably not get an overseas assignment as war correspondent until early March but has hopes for something earlier. You will see him before he leaves undoubtedly. He talks about you so much.

My role as pregnant hostess and assistant household manager has resumed and I do all I can to help Mum and Pop, who are simply wonderful as well as maddening.

Goodbye—my dearest one—my lover, my mate, my husband—every day is meaningless until you hold me in your arms again.

TENNESSEE MANEUVER AREA, NOV. 18, 1943

Our problem ended at noon today in total defeat. We "lost" 12 guns and crews and "knocked out" 2 jeeps. The infantry infiltrated our positions at night—a strange feeling, Janie, men coming on you in the dark—and we lost heavily. Our supply and service trains were cut off, our vehicles nearly ran out of gas. Luckily we managed to extricate ourselves and withdraw over the Cumberland River to new positions. The weather didn't help. Last night the thermometer dropped to 12, with some snow. Our metal vehicles absorb and hold the cold. We really shivered. More than ever I leave the Arctic regions to you.

I have not been to bed for quite a while (since Monday) and will just say I love you and plan to get into Nashville Friday and visit the Ashfords.

Don't worry if letters don't come; I'll write when I can.

LOS ANGELES, NOV. 18, 1943

I've spent some wakeful nights dreaming you are wounded and will not come back to me because you don't want to hurt me.

Surely you know that I love you and want you and need you, wounded or not. For the most part, I keep foolish notions about the war far away. I tie up my heart and say to myself: "No imagination to be used for the duration!" It usually helps me laugh at my fears.

You ask to know what goes on at home: rain, mostly—and indoors Pop (recovered from the reaction to his various vaccines) is concocting various complicated soups in his eternal mixer. This morning he gave himself a fright—his heart was *much* too fast (140), his breathing hard, knees weak. I got him lying flat and in a couple of hours he was better. He needs these jolts to make him cut down on cigarettes, coffee, liquor. He has been pretty good about the last, but I think he'll be more careful in all ways now. He worries about his physical condition for the correspondent job. I sometimes wonder if he will get over and back alive. The odds are heavily against it—as you can imagine.

Mum is brave but I know it's a constant fear in her soul.

TENNESSEE MANEUVER AREA, NOV. 28, 1943

Friday after our problem ended I went to Nashville, took a hotel room, showered, and phoned the Ashfords. Mrs. A. fairly shrieked when she heard my name. "Belvoir" is a good distance from downtown, as you remember, and do you recall how the driveway sweeps in over a bridge and up between huge trees and lawns to the portico that has stone columns nearly thirty feet high? There are chips in them from Civil War bullets. We didn't see these at first because we drove to the back under the porte-cochere. "I don't know why we always bring people to the back door," declares Mrs. A., "but we always do!" She's absolutely charming, graying, tweedy, says whatever comes into her head. She led me by the hand into that incredible downstairs hall with the circular staircase and cried: "Betty!"[2] A voice upstairs squealed joyfully: "Where *is* he? Let me *see* him!" It was Betty in bathrobe leaning over the rail and adding: "Is he as cute as Jane?"

I replied that she had me at disadvantage because I couldn't see her while she could see me, and challenged her to step into the light. She protested she had no clothes on and disappeared

2. Jane's roommate at Spence.

to get some, while Mrs. A. and I wandered through those mano-
rial rooms and settled ourselves in a salon fit for Queen Victoria.

There Betty burst on us, still squealing: "Now, *now*, NOW—
where *is* he?" She's not particularly good looking. It is her anima-
tion that makes her quite beautiful.

Luckily I'd brought photos and began with you at 18 on the
deck of the *Conte di Savoia*, which Betty adored, and ended with
the one taken just before Joan was born. "Two hundred pounds!"
squeals Betty. "Oh, *my*!"

Supper was divine. The long table supported constant hilar-
ity as well as yummy food. Father Ashford carved. Remember
the shrewd chuckling face, huge nose, bald dome? He's a sharp
operator if I ever saw one. More of that anon. For supper we had
spare ribs of pork ("poke"), corn biscuits and gravy, lemon pie
and so forth, all served by a colored woman who was included in
the never-ceasing conversation and teased and made to laugh like
everyone else. The two younger daughters must be fifteen and
eighteen and equally dynamic and fun-loving as Betty and her
mother—as almost everybody seems to be in this uppercrust
South. I must say I haven't laughed so much in a long time.

When time came to go catch my convoy back to camp, Mr.
A. would hear of nothing but driving me downtown. There he
took me to his club for a glass of his favorite Tennessee sour mash
whiskey called Jack Daniels, obtainable only locally,[3] and it is
delicious. It loosened us up beautifully and I soon discovered
there is indeed a gimlet lurking in old A. beneath all the fun. He
has ranches, he has oil, he even has a marvelous grass called
"lespedesia" (phonetic spelling),[4] native to China, ideal for live-
stock. It flourishes in Tennessee and was first imported by one of
his ancestors.

He introduced me to a fellow with a face as closely resembling
a hog's as I've ever seen and said: "Meet Guy Jenkins. Guy owns
more churches in this state than all our Christians put together,
don't you Guy?" Guy's game, apparently, is buying up mortgages
on churches. "Guy, you preach 'em one sermon and they pay—
right?" They poke each other and roar and Guy goes off, and A.
tells the bartender he wants a bottle of Jack Daniels for the
lieutenant to take to the commanding general of Second Army;

3. Now marketed nationally and internationally.
4. Actually "lespedeza."

and the lieutenant is provided with same and has delivered it to
Colonel M. with the explanation that it's a sample of Southern
hospitality, which it is.

Please have Pop send my last story so I can work it over
here.

LOS ANGELES, DEC. 1, 1943

Strange sensation to be the happiest woman alive—I *am* because
of your wonderful, long detailed letter—after 8 days of silence! I
jumped and shouted for joy when Mum brought it up at 9 A.M.!
I read and read and lived over again your visit at "Belvoir"—you
brought it all back to me so vividly. Did they tell you how
President William Howard Taft got stuck in a bathtub there,
because he was so fat, and it resulted in the invention of the first
American shower? I'm glad you had fun and a real taste of Southern aristocracy.

Let us always have friends all over the world! It is thrilling
to think of you seeing people I saw 6 years ago and being greeted
so warmly. I'm terribly proud of you. You are my greatest joy and
pride and it is because of you that Joan is so utterly enchanting.
She literally paralyzes people—of every sex and age. Her charm
and gaiety are a gift to humanity.

Mum has been saying how heavenly it would be if I could
go and stay with the Ashfords for a month. She is so sweet in
always thinking of our happiness.

I have no hopes the doctor will let me travel, so you had
better not give it a thought.

TENNESSEE MANEUVER AREA, DEC. 4, 1943

Shall I tell of the incredible hospitality of these hill people? At
the remotest log cabin, the housewife emerges with hot biscuits
or cookies as soon as the soldier boys arrive. And this despite the
fact the fields roundabout the cabin have been ripped up by tanks
and half-tracks, fences knocked down, cattle run off. Reparations
are paid by Uncle Sam but they do not account for the warmth
of hospitality. The paper stars hanging in windows tell where all
the young men have gone.

Two evenings ago I went to Division G-2 (intelligence officers at division and higher are called G-2) and stood in his huge

tent and looked at his huge situation map as tall as the wall, covered by acetate, which has red markings in grease pencil representing the enemy and blue ones representing us. While I was there General Fredendall,[5] commander of 2nd Army, arrived with three stars on his shoulders and the major general division commander greeted him and the two conferred about next day's "battle."

These professional warriors interest me. They are instruments of so much destruction and suffering, yet are also at this moment the saviors of the free world.

Enough for now. My love goes out of this C.P. tent and up through the cold night and over the stars to you.

LOS ANGELES, DEC. 6, 1943

I have moments of weakness when I consider another baby coming and the time not far ahead when I will have to take charge of two young souls as well as bodies. It is much too big a task for one parent—but I hope to keep them safely till your return.

Katherine is getting livelier by the hour and that pleases me. I have told her that it's her fault I can't go to Nashville. She doesn't mind upsetting plans at all! My poor tummy is definitely large. I feel an old hand at all this. My biggest joy is *eating*, and Rubens would find me large enough to paint with pleasure. Do you like me better fat or thin?

Please take a little moment out in which to think of me— Joan—and our unborn.

TENNESSEE, DEC. 8, 1943

We quote Sherman, "War is hell!" and are reminded that he soldiered in these parts, but went into winter quarters, as a rule, and chased Bragg during warmer weather. The temperature this morning at eight o'clock was 5 degrees.

Our rating at maneuver headquarters is the highest of any T. D. battalion. This is promising but not accurate because we make a world of errors that go unnoticed.

A curious thing today. Two enlisted men of my section

---

5. Lieutenant General Lloyd R. Fredendall, recently returned from commanding a corps in combat in North Africa.

informed me that an officer, who is a good friend of mine, severely criticized to the colonel a motor march I led yesterday. The men felt this unwarranted and unjust and thought, out of loyalty to me, I should be told. They did not suspect the trouble they might cause. I don't believe the officer maliciously informed the colonel. Yet did he? The question is sticky. Maybe the march wasn't any good. Maybe he had a right to criticize, maybe he didn't. Should I talk to him about it? Or to the colonel? Such experiences are disquieting and I try to shrug them away.

LOS ANGELES, DECEMBER 8, 1943

I sometimes think you may not miss or need me as much as I do you. Then I realize our love has no such aspects—I do believe there is no question of one loving or needing the other more—we both love to the same ultimate degree. Your letter tells me you are as lonely as I—so I feel better, strangely enough. I guess the great point is that every individual wants to feel essential to another. I admit I want you to desire me all your life—in the flesh and in the spirit—until we are parted in death. And that brings me to another point: I used to think death was final—that when one of us dies the other is forever cut off. I thought so very seriously when we slept together for the first time in our first home, our dear Rio Vista apartment.

For some reason, before we fell asleep, you said: "If I should die while you are young, I would want you to remarry." At the time I was revolted by the idea of remarriage and I still am, but now I know the reason for my instinct. I *do not* believe death is final when people love and are loved. I think that not seeing you is a kind of death—it is a death for seven months, at least—yet I am just as close to you in spirit. Do you understand?

The thought comforts me. I know I can never be alone, utterly alone, again—not even if you are killed in war or die long before I do—because there is something in our love that remains *alive* and stronger than death—as long as one of us can live to keep it burning.

A nice letter from Betty. She says, "Your old man is as wonderful as he should be. We're taking steps to adopt him for the duration."

Don't let Betty introduce you to any Southern belles—I am

always capable of being confoundedly jealous! I'm gradually going crazy thinking of the Ashfords being able to see you—while *I* am thousands of miles away!

NASHVILLE, TENN., DEC. 19, 1943 SUNDAY EVE.
Somehow the first keen edge of Southern society was dulled the second time at "Belvoir." I do want to talk further with the old grandfather, 89, who maintains simply (and rather remarkably I think) that Grant, Sherman, and Sheridan were the great generals of the Civil War—because they won! Otherwise the constant joking finally becomes a bit wearying and leads to a suspicion of emptiness below. But they are kind, oh, so kind, and speak constantly of you. Your last letters leave me believing more deeply in ourselves—just you and me. There is an abiding quality in what you say that makes the words stand strongly and beautifully as building stones; and I take from them the quality of our home-to-be, our daughter, our child-to-be, and yourself, who are most beautiful of all. I am never too busy to remember I love you.

LOS ANGELES, DEC. 23, 1943
John came last night—by plane—only took 24 hrs.—even with various stop-overs. He had a no. 4 priority, so he could get here on a 10-day furlough. He is very much older—quite brawny, more serious. Much of his work is secret and cannot be talked about but evidently he is going to interrogate prisoners at the front, and use his seven languages (including Russian). He expects to sail in January and is now, suddenly, a staff sergeant!

To think that he is 24 is incredible. You were that age when we met. John, thank God, has not fallen in love—he will leave for the war without that added wrench. I do give daily prayers for his safe survival of this mess—he is very fine, very deserving of a life ahead. Think of him, too, please, for me.

To show what a foolish, sentimental wife you have—I'm sending a little hanky of mine and I hope that when you hold it up to your face you will get a wiff of *me*. I never wear this special "smell" unless we are together—but tonight I put some on this hanky and send it to you—so you will know I love you always.

TENNESSEE MANEUVER AREA, SUNDAY EVE., DEC. 26, 1943
I spent Christmas here in the mud, though the Ashfords kindly
asked me to spend it with them, but something obstinate rose in
me and I said no. This C.P. tent in which I type is inches deep
with mud. We have slept, waked, lived all day and gone to bed
again in mud which must resemble on small scale the mud through
which Americans in Italy are fighting.

Actually I was glad to sweat it out, as we say, here with the
men, all of us cheered by packages from home such as you sent
and various bottles that somehow found their way. Chapin
brought Cresta Blanca sauterne. Doherty provided anchovy paste
and cheese crackers. I contributed a canteen of cold water. We
joined forces and made a party, and when the colonel appeared
in the doorway of the tent, dressed only in galoshes, blue shorts
and undershirt, irate at our over-loud conversation, we gave him
a canteen cup of wine and sent him to bed happy.

Some of the men have gone over the hill;[6] some just got
drunk. Several officers showed their colors by disappearing for
three days without permission. All-in-all, with the strain of the
maneuver, the constant labor of merely existing under these
conditions—let alone maintaining military equipment and disci-
pline—these holidays have been a test.

T.D. group S-2 just called on the radio. He wants the names
of our reconaissance boys who did an outstanding job on the last
problem. They hid in observation behind the enermy's lines,
watched him build his pontoon bridges and reported his armored
traffic over them, which enabled us to meet the tanks successfully
later.

You must continue your full days. I have no doubt that after
this child is born your energy will increase and with it desire for
self-expression beyond husband and children, important though
such things are. Over all of us is spread the larger meaning which
we occasionally grasp in moments by a word or a look.

The colonel has just reappeared in galoshes and blue shorts to
tell me my typing keeps him awake, blast his flamboyant old soul!

P.S. Pop wrote me a fine letter. He says, as he has so often, to
forget plot and cites Shakespeare and others who rarely invented
but often improvised, interpreted, selected. Good-night!

---

6. Absent without leave.

Next Day:

Big news. The rain is no longer falling—so far as I'm concerned—on the C.P. tent but on a green canvas tarpaulin ("gun tarp") designed to cover a 3-inch gun but now stretched over hickory poles in the form of a tent which holds the sleeping bags of Freeman, Eastabrooks and myself. There is a fire at the open end of the tarp and beyond it dark trees stand and the rain comes down. I have troop duty at last! Thirteen months on the staff was far too long. I should have had it to start with, as I wanted. This is B company and I am mighty glad to be here. The change probably means I lose all chance for promotion to captain. Colonels don't favor those who deliberately leave their staffs. And platoon leaders are supposed to be lowly lieutenants. Still I'm glad to be here.

Will tell you more as the days go by.

LOS ANGELES, JAN. 3, 1944, MONDAY A.M.

Pop has just heard that the war story he wrote while at Warners—called "After April"—has sold for fifteen thousand dollars to the *Sat. Eve. Post.*[7] This is a big relief—and rather unexpected! Pop is pleased as the money will be needed while he's overseas. The *Post* wants it under Frederick Faust, instead of Max Brand. I think that pleases Pop too—and I hope he gets back into that market and uses only his true name. I have read a good deal of "After April"—it is a beautiful story, humanly mature—fine writing and great suspense. The best picture of the fall of France, etc., I've read. The screen-play is in someone else's hands but Pop is busy with the Marine book. God rest its soul—it's been such a pest!

The mail just came. You can't imagine my joy! All the anxiety was ridiculous—I was not prepared for the havoc the holidays inflict even on mail! The letter you wrote Christmas Day took 9 days to get here air mail.

The best news, aside from the fact that you still love me, is that you are going to have a platoon. I'm so pleased the colonel has granted your request. Tell me how the first days go and if you feel like a new person.

Oh yes—it was better for you to be sweating it out with your

7. The weekly *Saturday Evening Post* was the country's leading popular magazine.

men during the holidays instead of going to Nashville where it was party, party. The old country club business! I find parties unbelievably hard to take without you, and even *with* you. I can think of a dozen ways I'd rather see our friends. But during the war, the old, stale, round of parties and the chat that goes with it, seems unbearable. As usual, we react in the same way.

Admiral King[8] predicts victory over Japan in 1945—you will be 30. The best years in our life will be beginning then. I cannot believe that you will die in this war.

Since Katherine is due early in April, you may not have sailed—I should love Katherine to turn into a boy for you. It would make me so happy to have a son—most of all for you, because I feel you'd be terribly pleased to have both a male and female offspring. Strange to think that our child months ago became a boy or girl—we have no way of telling which.

I'm glad you will see me for at least a few days of this pregnancy. I hope I'll not be *too* enormous by Feb. I should always like to be perfect for you—and a huge tummy is rather a distortion. I have a million hundred things to tell you. I am *so* happy! We have borne up under our longest separation. A reunion is near again! John said to Mum during his furlough: "I am glad Jane married Bob." He realizes how happy you've made me. Perhaps after the war we will all have time to know each other—it's all been so hurried ever since we were married! All I ever asked was *time* to live beside you. One day we shall be granted even that, I pray.

NEAR NASHVILLE, JAN. 13, 1944, THURS. EVE.

Maneuvers ended yesterday and we are waiting to move to a camp in Kentucky. We were lucky in our last problem, knocking out 15 tanks and 8 armored cars. B Co. shone with 7 tanks and 3 armored cars to its credit—the only real action our company got into during two months' maneuvers. Our positions were on a hill. The tanks came at us across a valley and through a town. We had them cold. Our big three-inch guns spoke with flame and smoke as in real battle. The hillside shook and the valley echoed. You should have seen how our usually listless men became transformed! They fired every round of blank ammunition we had!

8. Admiral Ernest J. King, head of the U.S. Navy.

I might add that the sky overhead was screaming full of P-40's and B-25's.

Despite all shortcomings the 825th made the best record of any unit in the manuever, so now we have something to be proud of. And overseas shipment may follow at last. There have been times when this seemed so improbable that I again considered transferring. But transfers even to the parachute toops are closed now. The Air Force is the only alternative and I can't stand the thought of 9 to 12 months schooling even if I should make the grade—I'm afraid my eyesight would bar me; I had to fudge a little to pass the paratroop physical. So it looks like I stay with the 825th and see what's next, for better, for worse.

As combined investment and security we'd bought a house in Santa Barbara. It had eight rooms and cost $16,000. Bob's parents generously offered us the down payment and we assumed the mortgage at $90 monthly. Our plan was for Jane to live there in close proximity to Mother and Father E. for the duration of the war. If Bob didn't survive, she and the children might remain indefinitely.

What was to be his last leave began February 6. Following happy days at 317 Burlingame, we went up to Santa Barbara and our wonderful new home at the corner of Padre and Anacapa Streets within sound of the Old Mission's bells. On the sweet side too was Bob's opportunity to hold Joan in his arms again, watch her first steps, hear her first words. Good news also came from New York. *Collier's*, which ranked next the *Post* in the popular magazine market, was buying one of Bob's stories for $400. It was twice what the highbrow *Atlantic* paid and indicated we might make at least part of our future income from writing.

Not so good was Jane's father's departure for overseas as war correspondent for *Harper's Magazine* and *The Infantry Journal*. Allied forces were stalemated in a bitter campaign in Italy and there was much criticism of American troops, particularly our infantry. At age 51, despite a fibrillating heart, Frederick Faust was determined to get to the front and send back dispatches that would do justice to the American foot soldier, and go on through the war with the infantry and write a book about the ordinary G.I. in action. Dorothy and Jane put the best front on it they could, feeling he was bound to go regardless of what they said or did. He felt Hitler represented much the same threat to civilization the Kaiser had. He'd missed out on the last war because of a physical disability and was determined to get into this one, for deeply personal as well as patriotic reasons.

As Bob's leave comes to an end, the thought is constantly in our minds that this may be the last time we'll see each other. But we carefully avoid mentioning such subjects and speak cheerfully of our next reunion. Again, our secret consolation is that millions are undergoing what we are, and much more. We sense the entire country bracing for the invasion of western Europe we all know is imminent, while in the Pacific bloody battles continue as MacArthur and the Marines and Navy capture one island after another in a triumphal progress toward the Philippines.

CAMP CAMPBELL,[9] KY., FEB. 24, 1944

Here at last after some adventures. Bad weather grounded all planes at El Paso for four days, including the Army and Navy, and you never saw such a frustrated mass of people. I spent 34 hours in the waiting room, minus three hours on a cot in a nearby Air Force barracks and a short night on a ping-pong table in an officers' lounge, and finally got a plane Monday night as far as a place called Big Spring, Texas, 296 miles nearer Dallas.

There we were grounded again and all took a train which put us at Dallas by 9:00 next morning, spent all day there, most of it in a book store buying some good western material one volume of which I sent you to keep. Left Dallas 5 o'clock yesterday but a bridge was out in central Tennessee and we had to take a bus, and finally, at 4:00 P.M., here I was.

There have been changes. A new captain commands B Co. I have the second platoon. There is a palpable sense that now we are on our way.

Somehow leaving you was less hard this time. I think because we were so happy. The days went by with such a complete joy that they seemed to move slowly and deliciously. I did feel they were a foretaste of our life to come, the one we knew existed, and suddenly, wonderfully, there it was. I am most deeply grateful.

9. Now Fort Campbell, near the Kentucky-Tennessee border.

Be well, please, and take exercise, write me long letters in which you fully describe Joan's days; and in the mornings when there is some free time, be alone and work on your stories.

P.S. On the subject of income tax, yes, go ahead and I can check your work. My base pay as a second lieutenant from Nov. 6, 1942 to July 10, 1943 was $150. That is what we pay taxes on; the remainder is living and ration allowance. As a first lieutenant my base—and therefore taxable—pay is $166.67 per month. For your information, a married 1st lt. is allowed $42 monthly to ration himself and wife and $75 monthly rental allowance, which accounts for my substantial pay check.

LOS ANGELES, MAR. 2, 1944

Four years ago I was just beginning to fall in love with you and by April it was only a question of waiting until you mentioned it. Will you ever forget our night tennis or our picnics in the spring hills and then when you kissed me? But how barren and very incomplete all that seems now—as I look back—compared to what we have built in these four years. This is what I used to dream of as a little girl of 14—a perfect, perfect marriage. And you came, like a prince, and made the dream come true!

Joan has developed a passion for grapefruit. She eats a half in no time at all and smacks her lips with pleasure! When I leave her in her room now to play alone on the floor she waves bye-bye and throws kisses without being told. She is so naturally lovely in all her reactions. I can hardly believe she is ours.

The western book came and I have it ready to move to our house in June—also the plays of Aeschylus which you want me to steal from Pop's shelf and pretend is *ours!* I forgot that I have the Harvard Classics which I was given, aged 15. We can take them to Santa Barbara—they include some useful volumes.

My diet keeps me in a state of continuous misery. No one wants the Milky Ways so I eye them maliciously all day. I will take some to the hospital and eat them as soon as I come out of the ether. I hate never being allowed to reach 200 lbs.—it may definitely stunt my soaring spirit.

Mum is having the glooms. Pop is still in N.Y. not knowing what day he sails. She is talking to him tonight. I get very cross inside when Mum behaves so. Why don't people learn self-control? She was a spoiled child and I guess that affects a whole lifetime.

I'm very like a huge benevolent cow and I feel very calm, as if nothing could disturb me. It will be good to have this baby out of me and feel myself returning to normal sensitivity again. Katherine kicks around tirelessly. I like her all the same.

I hope you still feel you can apply for a leave when she is born. I will be awfully disappointed if you sail without even a glimpse of her.

Goodbye. Every day and night are only half real to me—when you are away.

CAMP CAMPBELL, KY., MARCH 3, 1944

On the subject of women: there are many W.A.C.'s[10] here, a startling sight in their uniforms. I still think of war as a man's game. But don't worry. They aren't pin-up girls—though, to be frank, any woman looks good to our deprived eyes.

Janie, did I tell you I was named Class A Agent for B Co.? That means I draw money from the finance office and pay the men, as I did Tuesday. You can imagine the ordeal—being responsible for eight thousand dollars! However, despite great anguish, I came out only five dollars and ten cents short after everybody was paid, so my carelessness has robbed the food from the mouths of you and Joan to the sum of five dollars; because, you see, the Class A Agent must make up any shortages!

I had one lucky break. Although two of us officers counted out the money, one private got outside the orderly room and then came back with an extra $20 bill which had stuck to the one he was supposed to have. Without his honesty my pocket book really would hurt.

I am delighted about your keeping a diary of Joan. Isn't it fun and doesn't it impress upon you forever the loveliness in small detail that is, as you say, the baby changing into the child?

How I wish with all my heart I could shave tomorrow with the door open and watch you feeding Joan breakfast. I'm afraid she considers me the rather formidable figure of strange sounds

10. Women's Army Corps members were by now doing non-combat-related duty at nearly every Army post in the U.S., as well as overseas.

and actions in the early morning, silhouetted in the bathroom door. Tell me what she says.

Our new Captain K. and others are going down to Tennessee to umpire another battalion's combat-firing-test preparatory to overseas duty so I shall command B Co. next week. K. is Jewish, tall, dark, intelligent and has had his nose broken or altered so that it is almost pug. The other officers don't care for him much, partly because his manner verges on arrogance which doesn't help. Yet he is conscientious and thorough to the Nth degree. He seems to depend on me and I feel obliged to respond although I don't particularly warm to him.

LOS ANGELES, MAR. 4, 1944, SATURDAY, 7:30 P.M.

Mum and I, the two war widows, have had supper by the fire—Joan is nearly asleep—I hear her singing up there to herself. I never go to bed without thinking long and lovingly about you and wishing with all my heart I could have you by me. There is something so beautiful and peaceful in falling asleep near you and waking beside you and hearing your opening phrase: "There's the big eye!" I always like to sneak a look at you when you're still asleep and you invariably catch me at it. I adore you—every little as well as all the big things about you!

Goodnight—I must write Pop and add a few lines to Joan's diary. My soul and body and heart ache for you tonight and every night. Thank you for all you mean to me and for being my husband. You have never made me unhappy a moment.

CAMP CAMPBELL, KY., 6 MARCH 1944

Well, this was my first day as company commander, a memorable experience. I "took reveille," as we say—that is, rode up on the six o'clock truck and stood formation with the men, received the report of the first sgt. that all were present or accounted for, then went to the mess hall for a brief inspection and breakfast, then over to the orderly room to give directions and make plans for the day. First I signed the morning report—a sort of diary each company must keep and submit through channels daily. It contains full information about the men, how many present for duty, how many in the hospital, how many A.W.O.L. It tells how many officers are present, what men are on detached service at schools, or on special duty with some other company. It describes briefly any major events affecting the company, such as changes of station, long marches, engagements with the enemy, men killed in battle. The morning report is a permanent record of each unit and is eventually forwarded to Washington and filed there. Imagine the size of such a file!

Then I read the M.P.[11] report on one of our men picked up "disorderly" in a bus station in Hopkinsville with a pint of whiskey in his pocket. He had overstayed his pass—one signed by me—been brought back and turned over to the battalion duty officer and placed on K.P. by the first sgt.

Later I called him in—Hailey, Geo. T. Hailey—a good soldier, good worker when he's sober. I explained the Army's position and his, told him I must punish him "by the authority vested in me by the 104th Article of War" which empowers unit commanders to punish minor offenses within certain limits. My sentence was helping in the kitchen for a week.

After Hailey came a myriad of minor decisions. Where do the troops go *now*? Where is Area 3? Sir, what did you want to do about these reports of survey? Sir, will you sign these requisitions in your own name? Sir, would it be all right if I took this jeep down to the bank? Sir, would you give me some identification so I can collect my money at Western Union? Sir, these tables, we don't have any room for them in the kitchen, supply can't take them, we can't leave them here beside the mess hall till we go into the field again, can we? (Janie, this is it: father and children. The company commander—the oracle and confessor.) Then over to bn. hqs. where I'm acting S-2 and must maintain an office and read a few papers.

Then collecting necessary training aids and a 1-1/2 ton truck and a corporal and departing for the training area a mile away, there to set up and plan my class from 11 to 12 in the short-base theory of computing ranges, which involves the Pythagorean Formula—you remember?—from geometry: given A squared plus B squared equals C squared? And if you know two angles and a side you may solve for the unknown side of right triangles.

We worked with compasses, 18 three-inch guns with panoramic sights. (And when 18 three-inch guns come rolling up, by company, just where will you put them? In line facing west?

11. Military police.

What will be their aiming points? With half the bn. gone on furlough, how will you organize gun squads?) But first we must gather around Lt. Easton to hear what all this is about; and then we must go over in groups of 12 and pace off a hundred-yard course he has laid out to see exactly how many steps we take for 100 yds. And then we must group again around the back of the truck where he has unrolled such a big chart with lines and figures and different colored arcs, and where he stands now talking into the public address system. He is using as pointer a G.I. tent pole.

All this concerns what is called "indirect fire"—firing at something you can't see, as the artillery often does—because we may be called on to act as artillery. It involves little more than high school math. But remember many of our boys have not *been* to high school. Some cannot even *read* or *write*. We've actually conducted classes in how to read—first grade level. But now we are teaching indirect fire which is like teaching them Greek.

If the sergeants and corporals understand, that is all we really can expect—plus a few bright privates who may someday be noncoms.

And so, Janie, I reach noon, answering questions, arranging to leave one man from each company with the guns rather than haul them back to camp while we return for lunch, arranging to rush three men in to eat and quickly back to relieve the three who remained, arranging to dismantle the public address system, arranging to take it where it should go, arranging to collect and count the compasses and track down one somebody forgot to turn in. Arranging to get everyone back to camp in time for chow.

After lunch, I become S-2 for a while: "What will go in the daily battle experience bulletin?" Yes, here's an item: what a German prisoner of Jewish descent who got himself captured in Sicily thinks of us as soldiers. He says we ought to carry rifles low during night patrols. We always carry them at high port (across the breast diagonally) and the Germans recognize the silhouette. He was an antique dealer in Paris before they forced him into service.

Then I make a quick inspection of the barracks and latrines. Then to the motor park and talk with Padget, a half-track driver, who is spraying paint on all our vehicles with a paint gun and air compressor. He tells me we can use turpentine in place of paint thinner and make do. I say let's use turpentine.

Staff Sgt. Parrish, an Alabaman, dark and gaunt as an old

pine, comes and we all three talk. Parrish and I go inside the
motor shop. We watch our mechanics taking apart half-tracks for
the 6,000-mile checks. The vehicles are up on jacks and blocks,
wheels are off, engines pulled down, gears and wheels and greasy
tools and pots of grease litter the floor. Parrish explains that for
lack of a thirty-cent grease seal which is not being issued by
ordnance, he can't complete the job and put the vehicles together. He says the M-3 half-tracks are no good, with their White
engines. The M-5's *are* good with their Internationals. He says a
valve-in-head engine has more power than an L-type, though he
doesn't know why. Both have the same number of cylinders.

Back to the orderly room. Staff Officer Doherty appears. I
ask: "How's B Company's standing at battalion headquarters today?" "Great," he says, "except there was a company commanders'
meeting this morning at ten and you weren't there!" It's the first
I've heard of such a meeting. "Charge of Quarters," I call, "did
we receive word of that meeting?"

C.Q.: "No sir."

Doherty produces the buck slip. It is signed by my 1st sgt.
who denies signing it; says he never saw it. Who's lying? How
deep in hot water am I?

The mail orderly brings a letter from Mother with an absen-
tee voter's ballot to be signed and returned. I sign and return it.

The C.Q. is wearing a sweater, an unacceptable item of
uniform while on duty. I tell him to take it off.

Two drivers come with dispatch tickets for me to sign,
releasing their vehicles.

A query from the first sergeant, liar or no: "Sir, will we form
at close interval for retreat? Or normal?" How much distance
between companies? Will all personnel present arms, or just
officers? With so many men gone on leave, will we form in three
platoons, or four?

A letter arrives addressed to Lieutenant Commander, Co.
B. It is from a Miss Champagne and reads in part: "I am writing
a few lines to see if you could give me information about my
brother, Willie." Willie hasn't been heard from, she says, for five
months. I hand the letter to the first sergeant and tell him to
check on Willie.

We stand retreat. It is the ceremony for the lowering of the
flag at the end of the day which is said to date back to Roman

times. Then I return to the orderly room, pick up my green wool gloves and catch the truck back to officers' quarters.

At supper I learn of a meeting in the major's room at 6:45. It is now 6:30. I eat quickly and go to the major's room. He is in command while the col. is on leave. He tells us the results of the group commander's inspection today. Unsatisfactory. He's afraid we are letting down. "These things must be accomplished . . ."

And now at 10 P.M. the operator tells me there is a 3 to 4 hr. delay on California calls! Do I deserve such punishment?

LOS ANGELES, MAR. 6, 1944

I am in the sunny garden—just before lunch. Joan is asleep. Mum has gone up to her lot on Amalfi Drive and is planning her "shack" where Pop can work after the war on his writing—not on movies. He seems determined to give them up—which Mum and Brandt have advised for years. This little shack will occupy Mum's mind now and she is growing much calmer about Pop and getting a philosophy worked out. It's a big adjustment at first. I'll never forget those first weeks you were at Camp Roberts! I was in misery, literally, and scarcely felt alive at all. Now I know that husbands are silly conveniences and obviously it's better to see them twice a year instead of daily!

Four weeks ago tonight you came walking in with your cold—poor sweet. And I retired upstairs because I knew you and Pop would talk all night unless I dashed up and remained there as *bait*. Finally, you condescended to appear and I was glad when we were alone together. You are very attractive.

Oh, but this *is* a brilliant day! I wish you were here and we'd walk in the hills. We have actually been outdoors very little together, or indoors, for that matter! There are so many, many things we must do in the future. I can see only glorious happiness. As long as you love me—life is very simple and the work to be done will be only pleasure.

This must be a busy week for you as company commander. Good luck to you, my darling, you must know a great deal about human nature now, too. One day you will have a company to yourself and put in practice some of your ideas.

Yes, darling, I should love to be seen with you in public. I always am jealous when I think of the officers whose wives are near them and I so far away! But I know we are doing the right thing in having a companion for Joan while she is still so young. She will never remember being an only child—thank heavens.

Mum talked to Pop in New York today. He is very cheerful and doing 15 pages a day on various stories. He is enjoying himself; Mum feels quite gay too.

And I am happy too—because I am your wife and Joan's mother and am at last utilizing my time. I hope Katherine doesn't come until after April 10th so I can really accomplish some writing. It is immensely rewarding. And I adore being with Joan who is more delightful every hour and such a picture running on the grass and getting very brown.

In 4 to 5 weeks you will probably be here to see your second child—not to speak of your wife and *first* child! Won't that be amazing! Imagine having two children—it's unbelievable. And very soon I'll be 26—which is an awful age to have reached so quickly.

Goodbye and good night—I wish I could talk to you every day—or would it only make it harder not to see you?

CAMP CAMPBELL, KY., 8 MARCH '44

General Marshall,[12] Chief of Staff which means head of the Army, arrived an hour early in a spitting snow flurry and a wind that made your bones ache.

We'd just fired one order, six men, from the foxholes. Their rifle grenades had knocked down every target but one when a lieutenant drove in and said: "General Marshall is coming now!" And here he was: first two or three long green staff-car sedans, with red flags on fenders and generals' stars—gold on a red license plate—and then the old boy himself stepping out, with lieutenant and major and brigadier generals gathering around him, and all moving toward your husband who came at the double and reported with a salute.

Marshall smiled coolly and shook my hand. If he said anything I don't remember it. We walked together toward the firing line—and there were those six knocked-down targets and a bunch

---

12. George C. Marshall, later Secretary of State, author of the Marshall Plan for Europe's postwar economic recovery, and winner of the Nobel Peace Prize.

of men running around trying to tack them up! I thought: "This is it! This couldn't be worse! The Chief of Staff comes to inspect the firing of rifle grenades and what does he see? Men running around tacking up canvas in a snowstorm!" By some miracle the targets get tacked up.

At the suggestion of the major general conducting the tour we move nearer the foxholes. The major general asks: "Lieutenant, are these live grenades? Are you firing the bazooka today? What is the range to the targets?" Marshall says nothing. I steal a look at him from a distance of two feet. (Being the on-site commander I stand at his left, flanked by the major general and more brass than I can count.) He is a large, heavy man, every bit of six-two, I should say, and somewhat fleshy in the face as though he had spent too much time at a desk lately, which he undoubtedly has. His face is not refined, or very interesting beyond its strength and repose, but those are deeply imbedded. He has small eyes, light brown, and gave me the impression of a man submitting graciously to something he's experienced often before.

When the second order fired their grenades and got five perfect hits out of six at fifty yards, he smiled again. The sixth man's rifle jammed. We waited. My heart bled for the poor guy trying to clear his jam with Marshall watching. Finally he cleared it and fired. By then buck fever seized him and he was three feet over the target. "Well," exclaims the major general on my left, "if that had been a tank he'd still have hit it. Five out of six, that's pretty good, Lieutenant!"

Marshall smiles a third time and turns away, indicating the visit is over. We walk back silently side by side until we reach his car. There he turns to me with a final smile and holds out his hand. I salute and shake his hand, which was wrong—I should have shaken his hand and then saluted, and I thought of this as I did it, but it never bothered the general. He got back inside his big O.D. limousine and glided away, leaving us saluting the other cars in his retinue as they passed.

He wore pinks[13] and a short brown dress overcoat with all those sparklers on it and never uttered one word.

---

13. Light-brown trousers, part of winter semidress uniform.

I couldn't help thinking of the responsibility[14] resting under his great calmness.

LOS ANGELES, MAR. 23, 1944

Again I've had the terrifying fear that if you were badly wounded (blind, lame, sterile) you might not come back to me. It haunts me. You do know surely, that no matter what may befall—you are the only love I can ever have and nothing will change it. Tell me you understand and will never try to hide. I must know you will call for me and let me come to you—how little the physical outsides would matter!

Here are two excerpts of poems Daddy wrote recently. I thought you might get a little pleasure from them and send them back so I can keep them filed with his letters. What a great spirit he has!

Yesterday two pretty little hummingbirds did the loveliest mating dance and flight over the lawn! Joan was enchanted and I explained it to her though she had no idea what I was chattering about—except that she loves to watch "birds." She says "burrs."

Daddy leaves New York Tuesday for a port of embarkation and then sails. Thank God his wish is coming true!

I'm terribly glad you are optimistic about getting here next month. The later you make it, the better, for I shall be able to enjoy you more and we can read aloud and have music here together, and gaze at a very new baby which will look ugly to you and yet perhaps you will love its helpless little self. Joan will be talking a good deal more too, a few weeks make such incredible changes in them.

I really have no desire for this baby to come early. I love being outside in these lovely days with Joan. The thought of a hospital and bed and all the weakness of the first three weeks after birth do not appeal to me. On the other hand, the sooner here,

---

14. The Allied landings in Normandy were less than three months ahead. Marshall wanted to command them but F.D.R. decided he was too valuable in Washington to be spared, so Eisenhower got the job. But Marshall would be called the chief architect of Allied victory in the war. He was also the first to officially recognize the injustice done West Coast Japanese by relocating them in detention camps. As early as January 1943, he initiated programs to correct it—which led to formation of the all-Japanese-American 442nd Regimental Combat Team and to remunerative employment outside camps for other detainees. More than 18,000 Japanese-Americans would eventually serve in combat, suffering over 9,000 casualties.

General George C. Marshall presided over an army of 8.3 million men and women, was later secretary of state and winner of the Nobel Peace Prize. During their brief meeting what impressed Bob most was his great calm. (Wide World Photos)

the sooner over. The real point is that I am scarcely adjusted to the idea of a second baby and the thrill will be simply tremendous when I *do* look into the new little face and realize it is OUR child.

So you have been watching fencing bouts! Someday we will attempt that sport together. You are so quick you should be good at it. The Italians and French have the perfect temperaments, of course. Fencing is mixed in my mind with all my childhood and therefore a precious memory. As you know, my dear master in Florence was such a natural gentleman and somehow such a sad figure. I loved him very deeply. He was my first male love—and even if I was only nine when I first knew him, he paid me little attentions that made me almost a lady. He always opened the heavy wood door to let me out of the "sala di scherma" (fencing salon) and gave a lovely bow and such a gentle smile when we shook hands.

It's a very fast sport, sometimes impossible to follow unless you have a fencer's eye and know each movement of the foil or saber. The saber is a very heavy thing and quite formidable, but the foil is light and speedy and delicate.

When I went for my lessons as a child, I used to stand in a corner, hoping to be unnoticed, and watch the university students fencing among themselves. The master would wander round and criticize them. They were very thin, dark boys, eighteen and nineteen, incredibly quick. Their eyes shone like black stones behind those masks, and I must say they were like cats. The French are ever so much clumsier. Their style is almost heavy compared to the Italian. Why do I go on at such length about fencing? I remember my full black skirt and white jacket with high collar so well, and the way my long hair fell down the back and the noise it made on the canvas jacket, and my mask and how accustomed I became to seeing through it.

I was never very good because I was either at the timid age and had no special desire to kill anyone, or else I am just not competitive enough. The maestro used to shout: "Signorina, be more full of fire and lunge at your adversary with determination." But he said I had good *style*.

Judy comes tonight, for one week. How amazing that she is 16! At our wedding she was only 12 and a little girl!

I remember every bit of Sept. 25, 1940, our one-day honeymoon! I remember the heat and the grapes and the mist over the

Napa vineyards, and the wonderful peace of not saying goodbye to you, and how very tired and happy I was, and the lovely cool lake we suddenly discovered. And then on our way to our apartment at Rio Vista, you made me sleep in the car, and since then you have taken care of me as if I were some very fragile flower.

Goodbye. This is long and yet has said almost nothing. I think of you so constantly as the first spring days come, and my longing for you becomes the only real thing about me. Though my body is big with child I still want you to come and lie down and love me. The great miracle of that physical love is much more apparent to me now that we have made it fruitful and borne children. Because, though the children are the right and good outcome of such unions, the union itself stands for something beyond the physical and the reproductive. For even when I am quiet and full of child, there is the desire to have you love me, the desire to be made whole, and it is not the desire for another child, it is something very near to God and all beauty, it is the moment of complete oneness. You are the man and I am the woman, but in that lovely moment we cease to be individuals. Do you understand what I mean? I used to think that intercourse (I HATE that word) meant the woman wanted a child to be complete, or the man wanted a child to pass his name on to . . . but there is something even greater in that act.

I know now that I could never marry again, even if it meant lonely years ahead. I could not lie in another man's arms . . . there would be nothing in me to give to him. All I am and all I have and all I hope to be is entrusted to you forever. Can you understand? It cannot be explained, it is deeper than myself, but it is something that I can recognize.

Goodbye again. Will these adieus never end? My love for you grows, even in absence, like some wonderful fruit that does not need watering or sunshine or damp evenings. My love grows sufficient unto itself, though you should be taken from me for years and years.

CAMP BRECKINRIDGE,[15] KENTUCKY, APRIL 1, 1944, SAT. EVE
The move here was simple and tonight I'm alone in a quiet barracks typing away on "Old Colonel" who has grown to about fifty pages. The wind howls outside the window and I hear the

15. In northern Kentucky near the Ohio River.

slow step of the guard on the gravel. Pity him, poor fellow. He walks all night and works all day. He is a menial, a nobody, the private soldier. The more I see of his lot in garrison the more contemptible I find it.

For all its wisdom and achievement, I cannot condone the War Department for permitting a system that makes our men do housekeeping a third of the time, that draws them away to silly details like hauling coal, building shelves, scouring pans—men who should be out training in the field, learning to cook in their helmets, or whatever—I want the barracks burned down.

I am happier with my platoon than since I've been in the Army. Helms of North Carolina, my platoon sergeant, is a blond head of 22, short, peppery, always on the go, reminding you of a banty rooster. He's not the smartest noncom in the battalion but like so many Southerners knows how to handle men—how to command and still be respected and liked.

My gun commanders (buck sergeants: three stripes) are Desrochers of Maine, Burnell of Ohio, Golden of New York City and Thompson of Tennessee.

My security sergeant, also a buck, is Pate of Tennessee. Pate's face is from the older America—he looks like Davy Crockett—rangy, rough-hewn. He rides in a jeep and, with a corporal in another jeep, reconnoiters ahead of the platoon and acts as its security-outguard when we are in bivouac. With Pate on the job I feel safe.

I love you always and I love our babies, new and old, and wish I were with you to see this new one arrive. Our best work, Janie.

LOS ANGELES, APR. 2, 1944

I rarely have *moods*, but today I've been so mean and testy I could shoot myself. It makes me simply furious when I get this state of mind. I think it is passing as I write you. I'm a most unworthy wretch! And to top it all, poor sweet Joan lost her lunch (I may have fed her too quickly) with that lovely innocent look on her face!

I had to mop and clean and mop and she stood and stared at me and then I had to change every stitch on her and in the midst of it, with my breath and temper growing shorter every second, Renzo came to take color pictures of Joan! I was so cross inside that it must have shown outside too. Anyway, it's all over now and Joan is asleep and Judy at a movie.

I have some peace and am going to do your notes and tackle "Dr. Steele." What you say about the story is very true and I will work it out. As for poor Dr. S. himself, I wonder if he's alive or dead? He was with the Italian army in Africa and went back to Florence with a fever. The last letter I had from him said he was going to stop writing me (I told him about you and our early months of marriage) and give his full attention to trying to make something out of his family life, for he adored his two little girls, and I am sure his wife was not as bad as he thought. Also, he assured me that I must belong to you completely and that writing him was not right.

You say it was a good and beautiful experience. I wish I could think so—though in part I do believe it did *him* good. The wound I felt, and am ashamed of even now, is the ghastly deceit to his wife. He fell in love with me because I was very young and very brown and untouched. He was very lonely and believed life had passed him by—which it had. I renewed his faith—but I didn't actually build up his wife as I should have, or send him back to her fast enough. I rather enjoyed his adoration. How frail of me that was!

He wanted to kiss me one day by the pool and I said no, I don't want any man to kiss me who isn't going to be my husband. Suddenly that made him think me a goddess of some sort and he began adoring me until I was almost stifled with his admiration. How weird it all was!

And of course the whole business occurred exactly the last month we were in Florence and I was all confused about every-thing. I was wandering badly and trying to grasp something.

Two letters from John, at last! He's in England. He sounds very happy and wrote pages on the ghastly weather and lukewarm ale. He is evidently busy and happy and is hoping for a pass up to London. It is marvelous to hear from him after two months of silence.

We don't know anything about Pop. He must have sailed by now. I keep hoping a letter will come for Mum, though she is very brave and busy and I don't let her dwell on it and get maudlin. I tease her and joke.

Forgive me not sending a letter this morning. I was a little lax and very naughty. Your letters are my bread and butter and I love them all and always want more!

Judy is enjoying the Milky Ways and I have an occasional one too. With our third child I promise not to weigh more than 185! But I cannot be too miserable *now*!

Goodbye. . . . My thoughts are with you. I'm glad you and Captain K. get along. Everyone loves you—but your wife!

KENTUCKY, 6 APR. 1944

Last evening I was sitting here when K. came in. I'd hardly seen him all day. Sometimes his demands on my attention annoy me and this is often true Sundays when I'm writing and want to be alone. So I'd avoided him, perhaps noticeably. When he came in I remembered this with a small pang of guilt. I happened to be thinking of John the Baptist, so I said: "Did you ever think much about John the Baptist?"

"No," he said.

"Well," I said, "I never did either until lately, and now he seems to me a very great man, perhaps the greatest. You see, he was only a man but he baptized God. Isn't that the most remarkable experience anybody can have?"

"That depends," he replied. "You see, we Jews don't consider Jesus as God."

Then for an hour, while twilight gathered in the room, we talked. I learned he'd taken a master's degree in retailing at the University of Florida, managed one of three garment stores owned by his father in Miami, nearly died of boredom after a year and applied for active duty, having a commission in the organized reserves. So he got into the Army, and to being my commanding officer.

He loves music and has two dime-store piccolos he plays. Now he's just come bursting in to tell me to listen to music a radio downstairs is playing: "It's the 'Sorcerer's Apprentice!' " he exclaims. "That's the water! That's the water pouring in!"

He described the young apprentice who learned the sorcerer's magic word that brought water pouring from a stick. But the apprentice couldn't stop it. So he broke the stick. And then water poured from both ends. Just as the flood is filling the room and is about to overwhelm him, the sorcerer reappears . . . etc. You see what an unusual person K. is.

No letter for three days. I wonder how you are?

KENTUCKY, APRIL 11, 1944

Since Mum's telegram brought the news, I've tried to visualize Katherine. I believe she'll be a sturdy, noisy youngster given to slapping people on the back like her mother, and running the boys races and raising Cain generally. She will not be alarmingly precocious but immensely normal and rural, interested in horses, cattle, dogs, an earthy character in contrast to very feminine Joan.

Ahead I see two little girls in pigtails, going to school and asking their old dad how to work problems in arithmetic that he can't quite grasp; two young ladies at high school and the tempests in nutshells that are part of adolescence; then the flowering of the true character when we shall see what the woman will be— and finally the talks I'll have some day, as Pop and I had once, with semi-embarrassed young men—young thieves come to steal our girls and make them women, something you and I never can do no matter how much we love them.

And it always will be a love equally given to all our children, first and last.

I hope there will be many. This one born on our engagement day is different from Joan and must be celebrated in another way. She is continuing proof that our love is fertile and good. I love her and you, and hope you are resting quietly this evening with that thought, because I know the months have been long and the accomplishing of a child is hard, hard work. I very deeply admire you.

LOS ANGELES, APRIL 12, 1944, WEDNESDAY, IN THE HOSPITAL

Katherine has a wonderful face (for a wee baby)—it makes me very proud she is another *big*, 9 lbs., *strong* baby! I never dreamed I'd be so excited about a 2nd girl—but I am in a high state of elation and terribly thrilled over two children.

This birth was a song after Joan's. I only had two really big pains—then out under the heavenly anesthetic! And I don't feel all my bones are sore as after Joan!

Do you think we will ever have any boys? Just now I am so ecstatic and relieved and thankful once more to our good angel—that nothing matters. Not even the rather gruesome fact that I'm in a double room (all they could give me so far) with a gal who has her whole noisy family here all the time and it's pretty tiring. Wasn't I clever to have the baby on the 10th, our engagement day, as I sort of told you I would last Sunday?

I'm a little too hysterical about the miracle of birth to quite make sense in this letter—we must, *must* have two boys now—to follow our ladies. Think what fun Joan and Katherine will have! Mum has taught Joan to say "Katherine" already—and "sister." I miss lovely Joan. Who will Katherine look like? She gave me a deep frown once and looked like her serious Papa scowling in front of the fireplace!

I suppose all grandparents are hiding chagrin over no boy. You must have had a shock too. I was *pleased*, which quite amazed me—perhaps because I was prepared for her. She has a real *nose*. Where did it come from? *I* think she is beautiful but to everyone else I guess just a baby!

Oh, Bobbie—each baby makes me love you more. I am in a constant stream of joy. When will you, can you, come? Life is quite breathtaking. We must have some children *together*, not by telegram again, ever. Mum was wonderful, of course, and she worried, poor dear. Katherine came very fast and violently. I bled a lot and there was a little concern, evidently, and poor Mum was frantic. I'm glad you were spared the hours of wondering and waiting—it is exhausting. The relief to have two children safely here is enormous and I'm very happy and relaxed. Katherine is awfully lively and strong. Thank God we are a combination to produce fine, healthy children.

Hospital evenings are dreary affairs and I can hear young fathers walking down to see their wives and then to view their babies through the glass! They must all be 4F[16] as to draft—and though I want you here—I'd hate a 4F!

My arm is tired. It's hard to write lying flat—and there are so many things to say to you. I love you, darling. We have a little family now. How incredible!

---

16. Classified as unfit for military duty.

KENTUCKY, APR. 15, 1944

Frankly, being twice a father is a little difficult for me to grasp. It makes me the senior parent around here. But the whole thing is still on paper, so far as I'm concerned. I feel proud but in a remote way—about two thousand miles remote. Oddly enough I don't have much interest in Katherine when I know you are hospitalized because of her. Whenever these hospitalizings occur, I realize how little I care about anybody or anything except my wife, and I'm ever-such-a-little-bit jealous of the children that put her to bed painfully and leave her—if only for a short time— weak and tired.

What is the wrinkle-face saying this morning? I suppose she's hungry and not very pleased at being in this world after trying so hard to get here all these months. Kiss her for me, anyway.

Let me tell you of a great compliment. Some of my boys feel they know me well enough to borrow money from me. This often happens at the end of the month when funds are low. I had $35 out. And tonight in the P.X. a corporal who, I happen to know, has a wife in a nearby town and is probably out of money to pay bus fare, asked in a shy, embarrassed way for a couple of dollars. I tell you I was proud that he asked. You can imagine the difficulties of maintaining a family on $66 a month. Any help we can give these boys is far too little. They are good boys, the best.

LOS ANGELES, APR. 18, 1944, TUESDAY, 7 P.M., *HOME!*

Thought of you very hard this afternoon when we came home— even the ambulance was the same as 17 months ago! I missed you frightfully. I'm not much good as a single woman, darling.

Katherine has accepted the move beautifully. She eats well and sleeps soundly—not one cry since our arrival—she is very healthy and gaining weight. Her dark little head thrills me.

We had the nurse bring her to my room while I held Joan on my bed—and so they met. I shed a few tears because my heart was so full and I was witnessing the meeting of our two girls! It was a moment that needed you so badly and I cried for you— unashamedly—why pretend—just for once. I felt the tears and let them come as Joan bent over and said "baby" very clearly and put her hand out, oh, so delicately to touch her new sister!

Later Joan said "Go see Kath" to Mum and that is very advanced for 17 months—to actually be putting words together!

Pop is in N. Africa and quite well—slept on the upper berth in a three-tiered cabin on a troop ship. Will tell you about what he says after Mum reads me his letter.

I can hardly grasp it: Pop and John abroad! I have yet to face the inevitable going of *you*.

There are roses on the vine outside my window and after a high wind all day it is suddenly very still. Spring is in the air. I am glad for a spring baby.

Good night. I'd give anything to have you here tonight. What are you thinking and doing in Kentucky? Why are you always away from me?

KENTUCKY, 20 APRIL '44

De Rosa, the artist to whom I loaned your Van Gogh *Letters*, has returned it. I'd forgotten its excellence. My, what a genius, what a great, wracked soul crying out its pain in beauty! In my estimation Van Gogh was as great a writer as he was a painter!

Let me quote: "I have thought it over for four years . . . I have come to the conclusion that what was shown me formerly as duty was a *specter* of duty. They said: 'Earn money and your life will be straight.' Millet says to me: 'Make your life straight and even the earning of money will come in due course, and you will not become dishonest.' "

And again: "What I find moving is the great serenity of the great thinkers of the present. Voltaire, Diderot—they were the men who made the Revolution. It is the work of a genius to dominate time, and to make the minds that are thoughtless and passive strive in one direction and after one aim. . . . I think of the last walk of the two de Goncourts, the last days of old Turgenev, too. Sensitive, subtle, intelligent as women: sensitive to their own suffering also, yet always full of life and self-confidence—no indifferent stoicism, no contempt for life. These fellows die as women die; no fixed idea about God, no abstraction, always on the firm ground of life itself, and attached only to that."

Janie, this warm spring night is so gentle! It is like the very thought of you which is always in my heart and it is like Katherine, the small new flower born on the anniversary of the day we first pledged our love. She's dear to me and will be always, because she is you and me, our little masterpiece greater than all the masters could paint.

Don't worry about me coming home war crazy, or whatever they call it, or dead. I have a strange conviction I shall feel suddenly at home in battle, having dreaded it all my life. The irony, the absurdity of such a non-belligerent as I, such a peaceable, neighborly fellow, stalking around through the carnage! I shall be scared, horrified, sick at my stomach, or whatever, but I have a hunch I'm going all the way through with eyes and ears open and the certainty no terminations will happen to me.

Capt. K. is trying to sleep. Being a company commander is the most exhausting job in the world bar none, and he puts everything he has into it. It is the best and hardest job in the Army, everyone says. I don't agree. I think being a platoon leader is best, because there—and only there—do you work directly with the men; and the responsibility is not so great as to obscure the men and the moment, and is not so small as to let you forget it. So I'm quite happy.

LOS ANGELES, APRIL 24, 1944

Yes, I believe Van Gogh a greater writer than painter. Read him carefully and slowly—he's crammed with marvelous things. And some of his passages on love, God, work—all the major forces in life—are utterly stirring and deeply beautiful and amazingly wise. I never open the book without finding new and fine passages. And his descriptions of flowering fruit trees are heavenly. He makes you *feel* the spring of life—he who was so tortured and ugly—yet he saw past misery into beauty. I love that book.

No, darling, I don't worry about your becoming war crazy after battle. Nor do I worry about your state of mind after or during the horrors of war. I feel, with complete faith, that you are *well* within you—the ability to keep your eyes and ears open and retain what is good from the war, and cast off what is bad— you have it. So I am actually at peace about you. What would drive *me* crazy would be to have anyone other than *me* nurse you if you should be wounded. Does that sound stupid? It is not that I think you will fall in love with anyone (somehow, one outgrows such silly fears, when love as we have it is ours) but I cannot bear to be away when you are even mildly uncomfortable. And I have the conviction I could heal you more quickly. I want to be near you to help you through the bad days as well as good. "For better, for worse . . ."

There is a Negro infantry unit here, more blacks than I've ever seen at once. There were none in Santa Maria when I was growing up. The first I saw were Pullman porters and dining car waiters on the train going to San Francisco. In my childish innocence I thought black people inhabited only passenger trains. Now I learn they've soldiered in all our wars since the Revolution.

Today I heard our local unit being discussed derogatively in officers' mess. "You can't make soldiers out of jigaboos. Modern war's too complicated. Look what a man has to learn—pistol, rifle, carbine, light and heavy machine guns, Tommy guns, bazooka, mortars, 37-millimeter, 75, and 3-inch gun—not to mention mines, hand grenades, radios and the tactics of armor, infantry and field artillery. It's too much for a college graduate, let alone a jig!"

This afternoon I met a detachment of black infantry marching up the road toward me, in perfect step as usual. They were under command of one of their own sergeants, ranging alongside, and he was having them count slow cadence as they marched: "One . . . Two . . . Three . . ." as the feet came down in unison, "Four!" Then he put the proposition to them, also in cadence: "We're *in* the *Ar*-my *now!*" and they answered in chorus: "You're *right*, you're *right!*" And finally he put the big one: "We'll *fight* for *li*-ber-*ty!*" And they answered with one voice, as their right feet hit the ground: "You're *right!* You're *right!*" It was one of the most moving things I've ever witnessed.

Several German prisoners of war work at our quartermaster repair shops sewing old canvas. They stare at you as you walk by, then speak among themselves in a guttural jabber. You realize you're included in their hatred—you are their enemy. I've never been face to face with a mortal enemy before. It's a strange feeling. It strips both parties of their humanity in an ugly way. I did come across one tall blond fellow who spoke some English and was quite nice. Like the others he wore old blue fatigues stamped with a red "P.W." all over them.[17] He told of being on the Russian

17. By the war's end, around 400,000 German prisoners were held in the U.S.

front, then in North Africa with Rommel, which is where we captured him. He said the Russian winter was terrible, told with gestures how the German boys' hands and ears and faces froze— said they had no woolen shirts like mine, which he touched to show me, and that 20 German tanks in North Africa whipped 200 British tanks. He likes it here, says he gets plenty of sleep and the food is very good. All he wants is the end of the war and a chance to go home and see his wife and boy. He's been in the army six years, all of them no good, he says.

These privates are not hard to handle and often come around to something like our way of thinking. Not so the noncoms. They have to be segregated; likewise the officers. There is almost no changing them. The poison has gone too deep. As one colonel commanding a prison camp says: "The sons of bitches would kill you in a minute."

Every-so-often the officers and noncoms get the privates whipped up to singing songs of defiance. They know the Geneva Convention[18] by heart, know exactly what their rights and privileges are. If our commandant oversteps in the slightest, a committee of prisoners calls upon him and protests. For disciplinary action almost the only weapon he has is withholding a specified number of meals, which is said to be an effective remedy.

Better try a little Schubert now it is spring. Play the great C Major Symphony for Joan. How all of us are starving for some song, some great song to move us all with joy as this beastly war is moving us for destruction—something understandable to the privates like the poor German in the repair shop!

LOS ANGELES, APRIL 29, 1944

Dear sweet Mum gets so upset by little things, such as the letter from Pop yesterday. He is on the Italian front having a fascinating time, he says, but barely mentioned he loved her and missed her and didn't make enough fuss over her so she was depressed and full of self-pity and suspicion that he had picked up some great love while she slaves away with numerous household details and dozens of grandchildren.

Women are odd creatures. One of the first rules all men should understand is that wives never take it for granted they are

18. The international agreement establishing rules for treatment of prisoners of war.

loved or adored; they insist on being told over and over. I am no better than the rest, I should expect the same from you, only you always tell me what I want to hear. If you didn't I should mope as Mum did yesterday.

Of course, she's sure Pop will be killed any day. She is pathetic. I scarcely know what to say, and I do not even feel that I can say: "I know what you are suffering." I do not think anyone can understand fully until one's own husband is in it too.

I have that ahead of me. But dear Mum is a mixture of going to pieces and being very brave. I have tried to make her laugh as much as possible and not let her become morbid, or be alone too much. She will go off this afternoon to "the farm," as she calls the vacant lot on Amalfi Drive, and the sunshine there helps as much as any words a human being can say.

I keep my thoughts on Pop a good deal too. But he is not my husband, and the difference is something incredible. No two human beings can ever be as close as man and wife, not a mother and child even. I fully see that now. I hope I shall be able to take the days serenely when you are in combat. Mum dreams of Pop at night and imagines he's calling for her. Oh God, how terrible is this war! Anyway, no matter what happens, if anything should, Pop will be happy and he will go as he wanted to. How much better than a heart attack after a drinking bout! Mum realizes all this too.

The last few days I have been thinking about you and me in a shack in Texas, with only people like the Stileses as neighbors. I wonder whether we do not come nearer the eternal truths and beauties in such a life? I suppose it may be false to want to cast aside the stratum of society to which we have been born. But I often feel it is right for us. I have been particularly aware of it since the birth of Katherine. I should like to try it. We are already tied down to children, family, possessions. I always swore I didn't want possessions. Now I have them! But are they the stuff of our best dreams?

I hope we can abandon our babies temporarily and live really simply for a few months, either in Texas or in some other state that is open and appeals to us. I would even cook for you over a woodstove in the hot summer. I daresay running water and a soft bed would seem very pleasant after a while, but I'd like to try and live that way with neighbors like the Stileses, and have time to think and write and live, and lie on our backs and look at the sky at night and in the day! We never DO any of those simple things. We never look up enough. We may see trees in passing but we don't lie under one and really study all the beauty there is in it. Why do we waste such lovely, clear, eternal things? I am very guilty. I do want to drink more deeply and fully of life. Please take me with you.

Oh—how I hope you can see Katherine before you sail. To think that we have a child you haven't seen—is a *little* distressful! But I try to think only of the fact that I'm soon to be on my way to you—if we possibly can arrange it—and nothing else really matters!

KENTUCKY, MAY 16, 1944, TUESDAY

I was in the orderly room when your telegram came. Connell said this morning he heard Winchell[19] say something Sunday night about Pop being wounded. So when I saw the telegram I guessed the truth.[20] We don't get the metropolitan dailies but I understand they've been carrying the news. Naturally I called right away, inadequate as such calls are, but I wanted to hear your voice and you to hear mine.

You've been in my thoughts all day. The shock wears off me when I work. I only wish it were the same with you and Mum. Make it so if you can.

There is nothing, my heart tells me, that would please him more than to have us all busy and productive. As the good news comes from Italy somehow I take it as *his* victory, and in a very real way it is and will be all our lives.

I cannot in the deepest sense feel badly. He died for a great cause, a cause he believed in. He said Hitlerism could not exist in the same world with our ideas. God, but my heart breaks with the loss, though. He had so much to give, always to give, and the world is so hungry.

---

19. Walter Winchell, popular columnist and radio commentator.

20. While accompanying a platoon of the 88th Infantry Division in their attack on the German strongpoint of Santa Maria Infante, in mountainous country north of Naples on the night of May 11–12, Jane's father was struck in the chest by a mortar shell fragment. When the platoon sergeant bent over him, Faust said: "I'm all right. Take care of them," pointing to wounded men lying near. The sergeant thought he wasn't badly hurt. When the stretcher-bearers found him he was dead.

Now I know death is not final. I cannot believe Pop isn't very
close to us all. We must try and live by and with the ideals he
stood for. It is a large task but we can stretch ourselves for his
sake.

I am so thankful for so much: that he knew and loved my
husband, that he saw his John become a fine man, that Judy came
through the hard period with flying colors, that he held and
adored his first grandchild. I am thankful that he died in the land
which meant most to him, that it was a quick, clean death,
surrounded by the lovely Italian hills and with the young men
near him he admired. I can fairly see him as he must have been.
I am thankful it was May which is always a lovely month, and
the month of his wedding and birth. He had lived a rich, full life,
Bob, and he was happy during a great deal of it. Now that there
are only the good and beautiful things left of him, there is a kind
of peace for us to grasp and understand and through which we
may see him even more clearly.

This house is a mad rush. The telephone hasn't stopped
ringing since Daddy's death was announced yesterday morning.
It seems weeks ago, heavy weeks laden with a million things and
a million words and thoughts intertwined. Telegrams and flowers
keep pouring in. People come and go all day, and there are little
children to look after and keep on schedule. I go about doing all
I can yet it seems so very little. I am not tired. I am very lonely
in my deepest heart. There is only you now, darling. I felt that
you and Pop stood for the same things and how rich I was to have
you both. Now there is only you. The blow is lessened because
you are strong and wise and you love and believe in the things
he did. I cannot tell you how much this means to me. Thank
God for giving you to us, to me especially.

Mother is wonderful and brave and terribly sad. There is
little or nothing to say to her. She sees clearly that he died in the
best way and that there are so many blessings to be thankful for.
She talks of him constantly, she looks very beautiful, she is very
weak in her body and very strong in her spirit. The first days will
be totally unreal. Gradually she will feel worse, I think, before
she can feel better. She says I must stay here with the children
as long as you are away. It is the only thing to do. I do not know
how I feel about it, I am too tired tonight to think much. But

she wants me and clings to me, so I must just do what I can, small as it is.

There is no real comfort for her because a husband and wife are so close, the closest of all, and hers is taken away. There must forever be great voids in her. I'm glad the children are so fresh and lovely and such a joy to her and to us all. The terrible part is the little things: I cannot look at Katherine's tiny helplessness and realize that my dear, dear father never saw her. I don't even know whether he knew of her birth. When I see Joan and think of all the years that he would have adored her, it breaks my heart! He had so many happy days to come. But is it ever time for death? Who can say: "Yes, now I've had all I want from life!" He wanted so badly to live on a ranch near us and have hours in which to talk to you.

People from all over the country have volunteered to help in any way they can. Their kindness and love is incredible. Renzo, who feels he has lost his father and best friend, has done the marketing and fetched Mum's sedatives, and watered the garden. Aidan has come each evening after work and has written us such beautiful letters. Pinkey has been up too. Everyone is utterly broken and incredibly sad and the loss hits us all. We are drawn together now. Sorrow is a purifier. I have had so little of it in my life that I'm trying to rise and feel the inner beauty of it. I keep seeing Daddy in such living moments: standing before the fireplace reading Shakespeare aloud to us . . . in his chair in the big room with a beer in hand . . . bending over the flowers in the garden he planted . . . all such recollections are very alive and precious. I would give anything in the world to be with you but I am here where Mum needs me. Will you get a leave? I cannot face the fact that you may go over without my having a glimpse of you. And how terribly short a leave is! But I can't come to you now, not for months, and then I'm afraid you will be gone.

Judy comes tomorrow morning for a few days. We may have a memorial service in a little church Daddy liked, in Westwood. Everything seems vague and hard to plan. An hour seems a year. I have not said half of what I wanted to—but I must get to bed. I am strong, darling, but terribly tired now from a million little things. I have to take a sleeping pill these nights as I cannot quite let go enough to sleep.

KENTUCKY, MAY 20, 1944

Your letter nearly broke my heart but filled me right up again with pride and joy, that you are such a woman. I know Pop would be proud of you. He loved you, as you know, more than anything else on earth. These last days he has been closer to me than ever before. "How anyone so great could die?" is the question I keep asking myself. And the answer comes: "He did not die. Great things don't die unless we let them."

One point in your letter, Janie, I cannot agree with is the making of decisions now about the future. You see, we are all grief-stricken; we have lost something very precious, and when one has done that one instantly strives to repossess what remains, to go back in memories, to cherish a house, a book, a certain bed of flowers, because it was beloved by the person who is gone. This is not right, however natural. Therefore let's not be too hasty in deciding that you and the babies will stay with Mum at 317 Burlingame Avenue indefinitely. Just now it seems right. I doubt this will be true later. Because Pop once lived there, because we knew him there, would he want us to go on living backward, so to speak, cherishing memories for years and years, making a memorial of a mere place, rather than go out as he was forever showing us how to do, and *live*? What is Mum to do for thirty years, or more? Live on and help raise a second family in that house? I think she will not, in the end, want to.

I'm not suggesting you depart tomorrow for Santa Barbara but I strongly suggest that sometime you do. You will know when it is best. I should not even mention it now. I should give Mum every care and consideration, until the tide of this backward-cherishing has ebbed, as it will—and as we must make it ebb.

I wish I were there to help you carry the load. Regardless of any other desires the well-being of Mum does come first; but I want it to be a true well-being. To be that, plans for it must be laid now, with a long range in view.

All my love again.

LOS ANGELES, MAY 21, 1944, SUNDAY EVENING

I weep for Judy in my heart. Her loss is very great because she is sixteen and these are hard years and she depended so on Pop (as we all did as children) to guide her. She is wonderfully brave and has wept so little and has not thought of herself at all. I am sending you her two letters to Mum which she wrote from school because they are absolutely beautiful and they will show you what a person she is, how mature.

Mother is very weepy and yet very wonderful and I do admire her. I don't think any of us realize Daddy is dead. That is the point, it's still numbing. I am in a daze and we are all very tired. We've had days and days of people and telephones and a million things to plan and decide. I've been harassed because Joan caught a cold and decided that I was the only person she wanted around her! It is very difficult to cope with a sick child. However, she's better tonight and the nurse is back to look after Katherine, so we should get a little rest now.

When I see you I'll tell you about the memorial service. Many thoughts occurred to me while we sat there. I scarcely could look at Mum. Her face was beautiful with grief, and so moving and young. I hope we children and the grandchildren can make her feel that life still holds many happy moments. I try to imagine what it would be like for me with you gone. I've lived with that possibility in mind ever since we were married (for we knew then that war was coming to us eventually and I always knew you'd go). I have thought about it from every angle. Daddy's death makes me sure that death is not final. He seems so near to us and I know that I should feel even nearer you.

We will have to cut down here a lot and I must give Mum a hundred a month when we live on here (we, is me and the babes). Oh, I must see you to talk it all over with. I shall start getting a ticket tomorrow for June 22nd. I hope to heavens you will still be there then! Judy thinks I should go to you by all means. She says "husbands always come first." I know she's right. But because that is what I *want* to do I have a feeling I may be shirking here. Your parents are also eager that I go.

Goodnight. I am tired. Sweet Judy is in her bed beside me. She is absolutely tremendous. I think she is of Daddy's calibre. I love her very much and I want to make this summer a gay and happy time for her. I have *you*, darling, but she has no husband. I wonder if I could ever have stood losing Pop at her age. I shudder to think what she is going through so bravely.

Bless you, my love. We go the road alone now. What a loss Daddy is, but I think he is happy.

KENTUCKY, MAY 21, 1944

This letter is chiefly to tell you to be prepared not to hear from me for a while. Everything is all right and you might pass this word along to Mother and Father.

Your letters—all mail, in fact—will reach me, so keep writing.

I love you and my heart is strong because of that love.

317 BURLINGAME AVE., LOS ANGELES, MAY 28, 1944, SUNDAY

Yesterday morning the postman said: "I have bad news for you, your husband has gone overseas," and presented me with the famous little card the War Department has so thoughtfully provided for these occasions.[21]

You must be on the ocean now. This is the beginning of another phase of our life together. I say *together* because I do believe that even with thousands of miles between us we ARE together. We have said this before and I only say it again because it comforts me immeasurably! I hope it does you. I can picture you on the ship—attempting to get a little privacy, probably all of you very squeezed for room—and your notebook used whenever possible. This is the big adventure you've looked forward to so long.

It is a little staggering to have you actually gone. I knew it was coming soon, but I did not think quite so soon, because one is never actually prepared for such things. Considering it was only ten days ago we heard Daddy had been killed, I was a little shattered for a few hours. But I try to remember that you are really with me every moment and we have already talked of this separation and how we will carry on until we are together again. How many years will it be? How old will I look to your eyes?

Overseas-bound units often spend days, even weeks, at ports of embarkation. As my troop train moves eastward from Kentucky, I send Jane a telegram suggesting she come to New York on the chance we can see each other before I sail. But after only two

21. The card brought word that Bob's address would henceforth be A.P.O. (for Army Post Office) 403, c/o Postmaster, New York, N.Y.

nights at Camp Kilmer, New Jersey—all communication with
the outer world cut off—the 825th continues by train and ferry
to New York City and begins boarding the *Queen Elizabeth*. She
lies berthed in the Hudson River beside her smaller sister ship
the *Queen Mary*, their prows pointing toward the skyscrapers a
few blocks away. Years later the *Elizabeth* will burn and capsize
in Hong Kong Harbor and go to the scrap heap to be supplanted
by the *Q.E. II*, but now she's queen of the seas, largest and fastest
thing afloat.

Her gray camouflage paint advertises her new line of work.
She's designed to carry 2,000 luxury passengers. Instead she'll
carry 13,000 G.I.'s, few of whom could afford to sail on her in
peacetime. She's already carried thousands of troops overseas—
15,000 in one run to Australia, it's said. "See the world free of
charge with Uncle Sam!" Millions of us did.

As I walk up her gangplank, wondering where I'm headed,
I'm tempted to scribble a note giving my whereabouts, put it in
a bottle and toss it overboard in hopes someone will find it and
take it to Jane—who at this moment is boarding a train in
Los Angeles. She sleeps little that night. Thoughts of father so
recently dead, brother somewhere overseas in what danger she
can only imagine, husband about to embark, new daughter less
than two months old, heighten her awareness of the interrelat-
edness of life and death.

I fondly imagine the *Queen Elizabeth* will slip away in the
middle of the night so spies will not see and alert waiting U-
boats. As well try to conceal the departure of the Empire State
Building! At high noon on Memorial Day, right in front of
everybody, she backs into the Hudson, halting all other traffic.
Then, accompanied by a flotilla of tugs and small but armed escort
vessels, she proceeds down the harbor as if on parade.

Passing the Statue of Liberty is a throat tightening experience—followed by the harsh reality of the steel-mesh anti-submarine nets at the harbor entrance, open wide to let the *Queen* and
her cargo through into an unknown future.

As she picks up speed, one by one our little escort vessels
drop away. Traveling at nearly 35 miles an hour she'll go wherever
she's going unescorted, because no other ship can keep up with
her.

Suddenly she begins listing to port. We exchange startled
glances. Something wrong already? The list increases till it be-

The luxury liner *Queen Elizabeth*, largest and fastest thing afloat, carried tens of thousands of us overseas and back. Here she is, decks crowded, outward bound from New York in 1944. (National Archives)

comes difficult to stand upright and mess kits and cups, knives and forks slide from tables in the once-exclusive dining room, now starkly utilitarian, where supper of corned beef hash is being served to hundreds of G.I.'s in shift after shift. There is no explanation. Rumors fly.

Never slacking speed the *Queen* gradually rights herself—much to everyone's relief—and then begins listing as sharply to starboard. What now?

It's merely her standard evasive tactic. A torpedo can't be launched at her—a bomb can't be dropped on her—with much chance of success while she's swerving from side to side at such speed. She'll proceed in this manner all the way across the ocean, and we'll learn to live in a kind of perpetual tilt.

Waking next morning in balmy air in what seem southern waters, we think she's bound for North Africa or Australia. I go on deck in shirt-sleeves and watch target practice by anti-aircraft and anti-submarine gun crews at floating targets (crates or boxes) or at released balloons. Her captain and ship's crew are British but these gun crews are American. Later there's an emergency drill and all 13,000 of us come surging up wearing life preservers, amid loudspeaker warnings not to congregate on one side of the ship or the other but to stand only in assigned zones for fear of unbalancing her as she surges ahead on her zigzag course. Two million pounds more or less, on this side or that, might make a difference.

Now a four-engine B-17 ("Flying Fortress") bomber appears reassuringly overhead. It can warn of submarines and even bomb them. But the *Queen* tearing along at top speed, literally making the ocean froth, is her own best protection.

Once or twice during the war U-boats had her in their periscopes, we learned later, but never had anything like a good shot at her. We felt keenly at the time what a prize target she must be, how dearly the Nazis would like to send her and us to the bottom.

When not executing emergency drills or sleeping or eating or lolling in canvas bunks tiered five high, just space enough between to roll in and out, the G.I.'s spend their time shooting dice, playing cards, cussing the Army and the war, watching movies, speculating on what lies ahead or carving their initials into the *Queen*'s elegant mahogany rails. "Kilroy was here!"—the imprint of the anonymous but ubiquitous G.I.—appears there frequently.

The 825th's 800 men serve as ship's police force. As officer of the day I have full freedom to patrol her interior, from the officers' quarters up forward in what used to be luxury first-class cabins, to the hellhole down at her stern over the twin propeller shafts a few inches of steel away from her churning screws, where the air is almost unbreathably hot and the noise and vibration almost unbearable—and where a small contingent of Negro troops are quartered "down here at the asshole of the ship, Lieutenant," as their sergeant expresses it bitterly. I try to obtain relief for them but get nowhere.

Protecting the virtue of a contingent of nurses, some of them not too reluctant, from the depredations of thousands of sex-starved males proves almost equally futile. One creative lover boy devises a technique of stalling an elevator between decks so that events may take their course despite all efforts to the contrary.

The air grows colder, the sea grayer. Clearly we're northward bound. The move southward was merely a feint. The Flying Fortress no longer appears overhead daily. We're too far from land. Finally one morning I look off to the right and see a clump of rocks with foam splashing up them. They're the northern tip of Ireland.

Later that day, June 6, D-Day, the day of the Allied landings in Normandy, the *Queen* comes to anchor in the Firth of Clyde on Scotland's west coast. Knowing none of this, Jane has arrived in New York.

"They're over-fed, over-paid
over-sexed—and they're
over here!"
BRITISH COMPLAINT

Overseas

THE PLAZA, FIFTH AVENUE AT 59TH STREET, NEW YORK,
JUNE 3, '44

Every uniformed man in lobby or dining room makes me look
up and hope to see your face searching for mine! I cannot help
hoping. I have such a spooky feeling not knowing where you
are and still writing you! On the train I reached a number of
important decisions. Daddy's death has made me see a whole
new world—which I could only describe to you while lying
peacefully in your arms. The trip—yes it was fast and smooth.
In Chicago such a nice brakeman took me under his wing—
for no reason I could see. I was trying to look very mature and
practical but he carted my bags for me and put me on my train
and I never had a worry the entire trip. Last night in the
dining car I shared a table with a general. He was a silly but
I teased him about asking for more jelly and we had a laugh.
When I arose he said, "I wish you luck in your race with the
Army."

Dixie[1] met me at Grand Central this morning and got me a
lovely room here—twin beds so there is one for you. Without
pull like his it's impossible to get a room in this city on weekends.
I shall move to the Myers' apartment if you don't come by Monday
for this is awfully expensive.

Meanwhile Dixie dances attendance in style—gardenia to
wear and flowers in my room and constant phone calls. He is
longing to meet you. Tomorrow I'll stay close to the hotel in
case there's a message from you. Even a talk on the telephone
would be divine bliss! Why-oh-why is it so hard to live together
in lawful wedlock? This war makes everything impossible. I did
not marry you to spend my life—all my youth—on pen and
paper with you.

---

1. Her godfather, Dr. George Winthrop Fish.

SOMEWHERE[2] IN ENGLAND, JUNE 8, 1944
Well, I'm here, out in the sun with Connell beside me writing his Gayle. We are quartered in Niessen huts (counterpart of our Quonsets[3]) on the grounds of a suburban estate which is leased to U.S. military authorities. Its neo-classical 19th-century mansion serves as battalion headquarters. The men will remain here while officers go to private homes in the nearby town, also at Uncle Sam's expense. When I see you I'll tell you about our crossing and much more.

I'm going to walk around, now, and absorb this green English countryside, blue sky, fresh air. You will be following the Normandy invasion as closely as we. I wish we were part of it. How gallantly our side is doing, both there and in Italy! It does promise well, Janie. I wonder if you are in New York? I wonder when your first letter will reach me? I'm in no danger, so don't worry! Goodness, the thought of missing you is painful. But the thought of you gallivanting (in a mild way) around New York with friends is pleasant. Just watch your step, though! Love you and will let this go.

317 BURLINGAME AVE., LOS ANGELES, JUNE 22, 1944
After being home two days I feel my trip was a good idea—I needed a change and contact with other people. Things are peaceful here and I expect we shall have a constructive summer, though we must cut down a lot and watch expenses. The idea that we once had two full-time servants seems so remote as to be preposterous. Even if we could afford them now we couldn't get them. Like Morris and Ella Mae they're all at war plants making high wages. People say it's the end of the servant class in this country but I'm not complaining. Truly we get along beautifully.

Mum shops. I cook and look after the children. Judy washes dishes and does odd jobs and helps watch Joan in the garden. The healing power in a little child is so great and so pure. There are moments when the wound of Pop's death can only be helped by

2. At Macclesfield in Cheshire, central England. Security restrictions forbade saying precisely where you were or giving any other information that might be useful to the enemy. Officers were placed under orders to self-censor their letters and to censor those of their enlisted men.
3. Semicylindrical metal shelters having end walls.

the babies. Joan is utterly joyful and tender and lovely. As a matter of fact, I'm absolutely stirred by her nature—she is so *positively* happy. Katherine is nearly 2-1/2 months old and weighs 12 lbs. and looks rather like Pop and you combined. She's going to be taller and bigger than her sister and just as happy. She sleeps in the garden much of the day—and when awake lies on her back and plays happily, beginning to coo and notice trees above her. Her hair is light brown and her eyes enormous. I am pretty gloomy at times because you have not seen Katherine but perhaps she will be a lovely surprise to you when you get back.

Joan listens attentively when I recite "Hark! hark! the lark at heaven's gate sings," which was one of Pop's favorite Shakespeare lyrics. She is old enough to enjoy these things.

Your parents were here yesterday—they are so sweet and helpful and we discussed your whereabouts, etc. I'm quite sure we shall be in Santa Barbara by September—Mum with us there off and on. She will not want to live with any of her children indefinitely, so she must just come for visits. She's really amazing and very strong. Yet the coming of evening is always hard for her—as it is for all women without their husbands. I get a pang then too—for I can never fully live until you are back with me. But I would not have you with us *now*—you are where you must be and I am glad of it.

In N.Y. I found to my astonishment that people wanted to see me because they felt I had discovered a path in life. I told them it was *you* who made me—and they said *no* we must have found it together, which I hope is true. I look to the years ahead and see all the joy the earth holds before us.

SOMEWHERE IN ENGLAND [MACCLESFIELD], 11 JUNE 1944
I'm becoming friends with the family with whom I am billeted. They have a son in Burma, a daughter and son-in-law in N. Africa. I cannot say I was ever more hospitably treated. This Sunday morning, for instance, began with an honest-to-God *fresh egg* produced in the "hen run" in their back yard (to augment the national weekly ration of one egg per person). Then we strolled about the garden and vegetable plot and, despite the thin rain which is called "morning pride" for some unexplained reason, we rolled the grass tennis court preparatory to bowls or tennis later—

my host, Oswald, lean, graying, "frightfully"—as the English say—energetic, assuring me the weather would clear.

Sure enough about five it did and we started a game of bowls. First you roll a small wooden ball called a "jack" down the level grass for about fifteen yards. It serves as target. Then each player in turn rolls other balls (called "woods") toward the jack and you can curve your "wood" by means of a "bias" or weight with which each is loaded off-center; and you must be careful not to be "too merry" because the balls roll farther than you think on a smooth green. Later we played tennis on the same grass. The English are a vigorous race. I believe they became so energetic trying to keep warm. Since our arrival there has been hardly an hour of sunshine, yet little rain falls. The sky simply stays gray and lets down the "morning pride."

It makes for lovely flowers—rhododendrons a mass of brightest scarlet—and pansies, lupines, and others we know. There are also the noble English oaks and copper beeches, which latter are trimmed and branches laid away under the living-room carpet where they press out flat and keep till Christmas, then used for decoration.

You scarcely can imagine the disciplined way these people live, how they "queue up" at markets, walk or bicycle everywhere (even middle-aged women), do not complain and have plenty of time and food to give Americans. They even insist on doing our laundry. And they've discovered little tricks of thriftiness, such as sharpening a razor blade by rubbing it on the inside of a moist water glass. My host has used one blade for fifteen months and it's still sharp. The tennis balls we played with, purchased five years ago before the war began, are carefully washed, combed and dried after use. With this economy and care goes a lavishness of friendship and thoughtfulness. War has done this—people frankly admit they are better, more united, more involved with their community and each other, because of the war.

Take, for example, my host. To release young men for military service, he bicycles down to the police station and does three hours duty like any bobby—and this though he's past 50 and one of the most prominent and best-to-do citizens of the community.

He says he likes police work because it keeps him in touch with people he would not ordinarily see within the limits of his very responsible position.[4] He explains this as I walk beside him and his bicycle ("push-bike"); and when we finally reach the corner by the "robot" (stop-light) we are still chatting. He would have been late for his duty, so full of interest are these British in whatever they say or do, had not another middle-aged cyclist wheeled by, causing Oswald to exclaim: "There goes one of my colleagues!" and pedal off after him.

And all this is done in that casual fashion, with that understatement, which makes the British great. They say: "You chaps are putting on a good show, there in Normandy!"

LOS ANGELES, JUNE 26, 1944

Three letters from you today! Two air mail and one V-mail.[5] I think air mail is faster. I had one written June 7 and one June 13—so they arrive in batches.

I've always marveled at the goodness of life but I never cease to thank God for the stars that made us meet and belong to each other. I cannot take any such beautiful thing for granted. Your letters and the knowledge that you love me is all I ever want. And eventually to have YOU yourself. Sometimes I have a definite feeling that we will not be allowed to live together—something will happen to you or to me because we are so united and so happy in our love, perhaps it must not be allowed to any mortals to have so much. At other moments I feel sure that you will be brought back to me safely because we ARE so happy and a life together would be so beautiful and rich.

Are you still with the English family? You leave me in the dark about so many things. Has it stopped raining? I think it's disgraceful for you to have hot water bottles in your bed! I can see you will be quite impossible by the time you get back to me.

At the Plaza I saw Charles Evans Hughes[6] getting into the elevator. What a noble and yet human face! With his flowing white mustache he looked like God. I was deeply impressed. Also in N.Y., Dixie insisted I go to the blessed medical center with

4. Macclesfield was a silk manufacturing center, and H. O. Hambleton, a former manufacturer, was Controller of Silk (parachutes, etc.) for the British war effort.
5. A system whereby a microfilm of a letter was forwarded for printing in reduced size on photographic paper before delivery. The "V" stood for "victory."
6. Chief Justice of the U.S. Supreme Court.

him and wait there for three hours while he carved people up. He just wanted my company. Then he quite shocked me by keeping me up until 2:30 in the big Oak Room at the Plaza and telling me he thought I was the only perfect woman he'd ever known. Such things make one squirm—especially from a man of 48. I tried to change the subject and told him to beware of the 50s and growing foolish. He and everyone else asked me whether I was happily married. What a comment on the present state of matrimony! No one could believe their ears when I told how much I love you and how happy we are!

Joan is running around the bedroom now while I type. She talks to herself and comes to me once in a while to tell me what she's doing and smiles at me with such pure love that I tremble and wish you could see her. I think she may be mathematical because she loves order and puts me to shame with admonitions such as: "Hang up sweater, Mum-Mum!" I am terribly impressed.

It's not easy to finish a letter when there are two very young Eastons to look after. However, I would not miss their care and their smiles. When I fix Katherine all freshly, it gives me a little of the same thrill and abiding peace that laying out your clean clothes gave me after your bath.

I cannot tell you how wonderful your parents have been and how very sweet and gentle and understanding. They want to help me with money but I've told them I will let them know when I need help. So far we are on our own feet and I have not even touched the savings account.

Do not worry about me. I am what you asked me to be: steadfast and true. I mean true to you. By that I do not mean merely not going out with strange men or carrying on illicit affairs, but I mean true to your way of life and mine. I try to see what you see in the world because I think your vision is clearer and wiser. I have so much to learn from you. Try as I will, I see mostly the good and lovely things and I have a deplorable way of shrinking from the ugly and sad. You see it all and you give so much of yourself.

I never go to bed without missing you or awaken in the morning without thoughts of you.

ENGLAND [MACCLESFIELD], JUNE 27, 1944

We took advantage of fair weather last evening and left—my host, hostess and another officer—at 5:30, after tea, and bicycled thirty-five miles[7] calling at two homes and stopping for dinner at a fine inn, arriving back here at midnight. "We couldn't have done this five years ago," says my hostess. (Helena is 48, Oswald 56.) But since petrol has disappeared from private use due to the war, the British have returned to using their legs and have grown young again. Such a spin as we took is not very unusual. With double-daylight-saving-time at this latitude it was light all the way.

I've talked with many kinds of people about many subjects. Today it was a young idealistic Scottish-born doctor who lives here and belongs to the new Commonwealth Party headed by Sir Roger Acland. They are Socialists. Acland is said to have given his considerable fortune to the needy. They advocate public ownership of the means of production, which is to say land and factories, and would limit an individual's income to what he or she earns, plus a small capital that may accumulate. You may also own your house, lot, personal belongings and any small family business or shop you operate yourself or with a small number of helpers. They would standardize education, medicine, and other services and make them equally available to all—as we've done with our police and fire services.[8]

This group represents the "Left." The "Right" will doubtless be those favoring a return to the old order. Another group of which my host is a member believes the way lies somewhere between—that is, in retaining in peacetime the international machinery set up among the United Nations during the war. Thus we now have an excellent central economic control which is allocating production and distribution. Why could not this control be maintained after the war—to see more goods more sensibly produced and used worldwide, directing the process by statistics and fairness towards the needs of all, as we are doing now against the common enemy?

Oswald happens to be controller of a major commodity for the United Kingdom and therefore speaks with authority. Subject to audit by disinterested firms and to investigation by (and cooperation from) a parliamentary committee, his office governs the import, processing and distribution of this commod-

---

7. From Macclesfield to Chester and return.
8. After the war the British adopted some of the policies advocated by Acland and others, though he was the Commonwealth Party's only member in Parliament.

ity for the entire nation and is part of a system that seems, on the whole, to work eminently well. In fact we borrowed it from the British. "Now," he says, "when the war is over, let's continue the system!"

I thought of you at the Plaza waiting alone in your room for me to call, finally turning your back on that rather heartless stretch of water lying between us and going home unrewarded for all your effort and your hope. Did you go home calmer and more beautiful and readier to attack the job at hand? I believe so, though I've a jealous hunch you were for several days the glamorous war widow trotting the theaters and night spots, and being ogled by various men. Did you see *Oklahoma*?

War, even experienced stateside, enormously heightens the reproductive urge, witness our own. Over here, nearer the front line, it's like a mania. From officers to privates we're obsessed by sex, and much the same seems true of the civilian population. Nature's way of compensating, I suppose, for all the death. The more life is threatened, the more it asserts itself. Prune back a tree and you see the same result.

Keeping town girls (almost no young men around here since war began five years ago) out of our men's barracks and beds is a major housekeeping problem. Someday I'll sing you the bawdy ditty of endless verses which expresses the situation better than I can write. It's a G.I. creation, a true folk ballad, apparently. Suffice it to say the rollicking chorus goes:

> R-o-l-l me o-over
> Yankee s-o-oldier,
> Roll me over
> Lay me down
> And do it again!

My host's younger daughter (husband in N. Africa) drives for the local Red Cross but has no designs on me that I've noticed, or vice versa. So don't worry—yet!

There have been several brawls (one of them broken up by Oswald) between our boys and British Tommies, usually at pubs— the problem apparently being that our fellows have more money to spend and this helps make them more popular with the ladies, as does the fact they're from overseas.

LOS ANGELES, JULY 1, 1944

I never told you about D-Day in New York City. It was sunny
and warm—everyone walked a little faster, seemed more eagerly
alive. The flags looked very gay and confident and the buildings
looked severe and unable to rise to the occasion. The church
bells rang all day and sounded very serene—people rushed in and
prayed, and attended services, and some came out with eyes
swollen. I wanted badly to go in and kneel but I was very tired
and had a stomach ache and was very lonely for you and Pop and
afraid to cry in a church because I had so many appointments all
day and my foolish face does swell so abominably!

So I did not do what I wanted most to do—but I prayed all
day in my heart and had tea with your Aunt Alice Brown and we
ate masses of cinnamon toast. I shall always remember the taste
of that toast and the utter silence of the vast rooms of the
Republican Women's Club, and the church bells ringing outside.

There was a little wind as I walked along Fifth Avenue to
the Plaza to change clothes and dash out to dinner. How many
elevators I rode up and down that day! People looked stunned
and quite ready to understand that the big effort is *now* and
casualties will be heavy. On the whole there was no great jubi-
lance, just relief that one more step toward the end has come at
last. By contrast, those I saw in expensive restaurants were spending money hilariously and no one seemed to know there was a
war on. The rich French and German refugees were *revolting.*

Janet Hargrave is coming over Monday. She is a W.A.S.P.[9]
and has just obtained her wings at Sweetwater, Texas. She says
she loves Texas and hates the Texans. Perhaps you and I are
unique.

ENGLAND, JULY 4, 1944

Winsor and I just returned from the residence of "The Squire."
We were invited for "after supper" which means you arrive between 8:30 and 9:00 and stay till after the 12 o'clock B.B.C.
news.

We walked past a gatehouse, up a lane lined with magnificent

9. Women's Airforce Service Pilot. They were civilian volunteers who delivered
aircraft and performed other flying duties within the U.S.

sycamores and chestnuts to the manor on the crest of a rise surrounded by lawn and gardens. Cows grazed in a brilliantly green pasture beyond. In the spacious room where we sat was a fire, two grand pianos, easy chairs, fine antique tables, rugs, vases, family portraits, a sense of time and grace.

The Squire represents a successful business house which will be 200 years old next year. But in his youth he too fought for the civilization we enjoyed tonight. Thirty years ago he was captured by the Germans and spent eighteen months in the central prison in Berlin. He escaped twice and was retaken—once within sight of the Dutch border. The third time he succeeded.

He is a sturdy bachelor who lives with his mother aged 82, his sister and her daughter and the daughter's son aged three. After a glass or two of fine Irish whiskey he sang lusty old songs while sister and niece accompanied on the two pianos. Then we all sang that lovely piece of Handel's:

> Did you not hear my lady . . .
> Go down the garden singing?
> Blackbird & thrush were silent
> To hear the alleys ringing.
> Surely you saw my lady
> Out in the garden there.

Out there, in my mind, was only one lady!

Then we heard "Jesu, joy of man's desiring" and Sir Philip Sidney's "My true love has my heart, and I—and I have his . . . " And the lovely anonymous ballad you and I read aloud in Rio Vista:

> There is a lady sweet & kind,
> Was never face so pleased my mind.
> I did but see her passing by,
> And yet I love her till I die.

Remember?

So we passed hours in song and conversation, sipping tea, munching scones, while night came on and blackout curtains were closed, sealing the mellow old room into an unforgettable occasion.

The middle-aged sister is handsome and gracious: the niece,

Mary, beautiful and intelligent, with that clear English skin and clear-cut features. She and her husband were about to sail for the U.S. on a fellowship to Harvard when the war broke out. He's been in Burma three years. You would like her. We plan to keep in touch.

Winsor and I walked home in the rain under the dripping trees, agreeing that probably nowhere but England could we have spent such an evening.

I enclose some grasses from Wales where I was recently,[10] traveling by jeep, my half-tracks and guns clanking behind me through narrow lanes and cobbled streets, while people stared in amazement and smiled and cheered, holding thumbs up. I saw Harlech Castle built by Edward I in 1284 as part of his conquest of Wales. I saw rugged mountains that tumble into the sea like ours at Santa Monica. The gray-green dunes are lovely, the beach wide, and up the slope in gray stone homes that truly are clustered like aphids one finds the shy, half-suspicious, Welsh native against whom we were warned by some English but who, in the person of a tea room proprietress, proved quite the opposite and furnished us slices of Spam with a fried egg—and a fresh lettuce-and-tomato salad that was as delicious as anything since leaving home.

Still no letter from you. Is anything wrong?

LOS ANGELES, JULY 7, 1944

Last night I had a terrible nightmare. You and I were in a hotel. We had Katherine with us. She was tiny as she is now. I was out of the canned milk we give her and asked you to get up and go find some. You departed and went all over the little town and could not find the brand I used, so you came back with the very oddest, minute cans and I was in despair and Katherine lay on the bed looking up at us in bewilderment and tremendous hunger, while we stood there helplessly. It was very terrible. I don't think there is anything quite like the feeling of not being able to provide for one's babies. You are in my dreams often. Are my letters reaching you? Tell me you love me. I yearn for you always.

10. At the British Army's artillery range overlooking Cardigan Bay near Harlech.

I've just come from services in a Norman church a thousand years old. Arriving early I wandered around the empty nave reading inscriptions on walls: the vicar's wife interred here, the vicar there, smaller brass plaques showing where infants are embedded in those ancient stones; and for a moment the place became like a sacred old vessel, a cup used over and over.

I was standing meditating in silence—you know how quiet such places can be—when I heard children's voices approaching and thought grumpily: "No privacy even here!" Two boys about 13 entered by a side door. They wore typical dark-blue beanie caps, dark-blue jackets, dark-blue knee breeches. After a moment they decided I was a stranger who needed attention. One of them—a pleasant, fair-haired, fair-faced, courteous lad such as we shall have one day with bright cheeks and eyes—walked over to me: "Sir, do you see that window?" He pointed.

Above the altar was a large stained-glass window. One pane apparently had been broken and repaired, because only part of the figure of a saint remained in color, the rest being yellow glass. "A long time ago," my informant explained gravely, "an enemy race came and broke that window, and when they fixed it they couldn't find all the pieces." It was his contribution to making me feel at home in strange surroundings.

Both boys were evacuees, I discovered, moved here as part of a national program which removes children from bombed cities. One was from London, the other—the bright lovely one—from Manchester. He will have lived for five years this September in the little village where the church is. His mother and father see him regularly. He has two brothers in the army, one now in Normandy.

He asked if we had bombs falling in America. I told him no. He described them falling with a whistle, "*boom!*"—to "clout" buildings and destroy one Mrs. Morris and blow the head off the postman "who was walking down the street" and send it flying a hundred yards.

The service was almost exactly like our Episcopal ones but the vicar was gray and doddering. I thought, as he intoned endlessly from the Old Testament about David and Goliath, that if the church doesn't brighten up—lift off its old roof and let in some sun—it will die. But I shall always remember sitting there with those two boys beside me—three orphans in a row—and feeling contained by that ancient building as if we were a precious fluid held in a goblet hallowed by time and usage.

LOS ANGELES, JULY 14, 1944

I'm reading the early Italian poets, translated by Richard Aldington. They are romantic lyrics and I send you a few lines here.

June

by Folgore da San Gemignano (1250)

For June I give you a little mountain covered
    with fair trees, thirty villages and twelve
    towers surrounding the city.
And in its midst a little fountain with a
    thousand branches and rivulets flowering
    through gardens and little lawns to refresh
    the minute short grass.
Oranges, citrons, dates and limes and all other
    savory fruits made into long arches for the walks;
And let the people there be so amorous and do
    each other so much courtesy that they may
    be gracious to all the world.

Do you get anything out of this? It makes me long more than ever to spend my youth with you. I'm tired of being half dead. Thank you for holding my heart so gently and faithfully in yours.

ENGLAND [BIGHTON WOODS], 15 JULY 1944

I have seen a flying bomb[11] or two. They're particularly impressive at night. All you see at first is a streak of fire (the exhaust) proceeding steadily at constant height. Then the fire stops. Then the bomb dips steeply toward earth and a moment later there's a big flash as it strikes. By counting the seconds (sound travels at the rate of 1100 feet per second) from this flash till you hear the explosion you calculate the distance to the point of impact. The

---

11. Hitler's vaunted new "secret weapon," also known as the V-1 or buzz bomb. It was a cigar-shaped guided missile about 25 feet long powered by a pulse-jet engine, had a 16-foot wingspread and carried a 1-ton warhead. Bob's battalion had moved with many other units to a staging area on the south coast of England, preparatory to embarking for France, and the bombs were aimed at the concentration of men and equipment there. They were also striking London and other areas, causing much damage and loss of life.

whole experience is eerie, because after you've seen the flash and are counting, you still hear the motor puttering along like an outboard motor boat's, hear it break off abruptly—and then in a few seconds the detonation.

Far more interesting, more beautiful certainly, are the anti-aircraft beams searching the sky, or lying at rest upon some spot of cloud making a bright halo there and a long ladder of light descending. They are waiting for the German reconnaissance planes that come over to observe and photograph the effects of the flying bombs.

Nobody is greatly concerned about this weapon. You would be amazed to find yourself quickly resigned to it, feeling: "Oh well—if this one's for me it's for me!" Until then, why spoil a breakfast or a good sleep? This sounds as though I were a veteran Londoner under fire day and night. If I were I might feel differently.

Let me tell more about Captain K. He is one of the sharpest people I ever met. Nothing escapes him; there is no problem he will not attempt a reasonable solution for. He is utterly practical, utterly alert, quick to sum up and arrive at conclusions, prompt to act, courageous and fair. When he leads me into combat I'll feel myself in good hands.

Is it necessary to add—never be concerned when my letters don't come? I'm writing whenever I can.

P.S. My footlocker has been stored at the following address:

> Mr. H. O. Hambleton
> New Lodge, Ivy Lane
> Macclesfield, Cheshire
> England.

If anything happens to me (how dramatic—and all over a footlocker!)—if anything happens to me I seem unable to advise you on any course of action except how to regain a footlocker. Just write Mr. Hambleton, send funds, and the locker will, with luck, find its way home.

Time out—one of my boys just got badly burned. He was pouring gasoline into a stove he thought had gone out. The gas took fire. I held him for half an hour while the doctors worked over him, poor kid—he felt worst about going to the hospital and leaving the outfit. And he apologized to me. "Gee, Lieutenant, I'm sorry this happened!" He's a good man, one of the best.

Still later—I've just read your letters of June 22 and 26 for the third time and feel better than in weeks. Numbers 2 and 3 may be lost but at least I know you live and breathe, something I doubted all these days.

I am in a lovely lawn-and-garden behind a tea shop at Winchester. I've just walked up High Street to the West Gate built in thirteen-hundred-something, then dropped back a few yards to this tea room—on an afternoon so perfect, your letters so fresh in mind, that the only thing to do seemed to be to find a table in a corner of the lawn under a big chestnut tree and write, while sipping India tea and munching delicious toast & jam. The dense green leaves above my head are rustling with a most heavenly summer's sound, and the birds in the garden beside me sing mightily. Even the "victory chickens"—Rhode Island Reds & Leghorns—in the pen nearby chirp contentedly as a life-giving sun blesses us all. Planes are overhead. The phrase is: "The planes are going out!" It makes your spine tingle to hear them going out after midnight over the silent, blacked-out towns, with a roar so large all the sky echoes it and is never empty; and when they go by day as now—the "Marauders"[12] in small packs like wolves—straight off into the morning sun, one, two, three, a dozen, two dozen, graceful, dangerous—why, people stop whatever they're doing, look up, then grin at each other.

Pause for more tea. I offered my hostess a pound in settlement but she shook her head. Two cups of tea, two pieces of buttered toast and jam, two cakes have cost me a shilling—20¢.

John writes from Normandy enclosing Sgt. Delaney's piece on Pop from *Harper's*. Great news from Caen this morning.[13] I devour every word you write. Please feed me more. Love to all my girls.

LOS ANGELES, JULY 16, 1944

With every summer comes a longing for Italy—for Italy with you. Can we possibly manage it together? And see those hilltowns

---

12. B-26 twin-engine attack bombers.
13. British and Canadian forces had broken through the encircling Germans.

where each stone is a thousand years old and the faces of the peasants have the ages as marked in their eyes as the hills themselves? I cannot tell you how those rows of cypresses marching along the hills—surrounding castles and so straight against the blue sky—how they take my very heart and fill it with the brightest sunshine!

And the evenings in Florence, city of the flowers—oh I should love to wander there—where the hands of men have left such beauty! I wonder and wonder if we can do it. My youth was so very happy in that land and I should like to see it all again with you beside me. I want to talk again with the peasants—they represent the best of Italy, their expressions are as fine as those of the simple Americans we've grown to love and understand. I hope we can always judge a country by the people who work on the land—there you get the immutable quality and the *best*.

The main article in the last *Life* is on China—and it *is* marvelous! I yearn to go to those hills also—how large and peaceful. I could understand Tao there. The Chinese are an inspiration. Imagine 7½ years of war! It is incredible. They are the *enduring* people. Let us see them in their beautiful land!

How can we ever live long enough to do these million things? Tell me we shall have time.

ENGLAND [BIGHTON WOODS], 20 JULY 1944
Yesterday another dream of ours came true and I had lunch with Monty at Chequers.[14] We got on beautifully. When I phoned from the sentry post at the gate, she was a bit vague till I said, "Jane Faust's husband." Then my jeep was permitted to proceed down the sloping drive into the courtyard and stop before a house—part castle, part manor—that was mentioned by William the Conqueror in his Doomsday Book.

Monty met me at the door with a kiss, turned my driver over to a dozen A.T.S. (Auxiliary Territorial Service) girls (equivalent to our W.A.C.'s), who staff the place and led me into the grand drawing room which has a ceiling at least 20 feet high. Portraits of the illustrious adorn the walls, suits of armor stand around,

14. Grace Lamont, Jane's governess in Florence, was now manager and official hostess at Chequers, country residence of British prime ministers, not far from London in rural Buckinghamshire.

Chequers, rural retreat of British prime ministers, where Grace ("Monty") Lamont was hostess and manager for Winston Churchill in 1944. (Wide World Photos)

there is dark oak paneling, a fireplace large enough for trees to burn in, and every rug, every tapestry, every vase and chair must be priceless. In the middle of it all stands a huge new plastic globe, a recent present from F.D.R. to W.C.[15] Mysteriously, a cluster of brown spots has appeared in mid-Atlantic—which are simply defects in the material but W.C. jokingly tells F.D.R. they are islands and claims them for England.

We proceeded outside to a large lawn where Monty had been sitting in a canvas chair in the sun sipping a glass of sherry and talked there a while, and I did so deeply feel the way she cherishes all of you as dearly as if you were her own. What a decent, sensible, soul she is, with a touch of iron in her too. She looks very well and has that gray sandiness of the Scotch which endures forever.

15. Winston Churchill.

At lunch, which was served in her comfortable sitting-room-office, Grandson Winston,[16] aged 3½, bright, golden haired, and his governess joined us at a round table. I could see photographs of all Fausts on the wall and also on Monty's desk, including a lovely one of you taken the day in Florence you flung yourself down by the pool and said: "Now take me, Daddy, and I'll be a movie star!" Or so Monty says. It's ensconced in a position of honor beside Mr. C. and family.

Afterwards we all adjourned to the lawn and basked under a poet's summer sky and fleecy clouds, while Monty looked at my photographs and read my last letters from you. Winston was much interested in the picture of Joan. Turning to Monty he inquired politely: "Where is Joan?"

Monty replied: "In America."

"What does she say?"

"Why probably," said Monty gravely, "that she would like a lollipop."

"What's a lollipop, please?" asked Winston.

I asked Monty to choose one photo to keep and she chose the colored snap of you holding Joan. Please send her a copy of Pop's story in the *Post* (and send me one) and tell her the name of that last movie he wrote for Warners with Errol Flynn.[17]

There is a long room across one side of the second story lined with books. It has coats of arms done in stained glass of all the owners of the estate since time began. It's also used for movies. Mr. C. enjoyed *Dr. Kildare* there. Over the fireplace are two crossed swords that belonged to Oliver Cromwell. A daughter of his married into the family owning the estate, and a letter in his handwriting is framed beside the fireplace—advising one of his sons to love his wife even as Jesus loved all mankind. Other curios include Mrs. Cromwell's Bible, Napoleon's pistols, a steel collar worn by the last slave (white!) executed for thievery at Perth, Australia, in 1701.

While showing me the bedrooms Monty told of her run-in with Molotov[18] who stayed here with a delegation from the U.S.S.R. In making Molotov's bed, one of her girls found a pistol under his pillow. Monty confronted Molotov and told him in no

16. Winston Spencer Churchill, known as Winston II, later an author, journalist and member of Parliament.
17. *The Adventures of Don Juan.*
18. Russian foreign minister.

uncertain terms there was no need to sleep with a pistol under his pillow in any house where *she* was hostess! The pistol disappeared.

I'll see Monty again if I return to England. Much of what she told me, as well as the names I read in the guestbook, will keep until I see you. The Nazis apparently tried to bomb the house once but the bombs fell in a nearby wood. I spent from one to half-past five of the loveliest summer day with her. It was all like a chapter I'd read before, just as you and I spoke of it so often, even to the calm and absolutely sweet and dear old Monty who, barely raising her voice, would say: "I'm very excited. This *is* a wonderful day." She made no mention of Kenneth Clark[19] recommending her for her remarkably responsible position and I didn't bring it up. She did express a touching wish that Pop and Mr. C. had met. "They were so much alike. They would have had so much to say to each other."

Returning I saw London. It's in quite good state of preservation despite the devastating effects of the massive bombings of three and four years ago, and more recently, the V-2 rocket[20] attacks. I passed through Berkeley Square again for the first time since '37 and found it strangely unchanged, rather unreal.

LOS ANGELES, JULY 24, 1944

My darling, I was just being naughty when I said you were "self-sufficient." Please forgive me. I only wanted you to miss me— and your letters sounded so happy and gay. Naturally I want you happy—but I grew perverse one evening and suddenly decided you didn't *need* me and though you probably loved me, I was not essential. All of which I suppose you had surmised wisely and now I *do* ask your pardon. We are essential to each other—I've always known that in my heart.

Early in 1945 I should like to start another baby and so you had better hurry back. No—on second thought, I think I can postpone it until 1946! Does that meet with your approval?

I feel so relieved my words are reaching you! It was grim to

19. The art expert, then director of England's National Gallery in London. Monty had been his governess before going to the Fausts.

20. The Nazis' latest secret weapon, literally "Vengeance Weapon Two," was a liquid-fueled ballistic missile about 50 feet long carrying a 1-ton warhead at a speed of over 3,300 m.p.h. Arriving before people in its target area could hear it, it created much terror as well as destruction and death.

think you might never hear from me before going into action. Thank you for your dramatic telling of the address of your foot-locker. I shall keep it but I expect you to bring back the locker yourself!

I suppose you'll be kept away from me for many months after the end of the war in the West. I should not like it if you were sent to the South Pacific eventually. You speak of the ancient cathedrals and the heavenly roses! I can only barely *stand* being away from you.

Goodbye for this moment. Here is all my love.

———————————

The long low dark coast of Europe looms ahead.

At dusk on July 29th my convoy of ships, largest of the war since D-Day, reaches broad sandy Utah Beach on the Normandy Coast. Like Omaha Beach a few miles to the north and clearly visible below its bluffs, Utah was the scene of D-Day landings by our troops nearly two months ago. But here there are no bluffs and resistance was weak rather than strong as at Omaha. Gentle meadows spread inland. The beach swarms with men and ma-chines. It is the chief port of entry for U.S. forces invading France. In the distance anti-aircraft shells explode in the evening sky and a dull roar of heavy artillery marks the front line. Dozens of barrage balloons, like big sausages tethered to earth by cables, float close overhead to protect the landing area from low-level air attack.

Shortly before midnight our blunt-nosed L.S.T.'s[21] scrape their flat bottoms to a halt in shallow water three hundred yards from shore. In the morning when the tide recedes they open their bow doors and the jeeps and trucks of the 825th Tank Destroyer Battalion, followed by half-tracks towing 3-inch guns, emerge onto hard-packed sand nearly as firm as tarmac and move inland.

We're part of General George S. Patton's U.S. 3rd Army and Patton is already legendary. In Sicily he slapped the face of a combat-fatigued G.I. for speaking in a hysterical manner. But in Sicily as in North Africa he distinguished himself as a fighting leader. Now his mission is to lead the 3rd Army in a breakthrough

21. Landing Ships, Tank—designed to transport tanks and other vehicles of compa-rable size.

that will reach toward Paris and beyond. The fact he comes from Los Angeles adds to my interest. Before sailing I'd read with amusement his fiery exhortations included among routine information in the mimeographed poop sheets distributed daily to all 3rd Army units: "Grab the enemy by the nose and kick him in the tail!" Or: "When in doubt, do something!" I hope to catch a glimpse of the eccentric general who reportedly wears a six-shooter at his hip in open holster and addresses poems to the God of Battles.

Our first evidence of actual battle is anything but poetic. Behind a wall-like hedgerow is a series of abandoned foxholes, each surrounded by a litter of used K-ration cartons, tin cans, empty cartridge casings, dried human feces. This has been the front line. It is eloquent of a new reality, the feces perhaps most eloquent. There'd been no time to relieve yourself leisurely, cover your deposit afterward, and no such niceties as toilet paper. Like an animal afraid for your life you jumped out of your hole, excreted, jumped back in. The dead or wounded had of course been removed to the rear long before we passed. The able-bodied had gone forward as we were going. Again the courage and blood of others paved the way.

At Sotteville not far from Cherbourg the 825th is deployed as a security force guarding lines of communication, watching for German stragglers and French or German spies and saboteurs, while the rest of 3rd Army prepares for its historic breakout.

Meanwhile Jane is gently influencing her mother toward selling their home at 317 Burlingame Avenue and moving to Santa Barbara, as a decisive step in coping with the sorrow of her father's death. The children continue to be a source of life and hope for them both, as they crave yet dread each day's mail, newspaper, radio broadcast.

SOMEWHERE IN FRANCE,[22] AUG. 2, 1944

As you see I've made a short sea voyage and am here, back again after seven years, back in the same season too, apples not quite ripe, blackberries getting red in the hedgerows, fields and trees a lovely green. Despite man's worst efforts surprisingly little devastation has been wrought upon the earth itself, or that part of it we've seen. But what makes France really charming is the sun-

22. Again, security regulations prevented giving exact locations.

shine and mild air. I have sunned my old green sleeping bag and the Army blankets that fit inside it. I have stripped to the waist and dug a slit trench, bare feet wriggling in warm moist soil. I have had dahlias flung into my jeep by French girls as we passed. I probably need a bath but then so does everyone else in Europe.

The people appear subdued, though glad to see us, and the sign of the "V" made with the first and second fingers is the greeting between strangers here as in England. The French do not practice the "thumbs up." And instead of plaguing us with "Gum, chum?" or "Candy, dandy?" the children venture a mild: "Bon-bon?" Apparently they've been well nourished, neither have their elders suffered from lack of food, if one may judge from luscious vegetable gardens, herds of sheep and cattle, flocks of ducks and chickens, abundance of cider and wine, etc. Many wear wooden shoes but on the whole they are adequately dressed.

This afternoon I was walking a narrow path between high hedges and met a lovely fair-haired boy such as we'll have someday who comes to our camp regularly. He wore short pants, blue beret, and that readiness to smile some people are born with. We talked about the wheat fields where the grain is ripening and bright red poppies bloom. We discussed the fresh tracks of a hobnailed German boot, horses (Percherons, etc.) that have gone to America from France, and finally people who have gone—I told him we have many French and many Germans in America (his eyes widened), many Spanish, Italians, and Russians, but that they are all Americans. This was a big idea for him and suddenly it was for me too.

It reminded me of our first night at sea out of New York when the radio announced: "This is the Voice of America, one of the United Nations, broadcasting on the 16 meter band . . ." It sent a tingle up my spine, Janie, as we surged across the water, to hear that flat, absolutely unpretentious Mid-West voice bidding us look back and, as it were, view our country in perspective.

Our position here as conquerors is strange. Americans as conquerors? Absurd! Yet just a few weeks ago the Germans were using these roads, buildings, fields, chairs, tables, toilets, women, and now we are—and the look in the citizens' eye is not always one of acclaim but rather a question: "How will *you* treat me?"

I don't foresee a quick end to this bitter business. I don't foresee an easy healing of wounds. I begin to understand why older people anywhere grow disillusioned and tend to say to brash, hopeful youth: "Take it easy. Enjoy your small blessings. The world will change when it is ready."

From these ashes I hope better things will rise. Yet in some of these faces there is nothing left but ashes—grayness, giving off hardly any light at all. I suppose if President Roosevelt had sold out to Hitler and Generals Marshall and MacArthur and Eisenhower proved incompetent, we might look the same. We Americans never can know our good fortune until we look at it like this from 3,000 miles away.

LOS ANGELES, AUG. 5, 1944

Will we ever entertain together? Yesterday Raphael's brother Ripley Pumpelly and his delightful wife and their two children came as well as Dotha Lee and her nice husband Rod. I pined for you. The afternoon was warm and everyone in benevolent mood. I served white wine with soda, a drink you love and I might fix for you when we are in our own garden. Later Judy and I finished Act V of *Antony and Cleopatra* aloud. It is not nearly as good as Act IV which has Antony's death. Cleopatra applying asp to the bosom was really almost "de trop." But we found the rest of the play very fine, eloquent, simple. I miss you more and more. August climbs on and then September. I shall always like September, the month of our marriage.

FRANCE [LA HAYE-DU-PUITS], AUG. 10, 1944

We haven't seen any combat and, at the rate things are going, we'll have to hurry to catch up to the front line. But how grand it is, Janie, that our men and machines are successful, proving themselves as good as any in the world: 85 miles from Paris—we hear tonight; and today I lunched with a Frenchman and his family who live in an ancient inn by the sea. He fought in the last war and was wounded in the leg, as he showed me. He lived all through this one with a German fortification nearby. The drunken soldiers came and despoiled his inn, demanding wine at pistol point (but he had buried the wine in his garden). He has dug it up and shares it with us, and he and his wife raised their glasses to the health of America and France and the confusion of the Boches—who broke his windows, ravished his eighteen-year-old daughter and wounded him when he interfered.

Many good Russians, or "Georgians"[23] as these French call them, were with the Germans manning the invasion coasts; also many Poles and Austrians most of whom hated the Germans. But they were given their choice of death or serving in the German Army. Some chose death, some served. One Georgian, whose grave I saw, especially redeemed himself. He is buried in a little village churchyard overlooking the sea. Four Germans are buried at one end of the churchyard all alone. They were killed by American aircraft and their flamboyant wooden swastikas are already weathered and their graves overgrown with weeds; but the Georgian's grave has a headstone of granite, his photograph inlaid within it, and the French keep it freshly strewn with flowers, because rather than fight against the Americans he killed his German noncommissioned officer and was himself killed.

Beside him is the grave of an Englishman whose plane was shot down. Like the Georgian's it is kept fresh with flowers—while at the far end of the churchyard the Germans are relegated to oblivion.

This is a bitter thought but the mild little Frenchman who showed us the graves called it to our attention with a smile, saying that here we might see the true feelings of his people displayed, and adding with a gesture so very French: "Triste peuple, les Boches!"

These Russians or Georgians impressed into the German Army were made to wear a red shoulder patch marked "Géorgien." They and the Poles, Austrians, etc. were part of the inferior troops the Germans apparently hoped would cushion the impact of invasion, reserving their own men for counterattack. Whatever their strategy, it failed.

As a sidelight, a French seamstress described to me with relish the former Polish officer who, when made to lay wooden box-mines along the beaches, laid them all upside down so they wouldn't work. (This being a finesse especially pleasing to the French mind.) They snatch at such little things to help their self-respect. But I think my friend, the innkeeper, speaks for the majority when he declares proudly: "De Gaulle[24] is the heart of France!" His admiration for Big Charlie who never surrendered, who even in 1940 made the Boches retreat when his division, counter-attacked, is deeply

23. Actually "Géorgiens," after the Georgian Soviet Socialist Republic, birthplace of Joseph Stalin.
24. General Charles de Gaulle, leader of the Free French Forces now joining in the liberation of France.

touching. De Gaulle left France of his free will—to return and fight another day. And that day has come.

We get along. Food, clothing, all our supplies are first-rate. One fills with pride at the efficiency with which Americans function. And the term "American ingenuity" is a true one, Janie. You should see how quickly a deserted building or an empty field can be transformed and made livable by a few G.I.'s with the help of every conceivable odd and end and gadget.

The fog is in from the sea this morning like the fog at home. The smell on the grass makes me lonely for you. All my love!

LOS ANGELES, AUG. 11, 1944

I've been thinking of all the lovely little private things that constitute a marriage, or *our* marriage. I remember the early, early mornings, when you always swore it was my turn to light the stove in the freezing cold bathroom at the McCreery Ranch! And the mornings since you've been in the Army, when I've seen you struggle sleepily out of bed and put on your cap before anything else! And the feel of your feet beside mine in a double bed. And the sound of your breathing when asleep—and your rough cheek before you shaved. And you humming: "I've got you under my skin!" And your foolish smile of contentment when you brought home ice cream for our supper in Rio Vista. And I remember how pretty our little Rio Vista apartment looked when I came back from Berkeley after the miscarriage—you had bought plants for it and it was all clean and neat.

Do you recall Sunday afternoons at the McCreery when Josephine would bounce over and mow our back lawn and rake and sweep with a gust of energy and eventually we'd calm her enough so she'd stop and have tea with us before she dashed to San Francisco to see her dying father? I wish I knew how to reach Little Joe. He was my special treasure. We had tea and cookies in the Observation Post while looking and listening for Japanese planes. Can you ever forget his pride in his honorable discharge after World War I? As you say, that life was lovely but we could not return to it. What is so deathly about going back?

Exceptions: Italy and Greece—because I would be with you which would make it all so new and lovely. I don't want to raise our children abroad, even if we could afford it. Yet I have a deep desire for Europe. Where you grow up is forever pulling you back—if you were happy, that is to say, and I was breathlessly happy at seventeen, eighteen, nineteen. I looked for love (for you) around every corner, in every evening breeze and I remember wearing gardenias in my hair (picking them off the bushes in a corner of the garden); and we changed every evening for dinner and ate outside—fireflies in the fields below the terrace—and Pop in dinner jacket and Mum very beautiful in long dress. I remember feeling so awake and alive and reaching for something in that summer air that I knew not of.

I can see funny middle-aged men eyeing me and thinking: "Well, Faust's daughter has certainly grown up!" It was true. Suddenly I was ready for life, one summer, for that purest joy and optimism of eighteen years. I cannot help wishing you had come to me then. I was not meant for all the suitors who came and went and the attendant scenes and confusions. I began to loathe any man who took me for a prospective wife or flattered me with praise. How much simpler and more beautiful to have found you at once!

I have been wanting to tell you how upset I am over the six bridges destroyed across the Arno[25] by the Germans. I've always loved those stately old bridges—so simple and clear in line!

FRANCE [LESSAY], AUG. 15, 1944

Rumors fly. The latest is a bit of numerology as follows (to the effect the war will end Sept. 7 at 2 P.M.).

Take the word CHRIST

	Age	Years of Office	Date born	Year entered office
C=Churchill				
H=Hitler				
R=Roosevelt	57	11	1887	1933
I=Il Duce				
S=Stalin				
T=Tojo	60	4	1884	1940

Add up, as in the example, for each man and it gives you 3888. Divide by 2 and you get 1944. Divide by 2 and you get 972, that is to say: Sept. 7, 1944 at 2 P.M. the war will end. I

25. In Florence.

make no predictions except I shall go on loving you. There shall be no armistice there.

Have I mentioned the French, children and grownups, who come at mealtimes to eat what our men leave? When our boys finish, anything remaining is given to these hungry people. We feed a dozen or more at each meal. It is very pitiful—both the people and the fact we are so rich and never realize it. We eat, if anything, better here than at Camp Hood. You would be astounded. Tonight we had pork chops, mashed potatoes and gravy, choice canned peas, bread and butter and strawberry jam, prunes and coffee. This morning we had grapefruit juice, absolutely divine pancakes made with powdered egg and milk, bacon and coffee with canned milk and sugar. The richness of all America is lavished here. You've no conception of the equipment alone. Today, for example, I saw a huge locomotive marked "U. S. Army" hauling a train of cars!

Another item: our PX supplies: cigarettes, tobacco, soap, razor blades, candy, chewing gum, are all *free* now. But we accept all this almost without comment, though I hear an occasional voice raised: "Boy, they can take me home and I'll *never* complain, nossir!"

Must stop for darkness. I shall look out a while longer at the sea. The light is draining away from it down over the world to wake you up in the morning.

LOS ANGELES, AUG. 22, 1944

Miracle of miracles! A letter of yours this morning was actually written only eight days ago. I shrieked for joy. I can almost smell your face after you've shaved and I can imagine your touch and your voice and your eyes and your short hair and a thousand, thousand things that make you mine. Your letters are never censored and that gives me a pleasantly private feeling.

You say you are sorry Mum let me read the letter you wrote her before leaving England. She did NOT show it to me. I came in while she was reading it and said: "I bet that is Bob saying more foolish things about what and if he's killed!" Mum smiled and said: "Some day I may show you this letter." So I knew right away that you were back on the old subject of . . . well, as you say, NEVER let us mention it again! But I didn't want you to think that Mum had shown me anything you wrote her privately.

Judy and I will do Act IV of *Othello* tonight. I can never have enough of the good words. I need them as everyday food. After we read in the evenings, I type your notes. I usually write you at this time, between four and five in the afternoon, while Joan plays in my room with her toys. Then at five I undress her and get her ready for supper, and bring Katherine in from outside also and give her her prune juice. When I first took care of the children alone I was running all day and exhausted by 8 P.M. Now I feel very well and not a bit tired, though very sleepy by 10:00 when I switch off the light.

I long for you and sometimes wonder how I'll possibly last out through the years to come when you are absent. The children are a tremendous guard against all the worry a war brings, all the doubts about what the future holds and the possibilities etc. When I am with them I am obliged to smile and laugh and be gay and once that effort is made one begins to feel better.

I love you tenderly and proudly and humbly and with all the good there may be in my soul.

FRANCE [LESSAY], AUG. 22, 1944

Earlier this evening a woman who speaks English brought me her 19-year-old son. Like many he wants to join *our* Army. I told her about the Free French, asked if he did not wish to join them. No, he wanted to join the American Army. He was just a child, Janie, frail, undernourished, pathetic. I told him our Army was complimented by his wanting to join, then chatted a moment with the mother who was a girl of 17 when the last war brought Americans to France. She looks back, I gather, with nostalgic pride to those days and feels she's seeing history repeated.

Have I described my jeep and those who ride in it? My driver is pudgy, stocky George Hamilton of Brattleboro, Vt., who has cheeks like strawberries and a quality about his driving that reminds me of certain cowhorses I've known who, when you get them going after a steer, take the spirit of the moment and the bit in their teeth and go down country hell-bent.

Anthony Radovich of Watsonville, California, is my radio operator and general steward. Radovich is 20, tall, a little cocky and superior as 20 should be, when it has a certain amount of brains, artistic ability, and fine wavy dark hair. He was studying to be an interior decorator before the war. With his talent for painting he has given our jeep a name. It came as a big surprise. Hamilton asked me what I wanted the jeep named and I told him it was his jeep, he ought to name it. Nothing happened for a few days and then one afternoon he came up with a grin a yard long and said: "Lieutenant, come look at the jeep." I went and looked. On the lower front portion (exterior) of the windshield frame, just forward of where I sit, Radovich had painted, in white: "Daddy." I pretended displeasure with a certain amount of good-natured gruffness which seemed to please everybody, and Radovich explained I was the father of 51 men wasn't I? And so why not "Daddy"? The name has become a standing joke in the platoon.

The light is growing dim but see me now in what was once a fine chateau facing a circle of grass bordered by huge horse chestnuts. Now it is a weary ruin, a sort of horror of living decay, that once housed many Germans and now houses me and my men and some 14 French men, women and children, most of them refugees. I have a room upstairs over the front door and the sound of the super-fluid French language rises around me on the evening air. A jackass brays. Donkeys, horses, and goats wander at will on the unkempt grass of what was once the great lawn. Our kitchen and maintenance shops occupy outbuildings and stables. A radio loudly plays: "I have a song to sing, O!"—the lovely fool's song from "The Yeoman of the Guard." I cannot as I sit here help but recall *A Tale of Two Cities*. Remember when the mender of roads sees the carriage of the marquis pass, which has run over the child while leaving Paris, and beneath the carriage a man is hanging? And the carriage goes on to the great chateau, and that night the marquis in his bed imagines he hears a sound at the window but decides it's only the wind? And in the morning he's found with a knife pinning a note to his chest: "This from Jacques!"

Hearing the story read aloud as a child probably prejudiced me against chateaux and French aristocracy. But you keenly feel the degradation of the poor by the rich here. There are not enough wholesome middle-class people. God might do worse than send a flood and let the French start over. Maybe the war was the flood.

Am writing blind now. My love is yours. Please be sure of it every minute even when letters don't come. At times I just cannot get a moment for writing, and also the pen is such a heavy means of saying how light and bright my thoughts are as they fly to you.

LOS ANGELES, AUG. 24, 1944

I've been reading a depressing article in *Time* which points out how long it will be before our men are back. I am now prepared not to see you for two more years! Though I don't complain, I grow mortally hungry for you and at moments the ache is pretty bad. All the little things flood over me and I become quite gloomy.

When you speak of the wasted hours in life—in Pop's life— I understand so well what you mean and I do see that we must not do the same. For this reason, and others, we *must* break away from the pattern which our parents established. We must determine how we wish to live—what our goal is to be, and then *ruthlessly* follow the plan and fulfill it.

Talk to me always—of how we shall live when you are back. Let us begin planning by mail. We've done a good bit of living via letters—so let us continue, darling. But tell me—do you ever feel the need of a woman—a woman for merely physical contact? Do you feel tempted to sleep with anyone who might come along and don't do it merely because you know it would hurt me? I have wondered, a little. It is 6 months since you left. I can only hope that you feel as I do—that if either one of us were unfaithful physically or in any other way—we would be sinning against our love. I could never do this, ever. But is it fair to expect the same of you? What is all the talk about men needing it? I trust in you to do what is right for you and in your heart is just. You know how I feel—so let us be prepared. We cannot and must not hurt our love. If you ever did—I hope you would tell me—it would hurt me *more* not to know the truth of these months apart.

FRANCE [GRANVILLE], AUG. 25, '44

There have been some unpleasantries: piano wires strung across lonely roads at night to decapitate or otherwise mutilate members of our jeep patrols who drive with windshields down, some sniper fire too. No bloodshed yet, fortunately.

From time to time Germans come out of hiding and surrender. A number were married to French girls during the occupation, legally or de facto, and deliberately remained behind when their units departed. Others deserted for other reasons. The few I've seen are rather pathetic looking cases who leave you without much awe of "the master race."

Tell me of the notes you are making. I jotted down today:

"Taking hands is the most beautiful gesture, being that of friend and lover combined."

Darkness again. Love to all my girls.

LOS ANGELES, AUGUST 26, 1944

Katherine has stopped blowing her cereal and eats very nicely, flat on her back, and now has vegetables (pureed) for her lunch, as well as the eternal bottle. She likes carrots and hates peas because they stick to the roof of the mouth. I hated them as a child, too. Her appetite is excellent and her laughter my great joy. She likes me to throw her over my head and she really twinkles with mirth and expects no attention but adores to have company, especially Joan.

That awakening of companionship between the two is some-

Normandy Beachhead. Utah Beach looked much like this in July 1944. Half-tracks are towing antitank guns like ours. This is Omaha Beach a few miles to the north, where some of the bitterest fighting of the war took place. (National Archives)

Hedgerow fighting, Normandy. (Hearst Corporation)

thing I could almost weep about because it is so lovely and so true and you are not seeing it with me! Oh, it is a crime!

The other night I had them both in the nursery (Joan's room) and Mum was crying in her room and having a bad time and so I told Joan that after her supper we'd all go in and see Nin-Nin. When the meal was over, Katherine and Joan ready, Joan said: "Take hands with Katherine and say goodnight to Nin-Nin." I could not make it plain to her that K. is unable to walk, but I held her low and Joan took her hand and I carried Katherine in with Joan clutching at her and we saw Nin-Nin. Fortunately Joan does not realize when Mum has been crying, so pretty soon Mum was better while they sat on her bed happily smiling at each other.

There is bound to be a certain amount of fatigue in looking after babies and I like it. I never want to lie awake at night and wonder what's ahead. This way I turn my light out at ten and rarely wake before seven. There is absolutely NO creative energy left in me by evening as far as writing is concerned.

I suppose a good deal of creation goes on in every day with a child. This morning, for instance, while I was running Joan's bath and she was standing there naked (a sight I adore, tummy and all), I began singing a waltz and Joan held up her hands to

me saying: "Let's dance." So we hopped around the bathroom
and had a good laugh and then took the bath. So often one is
tempted to just say curtly: "No, this is bath time, no dancing!"
But they need laughter and pleasure, and making me a few minutes late in the routine of the day is not fatal, though I'm apt to
become a slave to routines.

How do you feel about routine? I don't see how else one can
accomplish the thousand things that go to make a woman's day.
I hope when we live together we can have some schedule. I mean,
at a certain time every evening we read aloud, and you spend a
half hour with the children in the study, or by the fire, reading
them poetry or Malory or Peter Rabbit or just talking with them
as they grow older.

I have it arranged so I can do all my duties and write you
daily and keep up other letters and do your notes at night and
read aloud with Judy. I make use of nearly every moment. And
then, yes, the children's diaries—I keep up that record, because
I think one should and Pop always begged me to.

Preston Ames telephoned yesterday to ask if I'd play tennis
with him today at 5, it being Saturday. I shall, over here on our
funny old court that is more and more full of cracks but has a new
net! My racket has a broken string but I shall be glad for the
exercise. Presty is very nice—39, which seems amazing. I always
think of him at about 25. We knew him abroad when he was
studying at the Sorbonne and we had a house outside Paris for
two summers at a tiny village called Giverny, near Vernon. I saw
that our troops went through Vernon the other day.

Judy was very flattered to have your letter this morning. She
is editor of the school paper next year. It starts Sept. 11. She may
very probably write. I hope so, for there is no greater satisfaction
on earth, as you know.

FRANCE [MAYET], AUG. 26, 1944

How your letters 44, 45 found me is something of a mystery
because we've moved a good deal. We left one old chateau and
moved to an older, grander one by a lake. An artist owned it.
His paintings and many others were on the walls. I saw a plaque
with coats of arms tracing the ancestry of the family from 1400.
There were beautiful carpets and priceless tapestries and figures
wearing suits of armour standing on each landing of the stairway.

A German general used the building as headquarters, and now the boys from the hills of Tennessee were traipsing wide-eyed up and down stairs peering and exclaiming—pondering old volumes of tax records written when Napoleon was emperor, sleeping on the beautiful hardwood floor of the grand salon where the feet of gentlemen and ladies waltzed.

Now we are farther into France where there are no hedgerows as in Normandy but lovely rolling country of great fertility un-touched by war—where there are fruits and flowers, ample food, and the people rush to touch your hand, kiss your hand, kiss your face, because we have liberated them. The girls bring bouquets of flowers, wine, cider, cognac, fresh tomatoes, pears, apples, eggs—every imaginable good thing.

We are the first troops to stay in this little town.[26] I am writing from my upstairs bedroom in the house of a doctor who is host to Lt. Eastabrooks also. One midnight the Gestapo came for the doctor. He left by the back door and lived four months in the woods until the Germans departed a fortnight ago. He has a wife and a daughter Joan's age with lovely blonde curls.

I took café au lait with them this morning. My French being about equal to his English, he would laboriously ask: "Do you desire the milk it is boil?" and I laboriously reply: "Il n'importe pas: si vous bouillir, je bouillir aussi."

So much has happened I hardly know where to start—in a little town I met a nun speaking English, Sister Patrick was her name, though her surname was Kelly, and she has a sister married to a Navy man at San Pedro, California, and speaks English as only the Irish can. I never heard all her story. It was a swift meeting in the street. She led us to barracks formerly occupied by Germans where we spent a hasty day and night. I must go back and talk with her for hours and learn how she came to the village of the Shining Door[27] overlooked by the great chateau of the seigneurs, where Lady Mary of the Shining Door lived in 1492 and her descendants ever since.

I must return also to the iron foundry in the same town where men and women go to work apparently through force of habit, because for months there has been nothing to do, no

26. Thirty-five miles north of Tours.
27. Port Brillet.

electricity, and the big buildings and great machines stand idle and rusting. Monsieur the mayor manages the foundry. We bought some iron stripping from him the morning Roumania asked for an armistice and Paris was liberated. I thanked him for his courtesy. "Ah," he said, "it is nothing! You have given us liberty!"

He took us to his house and we drank brandy to America and France and he gave me a bottle of finest red wine, Grand Vin Rouge, Chateau du Colombier Monselon, Pauillac, Haute-Médoc!

Children ran to take my hand as I passed in the street. Old men came out with a bottle and a glass to pour me cider. Janie, it was fantastic, dreamlike, repetition of a former joy after the other war ended; and I was not happy thinking of the misery experienced between those two wars by these poor people. They are diminished now. The owner of the great chateau is stooped though still a young man. His face is pale. He no longer lives in the chateau but in the porter's lodge at the gate.

Where have I been? Coutances, Laval, Mayenne, Le Mans and many more. What have I seen? A million 2½ ton General Motors trucks rolling thick and fast as Sunday traffic on a New York City parkway. A million jeeps, ambulances, guns, tanks, bulldozers, tractors, trailers that can carry houses, planes, trains—every machine imaginable—handled with the casual air of: "Hell, let's go! We'll use them up! Then we'll make better ones!"

I have watched my mechanics poring over a truck engine in the hours after midnight, the only light a trouble lamp, the only incentive the job itself and the love of the grease and gears and the tools that their fingers know. The maintenance crew is a clique of Southerners. Gay, prejudiced, charming as Southerners always were, I guess, and just as ready to fight as not. After midnight makes no difference. The conversation goes like this.

"Noles, get that hypoid and we'll administer a little grease to this lady!"—a 2½ ton truck they've put together out of parts found, begged or borrowed or stolen and it runs like one straight from the factory.

Noles gets the "gun," a grease gun on a hose attached to a pump you work by foot. He crawls under the truck with his trouble lamp while the sergeant works the gun. Noles, it seems, comes from Louisiana and is therefore suspected of living on fish and rice. While he's under the truck on his back, both hands full, grease dripping onto his face, is a good time to guy him about that fish and rice.

"Say, Noles, let's get this done before breakfast!"

"Get him a platter-full of rice. That'll fetch him!"

Noles responds: "Why, goddamn you guys, I'll come up there and stomp you to death!"

"Aw, Noles . . . !"

"Noles, he's like this here cal-avoosh [calvados] brandy. You gotta take a pine-top and beat the fire outa him 'fore he's fit to associate with."

Noles' grease gun runs over, drips on Noles, he begins squirming out from under, shouting: "That's enough! Hold it!"

"What's matter, Noles? Who's that coming out from under down there?"

"That's me and old Noles!" says Noles coming up nearly unrecognizable from underneath the truck. "Goddamn, I have a big time in the Army, though!"

"All right," says the motor sergeant, "now we'll get that universal on, turn the battery around and she'll be ready to roll in the morning." And he doesn't even bother to say who will do what because he knows some of the group standing around to guy Noles will take their turn now. They are not even regular mechanics; they are drivers and gun corporals who have stayed up till midnight just to watch the job go through and be around people they like.

Must get this to the mail clerk who will take it 60 miles to battalion headquarters this afternoon.

Tell Joan I am in a home with a little girl who looks like her.

                                        LOS ANGELES, SEPT. 2, 1944

I wonder where you are now, this Saturday night. I wonder if you're tired, hot, wet, or in danger, or laughing and sneezing. I would to heaven I could reach and touch you suddenly. What is there in the touch? I think I would surrender my eyes and my speech before my touch. How lonely the world would be without it. I should not be able to feel your body, your warmth and your heart beating, strangely apart from mine, yet nearer than mortals can ever be; and my children—I should be a sorry woman if I could not hold them and carry them and tickle them and rock them to sleep. Have you ever thought about touch? We can touch *life*. When I reach my hand to yours, in that most lovely gesture of lovers and friends, I am touching your life, your very being, your breath!

How incredible that we will never spend September, 1944, together! The lost, lost days of our life which I can rationalize but never understand. I could spend a hundred years of youth with you.

Why do I insist on having so much and such perfection? I can remember as a child saying: "I shall have a perfect marriage." And people laughed or smiled or pitied me and I still thought: "Life can be perfect, I must make mine so." So you see, you came and told me the same thing and together we have made a love and marriage that is perfect. Now we must spend a great part of it in different lands. Am I reconciled? No. I say only: "The time will come when our marriage will be a living day-to-day thing, always perfect, always young, with no goodbyes and no regrets."

FRANCE [MAYET], SEPT. 4, 1944

I'm writing on a little table by the fireplace in my room. There is a vase containing a mixed bouquet of lavender and white flowers resembling zinnias, under my nose. The maid has placed a fresh candle by my bed. The washstand has been tidied and re-equipped with water in the pitcher. Downstairs someone is playing the piano. The village children often sing sweetly these summer evenings: "Gentille Alouette" and others. Sunday as I went to breakfast I heard them in the church across the square, faint and sweet as though contained far down in the stone somewhere.

Yes, I admit French women are highly feminine. But they do not interest me. And all the manly French men must be prisoners in Germany because I see none, or almost none. I remember receiving the same impression in 1937 in Paris and elsewhere. After listening to a group of Frenchmen chatter in a barnyard over whether there are German stragglers hiding in a nearby wood, my men throw up their hands in disgust, declaring: "I never will believe a Frenchman! They talk too much!"

Am about to dine on C-rations. A complete meal for one person is contained in two small cans. One holds the "main course"—stew, hash, or meat and beans; the other large crackers called C-ration biscuits, plus such items as candy, sugar, and powdered fruit juice or coffee. But we eat it with a fresh tomato and red wine and it goes down not badly!

Tonight my friend the garage keeper has invited me for a drink after the cinema. We are showing two runnings of Bing Crosby in *Going My Way*, at 3:30 and at 6:30—for everybody, soldiers and girls, fathers and mothers, the whole town.

LOS ANGELES, SEPT. 4, 1944

In this same mail I'm sending off your story in *Collier's*. I think it *is* a good story—a competent one if not inspired. Tell me how it strikes you.

Yes, darling, the English holly came through in fine and prickly shape and Joan tried to grab it as I opened the letter. She always says: "Letter from Daddy!" when she sees me open an envelope. Of course, she cannot possibly remember you at 22 months, not having seen you for nearly 7, but it does help me to have her say "Daddy" and she knows your picture on my desk and when I cut her hair today she said: "Send curls to Daddy."

Katherine is also most satisfactory. Tell me you have a feeling for her—by the time you see her she will be Joan's age I suppose. I get quite a terror in my soul for all the long time ahead without you, and the children need you so much! I guess in some mysterious way the months *will* pass and the big day of your return arrive. Perhaps you are in the fight now. I wonder how, which, where! I don't often feel cut off, darling, but I sometimes am ghastly lonely.

Three weeks from today we will have been married four years. Do you remember eating tomato soup in Santa Rosa at midnight—that first night as we looked for a place to sleep after our wedding? How strange I felt! Walking through a dream and suddenly stumbling on tomato soup. It tasted *so* good!

FRANCE [MAYET], SEPT. 7, 1944

Tonight I dine with the Chief of Police on a special leg of "mouton." The chief is a pretty good old boy, head of the F.F.I.[28] hereabouts and has worked with us a time or two. His son is in

28. French Forces of the Interior, the underground or guerrilla fighters against German occupation, also known as "the resistance."

an American hospital nearby, minus an arm because he was mistaken for a German by some of our people—one of those mishaps incident to war. Daily we see the French streaming back into their liberated country, pushing carts, wheelbarrows, in trucks (funny old-fashioned high ones), low sleek Renault cars, on bicycles single and double, on horses and donkeys.

Cities like Le Mans, however, seem never to have deviated much from normal. Streets are crowded, shop windows appear as full as ever of lingerie, fine chinaware, even books. Food is plentiful.

Regions where our victory was swift display little hostility to Americans but back in Normandy, around places like St. Lô where destruction was heavy, some people reasoned: "When the Germans were here they did not trouble us greatly; at least they left us our homes. Now the Americans have left nothing."

De Gaulle recently visited St. Lô and explained why the destruction was necessary. His photograph is everywhere, on doors of town halls, in posters, "AVIS!" etc. etc., and bears the inscription: "President of the Provisional Government of the Republic of France."

These days are busy ones as I am company commander while K. is in the hospital with a minor burn. Do you have enough money? Enough help in the house? Have you been to the dentist? Are we able to meet the payments on the loan?

LOS ANGELES, FRIDAY, SEPTEMBER 8, 1944

The air changed last night at 9:30 precisely and today I can't decide if I am in Florence and just 17 or the Jane of 1940—about to get married—or Jane of the war years—or Jane of 1950! But the air has a promise in it and the heart rises to meet hope—no matter how many cruel facts such as, "Pop has been killed, Bob is in danger," try to blot it out.

This universal renewal is such a staggering and beautiful truth. You have found it in France—where the grass comes up again before the battle is far away, and the apples are ripening as usual. Then one sees how temporary the upheavals of even a great war are. The earth is willing to give us another chance at beauty, at peace, at fresh growth and young apples. We are offered all these and do we kneel down and give thanks?

Today I am sure that if you were here I'd talk to you clearly about our future, about what the years will do to us and for us. What life we will choose and how to carry it through so that the utmost drop of good and beauty is made of every day. The issues of living and dying and bringing forth children seem clearly defined in my mind. And when I am seeing clearly, I am seeing the good. That is why it has always seemed apparent to me that good and beauty are one and they surpass evil and sorrow by light years. When I'm muddled and depressed I see the ugly side of life—but it is never as powerful or as real to me as the other. This has been my experience ever since I can remember, even when people and events seemed to conspire to prove me wrong.

Perhaps this letter is too full of generalizations. But maybe— reading it on a bit of foreign soil—you will know what I am driving at.

The one thing I am never cloudy or muddled about is my love for you.

FRANCE [SENS], SEPT. 9, 1944

I'm writing in a pup tent in a green wood,[29] my back propped against my pack that contains my clothes: one set of O.D.'s,[30] one set of officer's greens, one officer's blouse, two pair shoes, underclothes, socks and a complete set of special O.D.'s impregnated against gas and consequently nearly as stiff and impermeable as cardboard. Carrying such stuff plus gas masks is a pest. But 'twould be a pity not to have it should the need arise.

We listen to the news: the British in Holland, our troops approaching Germany. Can the end be far away? Yet I hardly dare think about the end. What will the return to you be like? "Hello, how are you?" "Hello, how are *you?*"

I feel as if I'd been asleep two years. I wonder, in the end, what the Army will have given you and me and we the Army. Stories filter back from the front line . . . The Americans in combat become fighting fools with utter disregard . . . The Germans are afraid. They dread close combat with us . . . German officers do not lead their patrols as ours do. And so on.

We see truckloads of stunned prisoners who look as though

---

29. Sixty-five miles east of Paris.
30. The Army's olive-drab or brown wool uniform.

they'd been hit on the head by a mallet and stood up like logs in the trucks.

By contrast, a truckload of American nurses in steel helmets passed us yesterday on the road and they all waved and smiled. There are no women like American women. The British may have decency (some of them), the French *great* femininity, but . . . !

Every evening from 9:15 to 9:30 we listen to "Axis Sally." Her propaganda program from Germany is a favorite because she plays the best jazz recordings by Guy Lombardo and Duke Ellington in between her propaganda blurbs which are very absurd. One evening she tells us there is no food at home, that people are starving and lining their shoes with newspapers. Next evening she has all America going to wild parties at the Waldorf and disregarding the war and us poor forgotten boys overseas. She calls us "Roosevelt's cannon-fodder" and suggests we wake up to the fact we've been dragged unnecessarily into what is purely a European war. She is always honey tongued, the black-hearted witch, without trace of accent. As for her having any serious effect—none whatsoever.[31]

Following Axis Sally comes news from the American Broadcasting Station in Europe. Now the news is so very good there is always a group of us standing in the dark around the armored car containing the radio.

LOS ANGELES, SUNDAY, SEPT. 10, 1944

I've decided that you will feed my children on Sundays and holidays! I can imagine nothing more fun to watch than Papa trying his hand! This is brought on because I've just struggled through Joan's lunch and feel myself a failure as a mother. Joan will probably fade away as she ate only one pear and a cup of milk. I must be an idiot but I simply have NOT been able to face the idea of starving her, which I KNOW is the only way to break them of these annoying habits such as not chewing. The doctor, too, tells me it's the way.

Every once in a while you say that earthly bliss is not allowed and hence you are willing to bide your time until the war is over and we can be together. I don't agree that earthly bliss is out of

---

31. Axis Sally was an American, Mildred Elizabeth Gillars, who was teaching English in Berlin when the war broke out and soon defected.

the question. I expect to have a good deal of it! I consider bliss to be what I feel for you and being loved by you is certainly the same thing. I'm quite prepared to face the many trials we have ahead of us, such as the raising of children, being too poor for comfort at times no doubt, illness and other worries. We will have our share of these things which seem to make up almost every life, of course. But I consider none of them terrible. The only thing I am quite positive would make me miserable and really unhappy is if anything should happen to our love for each other. As long as we can stand together in perfect harmony, I dread nothing and feel equal to everything. That is what I call earthly bliss.

Judy leaves tomorrow for Miss Branson's and there is the attendant gloom upon her. Being a senior is such serious business! I love you and miss you always. Tell me when you will be back!

FRANCE [SENS], SEPT. 11, 1944

Up ahead on the Moselle, General Patton is forging two bridge-heads in torrential rain. They say the German soldiers pray for rain and curse the sunlight that brings out our planes.

Here the rain has stopped. Under a sky washed to a clear bright blue your letters 47 through 50 fill my heart with love and longing.

No, sweetheart, I have no need of other women and it's no great self-denial that keeps me true to you. It is the fact of our love. Also, enormously strong in me is the sense of wrongness involved in sexual relation with a person who is not one's mate for life. I honestly believe that had we not married and I lived all my life a bachelor, I never in my right mind would have inter-course with a woman I did not truly love to the exclusion of any other.

Interval—while a gun commander, buck sgt., deposits mail in the caliber .30 ammunition box we've painted O.D.-green and marked U.S. MAIL and keep in my tent. First thing after break-fast I censor mail. And I'll be busy tomorrow after tonight's big mail call.[32]

32. Delivery.

Lieutenant General George S. Patton, Jr., with his top subordinates and his white bull terrier "Willie." (U.S. Army)

LOS ANGELES, SEPT. 16, 1944

You would have laughed at your little family this afternoon. The day started off in a rush as I wanted to go and register to vote in Westwood. Hence, whisked through the morning routine and bounced both children into their beds for rests after their lunches. Then Mum and I dashed out and lunched at Bullock's Wilshire and I ate enormously and enjoyed being away from home immensely. Then to Republican headquarters to register. That was rather impressive and fun. Very nice people doing the job and nice ones coming in. Everyone is very excited about Dewey's[33] speech last night in reply to Roosevelt's really vile, mean one of a few days ago. I know you're still pro-Roosevelt, despite his third-term antics, but that didn't bother me at all![34] Many people believe Dewey stands a far better chance than ever. Earl Warren being on the ticket with him may help too. I'm not sending you the speeches because I think your father surely must be.

To go back—Mum and I came home and everything immediately went wrong with the afternoon in the most amazing way! And it's now only 4 P.M. so there is a good deal of time left—which is rather exciting, just to see *what* turns up. Anyway, Joan got up from her rest, came outside and promptly fell. She barely broke the skin on a knee so I took her upstairs and put iodine on it. She began to cry and begged me: "Wipe it off!" I explained as calmly as possible that the stain would come off in tomorrow's bath. But the wails continued!

She is so super-sensitive and nervous! We shall have to concentrate on a calm atmosphere for her. Then Katherine began crying because Joan was! I just laughed—the situation was really comical. They both looked so pathetic and I thought of all the years ahead with just such occasions!

Tomorrow, Sunday, a few people to lunch—a couple called Fuller, very nice indeed. He's a test pilot at Douglas and has won the Bendix Trophy twice.[35] She is a cripple (paralysis) but can fly her own plane. She is very beautiful—both about 40 and very devoted. I love to feel the deep love between man and wife—it's as obvious as bright sunlight.

FRANCE [SENS], SEPT. 17, 1944

Paris is quite unchanged, little damage, little sign of hardship, shop windows full of goods, people and vehicles crowding streets, liquor stores booming, many artistic posters proclaiming "LIBER-

33. Thomas E. Dewey, Republican candidate for president.
34. F.D.R.'s running for an unprecedented third term and now a fourth had turned many former supporters against him.
35. Frank Fuller, flying a Seversky SEV-S2 (P-35), won the famous Bendix Trophy Race for fastest aircraft in 1937 and 1939.

ATION!"—showing the figure of a woman flinging her arms upward against the dawn.[36] These overlie countless Vichy post-ers[37] depicting a man's muscular bare back and arms pushing against a wall holding Bolshevism out of Europe. Regardless of everything, I must confess that French women—despite five years of war—are the best dressed and best looking I've seen.

At a "perfumery" I bought a bottle of Chanel's Russia Leather. It cost 100 francs, about two dollars. You should receive it in due course if it doesn't break en route. As for us, we too shall be traveling soon.

Later:

An extra leaf (steel) inserted in the rear springs of our jeeps enables us to carry a vastly greater load. For example last night we started at 10 P.M. and traveled twelve hours with a load on "Daddy" estimated at 1300 lbs.—500 is theoretical capacity. We have seen new country—the Marne, Argonne Forest, Verdun— Verdun on a gray day that was like calamity itself and I recalled what these hills witnessed in the last war.[38]

Autumn is here. You see it in the leaves beginning to turn, in the pallor of the sunlight, and more frequent rain such as is falling now, not violently but very persistently. This over the battlegrounds of the last war gives you a picture like a dismal dream.

I have walked on the old battlements of Verdun. You can trace the zigzag outline of the trenches and the slightly deeper indentations where machine guns were set up. I've also followed subterranean passages through fortress walls that go interminably; and then you realize how long these poor, pathetic, burrowing people have been menaced by war! Now even their great fortress is rotting away, stinking of offal and corruption and the moist decay of earth herself. I long for sunlight.

Did I describe the woman who'd been a resistance leader in the little town just north of Tours?[39] My friend, the chief of police, took me to meet her one night. She was about 40 and lived in a small house up a side street with her old mother and

---

36. Paris was liberated August 24.
37. Of the overthrown pro-German Vichy government.
38. Approximately a million men, French and German, died during the struggle for Verdun, 1915–1917.
39. Mayet.

7-year-old son. A fire of faggots was burning as we entered and a copper kettle over it. Candles helped light the room.

She led us to a small dining room adjacent where a table was spread with her best lace cloth and there was a Singer sewing machine. First we were treated to a glass of brandy. Then we saw the parachutes—black, blue, green—dropped with weapons from Allied planes at a secret rendezvous in the woods where the F.F.I. was waiting. And they were waiting because of this woman's secret two-way radio which for two years talked to London and the planes at night. She even told me the code names—girls' names—Suzanne, Nicole, Jeanne—of those stations she talked to. She was brave, Janie. All day she worked in the fields and all night she worked for the liberation of France. Her house was the rendezvous for the resistance. And when time came for the men to emerge and join the fight for liberation openly, she sewed the Cross of Lorraine on their arm-bands.

Over a delicious peach tart and red wine we talked of democracy. She was thin, beautiful—angular face, lovely bright dark eyes and hair. Her husband is a prisoner in Germany. She reminded me of what I imagine Huguenot women were: more like an English woman than a French, because her character came before her femininity. Something rare in French women. Her young son slipped shyly into the room to look at the American. When she took him against her side with one arm, looked down and smiled, she had exactly the expression of Leonardo's *Madonna of the Rocks*, exactly. I think nothing lovelier exists.

I was going to return and get her entire story. But next morning we moved out.

317 BURLINGAME AVE., SEPT. 24, 1944

No letter for four days. I do rather worry about you being in the big battles near the Rhine now. How can anyone *not* worry? And the dreadful fact of the length of time it takes to notify the families when anything does happen, either captured or wounded or dead, is quite appalling. Often a month. Well, I can only silently pray and suppose that you are all right.

My confidence in that is very strong, but I suppose everyone thinks that their loved one will get back. Goodbye.

FRANCE [VERDUN], 27 SEPT. '44

Evoy is from Detroit. Both his father and grandfather were killed, he says, in labor disorders. He has been a labor organizer since he was 15, helped organize the C.I.O. at the Ford plant and elsewhere. He is warm, roly-poly, bright-eyed Irish and talks of a post-war organization of veterans of World War II similar to the American Legion but separate from it. Of course such an organization, 8 to 10 million strong, could rule the country.

Evoy was a liaison man at Ford—that is, he worked as intermediary between union and company. He tells of the great difficulty educating workers to the truth of employees' and employers' problems, tells of unscrupulous union men and employers, tells of sitting at table with old Henry Ford ("Hank"). You don't work at Ford you work at "Hank's." Typical conversation on a streetcar: "Where d'ya work?" "Hank's." "Same here!" "What at?" "Pressed steel." "How much you get?" "Dollar ten." "Dollar ten? I'm making 96 cents. My steward must be slipping!"

The main thing about Evoy is his honesty, his willingness to think and see both sides, and his faith in a youth that will take responsibility and make America a better place.

Spent this morning talking with Connell about Texas. My thoughts went something like this: after the war and a quiet period in Santa Barbara we strike out, you and I, into the Southwest and look around New Mexico and West Texas, and somewhere in the Big Bend country south of Marfa we find a small place, maybe twenty acres, maybe a hundred. Either it has a house and orchard or we build one and plant one. We buy 15 head of sheep and goats, 20 head of cattle, 3 horses. We develop 2 milk cows and plant a vegetable garden, dig out a spring and pipe water. We find a good man to help us, maybe one of the excellent Tennessee boys from my old platoon who can do anything with his hands and is loyal enough to trust with your whole life.

We are near a small town where there is a school and community life. We participate in this life and our children do likewise. We help our neighbors and they us. We work hard but the place is not so big that, after being established, it takes all our time and lots of money. It does not yield much ready cash but provides much of our food. There is time for reading and writing.

I can hire out my labor to neighbors whether or not cash is

necessary. We shall have simple comfort: a refrigerator, both a gas (butane) and a wood-burning stove, our gramophone and radio, a telephone, electricity, washing machine.

Our establishment is never so large it can't easily be closed or disposed of or left in responsible hands, while you and I travel abroad or live in the Middle West to accumulate background for stories, or whatever, while the children are away at school or with grandparents. What sayest thou to this?

Do you want such a home? Can you bring up children in such an environment? Will the care and labor of a household be too great? We have a man and wife to help us, the man in the field, the woman in the house?

That keeps the stage clear of all but you and me, Joan, Katherine, John and Roger, doesn't it? I rather like it—whether it's near Marfa or Lampasas.

LOS ANGELES, SUNDAY, OCTOBER 10, 1944
Having just paid my bills for this month, I shall be glad when you take care of our business affairs—*dear*!

I live in terror of forgetting the payment on the house. My *only* idea about finance is: don't spend more than you have in the bank. This, no doubt, *is* sound, but it's rather vague. I *do* hope we shall never be in debt. That is one of my horrors. Anyway, now the bills for this month are paid and all our dues, I feel very happy. When your check comes we will have $450 in our checking account. I want to have enough to pay for the expenses of living in our house in S.B.[40] for November and December.

Mum cannot decide what to do. It's not a good time to find another house, whether in Berkeley, San Francisco, or Santa Barbara. Also she does not feel emotionally up to the effort of shutting up this one and leaving—on the other hand she knows she will have to eventually. I think she'll feel readier when she's been away in S.B. for November and December. Naturally I'll come back here with her as long as she keeps this house and you are gone. We have talked it over and over.

She dreads leaving here because she will have to do away with Pop's clothes! Do you know how very precious the clothes are which were worn by the body one has loved? I know that I

40. Santa Barbara.

derived immense comfort from wearing your dressing gown when you went away to the Army that first March. I understand what Mum is going through now. I also try and think what I should do if you were killed. Could anyone pry me out of 34 East Padre for a long long time? No. So I'm trying not to rush Mum. I hope it will all adjust itself in time. The war has given us a horror of changes because they come so fast and there are so few stabilities to cling to.

I do so wish you could see Katherine. Nothing troubles her. She just watches with keen interest and grows bigger and better daily. For the most part she is incredibly fun. She begs to be read aloud to *all* day. Our main session takes place at night before bed. If it's chilly we have a fire in the living room and bring Katherine down. Katherine can't sit up alone yet but reclines propped on pillows, looking like a general. They both are really divine. I cannot possibly tell you what they mean to me, and I do not know how Mum would have come through Pop's death without them.

The news today is that MacArthur is nearing the Philippines again and Patton is moving up toward Metz through mud and rain and cold and the old trenches of another war! How gruesome that whole picture is! I worry about you. But on the other hand, I do not want you here in a safe job until the big victory is won. We have gone all through this before but I must say, I have moments of lying awake after being up at 4 A.M. with Joan, as I was last night, and just wondering if you are suffering or in a big tank battle or have lost any of your men, etc.

For the most part I plod along at my old routine and am doing not too badly. Eight months ago today you left me on that rainy February night! I thought I'd see you in two months, oh foolish lassie! When we have been apart a year I shall feel we have weathered every storm and nothing can ever hurt our love, though I know it now. I love you until death us do part, and 'way beyond that too!

FRANCE [VERDUN], 11 OCT. 1944

We sit through abominable weather, trying to content ourselves with inaction. Today we had a court martial and, as in so many back in the States, I was defense counsel—this time for a big, dark, Italian boy who left his sentry post to get an overcoat. Well, the night was growing cold and he was chilly. We are not in a position of danger but his crime is punishable by death. A "special court martial" within a tactical unit like ours can't render a sentence of death. But because of a technicality this case couldn't be taken before a "general court," and so we tried it and I'm afraid the boy will spend some time confined at hard labor.

At the trial my thoughts went back over thirty months I've participated in similar trials—and to once when I was "summary court martial," a court composed of one officer, and I recalled sentencing a fellow for being A.W.O.L. during a bitter freezing week of Tennessee maneuvers when the men suffered—sentencing him to a month's restriction to the area and loss of all but a few dollars pay, and then walking past a campfire the next Saturday night and having him give me a bottle of beer from the case he bought with the few dollars I'd left him!

Well, the time has crept around to early morning. The fire is out in the stove. Radovich is sound asleep, dark curls and a stretch of bare leg visible from among a scroll of blankets, and I hear the boys coming off guard and going to their tents to chop wood and stoke the fire, cook a few French fries with onions and coffee before turning in to sleep all morning. Tomorrow we leave for a new destination.

LOS ANGELES, OCT. 12, 1944

I become absolutely ecstatic just thinking what you say about our life after the war and all the stories you are going to write and our pioneering home in the Southwest. I am sure that very few of our friends and relatives will ever want to visit us in Texas—but perhaps those we *really* care about will. Oh—but how I ache to get started. It's rather sickening to think I'll be 30 before we get into that life. But I'm just as eager for a year or more, depending on your writing at 34 E. Padre. That is a sweet home for a while, and I do want a quiet and constructive existence there with you and our children. What do you say about a baby while there? I hate being nauseated at once but I do feel we should make the most of that time near good doctors and get our 3rd infant into the world. And also, I do want all our babies while I'm young. I'd hoped to have them all (4) here by the time I was 30, but with the war on it looks most unlikely. Please tell Patton you need to get back and to kindly push on toward Metz at breakneck pace. If only the weather were better! Last night I finished your notes. Now we have them in the file—from November 1939 to May 1944! It's quite a bunch. And now I am starting on those marked "overseas." I feel so pleased to have got things in order. I will take it all up to our study in S.B. I hope I can always type your notes. Oh, what busy days ahead! What fun too! Perhaps you will take me out to dinner once a month. *If* I behave?

When Germany is beaten, perhaps you'll get back here for a leave before starting off to Japan! I doubt whether I could let you go again—so perhaps you'd better not come back until it's for good. Think that over.

Goodbye for another day.

———————

The 825th T. D. Battalion is being divided. Headquarters company and two gun companies move fifty miles northwest to Luxembourg city in the Duchy of Luxembourg, where they'll act as security for General Omar N. Bradley's U.S. 12th Army Group Headquarters. The rest of us scatter over nearly 200 miles of Western Front—from Spa in Belgium, headquarters of 1st Army, to Nancy in France, headquarters of 3rd Army, down toward Switzerland. Our job is to guard a secret F.M. radio network connecting both armies with Bradley's command center in Luxembourg.

With half my platoon I reach Nancy and on a hilltop overlooking the city from the south we set up tents and post sentinels near a transmitter-tower which beams messages to the highest point of the old Verdun battleground of World War I. There Sergeant Helms and the rest of my platoon guard a similar tower which relays the messages to Luxembourg. Before airing, transmissions go into a scrambling machine which makes them unintelligible until unscrambled by a similar machine on reception. Thus Patton, or Hodges of 1st Army, and later Simpson of the 9th in Holland, can talk to Bradley or Eisenhower in Luxembourg as if talking on the phone and feel confident no one is eavesdropping. For further safeguard the broadcasts are carried by the newly invented F.M. directional beam which can be intercepted only by a receiver on the same axis as the beam.

I still hope to see Patton and get into action with his now famous 3rd Army. His dash through France nearly to the German border, often up front with his leading tanks, has made him a popular hero. I'm not really a super patriot itching for glory or to get shot at or even killed. But I continue to feel the horror and fascination for war that I believe most people share with me, plus a conviction this one must be got on with. For the moment, however, there isn't much to see or do beyond coping with rain and mud and seemingly endless inaction.

Censorship regulations continue to bedevil my letters to Jane. With foresight we might have devised a code. As it is I try to be as circumspect yet informative as possible on topics calculated not to rouse her anxiety, while she keeps trying to put the best possible face on things at home, where anxiety is like a heavy weight in the back of the mind day or night.

———————

LOS ANGELES, OCTOBER 19, 1944

We were all pretty shaken by Wendell Willkie's death. Did you read his *One World*? I thought it very fine. He had the fire and imagination Dewey lacks. I'm voting for Dewey of course, but I did think Willkie a great American and we all feel a big national as well as personal loss.

Mum and I made up Christmas packages to you and John today. We bought mostly eats, I fear, but it's hard to know what you need or want. I'm sending separately the 2 cartons of Chesterfields and 1 each of Camels and Lucky Strikes you requested for the men.

Here, separately too, is my love, all of it, very bright and clear and enduring forever. Your children are my delight but you are my very joy and life. Before them and after them, you and I stand alone as man and wife. Something like that can never be duplicated. I hope you will always like me and desire me. I should give a very great deal to have you in the bed beside me tonight. I suppose, on second thought, that you'd start popping on and off the light taking notes and giving me no peace whatever! I wonder why I ever married a writer. Heaven knows I always swore I wouldn't. Well, goodnight. Nearly half of October has gone. . . . Hurray!!

FRANCE [NANCY], OCT. 21, 1944

Your No. 84 came today with the good word Joan has decided to eat. Yes, I can imagine the trials of child rearing. You see, I have 51 children here—or in the platoon, I should say, because only half are with me. We left our old camp in the city of Verdun (actually at the old citadel there) at 9 a.m. in a raw wind and rain and followed the Meuse River eastward, the landscape indescribably bleak with this premature winter, as if summer had been given no chance and died abortively. Leaves have been torn from the apple trees before the fruit has fallen. The lowlands are flooded. The villages have that sickly pallor of age with not enough light. The ubiquitous manure piles in front yards stink and are leached out by the rain, discoloring the gutters.

But finally we came to our new area in a pine grove on a hill overlooking a cathedral city. Those spires are all that is left to me of the promise that was France. See them from a distance, above the tiled roofs, and your heart leaps with conviction that here beauty has aged well—here you will find mellowed civilization, culture, courtesy. What do you actually find? A hollow shell of defeat and despair, mostly.

As I write a great anti-aircraft fireworks is in progress, a veritable 4th of July. "Heinie" is overhead and the red streams of tracer shells are trying to burn him out of some scudding clouds the wind is driving into Germany. It is a south wind and as at home it brings rain. We are about 15 miles from the front. Great flashes periodically light the horizon. Minutes later you hear the guttural: boom! I'm almost embarrassed to say I'm again in a comfortable tent with stove and electric light. Sgts. Pate and Henderson, rawboned boys from Tennessee, are beside me writing their girls. Pate asks me: "How can you tell she's the right one to marry?" My answer: "*You* don't tell. Something tells you!" Profound?

Great news from the Philippines today. Can't you picture MacArthur as he waded ashore, making good his vow to return?[41]

The geese came over last night. I've not heard them since Rio Vista days—or nights, rather, because though they passed down the Sacramento Valley by day, it was at night we were most aware of them, as their cries fell out of the dark sky, remember?

---

41. MacArthur's forces landed on the island of Leyte, October 20.

These are en route from Sweden and Germany to the warm
Spanish lakes and the marshes of Algiers or tropical mid-Africa.
Some of my boys were on guard and could almost have knocked
down the leaders with a stick as they barely cleared the crest of
this hill which was hidden in mist.

Now let me tell you a few matters submitted for my decision
today: (1) whether the guard is to be four three-hour shifts, or
three four-hour shifts; (2) whether the ammunition trailer is to
be unloaded here or there; (3) whether the 10-in-1 rations are to
be issued by the box to squads or opened in the kitchen and
served from there; (4) whether we should use gas cans for water
cans, because we are short of water cans; (5) whether Pounds
goes with Rush for water, or somebody else drives Pounds so Rush
can stay and work on his half-track with Coville; (6) and so on
ad infinitum. Finally: two of my boys have syphilis and I must see
they get to the hospital tomorrow.

I've lost track of Monsman who was burned in England.
Lindstrom, whose letter I sent you, will probably not come back:
he has an enlarged liver and gall bladder. Anderson, my truck
driver, was killed in an auto accident near Mayet; and now
Sgt. Thompson of the 4th gun squad is hospitalized with kidney
trouble; while Jambard, our big French-Canadian, has an infection from decayed wisdom teeth.

In addition to all this I'm driving toward Verdun tomorrow
to check on Sergeant Helms and his half of the platoon, and so
goes each day—full of all 52 of our lives whether we're together
or not.

LOS ANGELES, SUNDAY 9 P.M., OCTOBER 29, 1944

Mum's leg is very bad. I am persuading her to get into a hospital
which is the only place Eikenberry can make all the tests necessary
and find out the cause of this sciatica. So we are postponing the
Santa Barbara trip. I shall stay here and telephone her twice a
day and see her in the hospital twice a week. When she is better
we'll go to S.B. It's bad to upset plans but I MUST get Mum well
before we undertake any move.

I suppose this will worry you but I simply had to tell you why
we are not going up as planned.

This is one of those days when things look dark but tomorrow
will be better. The thought of you makes me happy, always.

FRANCE [NANCY], 12 NOV., 1944

Spent two days in Luxembourg[42] since last writing—an odd city and country, fairly well riddled with collaborationists yet prosperous and solid, the people more like Dutch or Germans than French.

On my way I visited Helms and his men. They're camped at the highest point of the old Verdun battlefield where they occupy a concrete bunker dating from World War I days. The battlefield around them is so pockmarked by shell craters and criss-crossed by old trenches it looks like an abandoned quarry extending for miles across ravines and hillocks, where the earth has been devastated but green undergrowth and even some small trees are beginning to reappear at last after twenty-five years. I saw unexploded shells stacked like cordwood and unexploded hand grenades lying in piles, and cemeteries that covered acres, and pathetically lonely white crosses scattered here and there through the undergrowth to mark the spot where some beloved son or husband supposedly died. It was horrible, tragic, oppressive. Verdun was the Stalingrad of World War I, if you remember. "They shall not pass!" was the French war cry. They never did. The French never lost that crucial high ground where my boys are billeted. From it they poured murderous fire on the Germans below, inflicting nearly countless casualties and suffering similarly themselves. Incredible acts of heroism and foolhardiness were performed by both sides. But from Souville—it's called Souville Ridge—the German tide receded. An aura of horror, like an odor of death, hangs about the place. Helms and the boys tell me it's haunted.

The night I was there, a low-flying enemy plane circled and dropped two bright-red flares, about a mile from us. Then a parachute from which something was suspended—a man? a weapons container? explosives?—descended into the haunted wasteland of the battlefield. An attempt at sabotage? Aid to the French collaborateurs? We spent a sleepless night but all we found next day was a red parachute.

Big inspection yesterday, by big colonel, who said my set-up here is the best he's seen, which only confirms my judgment and pleases me too, because colonels are hard to please. More later.

---

42. At battalion headquarters.

Woke this morning to a world in white, a full inch of snow. Can hardly be comfortable thinking of the fellows up ahead fighting in this. It's almost as if God added this to what we must accomplish before we emerge into the springtime of peace. You describe our children playing before the guests in the living room and how proud you were of their straight limbs and clear happy eyes. I believe the blood is good. Shall we not continue it with other examples? Seventeen girls and a boy? How long will it take you to make a boy, Janie?

Rumble in the east night and day. Americans moving forward, night and day through rain, snow, mud. It is appalling, Janie, and a heroic, heroic thing.[43] Does anyone at home realize what's happening here? The abyss between what *is*, and what's printed or said about it, looms like the Grand Canyon.

Don't have nightmares of us parted in China, please. Your dream life is so strange, my sweet, so abnormal compared with your great waking normality, solid as the earth itself, which must tell you I never shall leave you till I die and then my soul flies to yours in some sweet place.

Until the war is over, I must say as my boys do in their letters that I'm obliged to read but seldom censor: "Love, Sugar! Sleep good!"

LOS ANGELES, SUNDAY, NOV. 19, 1944

I love you, I love you, I love you! That sums up what I feel today and every day. By now you must be tired of hearing it.

Last night we had quite a banquet with the Aldingtons and ancient Gilbert Emery and the young (40) pansy who has lived with him for years. It was a good evening of talk and I lay awake long after they'd gone (at 12:00) thinking about the intellectuals. Why are they so often queer? Either sexually or emotionally or in some other way, not able to fit into the pattern of ordinary life? I was fascinated by Richard Aldington's hands. The hands of a woman, and a small woman at that. But I believe everything he has done in his life he has done with manly honesty, at least what he thought was right.

I do like him immensely. He is very well versed in all subjects, very sensitive, very aware. His only give-away is his

---

43. The 3rd Army was moving toward the Rhine.

immense despair with the world and humanity. He simply has no hope. I think that shows a weakness. When they arrived last night, he burst into the room and the first thing he said was to me: "Where is your husband?" I explained where I imagined you were. He was very excited, very depressed, had been listening to the radio news, bitter fighting all along the western front. I know how hard a pill it is for him to swallow, having been through the four hard years there himself in the first war.

At dinner Gilbert Emery (75), actor and writer of plays and world traveller, turned to me and said: "I've missed your husband's stories in the *Atlantic*." I was very proud and pleased that he remembered them, as did his young pal, who was on my other side.

During the evening Gilbert regaled us with anecdotes of life in the old days, the old days that so many people hanker after and to me seem very well gone! The days of idle young men flitting about the country, kept by this woman or that man, the endless "teas," the comfort, the luxury for the few while others starved. The tales of his meeting Bernhardt when he was 19, and seeing the initials of Eleanora Duse carved on the windowpane of a cottage near Lake Como where she'd been on her honeymoon! And his continual use of the descriptive phrase about a woman: "An enchanting creature!"

He talks with savor and just the right word and expression, and makes it all seem frightfully important. He speaks of celebrities by their first names, and like so many he confuses celebrities with great people. What a mistake. And he pooh-poohed them, one and all, and told stories to make them out fools, but in his heart he was so very proud and pleased to have supped and "teaed" with them!

And yet, he knows history and languages and music and foreign lands and good poetry and good prose. I've met quite a few intellectuals like him. Why are they so often homosexuals? Is it a result of the last war? Will there be another lot of such young men after this one? (By the way, when they're young, this type always looks like a Greek God.)

Oh heavens! Do we blame the war again for everything? I felt very depressed when the evening was over. Why couldn't these intelligent men love their wives and rear children? Why, oh why? I see again and again how rare Pop was. No one could ever call him effeminate and God knows *he* was an artist! And no wonder he was lonely! The men who knew the facts and had the knowledge he had, were so often QUEER. Better perhaps to talk to a masculine bartender than these oddities.

Well, I got quite stirred up about the whole business and discussed it with Mum after they left and she agreed almost entirely. There was a bad taste after both those men. Aldington, by contrast, is very superior and I do want you to meet him, for his knowledge and his wit. But in the last analysis, I want GOOD people as my nearest and dearest. When the glamorous tales of Paris in 1910 and London in 1890 and Florence in 1920, are done and stale and unprofitable, the Weldons and the Little Joes and the Stileses will be shining as brightly as ever and far more deeply. I hope I have not been too harsh in the above. I simply grew up amongst a lot of that atmosphere abroad, and now I KNOW how evil it is, and I see that I might have been caught in it. People who have too much leisure cultivate vices as well as intellects.

I'm outside now, in the sunny air. The children are asleep. Mum and I had lunch out here. Soon I shall bring your little girls out too and I'll read while they play.

Tell me, darling, that you *do* believe you'll be back and we'll have time, a lifetime, together in love and work and play! I do so pray for it. Please make it come true. I've waited and you have waited so long and our little children are patiently waiting for their chance at a normal life of mother and father and home! Goodbye. It's 9 months tomorrow since you left me.

FRANCE [NANCY], 22 NOV. '44

To get champagne for our thanksgiving party I went yesterday to Reims with Monsieur André Péchard, in one of our 1½ ton trucks. Péchard is a "representant" (wine agent) I became acquainted with in Verdun. He's about 55 with a young wife and they live very well in an apartment with a maid and a well-stocked cellar. Knowing the great houses in Reims, like Mumm and Piper-Heidsieck, Péchard was able to get champagne for me and incidentally himself, a most difficult task because the Allied forces are requisitioning huge quantities—as much as 750,000 bottles monthly, mainly for officers—and there's a great shortage of bottles; so if you don't present empty bottles you are unsuccessful unless you have with you an advocate such as Monsieur Péchard.

We visited eight of the great houses and his pitch went like this, after the first greeting: "Here is Monsieur the Lieutenant. He is against the tanks at Luxembourg, Metz, Nancy . . . !" (Me and my boys holding about two hundred miles!) "He needs champagne for the American Feast of Thanksgiving for his brave men. Empty bottles? Ah, no! In the lines before Metz? Against the German tanks? Ah, no! No empty bottles!" After a few minutes of this sort of thing, delivered with the intensity of machine gun fire, the proprietor breaks out with enthusiasm for Les Americains or La Victoire or something such, and rings for a bottle of champagne (brought in on a tray with three glasses) and tells his garçon to prepare Monsieur Lieutenant a couple of cases to take back to the foxholes at Metz.

So it went all day. I saw the extremely tasteful, even swanky, homes of the proprietors, their panelled offices, their warehouses and wineries, a *cave* (cellar) 100 ft. below ground where the temperature is constant through five miles of corridors and 2½ million bottles of champagne lie in the making. We watched workers turn the bottles by hand one quarter turn, as they do daily for three months; saw them agitate the bottles with flagillators or flails made of loose pieces of metal which vibrate the glass and encourage the right fermentation; saw them above ground adding sweet alcohol syrup to the finished bottles—in proportion as the final product is to be "sweet," "demisec" or "sec"; saw them installing fat corks and fancy labels and laying away the final product in wrappings of straw from the fields around the nearby village.

Finally I paid 85 francs each or $1.70 for those bottles that will cost ten or twelve dollars in the U.S.

And so the boys and I had turkey and champagne for Thanksgiving, made many speeches, exchanged much merriment and conversation, and now write letters telling it all.

I was thankful for a number of things yesterday. Beyond you and the children was a gratitude for a nation which provides its soldiers 25-lb. turkeys and cranberry sauce 5,000 miles from home.

A word to finish Reims: it is lovely and prosperous. We were blessed with a clear day and the cathedral loomed majestic and unshakable above the rooftops and the rolling plain of the Champagne.

Break—This was the first clear day in a week. I knew it was before I was out of my sleeping bag because of the bombers. The sky rings with them the moment the rain stops.

Talked with a sergeant from a weather unit this afternoon—fascinating. I'd no idea how important forecasts are. He tells me the Norwegians were best at this game before the war and their most famous forecaster was badly wanted by the Germans but escaped to England and has served our cause well. You see, it's not the word of the commanding general that sends a thousand bombers on a shuttle flight to Russia, it is the word of the weather forecaster.

Then tonight at an evacuation hospital I talked with a surgeon about abdominal operations. "Looks like hell to have your belly shot open and your intestines out and around," he remarked casually, "but these [technical name] cases will be ready for duty again in thirty or forty days."

I ask about self-inflicted wounds.[44]

"There are so many it's disgusting! A second lieutenant today had just the tip of the little finger of his left hand shot off. Said he was fooling around with his carbine in a tank. How could you fool around with a carbine in a tank?"

"What will become of him?"

"He'll go back where he came from!" says the surgeon grimly.

Downstairs in the pharmacy there is a blood bank, Janie, consisting of a hotel-size Servel refrigerator on which are two signs: "*Don't Open!* (*Brother, it's not in here!*)" and another sign: "*Don't Use British Blood!* (*small bottle*); *Use American Blood!* (*large bottle*)."

Wind—early morning wind of 2 A.M.—is pecking at my tent, a Jerry plane is overhead, the hum of its motor coming and going as it passes between the clouds. The sound is unmistakably different from the forthright roar of our engines.

34 EAST PADRE STREET, SANTA BARBARA, CALIF.,
NOV. 28, 1944

We arrived yesterday and I've been rushing ever since trying to get our new home clean and pretty and the children presentable for callers and flowers in vases and clothes unpacked! To make it

---

44. Aimed at getting yourself out of combat to hospital or discharge.

all easier I have the curse and look about 35 and feel 40. But the truth is that work in one's own premises is fun and I am continually stopping to admire our little home. At the moment I'm on the terrace in the sun typing, the children are quiet, I've polished the silver water jug and finally decided I'd just better sit now and let the last suitcase wait a while.

The addition off the kitchen is very nice and does not destroy anything! It means extra room for the icebox and laundry sink and all other things that a running house needs. The fence around the garden is wonderful and soon Joan will be out there and Katherine sitting in her pen watching it all! It's very exciting indeed. On the terrace where I am now, the vine along the side forms a solid wall of green, shutting out the street and making the whole place more attractive than ever. I am thrilled. I need not tell you what it means not to have you here, though you feel close. Let me make clear that I like everything about you except that you NEVER get my age right. I've been 25 for three years according to you and I beg to inform you I am NOW 26, and will be 27 on March 29th, and I'd rather you got that firmly in mind, and realized that I want my children all here by the time I'm 32. So hurry up and get back. I have decided that four is ample, by the way, and when you have lived with some of them for a while I think you'll agree.

Our girls act as if they've occupied this house all their short lives and seem very happy indeed. They've not complained about strange beds or toilets or dishes or ANYTHING! Katherine has been an angel, which shows how normal she is, when I think back to Joan at 8 months. Mum comes day after tomorrow and the guest room looks adorable with only one bed in it and more room for her to move around. It's such a sunny gay room! All the rooms are, for that matter. I love this place, it's compact and easy to run. IF you were here I'd be happy, completely.

I do wonder when you'll get into action. Perhaps you were moved up in the big push which began the 16th. I keep waiting and waiting and living for some strange and utterly lovely day when you'll be through with war and walk in here to me and our babies. What will you say? I shall immediately spoil you beyond all hope and do all kinds of silly things for you. And we will sit on this very terrace and laugh and eye the sun and wait for the children to wake up and take them for a walk in the garden and round the block at dusk.

It's no use. We at home have only the vaguest idea of the war. The actuality of it is lost between the fact and the writing of it and the difference between the soldier and civilian and the man in action and the man at home. This is very hard to bear. I wish I could go through it all in the flesh with you!

I promise not to have any more odd dreams. I think I do it just so you won't get too *sure* I'm a normal, dull woman. How do you like a little suspense now and then? You didn't write between Nov. 5 and 11 which is a lot of days and I'm mad!

The first money order you asked for went off to you last week. Mum sent it but I gave her the money so don't think we're broke. I naturally hate to part with money! I hear that more divorces are caused by money disagreements than anything else. So I'm waiting a further demand and then watch out!

I love you through all this welter of moving and homemaking. I always have time to talk with you in my mind and to miss you with the most awful gnawing ache. When will this HELL end? That's what it is, and I shall continue to think so.

FRANCE [NANCY], 5 DEC. 1944

No snow lately but the same old rain and grayness that is despair written in the sky. Yesterday I talked with a Frenchman my age, formerly a lieutenant of chasseurs and a prisoner in Germany, who came home because of bad health. His eyes were large and friendly, his mind lucid as he explained: "France fell because her workmen would not work. She had no longer anything to offer them but money, and there never was enough of that."

He admires German efficiency. He says every egg he saw in Germany was stamped with the swastika. Being an officer he was not permitted to work in the prison or to leave quarters and work with farmers, as they tell me some did, so he turned his mind to reading and learning German. He says that on the whole older people are not for Hitler but the young ones are fanatically.

If he is typical of the Frenchmen held prisoner I revise my opinion of French men, but I'm afraid he is not. No matter, the French are busy making wine again and all the world is waiting to drink, and I imagine therein lies the genius of France.

Have just written a letter in French for Sgt. P., to a girl he met in Mayet who is now in Paris with her family and wants him to come down for Christmas. First I had to translate her letter to him: "Bien cher Lloyd. Being anxious over what has happened to you, I must write again and assure my heart that you are well. For too long a time I have not heard from you. Please, please dear Lloyd, write to me! If only you knew the expectancy with which I wait a letter that your hands have touched . . . !" And so forth.

I replied: "With all my heart I wish I might come to you and see you and speak to you, and touch you and keep me close to you. But the difficulty is the war. The war demands all! At the moment I may not quit my post, but in the spring, after the war, who knows?"

P. was very pleased with the letter. A thousand to one he'll never see the girl again (she's eighteen) but he may be the one in a thousand of our boys who will marry and remain here, or come back after the war to some dark-eyed child he hardly glimpsed in passing during this tempestuous year.

Till tomorrow, Janie. These letters are dim reflections by the light of yours. I'm immensely glad Joan has stopped stuttering and dances to Bach by schedule.

France, September 1944. With some members of my tank-destroyer platoon and one of our half-tracks. I'm crouching, second from left.

This is a banner day indeed. A letter from you written ten days ago, the day we arrived here! It is doubly marvelous because you spoke of the same moon I saw that night, the bright clear moon.

Speaking of shops with bells which ring when you open the door always will remind me of one small florist's in Vienna. I used to go there on winter afternoons when it was bitter and gray and I was quite lonely, or puzzled about some young man who was telephoning all the time and taking me out too often, and I remember the tremendous warmth of that humid air as I entered. The breathing of the plants was on the window panes, you know, and the fragrance of the watered earth in each pot, mingled with the smell of the blossoms was almost unbearably beautiful. It made me tingle all over and LONG for a lover. I mean a lover like you, a lover and a husband in one, because it seemed to me that I never could make anyone else understand such a moment. And there was a very old lady buried at the back of the shop who would come out and talk to me and I'd wander around for ages, pretending I couldn't make up my mind what I wanted, just so I could smell the shop a bit longer. Finally I'd walk off with some little plant, because they last better than cut flowers. The air outside was full of snow or rain, but as I clutched at the wrapped up plant, I felt terribly rich and secretly happy. No one knew what a lovely touch of spring I was carrying under the brown heavy paper.

I'm so glad you feel the story about Dynamite in your *blood*. You could write about him forever, you have him under your skin and in your very heart and soul. That's why you will write as well about him as Mark Twain did about Huck. I am sure it will be easy and fun and exciting to write, and REAL.

Have you seen pictures of Lew Ayres[45] at his work now as assistant to a chaplain on Leyte? I'm astounded by the man's face. Do you recall all the furor about his conscientious objection? And his stay in a detention camp? And finally he was given what he wanted, duty as a medical corpsman? And then what he wanted more still, work with a chaplain in combat? He said from the beginning he could not kill, but he did not say that he was honest and unafraid. His story is very moving. And his face has become hard-pressed and weary, so mature and so true.

---

45. Ayres played Dr. Kildare in movies based on Frederick Faust's stories.

For heaven's sake please stop referring to our child Katherine and her mother as "great good-natured vegetables." I hate the phrase and the lumpish qualities it represents and I think you should stop it at once. We are both very emotional and often unstable and we feel very artistic and NOT like vegetables at all. Have you understood now at last? We'll develop all kinds of strange quirks if you insist on calling us "normal" once more!!

FRANCE [NANCY], 15 DEC. 1944

We are about to move. The problem is what to do with the French boys who've served us so faithfully. They want to come with us to Germany, to America, anywhere. They are: Jacques, Jean-Albert, Maurice—15, 16, 17—and tomorrow I must go down and see their families in the village. The village is a suburb of the city, and what the boys say of the city would turn your heart cold. They say that when our planes dropped arms to the F.F.I. the Germans picked them up. They say that when the girls' heads were shaved for sleeping with Germans, the good girls' heads, not the bad, were shaved. They say the people do not sing the "Marseillaise" here. They want to be gone, these boys. I read that the French coal mines will be nationalized, that France will draw closer to Russia. But nationalization of everything to hairpins will not make a new France if people do not like the "Marseillaise."

Our own great disgrace, in my opinion, is our failure to nationalize our war effort and give government absolute control over all manpower and production. I'll say more about the 3 boys later. Barring a sojourn in Asia I may see you before we're gray-haired. Must run now.

SANTA BARBARA, DEC. 15, 1944

Today began at 5:30 with Joan waking. I really think I should feel like an Amazon if I got an unbroken night and slept nine hours. At breakfast I fed Kate her pablum while Joan grown-uppedly fed herself toast and applesauce. Then I did dishes and made beds, cleaned bathroom, etc. while children played in their room. Next I phoned our respective mothers with the daily morning report—which I must say is rather different from the one you described! Then I phoned Maier's Market to tell them what I wanted sent out—everything is quite plentiful now except butter and sugar which I don't miss at all, and of course cigarettes which have never tempted me. Old Mr. Maier is a dear, absolutely trustworthy, and keeps my coupon book as he does your mother's and others, detaching what's needed before he sends my order. Then I took the children for a walk, Kay regally upright in the pram cooing and crowing, Joan walking sedately beside. Then home to hang out the laundry and look at the blessed water heater in the cellar to see if it's still leaking. I lie awake nights hoping it will fix itself, dreading lest it burst and be irreplaceable because things like water heaters are impossible to obtain. Blessedly it seems to have stopped dripping for the moment.

Then I called Ouida B. to thank her for the lunch day before yesterday. By now it was time for a peanut butter and jelly sandwich for Joan and pureed vegetables and fruit for K. and of course milk. They ate pretty well because I'd deliberately starved them since breakfast. Then we all took rests though I didn't sleep but read quietly or thought of my absent husband. Then I took the children into the garden, and while I watered the flowers and vegetables they played about. Your mother dropped by bringing an apple pie and a letter from you. Evidently you're still in *France*! And have cold *feet*!

Finally it was evening, the hardest time of all, and we three solitaries must go into the shadowy house and create our own little life there, so far from yours, so desperately missing you. And then after supper and baths for babes it's reading aloud time: Beatrix Potter's *Peter Rabbit* for Joan. Then we sang "Three Blind Mice" with Joan enunciating every word perfectly and carrying the tune with me while Kate muttered along behind us or beat out an accompaniment with a wooden block on the floor. Usually I sing when I tuck them into bed or I tell them stories, "This Little Pig went to market," etc., etc. or made-up ones, and I always must tear myself away because they never have enough. But I want them to fall asleep in all the love and security I can possibly muster without you.

After which I betake myself to my lonely bed or to my typewriter and nearly but not quite fall asleep writing my wandering husband, wondering what you are doing and thinking at this moment.

The lunch at Ouida's was a pleasant surprise, if an odd one: wives all without husbands discussing the latest date of the last letter received, the Navy wives wondering WHEN his ship will come in, etc.—and all of us discussing life without men, children problems, etc. One girl has a husband in a Japanese prison whom she hasn't seen for three years. It's good to feel part of the times, to share. I realize what so many are missing. I do resent their unconcern about the war. They are scabs, on *our* backs!

[LUXEMBOURG] 18 DEC. 1944

I'm in a warmly lighted living room by a radio tuned to a German station that is playing Bach's "Air for the G String." Cox is writing at the table with me, while Captain K. sips a highball and listens to Bach. The house is not in France, by the way, but in a large city which has many solid stone houses, quite modern some of them, with chromium topped tables like this one and a nude over mantelpiece; and at last I have time to tell you all my heart, which is only yours.

I've left Nancy where we spent 2½ months on a hilltop in a grove of pines from where I wrote you many letters and read many of yours. It is the ancient capital of Lorraine, lies on a slope where high ground descends eastward to the Meurthe River, has a population of 120,000. The war did not hit it hard, though when we first arrived the front was only 10 or 12 miles away and the town received a few shells. Also there were some air raids and big ack-ack[46] shows in which some planes came down. The three French boys who'd worked for us so faithfully wanted to leave with us and never come back. They live in the poverty-stricken suburb of Vandoeuvre that climbs the heights outside the city toward the wooded hill we occupied. The day before we left I talked to their parents. Jacques' father is in Germany, "un travailleur volontaire"—how voluntary a worker is the question. His mother is an imbecilic with undone hair, dressed in rags, who lives with five or six children ranging from a babe in arms up to Jacques, in a filthy stinking room up some stairs (through some back yards and corridors first). She said she would not let Jacques go. She lost a son his age two years ago. He is the oldest and head of the family.

Jacques' heart was broken. I called him into my tent later and explained he was a man, now; that when you are a man

46. Anti-aircraft.

necessities govern, not personal inclinations; that his duty was to remain at home, etc.

The parents of Jalbert were quite willing for him to go. His father had served in the last war, sustaining three wounds. His mother and brother and sister were shining with excitement to think Jalbert might go to America, because there is little to eat in France and little money to be made. "It is necessary," I said, "that you understand the risks. There are mines. There are enemy airplanes. There is the enemy himself, and there are exposure and sickness. There are also higher authorities who may not approve if your son comes with us."

"Yes," says the old father who has four days' scraggly gray beard but a clear eye in which remain hope and faith, "but Jalbert is a man now and must accept a man's risks." He soon would go to the French army. "If he prefers giving his loyalty to the American Army, I shall not stand in his way because I too have been a soldier."

I tell you it was touching, the family giving away a son. I repeated: "I can't promise anything but if we possibly can we will take Jalbert to America with us." And then they did all shine with happiness!

The mother of Maurice is blind. His father is dead. Including two sisters the family lives in another of those two-room dungeons of darkness, in the solid stone, through a corridor up a smelly stairway. Yet there was no question in this blind woman's mind. She'd decided her son should go. He had hid with the F.F.I. for a year. There are the sisters to care for her and work at the tannery. She wants her son to go into a new future. Privately I could not help wondering if one less person in the house would not make more room; and one less chair at the table means more food, even though the lad is near self-supporting age.

At any rate, Jalbert and Maurice moved with us and Jacques stayed behind with a broken heart.

The whole experience reminded me of *Les Misérables*. Your wife and children are starving so you steal a loaf of bread and become a criminal. . . . Your wife and children are starving so you become a "voluntary worker" for the Germans in order that they may eat. . . . Your platoon is without tentage or coal to keep warm—a bottle of cognac to the right person will make the difference between the comfort and discomfort of 51 men who look to you for these things. . . . Where does principle stop and expediency begin? I can't say, though I've experienced both several times recently.

You may wonder why I'm in a large city with K., Cox and Winsor yet speak of moving into the hinterland from Nancy. The platoon and the French boys are moving but I am with them no longer.[47] Eastabrooks is in command and I leave here, early tomorrow, for an infantry division with the 9th Army. There are *many* reasons why I applied for this transfer. Chief among them are two: first, the infantry *is* the Army; the infantry and only the infantry is mankind nakedly at battle, and there I have wanted to be for a long time. Secondly: our present assignment—the 825th's—is an almost certain guarantee of inaction[48] till the war is over in Europe.

I should mention a third reason, which is that officers and men are needed in the infantry.

Accordingly I applied a month ago for a transfer, submitted my qualifications and let the authorities decide whether I could be of more service there or here. They decided there; so I know I'm doing the right thing for the Army as well as myself—rough as it is to pull up roots here and say goodbye to my boys. That, I may tell you, was just no fun at all. I found wads as big as wet washcloths in my throat when I came to tell them all goodbye. Vain as it may be, I wanted them to miss me and not like my successor quite as much as they like me.

My boys, good ones, Janie.

Henderson—I made him sgt.—is rough and skinny and tall, from away back in Tennessee and, at 23, has been everything from an able-bodied seaman to a bootlegger. He put it this way: "It's a hell of a note, Lieutenant. Getting us over here and then running out on us!" A tough question to answer.

I replied: "You might think of it this way. When you left home and entered the Army you left all you held most precious and liked best, didn't you? And you came into a kind of living you both hated and wanted, because you were obliged to do so? The same with me now—I feel obliged to go. I don't exactly want to go yet I can't stay. All I know is—just now I feel like hell."

Which was the truth and was still when I took leave of

---

47. Maurice and Jalbert eventually went home by order of higher authority.

48. Some units of the 825th did see action in the Battle of the Bulge and acquitted themselves gallantly.

friends like Connell and Fee, not to mention Evoy and Desrochers and Old Nick Nichols in the kitchen who used to work in the oil fields at Bakersfield. When some said they wanted to come with me I felt greatly complimented, more than repaid.

I know this is the right place for me to be—in the infantry, into the war as far as we can go; and I say "we" because you will be there with me.

Don't you agree? So I'm leaving tomorrow eagerly looking forward to this new chapter!

If my mail is irregular for a while, don't worry. I'll write as soon as I can. Meanwhile continue letters to the present A.P.O.

Yours of the 27th, the first from our new home, arrived today and made me happy indeed.

Your husband—doughfoot now!

CHAPTER 8

Look at an infantryman's eyes and
you can tell how much war
he has seen.
BILL MAULDIN

Up Front

Again we take a step in the dark. The infantry sustained far more casualties than any other branch of the service, as we both knew. But as I pointed out, the infantry *was* the Army and was thus at the heart of our personal commitment to the war. And if I were to spend all these years in uniform and never see action, I would never feel satisfied. Yet I felt I couldn't share the step with Jane until I'd taken it, or she would worry that much more. Besides, my application for transfer might be rejected and then all her extra anxiety would have been for nothing.

Oblivious to any of this for a few days longer, Jane is strengthened by moving to Santa Barbara with the children and her mother. It gives her a new lease on life and hope as it does Dorothy Faust—who insists on establishing a home there for Judy and herself, and for John when he returns after the war. The problem of finally closing and disposing of the Los Angeles house remains.

SANTA BARBARA, SUNDAY, DEC. 17, 1944

They are singing down at the church at the corner. It depresses me. The only church which hasn't depressed me is the one in the Santa Ynez Valley where we heard them singing that summer when I was big with child. Remember how we walked beside the creek and listened to the running water mixed with the voices from the old wooden building with the ripening grain all around it? I recall feeling as I've felt ever since we were married: "Drink fully, don't let a moment slip by unaware, be happy and good and kind to each other for the separation is drawing near and you will have to live on memories for a long, long time to come."

At 1:15 we go up to your parents' for lunch. Father is away at the ranch but Joan is always so thrilled to go to "Grandmother's house." She loves the big old rooms, feels quite at home, trots upstairs to "Daddy's room" and sits in your chair there. I wonder where you are, this Sunday.

29TH INFANTRY DIVISION TRAINING CENTER, GERMANY [ZOPP],
22 DEC. 1944

Here it is—the first from Germany to add to your collection from many lands.

I'm writing in the living room of what used to be a coal miner's neat white cottage, now officers' mess for our training center where I'll be spending several days brushing up on infantry tactics before receiving an assignment.

I wrote you last from Luxembourg. The German break-through[1] had begun two days earlier and things were going badly. To say the least, the atmosphere was tense. Fighting was less than twenty miles away and coming closer. Armored units of the 825th were preparing to evacuate General Bradley and his 12th Army Group staff if need be.[2] While I was writing, late at night, someone knocked at the door. It was a lieutenant I'd never seen before asking to come in and get warm. His anti-aircraft outfit was the line of trucks halted bumper to bumper behind him in the cobblestoned street, blackout lights glowing dimly in the foggy darkness. They were among thousands moving up that night of Dec. 18th from Patton's army to join the great battle.

The faint light showing through the blackout of our front door attracted more callers. From 1:00 to 5:00 A.M. I answered the bell twenty times. At one point fifteen strangers were sleeping in the cellar or finishing a loaf of dark bread that happened to be on the kitchen table. So if my letter was a bit disjointed, the interruptions and whiskey may have been the reason.

The following morning I left early for Maastricht in Holland. There was a ground mist like a tule fog in the Sacramento Valley and under it, that morning of the 19th, Von Runstedt's spear-heads were driving deep into Belgium. Not knowing this my jeep made its way out of town toward Arlon, among hundreds of vehicles. Like the ack-ack outfit of the night before they were rolling north but rolling fast.

At Arlon the Bastogne-Houffalize road—the shortest route

1. Later known as the Battle of the Bulge.
2. Portions of the staff were evacuated.

to Liège or Aachen and the one I travelled to see John[3] and along
which, at the tiny village of Baraque-Fraiture, I spent one snowy
night and watched the peasants spinning—was blocked off by
M.P.'s. So we swung west toward Rochefort. I wondered, as often
since, what has become of the Belgian family whose bit of wool
thread you have, for their village was on the through-road to
Vielsalm to La Roche and the Meuse, along which the Germans
drove hardest and farthest.

From Arlon toward Rochefort you climb into the Ardennes.
They are densely wooded with somber evergreens, cut by rocky
valleys from time to time. Everywhere our armor and infantry
were hastily moving in, or lined up alongside the road, or hur-
riedly breaking camp. About noon I asked two G.I.'s in a village
if they knew where a cafe was open and they said no, they were
looking for one. They'd had no supper and no breakfast but were
in good spirits, and although seeing one's army rushing around
getting a bit disorganized was not very reassuring, those cheery
guys were.

Spent the night of the 19th with some B Co. boys[4] in a
comfortable house on high ground five miles east of Liège. Flying
bombs, the infamous V-1's, came over steadily during the night,
exploding in the city below. Traffic kept moving toward the front
all night too. One of our fellows on guard suddenly appeared and
reported a Negro truck driver had picked up a Nazi wearing a
G.I. overcoat down at the corner. A number of them wearing
our uniforms were dropped behind the lines. At dawn, a single
plane laid a few eggs along the road nearby. Then all was quiet.

After breakfast we left in our jeep and continued along the
Meuse to 9th Army headquarters at Maastricht. Finally I found
my way into Germany and the 29th Division, said goodbye to
the jeep and the two boys who'd seen me through, and started
my new life here.

SANTA BARBARA, CHRISTMAS DAY, 1944

There's a full moon in a deep clear sky that is chilly and bright.
I think you may be looking up at the same sky and hearing planes

---

3. Jane's brother was with VII Corps headquarters, 1st Army, near Aachen on the
German-Belgian border, where Bob visited during his earlier trip to Luxembourg.
4. Of the 825th T. D. Battalion, guarding radio network installations.

going overhead by the thousand. Never has good weather meant so much for our side but the news *is* better. I am thinking of you so constantly that you seem nearer by the minute.

We sat in front of the tree at your house last night while Father passed the presents around as he's always done, your mother says. Joan was on the couch in the parlor in her nightie looking angelic. Katherine was tired and muted, also in her nightie, goggle-eyed at the tree and lights and the rustle of paper! The hope of mankind rests in such little children, the young flesh, the pure flesh, the believing flesh.

My heart aches that you cannot see them, touch them, watch them, hear Joan on her telephone, a little red toy one which is her favorite present, saying: "This is Mrs. Easton. I'll be right over. See you later, goodbye!" The voice, the tone! She is a child Renoir must have seen and painted many times. Her face as she unwrapped her packages was one to behold, and thank God we CAN give them gifts. She kept saying: "I wonder what's in here, now! Oh, this will be wonderful!" (a new word, this last).

Katherine spent much time chewing up wrapping paper and trying to get the silver balls off the tree, and crawling around like a locomotive and looking up at everyone—Grandfather is one of her favorites—and smiling broadly.

I thought of the many years ahead of just such nights, Christmas Eve, when our children will fall asleep with new toys and you and I will linger by the fire, discussing the children, the day, the future, the past. Will we talk of these Christmases apart? Or will they fade into a dream of nothingness?

No letter for a week and you know the complete despair I drop into at such times! I'm hoping for tomorrow. Thank God for this thing called hope. Your last was dated the 5th.

Goodnight once more! How little 1944 has given me of you! Ten days. And 1945 will give me nothing. Perhaps 1946 will do a better job, or is it 1947? You never speak to me enough of the future. Tell me what you will say when we meet again.

DIVISION TRAINING CENTER [ZOPP], GERMANY, 25 DEC. '44
Christmas Eve was clear and frosty with a moon and all the stars, and a curious plane that kept coming back and back over us, just as a reminder this isn't Santa Barbara. Today our fighters and

bombers are out, to celebrate the birthday of the Prince of Peace. Every once in a while we hear the artillery let go as further reminder, and all the time at the bottom of one's heart is the incurable ache of homesickness. I've been thinking about you all by the tree at 2442 and dreaming of a time I'll be there with you.

I've also been talking to Capt. Reynolds in charge of our school quarters. He comes from Waco, Texas, has a wife and a convertible Ford like ours, and a Texan's gift of gab. He was "up"—meaning "on the line"—for several weeks recently and likes to talk about it, mispronouncing the names of all the German towns he fought through and casually terming the Germans "Jerry," in that half-humorous manner with which these combat veterans personify their enemy as a kind of devil, with certain astute qualities—in fact so many you wonder who is winning the war, we or Jerry.

One of my jobs is censoring mail for the new men in school and men returning from hospital. I wish you might read some of them, especially those of husbands to wives, or fathers to children. Many of these fellows have been overseas nearly three years. Many have been in combat since D-Day. Many have been wounded, healed, and returned. Their deep humility, Janie, would wring your heart. I watch them line up for mess, the sturdy, weathered sergeants—the very best men we have—acute, humorous, clear eyed, with the free movement and casualness of free people—so mature and uncomplaining and anxious to get back to their buddies on the line, despite the frozen ground and the enemy and every physical hardship imaginable. Because up there with their buddies is their place and despite everything they want it.

You should hear them exclaim with disdain at the "comforts" of our camp: hot soup, "real houses to sleep in," movies at night in a cold (freezing) half-ruined barn. And you should hear them "bitch" (complain) about having to "go to school" after fighting from the Normandy beaches, to Brest, to Germany, just because it is "Uncle Charlie's" (Gen. Gerhardt's)[5] wish that every man returning take a brief refresher course. I heard one mutter today before going out to throw his compulsory hand grenade: "Hell, I've pulled the pin on 500 of these!"

Days without mail are hard. But I feel immensely clear and

5. Commander of the 29th Division, Major General Charles H. Gerhardt.

close to you forever, Janie, and know that life is running its course with us for a reason, for our share of joy and sorrow, and for our love which is unshakably strong. I wonder why I should feel this in the upstairs room of a white German cottage or at sea standing by the rail of the *Queen Elizabeth* watching bubbles rising from the green North Atlantic, or in England in the dim rain, or on Utah Beach—or Mayet, Verdun, Nancy, Luxembourg, or that Belgian cottage at a crossroads called Baraque-Fraiture above Bastogne, which I very much fear is now in German hands.[6]

SANTA BARBARA, DEC. 27, 1944

Two letters yesterday. I was getting anxious. I notice again that you do not mention your smoking to me. That makes me rather angry. Will you never learn to be quite frank? It's not WHAT you do that bothers me, for heaven's sake smoke two packs a day if it pleases you, but WHY not tell me?

Surely you know that I'll not be cross or unpleasant about it. I wonder why you are so secretive about small things? You've done this ever since we were married and perhaps I'm wrong to criticize you, but it does seem odd. Did you conceal things from your parents and then get in the habit? Surely I can be treated differently from parents or anyone else?

I am not as worked up over the smoking as I may sound, only slightly hurt that I've never seen you smoke and hence cannot visualize you in the process. I'm not going to mention it again, which I suppose is a lie. John just barely said: "Bob has taken up smoking" and nothing more. He didn't know you hadn't told me, I guess. Anyway, I shall tell *you* that some of your letters after a few bottles of Burgundy are quite gay and devilish and unlike the sober man I have known! Your writing gets very wild and unruly and you sound very sweet and silly and I love you terribly. What an old renegade, nothing but drink and smoke and talking to Hélène about "*Ich muss wieder einmal in Grinzing sein*"! I get so homesick for that Vienna and those gay Austrians (please be jealous) when I think of that song and the happy times they sang it while drinking the new wine down! I don't like you

6. A key crossroads, Baraque-de-Fraiture was the scene of bitter fighting during the Battle of the Bulge.

chatting with French girls, please stop it. I expect you to speak ONLY to men.

I am beginning to enjoy male company again. I don't think one can hibernate too long. But I think YOU *should*! There you are! Please sit down and write me a humdinger now, and let's have some spats across the 5,000 miles of land and water!

GERMANY [ZOPP], 28 DECEMBER 1944
Yesterday came my big adventure. I went to "the line" for 24 hrs. indoctrination with a rifle company. I arrived at dusk at a ruined house in a ruined German village[7] in snow-covered countryside with Jerry a few hundred yards away. I felt, a bit awesomely, that I was joining a new species of men, the combat infantry, and I was.

The captain, a gentle *Texan*, made me welcome and we ate, standing up in the ruins of a freezing cold house after the men had eaten first, a supper of fried dried eggs and bacon, French toast, coffee and stewed apples; and then we sat by a stove in what must have been the study of the once prosperous and intellectual household, where there are etchings and prints still on the wall, some books and a 50-caliber hole through the steel shutter and a long white rip where the bullet cut the wallpaper above the captain's head. It made me feel like an illegal intruder, occupying someone else's premises, but such considerations are among those overlooked in combat.

The core of this company is from Virginia and uses the distinctive "ou" sound, as in "about," which they make "aboot." They are great, great boys, outwardly cheerful and carefree as on a picnic, and spend spare time much as they would at home—eating, playing cards, telling stories. After dark I was out and around with them and could hear Jerry talking just across the river and firing bursts of his machine guns in our direction now and then to show us he was alert. Later he delivered some accurate mortar fire which caused us to hit the icy ground and thoroughly skin our knees and elbows and cuss Jerry. Under such circumstances he becomes "those goddamned Krauts!"

To complete my 24-hour course, I heard the whine of bullets close above my head—which is like the sound of large insects

7. Barmen on the Roer River.

passing at high speed—and their more palpable rattle against masonry; and I heard the louder whining of shells passing high above, our own and Jerry's, and even learned to control my ducking. Later I talked at length about Lampasas, Brownwood, California, Virginia apples, women, liquor, deer and pheasant hunting which are possible around here, and the innumerable facets—none of them pretty—of Jerry's character. He is fighting on his home ground now and has been very tough.

The most impressive personality I met was Tech. Sgt. Branham. Branham was a private in the States because he had a habit of saying what he really thought to colonels or anybody. Here he is a sergeant commanding a platoon (because no officer is available), holder of the Silver Star, Purple Heart, and I don't know what all—a sturdy figure of middle height who stands with feet apart, carries his carbine by the stock in one hand, moves with animal eagerness, lips parted. His face is chiseled in the strong old-English manner. What a man he would have made for Drake or Raleigh, and what a leader he makes now.

The captain has the Silver Star, too, I was told. Of course they don't wear their decorations, only their insignia of rank. There are two other officers (should be a total of six but the company was badly damaged recently and is understrength), but the men who make things tick are Branham and others like him—humorous, unruffled, casual, yet hard as steel. I left them unwillingly today to await my assignment.

The news isn't exactly heartening but maybe the Hun has overreached himself, and should these heaven-sent clear days continue much longer, allowing our planes to attack, we may yet destroy him once and for all.

I haven't told you about seeing Patton who is doing so much at the moment to repel the German break-through. My boys saw him on the street in Nancy wearing his pearl-handled six-shooter at his hip and his helmet strap buckled under his chin, but I missed him. I was on my way up to Luxembourg to transfer when I met a procession of three big olive-green sedans led by one with a brigadier's gold star centered in its red license plate, then a major general's with two stars, finally one with three and in it Patton. He was returning from that decisive conference with Ike and Bradley in which they decided to swing the 3rd Army north and hit the German offensive from the south. I just glimpsed his profile as he passed, jaw stuck out, eyes straight ahead, a few things on his mind no doubt. If anybody can stop this humiliating defeat, he can. We were caught with our pants down, Janie, absolutely down. Only a miracle and some hard fighting, even by cooks and clerks, saved Bradley's headquarters and Luxembourg.

I shan't kid you about anything. I've been under fire, been scared to death, but it's a good thing, Janie, and doesn't trouble me and should not trouble you, really, nearly so much as the thought of my *not* having such experience—in company with the best of our kind that I know.

317 BURLINGAME AVE., LOS ANGELES, DEC. 29, 1944
We're back here temporarily until Mum is strong enough to dispose of this house and make the move complete. I'm about to read Ernie Pyle's *Brave Men*.[8] I think of you at least a million times a day and with the result that there are moments when I do strange things in my absentmindedness and Joan suddenly says to me, when I am putting two shoes on one foot or dumping her on the toilet with her panties still buttoned: "Why, Mumsy, what a funny thing to do!" Poor wee one! But I have told her that Daddy is coming back one day and that you love her and Katherine and send them kisses. She likes to hold the large picture of you and kiss it. Goodnight. Will there come a night in 1947 when I can have your arms about me and feel you kiss me and know that I need never say goodbye again?

CO. K, 116TH INF., A.P.O. 29 C/O P.M., N.Y.C., 2 JAN. 1945
My assignment was another of those coincidences which lead me to believe a good angel is guiding us. By sheer luck, this is the very wonderful company to which I came for "battle indoctrination" three days ago. Out of all the companies in a division of 15,000 men, I was sent back to the very one I wanted most! K Company has been in action since D-Day—from Omaha Beach, to St. Lô, to Brest, to spearheading the current drive into Germany, and its members are, as I've written, a seasoned, good-humored, easy-going and hard-hitting bunch.

8. Pyle was a veteran war correspondent who specialized in covering the infantry, as close to the front as possible.

We are now sitting by the stove waiting for mail which a truck brings up after dark along with food and water, over the snow-covered landscape. Master Sergeant Purvis, a tall slow-speaking Virginian who holds a handful of decorations, is in the chair beside me. He will be a second lieutenant next week by "battlefield commission"—rather like being knighted on the field of battle—and will take the 1st platoon. I will have the 2nd, Sergeant Branham's.

Captain R., the slow-talking steady-eyed Texan, sits opposite me, wearing a regulation brown-wool knit cap such as we wear under our fiber helmet-liners and steel helmets when outdoors in cold weather, and indoors in these unheated premises. Occasionally he spits tobacco juice into a bucket beside his chair. He's small, cool, with great dignity and power.

The conversation has drifted to past experiences: "88 Alley" (the "88" is Jerry's most feared artillery weapon) back in Normandy, the capture of the submarine pens at Brest, the German cow the boys recently butchered and hung in the parlor of the half-ruined house we occupy. This morning I entered what remains of the church of this battered village, where we are now sole inhabitants. It was shot full of holes. The altars were strewn with debris and had either been looted or smashed by shellfire. On the central one was a small wooden crucifix with the left arm of the cross and Christ's arm blown off.

I also inspected several houses. Usually you enter these country houses through a brick arch leading into a cobblestoned courtyard onto which stables, storerooms and tool sheds face. The house door will be just to your right or left as you enter the arch. Its interior is usually a smashed and dusty litter, yet from beneath the debris—from the half loaves of black bread on the tables, the jam jar open, the hams soaking in a bucket, the apples on a plate, coffee pot on stove, even a bottle of French wine, St. Émilion 1937—from these you can tell the haste in which homes were abandoned—that people much like any other people lived in them and prayed to the same God as ours, for in every home there is a crucifix, plus a reproduction of *The Last Supper* in too-gaudy colors, or a Madonna's head, or some other icon. It is always the ordinary people who suffer most. Perhaps because there are more of them. But not only for that—they are the infantry of life. They bear the brunt.

Later I'll go down to the cellar, our sleeping quarters. One does not go abroad much by day and life is a good deal like that of a mole, until night comes.

Another change in our life together, or apart (except that I always feel you are with me)! Now you've begun the Infantry Phase and I am tagging along. I admit it was rather a shock at first. I cried for ten minutes and then felt better. I cried because you are more likely to be killed or wounded in the infantry. There is no sense in hiding from that. Now the initial burst of horror at the idea, and total surprise at your decision, is over, I am deeply proud of you.

I can tell how pleased you are, from the note you wrote Dec. 19. You were on your way then, with the German attack close to you. By now you've been fighting two weeks. I know you have what you want and that's what matters most to *me*. I am glad, darling, that we will be in the war as deeply as possible. It is our fate, somehow, and you have been moving toward that end for nearly three years.

I know how frustrated you have been to see no action. Now you will get it, all of it. Ernie Pyle has given me a close and vivid picture of the infantry. I'm reading his *Brave Men* right now. It is very inspiring stuff and I'm glad you are connected with it. I wired your parents, in Berkeley, the news. We have all been pretty anxious after two and half weeks of silence. I guess they will be distressed about the change. But as long as you felt the 825th was not going to get into the thick of it, I am all for the new assignment.

Hardest is the fact that I don't know your new A.P.O. I am depressed to think of the length of time it will take my letters to reach you. And when you are with the infantry, I daresay you will have very little time to write. I hate both those things! But there is a good deal I hate about the war. And there are many times when I think I'd be much happier in some kind of war work myself. Though in another way I know I simply have to be with our young children. I think I'd be a nurse and go overseas if I had no children. Would you have approved of that? There is such a demand for them!

How one wonders! I get quite excited trying to picture what you are doing, and where, as you read this. I wonder what kind of men you'll meet in the infantry. I wonder how they will compare to other soldiers you've been with. I do so ache to know. You will get all the fleas and wet shoes and hard ground to sleep on and hunger and exercise that even YOU could ask for. Tell me about it, every inch of the way.

I don't have to tell you how I miss you, my sweet doughfoot. I can't imagine why you were ever in the tank destroyers now. I feel very proud and happy about the infantry, dangerous as it is. The chance of your returning unharmed is much more slim but I believe in it all the same.

So you were in Nancy! Well, I loved your description of the town. It pleased me to think of the marketplace and the good evenings you spent. I was amazed by the French boys you took with you. I didn't know such things happened. You must speak a lot of French. I shall need lessons from you when you get back!

In April it will be Katherine's first birthday. And next month it will be a year since I've seen you. What does time mean now? It means nothing, it is all measured in terms, for me, of please, please fly by quickly, each and every day. I pray only for passage of time. How ever and ever more distant the day of your return seems to be.

I don't quite know what this letter says or means. I'm still bewildered by this change. I know you have always wanted it but I didn't realize you had gone through with it. And as usual you never tell me anything until it is settled. I suppose you will do that always. It's something primeval and strange about you and I know you put up with strange things from me, too. So I shall not say more. Bless you, my darling. May our good angel watch over you closely now and always, more carefully now than ever.

Give your division a good wish from me but remember how much I love you. I know you will take every risk possible and there is no use asking you to be cautious, but may I put in a plea that you try and be mildly sensible and not TOO foolhardy. There are three women waiting for you, Joan and Katherine and Jane, and a lot of others too.

I adore you now and forever. Please tell me when you join the submarines. I am expecting it.

Our sector of the front line consists of the village of Barmen and its outskirts. Facing us three hundred yards away across the Roer

River, about ninety feet wide at this point, is the German line. Between, on our side of the river, is a no man's land of snow-covered fields and scattered trees, some evergreen, some bare limbed, with here and there a drainage ditch or barbed wire fence.

There are nightly patrols in this no man's land which we look forward to, with various stages of apprehension, throughout the day. They consist of an officer and two enlisted men. To begin we follow a well-beaten path through the snow to our foremost foxhole where we exchange a few words with the fellows manning it, to make sure they know we're out there and won't mistake us for prowling Jerries when we return. Then we thread our way carefully on a very narrow path that meanders through hidden mines and very palpable rolls of concertina wire to the great unknown. There it is literally and figuratively a matter of taking steps in the dark.

Sometimes the blackness is so thick you can't see more than three or four yards. Sometimes there is bright moonlight which illuminates the scene with what seems merciless clarity, revealing you as an ideal target. In any case progress consists of a few steps, followed by long minutes of looking and listening, usually crouched, sometimes prone. A high degree of alertness is essential. The slightest sound carries long distances in the still cold air. A careless footstep on ice-encrusted snow can sound like an explosion. A cough or sneeze can be disastrous. The hardest part is sorting out imaginary images of danger from real ones. I once grenaded a band of small Rhineland deer which I mistook for an enemy patrol.

Lacking camouflage clothing we improvise it from bedsheets and towels taken from houses in Barmen and draped over uniforms and wrapped around helmets and even over the barrels and butts of rifles or submachine guns, so that we look like Halloween ghosts of a peculiar sort. By contrast the Germans wear the equivalent of form-fitting felt-lined white ski suits which not only conceal but keep them warm in the near-zero cold. Within an hour we were usually so cold we could hardly move, let alone pull a trigger accurately.

Nevertheless Lieutenant Art Dempsey leads a daring raid across the river during a snowstorm, takes a prisoner and brings him back under intense fire without suffering casualties, though the prisoner suffers a ducking in the Roer when he slips from the snowy trunk of the fallen tree serving as bridge. He proves to be a rather pathetic-looking middle-aged member of Hitler's "master race" who says his name is Willie, that he comes from Leipzig, and declares himself only too glad to be done with war and to have a cup of hot coffee in a warm cellar, after which he gives us the number of his division and other useful information.

A nearly successful counter-raid, likewise during a snowstorm, resulted in a courageous German sergeant being wounded and captured within a dozen steps of our foremost foxhole. He'd squirmed through two rows of concertina wire and over a number of mines so clogged with snow and ice they failed to explode, only to meet a rifle bullet fired by one of our imperturbable Tennessee hillbillies who'd sharpened his aim on tree squirrels as a boy. It ripped a bloody gash in the sergeant's side but he was fully conscious while Turton, who'd shot him, and others carried him to the nearest cellar where, by a warm stove, they gave him first aid, then brandy, then a cigarette. I was present and witnessed the expressions of mutual friendship and respect exchanged in two languages before the sergeant was taken away to a field hospital and prison camp.

From such episodes the realization comes to us, subconsciously more than consciously, that war, much like civilian life, is a matter of individual confrontations, individual courage and risk, and the point of decision is finally person to person—perhaps multiplied many times, on many fronts, in many situations—but still person to person. Along with it comes the realization that men can be comrades as well as adversaries.

All U.S. forces north of the Battle of the Bulge are now under command of British Field Marshal Bernard L. Montgomery. This has no perceptible effect on our daily lives but the fact that hundreds of thousands of G.I.'s served in combat under British command remains a little known feature of the war, as does the extent to which our top generals were surprised and divided by the German attack.

Hitler had hoped to come crashing through our thinly held line along the Roer while our high command was preoccupied with his Bulge thrust, and sweep down on Antwerp in Belgium, the Allied port of entry into northern Europe, and recover Holland too; but his reserves proved insufficient and the Bulge too consuming of his strength—so, perhaps fortunately for us, his grandiose flanking movement aimed at our sector never materialized.

On the home front Jane's no man's land is the long wait between my letters day after day, week after week, wondering if she is a widow and our two girls fatherless.

———

GERMANY [BARMEN], 6 JAN. 1945

Just came from a steak dinner with Sgt. Branham who will be my platoon sergeant. The steak came from a local cow and was cooked to order, rare, and served with pan gravy and coffee.

Branham hit Omaha Beach D-Day as a private. He thought he wouldn't survive that day and many of his buddies didn't. He cleaned his rifle three times by urinating into it, to get the sand out of it, as he lay on the beach under murderous fire. Before I was assigned a platoon he told the captain he wanted to work with me, which pleased me and had something to do with my assignment. So fortune is kind again. I'm looking forward to working with Felix and learning a lot. He told me about K Company. It is one of the oldest—perhaps the oldest—military organizations in the United States, having been in continuous service since 1745 when it was organized in the vicinity of Charlottesville, Virginia, as militia to fight Indians. The company served in the Revolution. Many years later when Lafayette visited Jefferson at Monticello (which is at Charlottesville in the Blue Ridge foothills), the company was on guard and Lafayette, glancing out the window, saw the men and asked: "Who are these soldiers, Mr. Jefferson, your Monticello Guards?" Monticello Guards they've been called ever since.

The D.A.R. has given them 64 colonial uniforms which they wear on dress occasions, complete with tri-cornered hat and gaiters. April 13th, apple blossom time, is the great celebration. Someday we must be there for it.

These Virginians fascinate me. But, as Capt. R. says drolly to Elwyn Walsh, our ruddy-faced first sergeant: "Walsh, if you was two men you couldn't lick a Texan!"

R. hails from Dallas, is married, has a daughter eight years old. He tells me all an infantry officer needs is common sense and a little guts at the right time and not to worry about a tank destroyer background because if your boys like you that's the main thing. He came to the company in the middle of the Brest[9]

9. Aimed at capturing the major German submarine base at Brest, on the French coast, from which U-boats preyed on Allied ships.

campaign as a first lieutenant fresh from a replacement center without a day's combat experience. On arriving he had difficulty finding any fellow officer since there was only one left and he was hiding in a foxhole—so broken psychologically that he didn't want to command, in fact refused to come out of his hole! So R. took charge of a company that was badly shot up and demoralized. He was its *ninth* commanding officer in two months of continuous combat since D-Day—his predecessors being dead, wounded, or relieved for incompetence or "combat fatigue." When the Brest campaign ended, K Co. had taken more ground, more prisoners, with fewer losses, than any other company in the regiment, while up against a crack German paratroop division.

We have many Irish: Hurley, Kelly, Kelliher, Mearin. Did you ever see an Irishman who wasn't jovial? Here they are invaluable. The monkey-business never is done; and yet Kelly's girl wrote the other day that she's grown tired of waiting and is getting married. Such things are what tear out a man's roots.

Today is D-plus-182.[10] Six months ago at dawn the L.C.V.P.'s—Landing Craft Vehicles, Personnel—hit Omaha Beach many hundreds of miles and many hundreds of unforgettable moments from here. I'm accumulating the story of these fellows day by day, being awed and feeling sorry I didn't have the good fortune to go the whole route with them.[11] The highest compliment they can pay is to call somebody a "good soldier." It's a vast understatement but it says everything. Janie, combat strips a man naked. Your true identity can't be hidden for long. All the props we rely on in civilian life—money, education, social status—are removed and you have to stand alone and define yourself from the ground up. The result is an extraordinary kind of democracy. All men are equal under fire.

"Jabos" are out this morning. "Jabo" is German for our P-47 fighter-bombers, the weapon the Jerries most fear.

Our little "cubs,"[12] fearless, cocky, are another omen of doom, bringing down on Jerry, as they do, the most accurate artillery fire.

10. D-Day plus 182 days.
11. Elements of the 29th and 1st Divisions made the initial landings at Omaha Beach, so often depicted in photos and print. They suffered heavy losses and near defeat. Had they been defeated, the entire Normandy invasion would have failed, according to some experts.
12. Piper Cubs, small single-engine high-wing monoplanes used for reconnaissance as well as directing artillery fire.

No mail in three weeks and the thought of another week or two till your letters arrive isn't pleasant.

I'm glad 1944 is gone. The faster the years run the better, till the one when I see you again.

LOS ANGELES, JAN. 8, 1945

I'm all trembling inside with joy! Your letter with the new address, at least the temporary one, came this morning. It was written the 22nd of December. I am quite convinced that your moving to the infantry is just right. I can imagine how dreary the prospect of never getting into combat must have seemed. Heaven knows, I never wanted that for you. We are in this business the whole way. I agree with what you say about things on the home front. It's not a pretty picture. I also don't think Washington has been above blame. It was from there that all those very optimistic words came a few months ago, so that people were betting on the Germans being done by Christmas—or even earlier! What madness.

Now everyone is very gloomy and depressed and it's hard to get back to work. The defense plants were badly hurt because workers felt the war was over and quit in an effort to find steady jobs they could keep for years. It's not their fault. Heaven knows they worked like mad, without any holidays, without letting up, many of them did.

There are the usual draft dodgers and people like F. who benefit by this country but never exert themselves, and there are many others who simply do nothing at all to help. It's infuriating. Perhaps one of the reasons is that back here we don't KNOW enough about the war. Swing[13] is rabid on the subject. "Let us know just how bad things are at the front and we will fight better. We will not believe the glossed-over reports." It is only now popping out, and then only vaguely, as to what this German breakthrough means.

Anyway, I wrote F. and L. another strong letter. I have for a long time felt a strange uneasiness in their presence and was beginning to dislike them, for they have neither of them done ONE thing toward the war. They've had four years together and never one day apart. They have not worked at the war in any

13. Raymond Gram Swing, prominent radio commentator.

way. They have not suffered or sacrificed, they have gone on living off the fat of the land. I sat down and wrote them very calmly and quietly that I felt the draft might now get F. and if it does it will be the best thing that ever happened to them. I went into it quite thoroughly, and just to make sure I showed the letter to Mum and she thought it very good. I wonder if it will awaken them in any way or they will never speak to me again?

Don't worry about me, ever. The children and I are very well. Wonder if you will read this in a foxhole?

GERMANY [BARMEN], 9 JAN. '45

I'm writing on the back of a beautiful volume bound in red leather trimmed with gold: *Die Malerei der Renaissance*. It resembles our large picture volumes of Van Gogh and Cézanne. Its first reproduction is *The Last Supper*. Then comes the *Mona Lisa*, samples of Luini, Buonarrotti, Botticelli, and others. You would be astonished at the number and quality of books in the simplest German homes. And I'm sleeping these nights in the new G.I. sack, Janie. You may have seen pictures of it: an olive green waterproof canvas covering with an inner blanket lining. I add a couple of blankets outside and sleep ten hours deliciously.

Sunday I went to services and sang "The Old Rugged Cross" in a candle-lit cellar crowded full of G.I.'s. The closer you get to the front, the more interest in religion there is. The young chaplain spoke of the promise far off that led Abraham. I thought of that same promise still leading us, still far off.

The snow is beautiful on the Christmas trees—the wild evergreens that grow between us and Jerry. Sometimes at night we prowl around in them and bump into him, like kids playing hide and seek, but not exactly.

Willy Russell of Oklahoma leads me to believe you and I must spend time in Oklahoma, because Oklahoma and its people are something special which Will Rogers epitomized. Russell, the oldest in the company, at about 42, is stooped, wry, dry, and endlessly humorous in Will Rogers fashion. He and his "Sweet Pea" used to get in their car and make the fruit-circuit of California just for a sightseeing holiday. He would pick the cherries and she would pack them. They would take time off to see Sequoia Park or the Golden Gate Bridge. . . . Let's us do it, Janie. I'll pick the cherries, you pack them. We'll live from day to day in the open air and never fret about tomorrow. We'll buy an old touring car, put on blue jeans and old hats, take $20 and not tell anyone where we're going.

Our medic here, age 20, is from Yazoo, Mississippi. He hit the beach D-Day and is widely respected. But he hates "niggers" and do you know what his complaint is? (Wonderful and terrible, the human mind!) His complaint is "that the bastards ride around in closed-cab two-and-a-halves [2½ ton trucks] while we walk and freeze!"—meaning that they have service jobs in rear areas and none in our sector are in combat. Of course it is largely discrimination like his that keeps them where they are.

Cpl. Bang, 21, is from Brooklyn, glib, cocky. His father was a Danish sea captain from Schleswig-Holstein and his mother a German from Magdeburg. The family left Germany when he was one year old. He dislikes Germans and enjoys his job as company interpreter. He can speak high, low, and seafaring German and has given me a few lessons.

Lt. Martin of our weapons platoon (4th platoon—the other three are rifle platoons) is from Long Island and directs operations of three 60-mm. mortars and four light machine guns.

Lt. Dempsey is from up-state New York, was with an A.A.[14] outfit that fired on the "Japanese planes" that night in February of 1942 when you and I were staying at 317 Burlingame and Los Angeles had its famous "air raid." Remember what a barrage went up? Dempsey is an eccentric who plays the flute, prowls by daylight in the woods between us and Jerry, and has made a Daniel Boone hat from rabbit skins and the tail of a stuffed fox.

Had the pleasure yesterday of "battle indoctrinating" an officer as I was indoctrinated two weeks ago. He was a little dark intense Frenchman named Marco who owns a laundry in Boston, and somehow it was good and interesting to hear him tell about his labor problems, cost problems, home problems. We pressed him for news of the States as he left them Dec. 12. He came down for 24 hrs. of which he slept 2 and departed filled with stories and with very wet legs from falling into a snow-and-ice-covered drainage ditch while with me on patrol.

If anyone inquires, you might tell them the best thing they can do at home to help us over here is to urge Congress to

14. Anti-aircraft artillery.

pass the National Service Act.[15] Quite rightly, the boys can't understand a dual standard of service—one for soldiers, another for civilians. As I frequently hear: "A few bombs dropped on the U.S.A. might wake people up, make them realize what war is all about." Must wash underclothes that are boiling on the stove. Continue hungry for mail. I only hope mine is reaching you. This gray winter, the bare trees, dim light and cold make me yearn till I hurt for your warmth and sunlight and the beaches and broad blue sky.

LOS ANGELES, JAN. 9, 1945

Tell me all, all, everything. From how dirty you are to what a foxhole smells like and what you dream about when you *do* sleep, and what death is like so close, and how cold your hands grow and anything and everything that you can possibly take time to write me. I am so much more interested in this phase than I was in the T. D.'s which always remained rather a mystery.

Mum is in the hospital for x-rays of her leg and an attempt to find out the cause of this pain, but DO NOT TELL JOHN anything about it—he gets so worried and is so gloomy anyway! I have Janet Hargrave here for a week so I shall not begin talking baby talk to myself. Dotha Lee and Margery Henshaw came for lunch. It was pleasant, though rather long and they stayed until nearly 4. I sometimes lie down for twenty minutes in the P.M. and that rests me.

Most of all, I am glad and pleased and thankful that you feel so happy now. That really makes me happy too. I hate to think of how dirty you'll get and how tired and how sore your feet. I simply cannot grow accustomed to your suffering. But I shall have to go on living in this strange, indistinct way, half alive, until I can be in your arms once more. The way seems long and cloudy, but I believe it will come to an end, that is all I pin my faith on. The rest means nothing at all: just your return. So please be a little careful. Joan says every night when I kiss her: "Some day Daddy is coming." And heaven knows I say a prayer for that.

---

15. The National War Service Act, opposed by organized labor and management and not actively supported by F.D.R., failed to pass Congress, despite pleas by General Marshall and other leaders; and consequently there was no mobilization of civilians to help in the war effort, despite the urgency caused by the Battle of the Bulge. England and Germany, by contrast, had total mobilization of men and women for their war efforts.

GERMANY [BARMEN], SAT. 3 P.M., 17 JAN. 1945

I loved your letter describing Aldington and Emery, agree with all you say, and desperately wish I'd been present.

Instead I give you Hurley. He is a deep-voiced, burly Irishman, 35, who has been "all the way through from the beaches." He moves like a bear and looks out from those touchingly honest eyes some faithful animals have. He fires a light machine gun from his hip commando style, his body wreathed in a belt of ammunition. The machine gun weighs forty lbs. but is as nothing to H. who used to be a mucker in the great tunnels like the Holland[16] and has a bear's paws—one of those laboring Irish, he is, who immigrated by the million to build our railroads and our tunnels and fight our wars. But there is a sadness in him that has nothing to do with the war. Today I found out what it was. His girl has written she's marrying "a banker."

The very good news this evening from all fronts goes right with my mood and brings that Texas shack up over the horizon in full view. No silver trays there, Janie. No tea cups. You know what will be there and with it always my abiding love. Goodnight, now.

LOS ANGELES, JAN. 26, 1945

I hated the tale you told about Hurley and his girl. That is more than man deserves, and heaven knows the soldiers should be spared these things, but the animals go on living at home, and the females want the males and they must reproduce and waiting seems impossible to them. I just hate to think of the men who are disappointed in the home front. It's tough on them, and it makes soldiering a thankless job. It must be pleasant to be with only men. I shouldn't like to be with women alone but it works out differently in the male species. I know that you are with the fine men that count and have made our infantry such a proud thing. I go around blowing the horn for K Company, I assure you.

I have a copy of *Life* nearby. It has the tragic news of Bill Chickering's death.[17] On a battleship in the Philippines on Jan.

16. Connecting New York and New Jersey under the Hudson River.
17. William H. Chickering, correspondent for *Life* and friend of Bob's.

6. What can one say? A son four years old and a baby due any day.

The Russians are making gigantic strides. 150 miles from Berlin!! The war in Europe may be over sooner than we think. A great wave of gloom as to the final outcome, however, has settled over the country—I mean, as to the length. But perhaps it will be early summer, if the Russians continue. The spring of 1945 sounds as if it had something good up its sleeve, doesn't it? Oh, how I pray for the weeks and months to pass and pass. It seems already a thousand years since D-Day, and to those who fought through it and beyond it and are still fighting, it must seem longer yet! We must all hang on hard, for there is peace and happiness and reunion at the end of this, and perhaps a better world. And work and work and work. So much work to be done and I can hardly wait to get my hands and heart into it, with you beside me night and day until we are old and tired and even then we will never say goodbye. I do not dread death if I can die with you, at the end of many, many years.

GERMANY [BARMEN], 6 FEB. 1945

I write from our 2nd platoon C.P., my back to the stove. Sergeant Branham sits beyond the candle, finishing a "sugar report" to the girl in Charlottesville he hopes to go home and marry any day now. He's next on the rotation plan after more than two years overseas. He pauses to recall one payday night in England when they were preparing for the D-Day landings in Normandy. He and two other G.I.'s returned, quite tight, to camp with several bottles of whiskey which the officer of the day took away from them. They were mad enough and tight enough not to care what they did next, so they went to Colonel Canham's, the regimental commander's, room at a few minutes before 1:00 A.M. and pounded on his door. Canham didn't open so they went in, found him asleep, shook him awake and complained: "Colonel, the O.D. just took our whiskey! What the hell good is payday if a fellow can't go out and buy some whiskey and bring it home?"

"Boys," said the colonel calmly, "you'll have your whiskey back in the morning. Now go to bed!"

They got their whiskey back and the colonel chided his officers: "Those men have more nerve than any of you!"

Bedcheck Charlie is overhead, the lone Jerry reconnaissance plane whose nightly visits began—and whose name was given—back on the beaches so long ago and far away.

The Big Push begins in the darkness of that frigid early morning in February when we jump off to cross the Roer, a wide stream now owing to the destruction of dams near its headwaters. The push carries us past Jülich, across the Rhine, deeper and deeper into the heart of Germany. We don't feel much hatred, mainly an inexorable sense that this has to be done, justice served, the world righted. Mostly we wonder if we will survive.

Germany, February 1945. Members of my infantry platoon prepare to cross the Roer River during the attack on Jülich. I'm standing in background. (National Archives)

GERMANY [NEAR MÜNSTER], 8 APRIL 1945

These are the glimpses you have during the invasion of the Reich: a copy of *Mein Kampf*[18] lying open in the middle of a ruined street, its muddy pages (where somebody has trampled muddy feet) idly flipping over in the breeze; on the bank of a canal, a dead German soldier, a boy no more than fifteen who has undertaken a man's game; British Tommies passing in an armored car, brown berets, broad grins and our boys calling: "Hya, bloody bloke?" and the Tommies replying with thumbs up: "Okay, Yank!"; Purvis walking into an air-raid shelter where 2,000 men, women and children are sitting rigid with fear in as jammed, evil-smelling a hole as you can imagine, absolutely silent with anxiety as the first of the conquerors enters—the tall slender officer with the pistol at his hip. He looks at them and they at him. There is no sound, except for a crying child, finger in its mouth. Purvis pats the child on the head, and suddenly everybody is talking and laughing with relief.

The deep tracks of our advancing tanks will not be erased from the German mind for many years—nor will the sight of the truckloads of prisoners, huge semi-trailers like those that used to carry hay to the mill at the B. B., moving to our rear. These carry more than a hundred men jammed upright like posts on end.

You feel our great army in your heart, in your bones, moving forward, thrusting deep into decadent, corrupt, tyrannical, enslaved old Europe, letting out the poison, letting in the health. We are the great westward emigration to America coming back on itself, renewing the source, liberating it for freedom—let's hope.

Anyhow, the excited children are learning to say: "Chocolate, uncle?" as the children of England, France, Belgium, Holland. I think of us as reluctant conquerors, Janie. Whenever was so much conquered against the inclination of the conquerors? I think of Plato saying the best public officials are those who serve against their will, from a sense of duty.

I remember the nun who suddenly appeared in the basement of the supposedly deserted school building where we'd hastily taken refuge from shellfire, calmly saying in perfect English that

18. Hitler's autobiography.

she was sorry she didn't have any food to offer us, shaming us
with her serene courage.

I remember those burning haystacks lighting our way during
night attacks. They were the scene of some strange happenings
during the day. We'd heard that loot was often hidden in them.
Approaching one and remembering this, a lieutenant friend of
mine decided to check it out. He went around the stack prodding
it with the muzzle of his carbine. Part way around he hit something
soft with give to it, so he removed some of the hay and there was
a very scared blonde girl shrinking away from him. He backed off
a little, leaned his carbine against the stack and asked her if she
was cold, which was almost the only German he could speak. No
response. Then he asked if she was hungry and pulled out the bar
of very hard chocolate he carried in his shirt pocket, to stop a
bullet as the saying is. She didn't answer but kept looking at the
bar, so he broke it in two across the carbine barrel, set the gun
back against the stack and sat down and handed her half. When
she finally accepted, he showed her how to nibble on the edges
of it so as not to break a tooth. Not long later she moved over
and invited him in. See what you're missing?

And I won't forget the everlastingly American Irishman who
carried a jar of fresh eggs across a minefield, came under fire, ran
for his life, spent all night in a hole, returned to us next morning
in a farmhouse with the eggs still unbroken and cooked them for
breakfast. Until you've gone months without a fresh egg, you
can't fully appreciate this.

And I remember the mail being distributed at dusk just as
we formed up, ready to move out—and the column of dirty,
weather-beaten, heavily laden G.I.'s moving out into the darkness and the battle, tearing open and reading letters, calling out
and kidding and showing clippings and pictures from home.

Well, Prusse, among those letters were three of yours—and
yours are the standing tease of the boys here, not a few of whom
used to receive letters from women they thought loved them but
whose letters have stopped coming. All I find to tell them is:
"Maybe it's for the best. Had you stayed home you might never
have found out till later, and that might have been worse."

As executive officer, I've taken over the company in a few
instances. I've slept beside and spent every day close to a man I
regard more highly than any I've met in the Army, Capt. R. He

is a great leader as well as a fine, thoughtful, sensitive person. I hope you'll meet him someday.

SANTA BARBARA, APRIL 10, 1945

I was shocked and stricken to hear of the men you admire whose wives are unfaithful to them. But please remember that there are a greater number who are virtuous. I know there are. It's the bad news that travels fast. Believe me, there are true mates waiting over here for their soldiers. This doesn't help those you mention, I know, and I share with you the heartache it gives them. It would wound me to the core to know you had slept with another woman and I would consider myself unfaithful to you if I held the hand of a man, much less slept with him (this last is utterly incomprehensible to me, even if you were dead).

To explain a little of these erring females: beyond missing the touch and love of a man, I think the hardest thing is not being able to GIVE your love. I know that I miss it horribly. It's the loneliness of not being able to wash your man's shorts or help him to keep clean in every way, of not being able to cherish him with all your soul and body, not to be able to GIVE. Naturally, it's very pleasant to receive love too, but surely as in all life, the greatest privilege is to make a gift of yourself, whether it be your love or your time or your body or all of you.

I'm going to another women's get-together this afternoon. I dare not tell you how awful most of these hen parties are. I keep hoping my work at the hospital will begin soon and give me something worthwhile to do.

GERMANY [NEAR BIELEFELD], 14 APRIL 1945

We're in a rich section of small and large farms and rolling hills with patches of woods, all very beautiful with spring and blossoms. The weather is heavenly, fair beyond belief, and even the countless liberated slave workers do not look unhappy. The Germans look likewise. The truth is that the approaching peace and spring have lifted a load off friend and foe alike, and farmers do not even look up when the planes fly over but continue planting their potatoes and wheat—by hand, usually.

News of F.D.R.'s death comes as a shock. Nobody here knew he was ill. I didn't vote for him in '40 because of the third term issue but I did last year, as you know, because I thought him best fitted to see us through the war. Now there's a real sense of loss. I can imagine how shaken everyone at home must be. Yet the end is in sight here and there is even a feeling we will not let Roosevelt's death bother us but will fight harder because of it. But how can Truman, who looks like Mr. Milk Toast incarnate, ever fill his shoes?

I've seen enough to convince me Germany is the richest and most industrially advanced nation of Europe. An example of its well-organized war production is the factory I visited yesterday— a huge place which employed many hundreds of German workers besides the Poles and Russians who lived in the enclosure beside it. Among its products were machine gun bolts, operating levers for artillery breechblocks, two types of radio antennae, leather pouches, back-pack carriers, cinches for saddles, wooden boxes for special signal equipment, the base of an airplane joy-stick and adjoining foot pedals, and much more. Originally it was a sewing machine factory. Evidently it was deliberately redesigned to produce a variety of products, with the strategic reasoning that if the place were bombed (which it partially was) only a small percentage of the total national output of each product would be lost.

In the big lathe room on the ground floor black machines— lathes—stretched solidly in rows for about a hundred yards, and an aged Russian worker, recently liberated, was sitting on the floor in the central aisle drunk and singing happily amid disorder and ruin—singing a wild song from his younger days, such as you hear at performances of professional Russian folk dancers. While trying to roll a cigarette he invited us to sing with him. Sitting on the floor at either side of him were two empty 10-gallon cans of commercial alcohol from the paint room. Maybe he hadn't drained them both but he'd taken his fair share.

The ex-slaveworkers loot thoroughly, rifling every nook and cranny, ripping portraits of Nazis from the office wall, drawing great Victory V's in chalk on walls everywhere, even tearing off the clock hands which marked their time in servitude. A few were still loitering on upper floors of the huge, shadowy, otherwise deserted building. They reminded me of stray dogs at evening prowling a city dump. They didn't bother to look up as Purvis and I passed.

Today we became honored guests at an incredible celebration. They'd dragged an old upright piano out onto the hard-packed earth at the center of the compound where they all live in miserable shanties enclosed by a high barbed wire fence, and a long-haired Yugoslav dressed more or less in rags was pounding away at it while around him all nations of Europe, just about, danced by proxy in a wild delirium. These are called "displaced persons" and at times are causing us more trouble than the enemy because they swarm the countryside by the thousand and must be rounded up and cared for.[19] As a matter of diplomacy, I joined in the party. Now don't be jealous and I'll give particulars. I danced with—*was danced with by*, would be more accurate—a hefty Russian gal who outweighed me twenty pounds at least and whirled me around as if I were a leaf, to the strains of, guess what— "Yessir, she's my baby; nossir, I don't mean maybe . . . !" It was fantastic. So much for international relations. Ah, but that *tovarich*[20]—she was *quite* an armful!

"Ich muss schlafen jetzt."[21] I'm learning a little German, as you see.

Never mind candles for a while; thank you for so many.[22]

SANTA BARBARA, APRIL 15, 1945

This morning I was making our bed and the children were playing about, when Katherine stood up for the first time without aid of chair or any prop, and took three or four steps alone, tumbled down, and repeated the process! She was overjoyed at this walking instead of crawling. Kaff is two and a half months ahead of Joan in walking but I doubt if she will talk as soon.

I took them out in the lower garden and immediately Kaffie was into the "good earth" as Joan calls it (but doesn't care much for touching it) and was eating it before I could stop her. She crumbles it and pats it and plays about happily with it and then crawls off and picks leaves off the shrubs near the gates.

Joan watched butterflies and was very sorry they wouldn't stop and let her touch them, but explained to me: "Butterflies like dandelions!"

19. Congressional action enabled many of these displaced people to find homes in the U.S. eventually.
20. Comrade.
21. I must sleep now.
22. Jane was also sending dried fruit, nuts, hard candy and cookies plus such delicacies as canned oysters.

You speak of the children's education. I've not made up my mind about a good deal of their future because I want to do it with you. I like what you say. But we must be careful not to force on them what we've found important. Sometimes Daddy swamped John and me with his beliefs so that we lost our own and were under a heavy weight. The same applies to our belief, yours and mine, in the life of the open, action, etc. We must not make them think that only the poor are the real or the earnest. This will make them seek the cities and the rich. I hope we can achieve a balance.

God knows, I long for a simple life, in a community far different from this one. Here there are no neighbors like we knew in the small towns of Texas. The rich live here and the idle and the would-be artists. We must get away after you have had your rest and maybe we have sandwiched in another child—I hope, a boy. I worry about your constant reference to "a son" or "sons." I hope you realize I may not have any. Such things DO happen. I am hoping that when we have had four children we will have at least one boy.

Must go. I love you terribly much always.

GERMANY, APRIL 18, 1945

We've been rounding up displaced persons, mainly Russians, former slave workers in the lager[23] I told you about in my last letter, many of whom have started roaming the countryside looking for food or freedom, or both. This afternoon I overtook a big fellow and a smaller companion on a lonely road in some woods. When my jeep pulled alongside, the big fellow stopped and turned to me grinning—jeep and uniform meaning we were Americans.

I held out my hand. "Americanski!"

He grabbed it and pounded his big fist into it. "Ukrainski!," grinning a mile wide.

But when I explained—in broken German with many gestures—we would take him back to the lager if he climbed in, and he would be sent home, he stopped smiling and shook his head.

"Nyet!"

He didn't want to go home. He wanted to go to the West to freedom and Democracy. He came from Kiev where there has

23. Camp.

Santa Barbara. Jane with Joan and Katherine and our blue Ford convertible coupe.

long been an "anti-Russian"—a new idea for me—movement for autonomy.

Anyway, we let him wander, since he was too big and strong to let do anything else.[24]

Our boys are getting fed up with this police work and want to be back in action. I likewise. The end cannot be far off, and we talk of celebrating in Berlin.

We also talk of usual subjects, chiefly women. Over doppel-korn, which is German whiskey, I'm telling Captain R. that many young people marry through sexual attraction alone. "Something like that happened to me," he replies. "You might say I married above my station, or maybe below it." His wife comes from a not-well-to-do branch of a wealthy family. "Her mother was 'a lady' with tastes for art, music, etc. But her father was a druggist and you know druggists aren't rich or fashionable. She went to live with a rich aunt when she was 12, later attended a girls' school on Long Island, one of those places where the daughters of the rich go, though I swear I can't figure out what they do there. She didn't know whether Texas was north or south of Kansas. But she was what you'd call attractive to men. I was a gay young blade so I married her. But it didn't work out." He passed over in a sentence the fact she was unfaithful. "I guess there are women like that at every level of life—who see some member of the opposite sex and can't resist the attraction."

To compensate, he has the devotion of 162[25] fighting men. They'll do anything for him and he for them. He listens to them with infinite patience, truly loves them. Yet it's his job to order them into combat, perhaps to their deaths, and his manner expresses that he knows this, knows the relentlessness of life as well as its tenderness, and they know it too which is the beauty, the deep dark terrible wonderful beauty of it all. In the hottest moments I've never seen him excited—maybe the wad of tobacco in his cheek becomes a little more prominent, that's all. In one action we attacked all day, took 129 prisoners and afterwards all he did was grin and drawl: "Makes a fellow proud to see the boys work like they did today!"

24. Thousands of such Russians were shipped back to Russia by the Allies, many to be sent to prison camps or executed by Stalin as having been contaminated by Western ideas.

25. The company was nearly 40 men under full strength, infantrymen being in short supply.

He is the greatest leader of men I've known, bar none. Yet he'd give anything, I think, for a woman who truly loved him.

Unknown to any of us on the line, a drama of momentous significance has been playing at highest Allied command levels. While the Russians are still twenty miles east of the city, 9th Army armored patrols reach the western outskirts of Berlin almost unopposed. General Simpson informs Eisenhower and urges him to let the 9th take the German capital, possibly capture Hitler, possibly end the war at one stroke, certainly change the nature of the postwar world.

Simpson assures Ike he can reach Berlin with his advance elements within twenty-four hours and follow with his entire army within four days. It is April 14. Ike is so strongly tempted by Simpson's proposals that he passes the decision to higher authority, the combined Chiefs of Staff of Allied Forces, and asks for direction. When no orders come back, he tells Simpson to

German prisoners taken during the crossing of the Roer River, February 23, 1945. (Photo by George Silk. Life Magazine, © Time Warner, Inc.)

halt the 9th Army at the west bank of the Elbe River, some fifty miles from Berlin, as previously agreed.

So instead of rushing toward the German capital, K Company moves sedately northward by truck convoy up the Rhine-to-Berlin autobahn or freeway. We've never seen anything like it. We don't have such freeways in the U.S. To our eyes it's a marvel of engineering—an elevated speedway atop an earthen fill, two lanes in either direction separated by a grass divider, underpasses for crossroads. It reminds us again of German technology, in many respects superior to ours or anybody's.

Hitler built these autobahns to connect all parts of Germany with Berlin. On them he could move troops quickly to any border. But he never intended them for use by American invaders.

We pass the large city of Hannover, bombed nearly to extinction, looking as desolate as a city on the moon. Near Braunschweig we turn off northward and follow side roads to a gap opening between the 9th Army's left flank and the British 2nd Army which we're to fill. By the time we approach the Elbe near Dannenberg, sixty miles from the Baltic Sea, we're among the northernmost U.S. troops in Europe—on a front extending more than 400 air line miles to Patton's 3rd Army spearheads in eastern Austria, surging toward the Hungarian and Czechoslovakian borders. We de-truck, set up headquarters in a village and spread out in preparation to attack through dense woods lying between us and the riverbank.

The end cannot be far off now, but people are still being killed.

SANTA BARBARA APRIL 22, 1945

The news today is that the Russians are in Berlin. It seems fitting they be there first, after their long pull and Stalingrad. It means more to them than to us. But the stories of the atrocities of the Germans to our American prisoners and to the inmates of the concentration camps[26] are something incredibly terrible. Surely such things will affect our treatment of the German nation. Thank God the Pereiras[27] have survived, or had the last we knew.

26. With the Allied advance, the realities of Nazi concentration camps such as Belsen and Buchenwald became known to the public for the first time.
27. The Jewish family with whom Jane lived in Vienna in 1937–1938.

Winston Churchill (center, with visored cap) crosses the Rhine in our sector, flanked by Field Marshal Bernard L. Montgomery with beret (left) and U.S. 9th Army Commander Lieutenant General William H. Simpson (next Montgomery with three stars on helmet). Several hundred thousand G.I.'s were under British command in the early months of 1945, during and after the Battle of the Bulge. (U.S. Army)

How can we forget or be lenient after this? What do you feel about it? It's a ghastly condemnation of a race. Can it all be attributed to the wrong leaders? I don't think so. There is something wrong in the blood, some desire for superiority, something bad and dangerous. We must not forget. The San Francisco Conference[28] and all the talk about Russia and the Polish Communist gov't. the Russians recognize and we do not, seems awfully bad as an omen of allied cooperation. I must say it makes one shudder.

There is little elation over the prospect of Germany's defeat. People realize the way is long before we have peace and our men back. Long after Germany is done, there will be Japan.

Last night Mrs. Calhoun told a story about a tough cabaret singer who went into a ward of wounded men, all totally blind, and asked what they would like her to sing. There was silence. Then one of them said in a clear, low voice: "I Walk Alone." Such things make one stop and think, but there is nothing to do to cure the men who have no eyes or no ears or no legs or no

28. To create a permanent United Nations organization.

arms; for the dead maybe there is a peace, even though cut off in their prime, but for the wounded and maimed we have such a job ahead, such a time to prove our love and our faith and our tenderness without too much sympathy. God, what a sacrifice they have made! If this be in vain . . .

No letter for several days. Perhaps tomorrow. You cannot imagine how my heart thumps when there is your handwriting in the mailbox in the downstairs cupboard!

GERMANY [NEAR DANNENBERG], 27 APRIL 1945

We can smell the Baltic Sea when the wind is right and Oklahoma Willy has calculated it's 900 miles back to Omaha Beach, via Brest, where the company was sent to capture the submarine pens, and 4,850 more to Oklahoma and his Sweet Pea. He says that when he gets back there he's going to stick his rifle into his front yard by its muzzle, sit him down in a rocking chair on the front porch and watch it rust. I agree with him home, not here, is the place to be. Here the country is absolutely flat and quite densely wooded with smallish pines that grow out of sandy red soil, but the people are friendly and bring us food.

Two more boys from my old B Company of the 825th joined us today—one a sergeant who beat up the new 2nd lieutenant (my successor) at a dance and accordingly transferred. Captain K. has returned to the States with serious arthritis. Fee commands B Co. Evoy threw a cognac bottle at the colonel, and 35 men were applying for transfer at last report.

More anon. I feel an extra abundance of love for you these heavenly spring days and the promise of you is as bright for me as they are.

SANTA BARBARA, APRIL 27, 1945

What does this fragrance of sage remind you of? Remember that late afternoon on the golden hill when we talked till dark and walked back down to the ranch house? Your jacket smelled of sage and the one you made me wear did too. I can see you beside me, we were not engaged or even in love, but something was happening even then—that first weekend.

And we talked by the fire after your parents went to bed. And you drank beer and you lit the light to my room and said:

"Goodnight!" I was lonely then. Next morning you were gone and never was I lonelier.

What a long way we've come! We have lived together and apart, and borne the fruit of our bodies, and the fruit of our minds, and somewhere the sage is waiting again for us.

GERMANY [NEAR DANNENBERG], 28 APRIL '45

We've pushed Jerry about as far as he can be pushed in the direction of Uncle Joe's boys.[29] In one spirited little action right on the bank of a great river which must remain nameless, I rounded the corner of a house with carbine ready to fire and came face to face with a major general with .45 automatic pistol ready to fire, apparently at me. It was Uncle Charlie[30] himself come to help us clear the village. I couldn't think what to say so just grinned. He grinned back. We proceeded to clear the house together. On its dirt floor lay a kid in German uniform aged about 14 ripped nearly in two by an M-1 bullet. One of our medics was already treating him. So Uncle Charlie and I and the two aides with him kept on, right up to the river bank and the high levee there, helping capture in all more than 200 prisoners.

That was two days ago. Now our big excitement is 1st Sgt. Walsh's pending departure for a 7-day furlough in England and his girl in Liverpool. She's a Welsh dancer, one of many who find the American boys preferable to the British. The German girls do too (the official non-fraternization policy notwithstanding), as did the French, Belgian, and Dutch girls before them. "The Americans are so carefree!" they say. And when you realize how careworn these Europeans are, how prematurely aged and tired, you understand what they mean.

The German country people are much like country folk anywhere. Those of our present area, for instance, concealed ten American prisoners who escaped from a marching column and hid them two weeks until we came. And having been warned we would rape and burn and murder, they cannot show enough appreciation when we don't, wanting to cook for us, scrub the floor, make up beds with sheets—one old woman still unbelieving asking: "When you leave will you burn the house down?"

29. Joseph Stalin's Russian troops.
30. General Gerhardt, commanding the 29th.

My three years in the Army, March 11th, brought an in-crease in pay of a few dollars—5% of $166.66 (which would be what, sweet?)—called "longevity pay," so I'm going to send another ten dollars home monthly making you $250.[31] With dividends quarterly totaling around $90, you should have $280 or $290 income per month. Subtract $90 payment on the loan and you have $200 for the household and savings. Are these figures correct and do they take care of your needs adequately?

Walsh has just come in nude from taking what the G.I.'s have chosen to call a "whore's bath," out in a bucket by the pump, and is prattling about Plymouth, Liverpool, and his girl's eyes. Capt. R. is reading *Yank* and Cpl. Hans Bang, communica-tions chief since Don Mearin went home, is reporting to us the exciting news from the radio. The end seems in sight.

Next evening:

Captain R. left at noon for ten days' holiday on the Riviera. When these leave-orders come you drop everything and obey immediately, unless in actual combat. As he rode in his open jeep past the chow line, all dressed up in a new waist-length "Eisenhower" jacket, wearing all his decorations and a dark green overseas cap, everybody had a grin for him and a good word: "Don't do anything I wouldn't do, Captain! Don't forget to come back!" Croesus was never so rich as this Texas country boy.

Because of him I'm enjoying being company executive. We share many things, including when necessary a bed. We go on reconnaissance, formulate a plan of attack, study German, talk of wives, review today, tomorrow, yesterday; or we share a bottle of whiskey with mutual enjoyment. He is one of those rare humans with all the qualities of greatness: complete simplicity, complete modesty, complete courtesy which is to say respect, plus cour-age—courage to implement all the rest.

He has told me, in deepest confidence and soul baring, of trying to get himself killed during his first days in combat. When he discovered his wife's unfaithfulness, he lost all desire to live, volunteered for overseas as a replacement officer, and in a matter of weeks was at the front commanding K Company as I've de-scribed. In those first days he repeatedly tried to commit suicide by exposing himself to heavy fire, asking that it hit him, asking

31. About $1,750 in today's dollars.

God to take him; but God did not let it happen. Men all around him were killed. Miraculously he was untouched. Finally he decided he wasn't meant to die but to live, and he began to live for the men, for his work as their leader, his responsibility for them. Thus he's been gradually transformed into the person I know today. Like the men I recognize in him another order of being. Someone touched by the divine. I've seen men look at him as at a saint, or a Christ, and inwardly and even outwardly reach out to touch him because they've seen him willing to die for them. It is a wonderfully sacred and moving thing, Janie.

Tonight I'm signing for him recommendations for the award of the Bronze Star Medal to six of his men, some of whom distinguished themselves for gallantry in action; some of whom, day-in-and-out for six months, have simply done their duty.

Night has fallen. The dusky spring darkness—"dusky dark," the Southern boys call it, recalling times they went up under the banks of "shoemakes" (sumacs) and wild red haws in blossom to meet their girls—my dusky dark has flowed out from the east and spreads under the trees but every higher outline is clear, including the sky from which the clouds are passing. Wish I had a girl to meet me!

Daily now, eastward in the distance, I see a towering column of black smoke. Berlin is burning. As the Russians come on toward the Elbe, fleeing German soldiers begin crossing the half-mile-wide river and surrendering to the Americans.

Soon the elite V-2 Rocket Division appears. It's been based at Peenemunde on the Baltic coast, center for development of the V-1 and V-2 guided missiles which have caused devastation and thousands of casualties in England, France and Belgium. It has even developed plans to tow containerized V-2's to the U.S. coast by submarine and fire them at New York City and Washington. The Rocket Division is ferried across the Elbe in boats and makeshift rafts and its arcane secrets become part of U.S. military technology. All resistance ends.

On May 2 a patrol from our 175th Regiment crosses the river and spots a group of saddled horses and sees men standing near them wearing long gray overcoats and round furred hats. Private Russell Frederick calls out in Russian: "We're friends! We're

American soldiers!" Hearty handshakes follow. The Russians are members of the 6th Guards Cavalry Division. Other Russian soldiers shook hands with members of the U.S. 69th Division on the upper Elbe a week earlier, in a celebrated first linkage between American and Soviet forces. The war in Europe is as good as over.

With the captain still away at the Riviera, my jeep and I lead our truck convoy back down the autobahn to Bielefeld, in pastoral Westphalia, to await a new assignment.

GERMANY [NEAR BIELEFELD], 5 MAY 1945

The German collapse has been total, of mind even more than of body, and now if there were a great prophet, or even a skillful director of a peace program among us, most Germans would receive him with open arms. They have been drugged so long by lies that when the daily dosage stops they are like addicts without their opiate. It is a ghastly fact. The mind of Germany is a huge vacuum. If we can step in and give it something it can believe, we shall truly have won.

To temper the celebration here, there is the Russian who helps in our kitchen, a sturdy blond of 30 with broad face and nose who was brought to Germany five years ago from a village near Moscow and compelled to work in mines and build roads. For four years he did not hear a word from his wife and two children. He knows his home was burned by the Germans. He does not want the Germans to help him rebuild it. He says he would kill them.

A Russian girl told her experience to our Russian cook, Zalo. She showed him the bluish-purple scars of the whip across her shoulders. A German officer wanted her but she refused him and was whipped and kept two weeks in a dungeon, then treated kindly in hopes she would give in. But she didn't. She told Zalo she would rather die first. She said the Russian girls would lie down for any Russian man to make male children to kill Germans, and if the baby was a girl it was disposed of. She said the best defense against being molested was never to wash so that you smelled so bad no man wanted you.

Though there is degradation and filth, you would be astonished how clean and decent most of the slave-labor camps are. Each has its own commandant. If several nationalities are present, each has a leader and one of them is chosen to represent all. At a camp I visited today this head man was an Italian officer, an engineer from Bologna. He spoke for 500 Russians, French, Poles, Dutch, Belgians, Italians. I had a long talk with him in French and told him about you and Florence and what I knew of Italy from my travels there. He was captured on the island of Corfu by the Germans. He said the Germans shot several officers in his group for no apparent reason.

Throughout the camp men and women live together as man and wife. "One day they just tell you they are married," he says with a smile and a shrug, "and that is it!" In general everyone is well behaved. "Only when some prisoners of war were here did we have trouble. But now all is forgotten—all!" And we raised our glasses to freedom.

GERMANY [NEAR BIELEFELD], 9 MAY 1945

A word on Victory Day.[32] It's a heavenly spring day, all the trees suddenly in leaf, all the world so green. You look up at the sky and think: nothing more to fear from there! You look back across the fields and they are just fields now without a menace from that ditch or that clump of trees. Sharp sounds don't startle you. There is no more alarm. And the horrible scream of an incoming shell is something to be slowly forgotten.

Uniforms may soon be out of place. But today they were a fitting and grand sight, the whole regiment of them, in a green field under a blue sky, to commemorate this moment of victory and honor the dead who could not be with us.

First a Protestant chaplain led us in a hymn, 3000 men standing with bowed heads. Then a Catholic chaplain led a prayer. Then a Jew recited the 23rd Psalm. And then taps was sounded as we all stood silently in the midst of that warm green morning.

Passing in review for General Gerhardt was by columns of companies so he could get a good look. He was standing close to the microphone of the public address system and we overheard him asking Colonel Bingham, the regimental commander, impa-

---

32. V-E Day (Victory in Europe Day) was later designated as May 8 when final surrender documents were ratified.

tiently: "Has K Company gone by yet?" And then complaining because the identifying guidons were not out so he could recognize each company.

K is his favorite, the best in the division. I was proud to lead it by him and sorry Capt. R. could not, because more then anyone he brought us safely through.

I never liked parading in the States but I do now. Marching with these fellows with whom I've shared so much brings us all closer, like good conversation, only much, much better. And we all feel this and silently respect it. In step, easy, tested, strong, we are right as never before and perhaps never again. And if peace could be established in the spirit we have now, or if (and this may seem a strange thought) we should all die now, it would be a just and lasting peace, or it would be the finest moment of our lives.

Later there was a thanksgiving and memorial service just for our battalion. It was held in the Lutheran church of the village where we are quartered, an old and very dark church where you would not expect God to come when all outdoors was so green and lovely. But if it is true that when two or three are gathered together earnestly God comes to them, he was there this afternoon, the pews solid with O.D. uniforms and the young chaplain in brown combat jacket at the lectern.

We laid our rifles in the aisles, those of us at the ends of the pews, and the rest held theirs between their knees, and during the prayer you could see the black muzzles of the M-1s sticking up between the bowed heads.

The first hymn was "Come Thou Almighty King" and as with everything now the words had meaning as never before. It occurred to me we were released at last, were free again.

In front of me two boys shared the same hymn book. I saw them sharing the same frozen foxhole on an outpost along the Roer River, and when we jumped off and crossed the river they came one behind the other on the footbridge you saw pictured in *Life* which a mortar shell cut later and on which the dead floated all day. Those two men have eaten, slept, prayed, gotten drunk, argued, laughed, bitched about the Army and gone to the latrine together for six months and they've fought together, if there is such a thing. Actually nobody fights, you know. You just get up and go, scared to death, and hope you don't get killed this time, and then not *this* time, and so on through all the times. But if you have a buddy it isn't so bad and without ever saying it you cling to him and depend on him.

The sermon didn't matter. The chaplain suffers from what you might call the ecclesiastical approach. Talk to him around the mess line and he sounds like anybody else, but in preaching he must say "utilize" instead of "use" and many "thou's" and "thee's." What really mattered was that he was dressed like we were and had been through what we had.

Then we prayed silently for the dead, each for his own particular friends and for the great figures in whose glory we all share, like Peregory who advanced alone across an open field with his B.A.R.,[33] killed 8 and captured 35, so the battalion could advance; or the especially pathetic cases like Simone. He had been with us only a few days. I saw him last lying in a plowed field in a drizzle of gray rain. They had laid his poncho over him and marked him with his own rifle, stuck in by the muzzle with his helmet over the butt. He was my man, Janie. I had led him where he was. He was following me. Perhaps the bullet intended for me hit him. If I live a hundred years, the thought of him will never leave me. Recently I received a letter from his widow, wanting to know . . . "wanting to know, as I cannot rest."

At the end we sang "America, Sweet Land of Liberty."

Going out I heard this conversation:

"Remember the first one at Fort Meade?"

"Yeah."

"It's been a long way."

"Yeah."

"You heard Stevens was killed?"

"Yeah, Bellemere too. He got it that last push."

"Yeah?"

"Yeah."

A day always seems brighter when you come out of church but this afternoon I believe there was something more. Until you have been in combat and come out you do not realize under what a shadow you have been, even on the brightest day; and until you've been through a war and come to peace you cannot realize the blessing of a clear blue sky without any menace in it at all.

33. Browning Automatic Rifle.

Bless you, and keep you. I am happy today and every day I have your love.

P.S. The above may sound somber. I know it does. We had the joyous celebration—the bottle-emptying, the bottoms-upping—yesterday afternoon when the news first came. This was the somber part—because we know we're at the end of much, the beginning of much. Victory, Peace, Spring, on to Japan—they're all intermingled incomprehensibly, grandly, gloriously, and somberly! I love you.

SANTA BARBARA, MAY 9, 1945

V-E Day was a solemn occasion here as it must have been with you. All the stores downtown were closed. The Mission bells rang as did the bells of other churches. All church doors were open and people went inside to pray. We exchanged prayers of thanksgiving

Members of K Company receive the Silver Star and other decorations. Felix Branham is at left, front row. (National Archives)

Germany, 1945. Many slave-workers we liberated were penned up again and sent back to Russia, where they were murdered on Stalin's orders or sent to Siberian labor camps for supposedly being contaminated by western ideas. (Photo by David Scherman. Life Magazine, © Time Warner, Inc.)

Members of the elite German V-2 Rocket Division, fleeing pursuing Russians, are helped across the Elbe to surrender to our 29th Division. (National Archives)

over the phone, your mother, Mum, and I, and tonight when
Father gets home we shall all have dinner at 2442 Garden.

I cannot quite grasp it—this war which has taken Pop and
still holds you and John—and now you both must go on to the
Pacific. The paper says nearly three million troops will be moved
out of Europe in the next nine months, leaving an occupation
force of perhaps 400,000. Some are already on their way to the
Pacific. Dear God, will there be no end? Yet I am thankful, most
terribly thankful, that for the moment the danger is over for you
and for John. And I pray that you will be given an opportunity
to return and see, if only briefly, those who love you.

I feel very middle-aged in our garden. Two little girls in
overalls are playing about me, rushing up every so often for a kiss
on some bump, or a reassurance about some menacing bee or
passing dog or cat. It seems just a moment ago I was playing in
the garden in Florence and Monty was reassuring *me*. And now
I, we, are the old and these little creatures we have made are the
young. And the great tide of life rolls on, past these milestones
such as yesterday.

There was a great gathering of citizens in the County Bowl

Only fifty-seven miles to Berlin . . . (U.S. Army)

put on by Aunt Pearl Chase. Hermann Hagedorn[34] who lives here now, was chief speaker. I thought some of what he said was very fine:

"A war is over . . . but intangible yet dynamic forces do not end when the last enemy ship is sunk, the last enemy soldier killed or captured . . . Hitler is beaten and appears to be dead, but the satanic spirit he roused and organized is going to be a power in the world for a long time to come."

Hagedorn especially mentioned anti-Semitism in this country as one of Hitler's slimy marks upon us. "There is no defeating such forces with pious hopes or fifty cents in the collection plate. Militant corruption can be overcome only by militant integrity, militant barbarism only by militant humanity, the propaganda of hate and death only by the gospel of love and life, speaking to the least and the greatest among us through the still small voice of the heart."

I thought that very fine. Don't you? We must stretch with every nerve and muscle to make the post-war world a better one.

All my love, my darling, all my love and that of our two daughters, goes to you with these words, along with the fervent hope that you can somehow find a way to let us see you, how ever briefly, before going on toward Japan.

34. Poet and biographer.

CHAPTER 9

*The invasion of Japan will
cost over a million casualties
to American forces alone.*
DOUGLAS MACARTHUR

On Toward Japan

On toward Japan. The words rise like Mt. Everest before us. Already we've been climbing, so it seems, for three and a half long years, together yet seemingly forever separated and no end in sight and we've already traversed what seems like a Himalayan expanse of base camps and monsoon storms, escaping avalanches and ice falls.

From the Normandy beaches to V-E Day and the German surrender took eleven bitter months. But even more bitter seems the prospect of what lies ahead. Adding poignancy comes news that Bob's college roommate, Sylvester Cunningham, has been killed by a Japanese kamikaze which struck the deck of his destroyer off the Philippines. Sylvester and Amy were married about the same time we were and have a three-year-old daughter. As sorrow sweeps up and grips us again, with it comes the conviction that no one in this war is dying or suffering in vain, that there must be a better world ahead. We hold to this idea with all our might because anything less seems intolerable. Our long uphill climb hasn't ended, it appears. We've merely stopped for breath.

Preparations for the invasion of Japan, scheduled for November 1, 1945, code name Operation Olympic, were well under way by early summer. Admiral William F. ("Bull") Halsey took his U.S. Third Fleet into Japanese home waters and bombarded shore installations from battleships in addition to launching 1,000-plane carrier attacks. A British carrier force joined these operations. U.S. Air Force B-29 bombers had already devastated Tokyo, while our submarines took deadly toll of the Japanese merchant fleet on which the home islands depended for supplies.

Even so, an invasion of Japan will cost a million American casualties according to reliable estimates. The Japanese are gathering a defensive force of 35 million, more than the combined armies of the U.S., England, and Nazi Germany. It includes women and children prepared to strap explosives to their bodies and sacrifice their lives as human kamikazes, and a thousand deadly kamikaze planes are ready to strike our ships in suicidal attacks.

Against this background, President Truman and his advisors will debate whether to drop the newly invented atomic bomb, which may force Japan to surrender without further loss of life by either side.

For the moment the two of us breathe a sigh of relief as the 29th Division goes to Bremerhaven, on the North Sea coast of Germany, to take it over from the British who'd captured it and to help make it the main port of entry for U.S. troops and supplies bound for occupied Germany. Jane begins part-time work in an Army hospital in Santa Barbara.

BREMERHAVEN, GERMANY, 19 MAY 1945

At last I can say where we are—Bremerhaven at the mouth of the Weser. Just a moment ago I stepped out of this guardhouse onto the dock and took a look at the *Europa*[1] by moonlight, a stone's throw away. She's spent the war moored here, resting now in five feet of mud, and it is our duty among other things to guard her as a war prize. The British bombed everything else along this waterfront but carefully spared her.

Outwardly she's little changed from the night I first made her acquaintance in New York City. I vividly recall that humid June 30, 1937! We[2] went up on deck for a breath of fresh air before sailing and noticed the glaring red Nazi flag with its white circle and black swastika at her lighted masthead above us. It gave us a creepy feeling even then—and little did we know!

Yesterday I boarded her again. She was absolutely deserted, silent as a tomb, everything coated with dust, and my footsteps went echoing ahead of me along her corridors. I found my old cabin and other places frequented during the voyage, even the location of chairs and tables where Harris, Henley and I and fellow collegians sat and quaffed beer with certain young ladies

---

1. German passenger liner, famous as holder of the blue ribbon for fastest transatlantic crossing (4-1/2 days) prior to the advent of the French *Normandie* and English *Queen Mary* and *Queen Elizabeth*. The *Europa* was Hitler's challenge to the democracies' supremacy in transatlantic passenger service.
2. College students, at the beginning of the trip that led eventually to Moscow and Berlin.

while we plowed the mid-Atlantic. I can't say I recall sitting on deck with a steamer rug across my knees being served hot consommé by a steward in white jacket. All that happened up in first class, far above us. We were in third. But we used to sneak up to first at night, while the stewards winked, because there were far more girls up there traveling with parents than boys, and dancing partners were needed. My first experience as gigolo. Being aboard her again under present circumstances gave me a mighty queer feeling, believe me.

Much speculation hereabouts. Do we remain as Army of Occupation? Do we go home? Do we go to the Pacific? Best guess: we go home on leave before we go to the C.B.I.[3]—if we go.

Home. You can imagine how much it is in the minds of everyone and what a madness of guessings and rumors and gripings there is about the "point system" that's going to take us home. Officers are on a different basis from enlisted men. For us there are two systems. The first is the same as that of the men, based on length of service overseas. Under it I score 84 points. The second is based on our efficiency ratings. Every six months a commanding officer rates the efficiency of his junior officers—as to whether their work has been unsatisfactory, satisfactory, very satisfactory, excellent, or superior. My ratings until I left the 825th were excellent. What I've received since I don't know. But my final point total will be a combination of the two systems I mention.

Anyway, there may be home leave. Shall I come home first, if I must go to the C.B.I., or would you rather continue without me, now you are adjusted to widowhood, and not go through the upheaval and readjustment?

You say. Sometimes I think it would be easier on both of us for me to slip off through the Suez. Frankly I go through seven kinds of hell just departing from you after a ten-day leave. And to come home but not to stay home would not be much pleasure. And yet it would be the most acute pleasure imaginable.

Well, this is more of "what if" and "maybe," because nobody knows anything and we may be here a long or short time and I may go individually to the States or the C.B.I., willy-nilly, without benefit of K Co. and the 29th; or we may go as a unit; or we

---

3. China, Burma, India Theater of Operations.

may stay here ten years as Army of Occupation; or a dozen possibilities.

34 E. PADRE ST., SANTA BARBARA, MAY 20, 1945

Another Sunday dead and gone. Thank God for that. I've never liked the day, not since I was a child. I used to look forward to it because of no school and then I was always disappointed, probably because I had all the free time I wanted and didn't realize I was bored.

Anyway, I still feel that same oppression at the end of a Sunday. I hate it even more when I have to go to church. I shall enjoy going with you, I am sure, but church for church sake is pretty dead to me. I don't suppose we will ever completely see eye to eye on religion. I can't stomach much of it. I suppose this shows a lack on my part but I'm not sure I'll be able to change.

I hope you won't think the children have to go to Sunday school; I hate the idea. I don't think I'd mind it in a small and wild community in Texas, but in a genteel place like S.B. there is something rather awful about all the little dressed up children traipsing to Sunday school—that "holy" speech and attitude, etc. If they were allowed to follow my instincts, ours would never go near a church. When they are adults they can make their choices. I've never felt a desire for religion. But perhaps my desire for sunshine and country and music and poetry and little children are my religion. I find them the working, everyday things by which I live.

BREMERHAVEN, GERMANY, 20 MAY 1945

More than once after we jumped off across the Roer your letters came when we were on the line, as I've told you, brought up at night by the jeep that brings the ammunition, K-rations, and water; and by candlelight in the cellar of some ruined house I opened the blue envelopes I know so well, that have become part of you, and read your words and at the same time thought how strange I should be where I was, and you there, and the scrap of blue paper between us, as it has been for so long and in so many different places.

The enclosures are from those letters. I saved your best but was forbidden by regulations to carry them in action, lest they reveal useful information to the enemy, so would tear out parts that meant most, unwrap my wallet from its oilskin sack and carry those fragments in it until we went into a rest area again and my bedroll and other belongings caught up.

There is such a world of things I haven't told you. If I wrote from now till morning I scarcely could describe one day in action, time is so crowded full then. Let me tell about a particularly moving experience. One morning at dawn we attacked the big city of Dortmund, back in the Ruhr. It was a little like attacking New York City. Imagine a long meadow resembling Central Park but V-shaped, its apex pointing from the suburbs into the heart of downtown—right down to the skyscrapers. That's how you enter Dortmund from the west or how we did, anyway. The German F.O.'s (forward artillery observers) were up in the sky-scrapers and had a truly beautiful view of us. Snipers were in the suburban buildings on our flanks. We advanced rather grandly if absurdly in a broad skirmish line down the meadow toward the rising sun, dew on the grass, shot and shell flying around. Really it was fantastic, a covey of brown-clothed men scattered over the meadow, those skyscrapers rearing up in front of us like mountain peaks with the sun coming over their summits.

We'd got about halfway toward them when the artillery barrage hit us. We started to run forward out of it (better to run forward than backward in such cases) and head for some old Jerry trenches in the lee of a railroad embankment which bisected the meadow. And just as we got there—you can't imagine how gratefully—M., the boy I shall write a story about, the boy who "went back" (turned coward a few weeks earlier and headed for the rear) and who had come forward again and made good with us—M. took a direct hit from a shell. "It had his name on it," as the boys say. End of M. End of that pale uncourageous but finally gallant young boy whom I'd talked to heart-to-heart the night he came back to us from detention, advising him not to worry, the past was the past, I'd give him another chance.

He'd made good, stayed in there solidly—all the way till now. And I'd seen the pride and manhood return to his eyes and spine. And then this. It was heartbreaking, really.[4]

4. Bob's story about M. was published in *Collier's* for May 8, 1948, and is scheduled to appear in 1991 in the New American Library anthology *Combat!*, edited by Martin H. Greenberg and Bill Pronzini.

Garrison duty quickly becomes a routine. Already some are saying they would rather be back on the line. You know this life—the same old story of petty details and restrictions. A man ceases being an individual and becomes a number, a name on the bunk tag, etc. And tomorrow morning our combined Army and Navy officers' mess opens, with colored boys in white jackets serving us. I don't like the idea.

SANTA BARBARA, MAY 23, 1945

It has taken me exactly two months to achieve what I did today! I got out to the hospital[5] for the afternoon and worked at the recreation room of the Red Cross. I played ping-pong for nearly three hours so my back and legs are tired tonight. Two men were excellent and beat me after some close rallies and much fun for them. They love to win.

Then I played a foursome with a very nervous tall dark and handsome partner. He appeared to have no ailments but wore a hearing aid (many of these at this hospital) and was terribly upset whenever I missed a shot. Then, having been gruff with me, would suddenly remember, as it were, that I was not the cause of his nerves and would excuse himself. I was sorry for him and for others I saw. All were able to move around, but there were some with such sad faces and some with such serious wounds: arms and legs in slings and casts which mean months and months of life like that.

The first time is a bit strange and one feels rather hopeless and helpless but I shall manage better. I did feel awfully queer when rebuffed by some, who merely grunted and turned away when asked if they would like to play ping-pong. They must be SO sick of well-meaning women, and yet the doctors want them to mix with us and do SOMETHING. Games are what they like most. I shall need to learn card games galore because they love cards. Cards, and crossword puzzles, or picture puzzles. It lends a strange degree of fun and interest to a game for them if they can play it with a woman or girl. There were two much older women on the shift with me today but nice, and gradually the younger volunteers are coming.

At one point I sat in the lounge and talked to four or five

5. The Army's Hoff General Hospital at the western outskirts of Santa Barbara.

fellows, all arguing about citizenship questions. They all wore "reds," that is, hospital gowns. One, a top sergeant and apparently very well though evidently he has been here ages, was bawling the others out. He was a French-Canadian, very husky, awfully tough. I wanted to sock him but of course merely smiled warmly. He complained about EVERYTHING! And I wish you could see what the Red Cross, alone, does for these men—everything free and amusements galore and comfort and treats of every kind!

One awfully shy and nice boy from Pasadena, with an arm in a sling, only back in this country seven days, told me he hadn't played ping-pong for three years. I guess he meant he'd been in the war zones that length of time. He was nice and asked if I came from Boston! So there you are. My first day. If in any way I helped or amused those men I am awfully glad. I hope sometime to be able to pick out a lonely one and make him happier or help build up his faith in life and the years to come. But it's not easy when lots of them would rather be alone and grump or silently be wretched and tortured.

I feel amazingly tired. I think being with utter strangers and the added emotional strain of seeing their wounds or discontent is quite exhausting. But that's where I'd rather go on my afternoons away from the children. It is a change and it's a help, however minor, to the war effort.

No letter from you for five days. We may hear from John any day that he is on his way here for a furlough before going to the Pacific.

Joan talks a lot about you lately. This morning as we were starting downstairs to get breakfast, I asked her to go to my room and carry down the letters on the low table with us, and as she came back she said: "These are letters Mumsie has wrote to Daddy." And tonight I asked her what I should write you. She said: "Dear Daddy, come back today." And she has already planned: "When Daddy comes back Joan and Kaffie and Daddy and Mum-Mum will all bounce on Mumsie's bed together." So you see we are in for a lovely time of broken springs and won't it be fun?

BREMERHAVEN, 23 MAY 1945

Six of us including Capt. R., Lts. Proffitt, France, Snipas, Martin have a magnificent suite consisting of a sitting room, two large

bedrooms, a bath, kitchen, attic, and cellar. The whole is connected with the men's barracks, a fine four-story brick building
once a school for German Navy warrant officers. The entire
battalion and many of our own Navy people are quartered similarly and there is a fine drill field in the center of the barracks
quadrangle where we all stand formations and march. All very
much a military post.

Today I was thinking of a year ago this time—thinking that
the first year without Pop, the hardest, has passed. At times I tell
people here the story of his death in action with the infantry,
feeling that those who know Max Brand, the writer, should also
know Frederick Faust. I believe he would be glad to see veteran
infantrymen taking such pleasure in *Destry Rides Again* and *Singing
Guns* and his other books. They have a place among the familiar
daily requests one overhears. "Got a *Stars and Stripes*? Got a *Yank*,
Buddy? Seen that Max Brand anywhere?" He would be glad, I
think, to know he is with the infantry here as he was in Italy.

Tell me about Judy and John. And give my love to Mum.
Does she continue gaining her way back into life? I love your
mother very much and want her always to feel that I do, a triteness
perhaps, but the mere suggestion one is not wanted or loved
always has seemed to me one of the cruelest punishments a human
being can be subjected to.

Have I told of the return of the great Chubby Proffitt from
a hospital in England? He's a second lieutenant by virtue of a
battlefield commission last October, one of the old Charlottesville
originals, cut from the same mold as Purvis, tall, smiling, gentle-
mannered Virginian, with that granite courage and fighting instinct. He was wounded three times, holds the D.S.C., Silver
Star, Bronze Star with cluster. We expect him to go home any
day for discharge and shall miss him. Purvis already is on his way
as are most of the oldtimers.

My former platoon sergeant, Keating, was hit after our crossing of the Dortmund-Ems Canal but should eventually return. I
never told you about Keating. He was of the best. His wound was
a little round pink spot slightly indented at the center, well above
the heart, thank God. We'd been attacking a roadblock, crawling
on our bellies in ditches on either side of a tree-lined road, bullets
snapping around our heads. It was old-fashioned war, all rifle fire.
Keating must have raised himself to shoot. When I saw him he
was lying on a stretcher, shirt off, conscious but pale as a ghost,

and I had just the glimpse of that pink hole, like a spot of jelly, as I gripped his hand.

A few days earlier I'd nearly got mine. We were about to attack a village across a large open field and were lying in a ditch (thank God for roadside ditches!), waiting for the captain's hand signal. A platoon of five tanks came waddling down the road to help us, a welcome sight, much resembling trees in a desert to men suffocating from heat. Waiting to jump off *is* a kind of suffocation, by the way.

Finally the captain gives the signal and as the tanks deploy and waddle out into the field on my left, I stand up—one of life's more difficult moves under the circumstances—and my men follow suit and we advance in a long ragged line, the standard five paces between each of us. But invariably when you come under fire in the open you draw closer for physical and moral support. Even the tanks did. Pretty soon we're all moving forward in a confused mass, the tanks blasting away at everything in sight, our B.A.R. men spraying red tracers like water from a hose, the rest of us firing at random in the new technique called "marching fire"—which is to spray as much lead as possible in order to make the opposition keep its head down and finger presumably off its trigger, while upping our own morale. If you hit anybody in such confusion you seldom know it, which may be a blessing.

Well, things began going wrong. Instead of heading for the village, the tanks began veering to the right across our front as if they wanted to avoid it and go south for the spring. I climbed on the rear deck of the nearest one, far too excited to think about anything except getting the tank commander's attention and steering him straight. Bullets pinged off the steel around me but I hardly noticed. I pounded on the turret with the butt of my carbine and yelled until the hatch opened and a head wearing what looked like a football helmet poked gingerly out. I pointed with my carbine toward the village directly in front of us and shouted: "That's the objective! Fire on that!"

He nodded, pulled his head down, shut the hatch. By this time the tank had come to a stop, so had everything else. After what seemed an eternity its big gun swiveled around and there was a mighty blast of flame and smoke which nearly deafened me and the nearest house caved in. Then there was more blasting and the same thing happened to the next house, and the next, as other tanks got the idea. And as we all began to move forward toward the village, gray uniforms began to emerge from holes in front of it, and from the remaining houses, with their hands up. By which time I'd dismounted from my charger, glad enough to be on solid ground again and no longer the object of any special attention from anyone.

Well to resume: with Keating and others gone, my old 2nd Platoon will be almost entirely new faces before long. So, in a way, I'm glad to be where I am—executive officer identified with the company as a whole.

The new battle star[6] for Germany gives me 89 points. Capt. R. has 98. The two of us *may*, therefore, be with the 29th for a while, or go wherever such scores go. Would you like to see the old husband before he's 30? I count these years in abeyance and consider myself as returning to you at 27, when I left so early one morning for the recruiting office.

I'm enchanted to know Kaffie can build a castle with her blocks. I want to spend whole days with that young fraulein, fraternizing, and be sure she takes to her old Daddy as to all those other males. I think you are terribly sweet to bring the children up with me a living, breathing father capable of taking tea with Joan and Panda, eating oranges from the garden, building block castles.

I'm glad you have begun work at Hoff Hospital. And what will the men say? I'm eager to hear every detail. First they'll ask if you're married. Then where your husband is. Then why you are there. (Damn their souls, they will recognize a beautiful woman!) And then they will tell you about themselves and that is what I want to hear, because I believe I can pay you my own compliments and I want to know the thoughts and hopes of those poor devils who've had their bodies and minds wounded, and about the people in charge and whether their program is good or bad.

The radio is going on in detail about the suicide of Himmler,[7] the honors being accorded Eisenhower, Montgomery and the rest, and yet all is anticlimax, a quick decline from the high excitement. Impatience will be the mood here, coupled with a willingness to stay put in preference to the C.B.I.

Can't you send me a piece of your sweet flesh to go with the

6. Small bronze star worn on a campaign ribbon.
7. Heinrich Himmler, head of German police including the Gestapo.

scent of you I carry with me, on the handkerchief I received so long ago at Schleiden in the dark cold days before we attacked? This is spring and I had forgotten those days but for the handkerchief, and the scent of you whom I love.

SANTA BARBARA, MAY 24, 1945

I was awfully pleased this morning when the woman who heads my section of the Red Cross at the hospital telephoned and asked if I could possibly go tomorrow as an extra day, since four volunteers dropped out and they were shorthanded.

I managed to contact another woman, also in my class and about 45, who said she'd go with me so we'll drive out together. It's out on the 3000 block of Hollister. I must say there is nothing much better than the feeling you are helping someone. I revel in it! It elates and purifies me. It's the best tonic for morale that I know. I love the feeling that people are depending on me and when I can deliver the goods I am about the happiest mortal on earth. You know what I mean? To once in a while not live for one's own ends, to stretch out and see the other person's viewpoint? I must make a special effort tomorrow to play ping-pong or cards or whatever with the Negroes. It is so touching to see them. There are not many. Yet even here among the wounded they are still often treated like outsiders. A greater effort is needed, Bobbie.

My whole outlook on life has changed now that I can be in the war more fully. I think the summer will pass faster and better if I have Wednesdays and occasional other days at the hospital, not even thinking about the children for three hours!

AT AN AIRPORT NEAR HANNOVER, 28 MAY 1945

I'm waiting here for a C-47[8] to take me to the Riviera for seven days' leave. Doubtless we shall fly down the Rhone and see the Alps and come to Cannes along the coast. If the day is bright I'll be watching for Corsica, where your little friend[9] lived 150 years ago. Of all leaves available, Paris, Brussels, England, this is the one I most wanted and am very pleased and excited.

8. The military version of the Douglas DC-3 commercial transport plane.
9. Napoleon.

I wish you were with me. Being alone in the Army is bad enough but to be alone like this, practically a civilian, doing fun things, is worse. All I look forward to is a quiet room, time in the sun, many walks in back streets or bicycling in the hills—to find some inn where I may sip wine under olive trees and look down upon clusters of tile roofs and the blue Mediterranean. All I carry is what I wear, and a field pack with fresh underwear and socks, a borrowed pair of swim trunks, paper and envelopes, and notebooks I hope to fill. And I'm ready to go, Prusse. Can't you fly quickly to Cannes tomorrow? A bicycle built for two will be the thing, fitting to your long brown legs, and I'll take the rear seat to watch and make sure you're not loafing.

While waiting here I discovered Vallentin's *Leonardo Da Vinci* and am reading ardently. I feel we have never studied Leonardo enough. Look in his *Notebooks* at the reproduction of the cartoon for *The Virgin and St. Anne*, the mother's head. Her expression is a pure bit of heaven on earth. Do you know I have seen you look like that? I love that expression beyond any other.

SANTA BARBARA, MAY 28, 1945

Now I know how you felt when you came out of church on V-E Day after the service, and how you felt when marching by the general. I have almost written to Capt. R. several times to tell him how proud I am of all he has done, and that there are so many other wives who feel the same and may not be able to express it. Anyway, your letter was dated May 12th. That seems fairly long ago and V-E Day equally distant. Already we want the rest, the total end of the war. I know there are likely two more years before we can have our husbands back for good, but one has vague hopes of a leave before the next pitched battle, somehow, though one tries to put such thoughts away.

The main thing, as you aptly say, is to be thankful that there is a Bob on the receiving end of the line at all, that letters reach you and come from you, that for the time you are out of danger, that we have come through the German war with no loss of limbs, or of each other's love. One must remember and thank the sky and the spring and the warm summer coming to us. I do feel so numbed by all this living in war and then the partial peace. The relief of knowing you are well and safe, and that you are my husband still and in one piece, is something very strange. I can breathe more freely, but still the inmost tension which did grip my heart for months and months is only slowly dissolving and I suppose it will melt away soon. Then one silently and with faith must prepare for the next siege.

Your description of services for men who were not with you and your thoughts about poor Simone and his wife moved me deeply. Such people are part of us and will live on in us. As you once said, we have lived too long with catastrophe and horror and aching hearts and it will take time to return to life again. But we need never forget. The summer helps. I can see you sitting in shorts! Is it hot already? I will send shirts to you, undershirts soon.

Am having some bad days now with the knowledge that my depressed letters must be reaching you. There was a gap in the mail with ten days of nothing from you so I felt very grim; perhaps because it was just after V-E Day and I did want actual word that you were alright. I hate myself for writing when in those moods of despair and longing, but I find it hard to conceal my emotions when I must write every day! It is nearly June. Thank God the months are passing! The casualties on Okinawa[10] are staring us in the face in the papers daily. It is horrible and yet we are growing numbed, at least those of us who have no men in the thick of it.

I know how you must be feeling since the fields and the clumps of trees no longer mean shells and death. I understand your sense of renewed life, for I had it when I emerged from pneumonia in the hospital in Santa Monica seven years ago. I thought then I would never take a day of sunlight for granted or a flower in the breeze or the smell of pines by the ocean, or the eyes of a little child at play, or a thousand other things that are so closely immortal. Out of this war may come a thankfulness strong enough to give peace to the world. Yet I wonder. The squabbles already in progress are so old and yet so horribly new— after all our high hopes and faith in the future when we were at grips with Germany.

I've been asked to an officers' wives tea on Thursday, to a children's party with Joan on Saturday, and to a lunch on Tuesday. I am only going to the children's party because I cannot do

10. Island in the Ryukyus, last stepping stone in the drive toward the Japanese homeland. U.S. casualties would total over 50,000 and include 36 ships sunk and 368 damaged, and 763 planes lost. If Okinawa was any measure, the invasion of Japan would be bloody business indeed.

so many social things in one week and because I loathe mass gatherings of women. While the war lasts my outings are only good and profitable when I can go to the hospital and help a little toward the war effort in that way. For the rest, I'd rather type your notes and be with our children who have rather a raw deal with only a mother when they need a daddy so badly too.

Tell me as soon as you know what the future will hold, at least the immediate future. I suppose officers will stay on until six months after the end in the Pacific, or even longer for the policing of Japan.

CANNES-ON-THE-RIVIERA, 31 MAY 1945

The clouds cleared as we flew out over Marseilles and saw the unbelievable Mediterranean, skirted the coast and within half an hour were landing at an airport on the waterfront at Nice. Nice is the enlisted men's playground, off-limits to officers. A bus brought us over here to Cannes and we have been distributed to various hotels. By great good luck I escaped the large, once-fashionable hostelries at the beach, which are more or less in a continuous state of fiesta, and was assigned to this small Hotel Campestra up the hillside. It is hardly larger than a villa, twenty minutes' walk to the waterfront, on a quiet side street of the residential section, which spreads up the slope as in Santa Barbara. In fact the whole region reminds me of Santa Barbara. White houses with red-tile roofs scatter back into barren-looking hills, nestled under olives or palms, and then the green brush begins and climbs on back, as does our chaparral.

The Riviera is not as steep here as at Genoa and Santa Margherita and I'm planning to wander back into it. Already I've located a nearby wine shop frequented by the French where the proprietress unthinkingly charges only 8 francs for a cup of vin rouge compared to three times that in the big bars downtown. Now at 9:00 A.M. I'm going out to change my marks to francs and see the sights, perhaps buy a khaki shirt, for there are no uniform regulations here. You can wear anything. Everyone is incognito so far as rank is concerned. All insignia is *verboten*. So you can't tell a lieutenant from a colonel except by age. The result is a delightful feeling of freedom. I passed General Simpson, commander of the 9th Army, wearing sun-tans much like a Texas farmer's, and identified him only from his photo in *Stars and Stripes*.

I miss you more here. My room looks west over an enchanting garden. The sky is clear, the air just cool enough. I feel so well, so happy and so miserable at heart—because I could make such a joy of this place with you.

Only along the beaches occasional empty concrete pillboxes and rusty barbed wire remind us there was a war here too.[11]

I've resolved to use this week for reading and writing and walking and the privacy I simply don't have when with the company. I've given up trying to find it there. You can't find it without hurting someone's feelings or making yourself a prima donna.

SANTA BARBARA, MAY 30, 1945, MEMORIAL DAY

Today at the hospital proved much less depressing. I walked over to the ping-pong bats when I first arrived and at once a soldier in "reds" came up and asked if I'd play with him. I felt very pleased. When I have my uniform I will feel more secure. This way they often don't know what job I'm doing. So we played for nearly an hour and then managed to get two more interested and played doubles. Doubles is good because it's fun to see people scrambling to get away and give their partner his shot, and this makes for laughter and relaxation and pretty soon even the glummest take pleasure and laugh along with you.

Of course I try to tease them, too, and they get excited about beating me and so on. I felt very rewarded because I didn't have a free minute and played with many sets of boys and their buddies and pretty soon they all were friendly and thanked me for playing.

I sat down at one point, a boy beside me, and pretty soon he asked: "Are you married now?" And I said I was and then he wanted to know where my husband was and I told him and he grew more and more interested. They all seem to feel better about me when they know I have a husband doing his stuff. It makes us all feel closer and safer somehow, all in the big thing together.

This one was from Michigan and had a three-months-old son and we discussed weights of babies and which sex was best to

11. U.S. 7th Army troops came ashore between Cannes and St. Tropez, shortly after dawn August 15, 1944, meeting only light resistance.

have first, etc. He was with the 7th Army and got as far as Strasbourg! He was nice and said he'd see me next Wednesday and show me a picture of his baby. I was able to tell many of them to look me up next Wednesday and I must say I was glad when a youngster only 20 came and spoke to me, because I played cards with him two weeks ago on my first day there. He lives in New Mexico, has been to England, Belgium and Holland. He hates all those countries and found nothing more to say than: "They are so backward and funny!" That finished Europe and we began talking about his girl whom he hopes to marry when he gets out.

I like to hear them talk and kid each other (though this last vast American form of amusement I'd find very tiring if I had to live with it). At one point a boy came in led by a nurse. He was deaf and wore an instrument around his neck, had an arm out of commission and was blind in both eyes. His face was terribly scarred, too. But he called to the boy who was playing ping-pong with me: "What's the name of the girl you're playing with, Joe?" Joe, who's also hard of hearing, shouts at me: "What's your name?" And I shout back: "Jane!" And so it went. And somehow no matter how little I do, I feel better for having been there. It's good to be with men, and they are nice and not fresh or intimate. They know I have a husband and children and they know I donate my time for them, and I know what they have done for me, and it all adds up to something.

CANNES, 2 JUNE 1945

By half past eight I've breakfasted and am at work writing in what was once the dining room of this hotel. It has large windows and French doors that let in the sun. The ceiling is high, there is no one to disturb me as the room is not used for dining—we eat four blocks away at another hotel. So I write. And I write with more pleasure than in a long time because I feel so well and you love me. I write till one o'clock or perhaps two, then go to lunch.

Afterward I don't come back but climb the hill above the city, up winding streets among tangled fragrant gardens to a high point under some pines, where the sweet-smelling wild thyme begins and also the broom and wild roses. Standing there today watching the blue sea and the ships and the planes sailing in, I met a young man pushing a handcart. We exchanged greetings.

I asked where he was going. He said picking cherries over the hill. So I went with him.

We climbed the ridge separating Cannes from Antibes and from the top could see a hundred miles, all the Côte d'Azur— the blue coast of famous beauty—and right below us another hillside terracing down, with grapes and olive trees and occasional red roof. Then we descended toward the cherry trees. My friend picks cherries for a living just now. He is 31, lean, bright eyed, nervous, with that tireless energy some of these slight Frenchmen have. He was an infantry noncom in 1940, "en quarante." Then for six months he was a prisoner in occupied France till he escaped by digging under the wire and came to Nice. Now his wife and two children are here.

He wanted to know how much cherries cost in America and how much a worker made there in a day and why the French freight cars the Germans stole weren't returned, so that meat could be brought to Cannes. He says he's in good health but lacks stamina because he lacks meat. He described, laughing, the lack of stamina of his lieutenant in '40. A few kilometers and the lt. is sitting on a rock exhausted, and he, the sergeant, is urging the men on. He says reservist officers like that were the trouble with the French Army.

We picked cherries for an hour, fine black ones from three trees that seemed to belong to nobody and just grew beside the path on that warm hillside. We walked back, shirtless, both of us, and then I slept two hours, bathed, and dined at 8:30. Since half past nine I've been writing and it is midnight now.

For three days I've managed seven to eight hours' work a day and have written a story a day—except today when I did two— and have redone the long one about Major Dean of "The Commander" which must be 20,000 words. I haven't felt the muse stirring so keenly since the days of our first stories. Maybe it's an aftermath of war. I suddenly realize time is all that's required— time and quiet. What can be accomplished in four uninterrupted hours is astounding!

For reading I have Shakespeare and Jack London. Why has no one ever told me of Jack London? I mean the mature London beyond *Call of the Wild*? He's far better than I realized. When in heaven are you going to tell me you've read his autobiographical *Martin Eden*?

I'm hungry to explore American literature with you. And

when I think that I majored in English at our country's leading university and wasn't required to take a single course in American lit, *wasn't even offered one*, I wonder what's going on in Higher Education.

I think of you playing ping-pong at Hoff Hospital and drawing from hurt minds and bodies the pain that brings them there. I hope this work is rewarding. If not, leave it.

Will you kiss our babies and show them the thyme (the gray sprig enclosed) and the broom and poppies from a sunny place called Cannes?

SANTA BARBARA, JUNE 2, 1945

I try to picture what the next step may be; and from President Truman's speech that all men who have not yet been overseas will be the first to go to the Pacific and some veterans will return and hold jobs in this country, it looks as if you might have a chance of getting back, even if not discharged. About a leave and then return to combat, I cannot say. You ask me what I wish. I don't know. It's just a question of constantly being torn apart, whatever happens. I should adore to see you and hear you and touch you, if only for thirty days, but I don't know how one could stand the next parting and the agony of those first months again when all around there is loneliness and only loneliness and the acute awareness of how empty life can be! But on the other hand, as you say, a small breath of life together, or life with the children and life alone—maybe that would restore us a little and give us faith and strength to carry on for the next separation.

I hardly dare say what I think, because something else will surely develop. But I hear that if you are to be sent home, if only for a leave, you are allowed to cable your family. Please do that. It will be something to look forward to!

I took Joan to a party today. It was a little boy's two-year-old birthday and Joan behaved very nicely, playing by herself of course, because until they are nearly four they never play together, but just in little separate games. She ate her ice cream and cake at the table very grown-uppedly and adored it all and drank her milk and had a lovely time staring at the other little children. I must say they looked nice.

Your mother is 69 today. The longer I live the more I realize what a strong and fine person she is and how much we owe to her! Perfectly enough, there was a long letter from you awaiting her this morning when she went home after being here watering my corn and inspecting the berries which are nearly ripe. The estate is looking very lush and productive and our young trees and plants are doing well. I harvest lettuce and beets and carrots and squash from the garden daily and oranges galore! It's a fine feeling and it will be even better when you are here and can work with the children playing around you and me dashing in and out of the house because I cannot bear to be away from you longer than five seconds.

Darling, if I were unwed or married to someone else, you could win me again and again and again. No matter what obstacles were in the way, I should inevitably as the night follows the day, have been drawn toward you. I'm afraid that nothing could ever stop me from finding you the most mentally attractive and physically desirable man on earth. I shall always expect you to woo me and I shall be won. The greatest miracle on earth is that we met and loved and were married and have had children. If we had nothing else on earth, ever again, we would already have had the best that life can offer.

You ask about the hospital and I have already written detailed accounts. The other women are mostly a good deal older. Some are marvelously strong and gay and valiant as the soil of this land. There is one, a Mrs. Dennison, about 35, with two children—her husband was killed two years ago. She is not only lovely to look at but lovely to work with and talk to. She works eight hours a day at the information desk and never gets a penny. She is wonderful. Still, our efforts seem inconsequential enough though the doctors think we help the men and that the atmosphere we create is a good one. There are some pretty morose faces, you know, and some mental wrecks, but by and large there is still the old gusto for life.

Goodnight darling. I love you with my poor empty soul and lonely body. There will come a night and day when we can be together.

CANNES, 5 JUNE '45

Today I mailed a box of presents for all the family. Let me know if it comes. Between you and me *only*, the three cans of pâté de foie gras for our parents cost $11 each, a prohibitive sum, yet I gladly paid it because I wanted them to have genuine pâté and because I wanted—once—to pay the black market price. Said market flourishes here. There's still very little transport in France and back corners like this suffer—no meat whatsoever for months in the open market and $30 for a decent piece on the "marché noir."

I never told you of my big adventure on the flight down here, and now I am ready to go home. I stayed at Hildesheim near Hannover for three days waiting for the weather to break and finally on a perfect morning we took off—26 of us in a big C-47 that had hauled parachutists during the Rhine crossing and gasoline for Patton's tanks and was patched in many places where shrapnel hit it.

The pilot was a lanky kid of a first lieutenant, oddly young in connection with such a large plane and its history. He brought us south to cross the Rhine at Coblentz. Imagine the beautiful scene: dark forests, fields alternating green and brown, the rivers and the bright red roofs of villages. We stopped for gas at Thionville near Metz. The weather was closing in and from there got no better so we landed for the night at Lyons and were billeted in the Grand Hotel Nouvelle beside the Rhone.

After supper another lieutenant and I went to the Red Cross to get our marks changed to francs. The girl at the desk informed us the finance office was closed but that she could send us to a party where we wouldn't need any money—a woman had telephoned for two American officers, young ones, to come to a party that evening. Well, this sounded interesting so we decided to see who Madame Morrel Beguin was and what she had in mind for us.

We walked down to the Saone (it parallels the Rhone) through the town, caught a trolley bus up to the heights overlooking the city on the west, explored winding streets, were drenched by a rain shower, finally found our house number—a door in a deceptively unprepossessing old stone wall.

We rang. A pretty girl opened. She led us down a sumptuous hall to a spacious parlor which opened onto broad lawns and gardens overlooking Lyons and all of France beyond it clear to the Alps. There she introduced an attractive sister and a distinguished mother and father, the type of French I'd not yet seen, of the true aristocracy, I judged—the father straight and severely dressed in black with a small mustache and thin dark hair slicked down, reserved, polite, and giving the impression of being deeply sad, perhaps about France; and the mother delightful as only older women of grace can be, slender, tastefully dressed, with gray hair done back to a bun like our mothers'.

My friend spoke no French and none of these people had more than a few sentences of English so I (get this, Prusse)—I maintained conversation in French for the better part of an hour, until other guests arrived and gave me a chance to look around. The house dates from the Second Empire. The rooms were actually chambers with panelling, tapestries and lofty ceilings. The floor was inlaid squares of hardwood set with the grain at opposing angles to make a pattern. There were ornate sideboards and Chinese vases and a portrait of grandfather over the mantel. He'd been killed at Sedan in the Franco-Prussian War.

I watched the guests arrive, nice looking, though the young men, as in all France, seemed suffering from lack of fresh air and exercise. I watched them kiss the hand of the mother and realized I was witnessing the carefully controlled entertainment of the daughters of fine families, who are not free to go out alone with men or to meet Americans of their own choosing. Doubtless their marriages will be traditional affairs arranged between parents.

Well, we danced to phonograph records of U.S.A. jazz, refreshed ourselves on champagne and delicious sandwiches and cups of the season's fresh fruits, and my friend and I answered many questions about our battle stars, our ribbons, our combat boots, our flight from Germany and our destination at Cannes, until we felt mighty glamorous indeed and nearly forgot we were 29 years old, with wives and children. Now are you jealous, green eyes? Well, we nearly forgot but didn't quite—and after a long time took our leave and went downtown to deep white beds, saying we missed our mates a little.

Next morning we came on here. I tell you all this at length because it was my first acquaintance with the French upper class. Yet scarcely one out of the twenty in that room could have been called a whole man in our sense of the word. They are effeminate, wordy, nervous, excitable with a large helping of the gigolo and I cannot greatly like them. The women are their superiors and live up to their role as women with traditional French perfection.

The plane for Hannover leaves tomorrow morning at 7. I hope we go straight through and I'm home to K Company for supper. I miss the company and I don't. My stay here has been exactly the kind I planned—by the grace of heaven. Think what a bore sharing a room with someone might have been! Now I'm going back to the old gregarious life, plus a great pile of letters from you, I hope. I feel a little as in that terrible 5-week hiatus in England last June and July when there was no word from you. A year ago today, the *Queen Elizabeth* deposited us at Greenock. I wouldn't have missed it, Prusse. Not for the world.

SANTA BARBARA, JUNE 8, 1945

Your father thinks you'll be back by Christmas. I simply have decided that until I hear anything *positive*, it's better to go along and love by mail, as we have for such years and years and years! God, how long it is and how futile life without one's love is! Why, even the dear little ones mean nothing without you. Our life here could be so happy for a few years, producing some writing and some more children, etc. Each day would be an untold richness. Now, I live alone in the numbness of a mule and feel deader and deader as time goes by. I sometimes wonder how long it will take me to live fully again after you come back. Will it be a sudden breath of life? Will a few hours wipe out all the misery of years? Or will it be a gradual reawakening?

In July you'll be thirty. Three years ago this summer I thought surely you would be home for good by this birthday. Isn't it lucky one doesn't know what's ahead? Thank heavens we aren't back in June 1944! A year ago, all our anxiety lay ahead and the full impact of Pop's death just dawning, and I was in New York and you were in London and the children were in Los Angeles and John was in France and your parents were in Santa Barbara. Thank heavens it's over, that part, that year! Now we can face the future—always with the conviction it will be better than the past. One has such amazing faith because one loves so strongly that there can be nothing else left *but* faith!

Yesterday I went to the hospital again. When I started working there, I saw myself as a woman talking to men of their past and present and their anxieties and troubles. Now I don't. I just play ping-pong and in between games let the talk happen. I was pleased that two or three came and asked me to play, one very surprised I'd recognized him when he entered the room. I told him I always remember faces (I'm trying hard to because they all love you to speak spontaneously or to shout some greeting

across the table when they come in). This boy said he'd been in
the U.S.A. thirteen days. I did not, as I was tempted, ask where
he came from, etc. They warn us not to dwell on battles or
mishaps unless the men insist and feel like talking.

I could not forget this one because it seemed to me he had
the darkest, most sinisterly tortured eyes I've ever seen. His face
was all nerves. After we played a while he began to smile and
laugh and even laughed so much at one point that I was afraid
he wouldn't be able to stop.

I end up making a lot of noise because *all* these poor fellows
are terribly deaf. They often don't wear hearing aids and that
makes conversation difficult. I shout and shout and speak slowly
and it gets rather tiring. But, honestly, to see them give you a good
smile and to know, somehow—for they never pay compliments—
that you may have given them a five minutes' absence, as it were,
from hospital life, is really a great reward. I wish I could go out
there two afternoons a week but it's pretty hard to get a baby
sitter or grandmother more than once. I come back quite sore
from having chased ping-pong balls all over the big hall!

I also had a talk with a man (very nervous, perhaps Jewish,
older than many) who was to be discharged in a few days. In the
Army three years. No apparent wounds. But deaf. He kept saying:
"This is the worst time of the whole damned war. My poor wife.
Why, she's going nuts up at Rio del Mar waiting for me!" They
get very fidgety these last days. He was also very gloomy about
the world situation. "It's all been for nothing. The only heroes
are the dead ones. All those countries over there are hanging on
to the old world, to old ways that are gone. Churchill should be
gone. The British Empire is out of date. The world is moving
on!"

But they don't all have such dark outlooks. Some just see as
far as getting out of uniform and back to "my girl." One kept
repeating that all the girls had been married since he left the
country. "And sure enough, all to 4Fs!" They have many com-
plaints which a little more education might eradicate. I've met
none from the educated brackets—none I can identify as officers.
But all are in "reds" so I cannot tell for sure.

Lots of dark-skinned boys from New Mexico. One very
pathetic one sat near the door with a huge cast on his leg. He
looked horribly worn and tired as if in pain. I managed to sit by
him a while. He had a soft voice and was NOT deaf, thank

heavens. He wants to move to Colorado. So many of these New Mexicans want to go there for some unexplained reason. Lots of them ask me if I am English! How many times I have been asked that! And immediately they add: "I don't mean to insult you!"

All in all it's very interesting and somehow emotionally exhausting. I come home and sink into bed, like last night, and can't even write you. I never realize while I'm out there, making the effort, that I'm really terribly worked up about their minds and bodies and problems.

There are blossoms on the jasmine plants you gave me for my birthday. I'll send you some in tomorrow's letter.

BREMERHAVEN, 14 JUNE 1945

None other than Captain Roger Fee of the 825th T. D. Battalion dropped in today for lunch, a fat and friendly ghost from the past. The sight of him reminded me how much I've left behind, and gladly—yet not all gladly. He commands B Co. and has men scattered from Augsberg (near Munich) to Bremen on the same radio security duty we did in my day.

Several officers have transferred as I did or gone home. Fee said, over brandy and soda in our quarters, he hoped the battalion would be broken up. He wants to go to the Pacific with what he called a "ground floor outfit," if he has to go. I liked him as much as ever, and yet strangely was not grateful for a reminder of people and events, remote by light years from where I am now.

The Navy is here with us, as I mentioned. They are members of a "port battalion" whose job is to operate a port such as this, have spent the war till now in cozy quarters in Scotland and never heard a shot fired in anger and probably never will. I've just come from breakfast with them at our combined officers' mess: 100 Navy, 40 Army. We eat from white tablecloths (the enemy's) set with the enemy's silverware and china, begin breakfast with oranges from Spain, then good American oatmeal, scrambled eggs and bacon, toast and coffee, served by colored boys in snappy white jackets. Soft music accompanies from a radio loudspeaker.

The Navy in "blues" and stiff white collars far outdresses us in our combat O.D. woolens open at the neck. For supper, however, we're required to wear the new waist-length dress jacket, Eisenhower style. A bar is being prepared and everything points to garrison life complete except for wives. Now get this! The colored waiters are departing soon, to be replaced by beautiful *fräuleins* from the town—so what do you think? Actually these German women are handsomer and better proportioned—on the whole more wholesome in appearance—than any I've seen in Europe, unless it's the Dutch. And their attraction for our female-starved men and officers is such as to make the official non-fraternization policy absurd, and this may have a truly deleterious effect on all our other "laws," which the Germans may learn to hold as lightly as we hold this one.

I've gone on record as not wanting to remain in the Army and will not *volunteer* for service in the Pacific.[12] If they want me there they can send me. The yearning for the Flying Submarine Corps is gone, Prusse. I hate to admit such evidence of age—I'll be 30 about the time you get this—but the fact remains. And with it comes a feeling the 30s will be better than the 20s, the 40s than the 30s and so on till the optimum is reached about 83. What say? "When your hair has turned to silver I shall love you just the same!" And you, me?

If you were here I might fraternize with you a bit, this spring evening.

BREMERHAVEN, 17 JUNE 1945

Let me tell you about the "good" Germans. Being desirous of acquiring typewriter ribbons, paper, and if possible a typewriter of my own, I was given an address at which stationery was reportedly sold. It proved to be a nice home in the best part of town, neat lawn, roses in bloom along the window ledges—residence of the proprietor whose downtown store had been bombed out. He is a cripple about 50, with very nice eyes and a cane to help him get about, reminding me of book-and-stationery-store people the world over—gentle, eager to please. You know the type.

He had everything I wanted including portable typewriters at 150 marks or $15. They are war products, cheaply made, yet a bargain, so I bought one intending to give it to the company clerk in exchange for his big upright which I've been borrowing. However, I did not have the right kind of marks. Allied-issue marks are not acceptable to German banks, so I told the proprietor I'd leave my purchases and return with proper marks—and was

12. Thirty divisions would be sent from Europe to the Pacific by the end of July.

surprised when he insisted I take what I'd bought and return with the money at my convenience! Well, the money was no problem. We have wads of old German marks issued in the '20s during the inflation and hardly thought them worth the trouble of collecting. But they are now! And with them I returned and paid this trusting man.

He has a wife and two grown daughters, all nice looking, and a rather severe-faced friend, a man about his age, who seems to be sharing the residence. This friend speaks good English where the proprietor is shaky. During the second transaction I wandered to the bookcase in the combination living room-salesroom-office and noticed a set of Byron and other English titles. I asked the severe-faced friend if English books were not banned under the Nazis and he said yes. He said Schiller was also banned and asked if I knew Schiller.

While we were talking I noticed, on the wall over the desk, the inevitable picture of the son of the household in uniform, and on the desk the son in civilian clothes, and then on another wall the son in oils. And like many such portraits these were wreathed in faded leaves and flowers. But unlike all others I've seen these were of as fine a face as there could be. It was outstanding, noble, kindly, like the crippled proprietor who is the father of this boy of 25, an infantryman killed in Russia.

I was so deeply impressed that I spoke my admiration to both men. By now the friend's severe face relaxed and he told me *his* son was last heard from in Roumania last August. So it goes with all these people. The dereliction here is ghastly: husbandless women, fatherless children, people without houses, men returning from prison camps to find both house and family gone. It is a dreadful horror, actually, and yet in the streets the life of everyday goes on. We have no trouble. The people show no hostility and considerable friendliness.

We spent yesterday rounding up Hitler Jugend[13] some of whom were caught stealing explosives from a dump we guard, and these revealed others till we had insight into the whole gang. We picked up three as a starter, three as murderous little criminals at 15 and 16 as you would ever see, nothing youthful about them

---

13. Hitler Youth, members of the Nazi organization which became an important element in National Socialism's program of establishing complete control over every aspect of German life.

except undeveloped features and body. All I could see in their faces was evil. They lied up and down and, when we found them out, grew tearful and lied some more. One, the weak one, the follower, broke down and told us much, saying: "Don't let them think me a traitor! I mustn't be a traitor!" They'll probably kill him when they get out of jail.

In a house we searched I discovered an entire Hitler Jugend Series of books like the Rover Boys Series our youngsters read. All were devoted to destruction and war. Also in the bedside cabinet were tales of the Norse Gods, not part of the actual series but like it in terms of content; and then tales of the Huns with cover illustrations showing Attila and friends on horseback, riding down and beheading some poor devils on foot. And there were also souped-up history books Herr Goebbels[14] devised, lies with enough truth to make them plausible; and then a set of postcard portraits, also in the Jugend Series, of all Nazi leaders—but chiefly Hitler in every imaginable pose.

Our Counter Intelligence Corps was glad to have the Jugend Books. They are collecting a library of them and showed me a list of titles they need, for the preservation of these vicious lies into the future.

On a lighter note: without incriminating myself on a fraternization charge, let me tell you about German girls' wedding rings. When they become engaged they wear a single gold band on the third finger of the left hand. When they marry they gain a second gold band on the corresponding finger of the right hand. And when their husbands die both rings are united on the finger of the right hand.

We are taking a census at mealtime and so far have spotted three waitresses with dead husbands. Pleasant atmosphere, you say? Ah, but it is, and the pretty *fräuleins* are *so* happy to be serving the American officers where they eat three delicious meals a day and are paid 5 marks, or 50¢, an hour!

SANTA BARBARA, JUNE 22, 1945

Exactly a year ago I began numbering my letters. This would be No. 365 instead of 333 if I had written every day, but out of a

---

14. Hitler's minister for propaganda, Paul Joseph Goebbels.

year to miss only thirty days is pretty good, don't you think? I started by allowing myself one day off a week. Now I don't even take that day unless I'm absolutely swamped with other things.

This morning over my meager breakfast, which I always eat in the kitchen, I saw that your division is definitely detailed to stay in Bremen with the occupation forces. I'm terribly relieved you are not coming this way to the Pacific. Perhaps our good angel knows we have suffered enough and now can relax a little. Naturally, human nature being very demanding, I at once moaned because I will not see you for another year probably—instead of getting down on my knees and giving thanks that you are alive and well! However, I am thankful! How deeply no one can ever know who has not been through the months of continual doubt and wondering. I feel as if our future life had already begun, our fifteen-year plan, and our third child. Before this, it has seemed rather futile to plan too much, because there was always the question: "Will we be given more time together or have we had it all?" Now it seems fairly safe to say we WILL have a life.

The whole thing is a bit large to grasp but gradually the enormous rejoicing and relief will set in. I already don't jump when the doorbell rings at an odd hour, as I used to, thinking of a telegram from the War Dept.

Your thirtieth birthday is coming soon. I wish for you the same great and lasting things I have always wished ever since I fell in love with you years and years and years ago. I can see you now as a mature young man, not the groping one I first met that summer at the station here. I think you have grown and developed in all the best possible ways. I know Pop felt that too. I am so glad he died with that knowledge: believing you and I together could live a life that in many ways he wanted to live himself. For God's sake let us be true to all the heritage he left us and true to our own highest ideals. I know the war has not been wholly wasted but now, with the years creeping on, we must never waste time. Time looms so very important now. I'm still glad to see the night come and to know that one more day away from you is over forever. But when you come and we can live again like a youthful, growing family, I shall never want the sun to set or rise, I shall hope to make each day a small eternity of wonderful richness and work and laughter.

Capt. R. was operated on today for acute appendicitis and will
be hospitalized three weeks. Also today I was asked to take
command of L Company but declined. Garrison Army is bad
enough without the wear of making yourself a new home in it
once again. I do not want the promotion. If it comes to me here
in K Co. I'll take it. I am perfectly happy here in any capacity.
Being with congenial people is about all that makes the above-
mentioned Army bearable.

Actually events are moving so swiftly nothing is settled from
one day to the next. Tomorrow I may be en route home or to the
C.B.I. or wherever—so all I'm counting on is making life as
pleasant and useful as possible.

Papers have come from Father picturing and telling of the
great receptions for Patton and Doolittle. Don't you think old
Blood-and-Guts Patton's pronouncements pretty good? And
aren't those of Eisenhower remarkably fine? He is beginning to
appear as a great man.

Radio Stuttgart is signing off its evening symphony program,
promising Mozart tomorrow. Both British and American stations
are giving the Germans their own good music, which I must say
makes our jazz-racket programs suffer by comparison.

And now taps is sounding and I'm very sleepy. Prusse, can
you wait a little longer for me? I am coming and I'm going to hold
you very close to me and kiss the tip of your nose.

I've been chosen from among many volunteers and given ward
duty. Which sounds very complimentary until you know that
what I do is pass cookies to bedridden men and barely stop to
chat with them. I must say it was grim at first.

I arrived early, played some very violent ping-pong, then
from two to four o'clock went tramping the wards. I wondered at
first if I could make it, because the wards are kept so terribly hot
and stuffy, but then got used to it and even the aches in my back
and legs didn't bother much. An extremely attractive young
woman about 35 showed me how to offer cookies and talk a
moment with each man. We are not supposed to become intimate
or offer to see them next week or anything like that. Some were
so sick and so white in the face, some with their legs strung up

in traction above the bed, some with distorted arms, etc. It's a horrid business, this war, when you see rows and rows of beds with victims; and then other wards where the psychoneurotic are kept behind gates, my heavens, which a male nurse unlocks for you, and then the men look up at you rather blankly, or very resentfully, and always with little hope in their eyes, and as you leave they are locked in again. For them, the clang of those barred gates must be something!

I was continually amazed at how few are fresh or intimate; many are too depressed to care what you do or say and most of all they look for the wedding ring on your finger and then they know you are not for them. Only one, sitting on the edge of his bed said to me: "Why, I'd rather look at you than eat a cookie, any day!" You toss off such remarks quickly and pretty soon are not bothered by anything.

I must say my tummy felt queer a time or two when I saw the very disfigured or morose. But I truly hope my work is useful.

Anyway, I was pleased. I had to borrow a uniform, which is gray with white collar and cuffs, and felt proud wearing the Red Cross on my left bosom.

BREMERHAVEN, 3 JULY 1945

Yesterday in the Bremen hospital while visiting R. I saw some American nurses. "Plain old country girls," he calls them. Yet how the luster of the *fräuleins* dims by comparison! How richly and warmly their eyes sparkle with friendship, how jaunty their carriage and carefree their manner—compared to the pale animal-like eyes of these Germans with their intelligent fleshy look! Protoplasm, they strike me as, most of them. For a heart they have a bivalvular mechanism which very efficiently operates their bodies. For feelings they have sentiment, for a soul a brain. They are psychological beings and just as dangerous in our modern world as machines. Witness their atom-smashing and sun-concentrating designs, not for good but for evil, not to build but to gain power to destroy! Truly they live in the Age of the Fish,[15] with biological juices operating them and not blood.

We are nearing total victory. And yet the most horrible possibilities remain, not those for good—not the world courts

15. Title of an anti-Nazi novel by Ödön von Horvath.

and charters—but the spine-chilling "ifs" suggesting a total rigor mortis for the world.

I can't tell you how ineffective I feel the United Nations peace plans are. Yet they're as good as can be expected. But the premise is still wrong. Until we erase that premise and write down a new one, a totally new kind of human relationship, we never, never, never shall solve the problem. And complicating factors always are intruding, like the boy today—the second in three weeks—who asked how he could volunteer for the C.B.I. I know and so does he that the moment he hears the first shell scream he will give ten years of his life to be back in Bremerhaven doing guard duty and catching gonorrhea from the *fräuleins*, but I admire him for trying to go. Anything but boredom!

SANTA BARBARA, JULY 3, 1945

I've asked to be put back in the recreation room where there is real need for me. This cookie thing is nonsense. The authorities act as if it were a great honor and are very hush-hush about my being allowed in the wards. But I think it's all a lot of hooey. It's unpleasant at times, yes. Still I could put up with that if I felt it truly important. There are sickening scenes when doctors are changing casts and sickening scenes when men come out from anesthesia, yes, and there are tough nurses, male and female, and there are large assortments of indifferent and indefinable patients—some very thin ones, so thin their bones seem to be under the first layer of skin, and some with so many wounds that you wonder how they are alive. But the point is that I can't do them any significant good by passing cookies and dropping a word or two, whereas out in the recreation room I can truly help.

Also I heard a ward nurse today ask a boy to go and see his colonel (a doctor) and the boy looked up from his book and didn't understand at once, so she shouted at him and was very rude. I was ashamed that any human being should be treated as that boy was. By and large the gals who go in for nursing lose something very important: gentleness. They have to. They see too many bedpans and wounds and tough doctors and they are too close to the men. The result often is that the nurses resent the men and the men don't as a rule like the nurses.

That is true here, at least. In the field and in other hospitals overseas, maybe they are made greater people by the closeness of battle and the sacrifice all around. But I should be very distressed if Judy or Joan or Katherine ever wanted to be a nurse. A strange thing happens to all of their eyes: a hard coldness and a nothing-is-sacred attitude. I shall be glad when I'm back in my more useful job of playing games with the men and talking to them.

Today I managed a little ping-pong with a boy who asked me to play a few weeks ago, and was just beginning to talk to an older man when I had to leave. The older man spoke of a year and a half in the South Pacific, New Guinea, etc., ending with: "I couldn't take it." I tried to explain that anyone over there for a year and a half and in two campaigns had certainly shown he "could take it." It is funny the ideas they get. No, it isn't strange really, it's terribly human. I try to pump a little ego into most of them.

This one is about to be discharged, something in his lung. He told me his wife divorced him because he enlisted in the Army. I wonder how many wives have done that? Everyone was confused and that woman knew little about war. And the natural instinct of a female is to make a home and hold the man down to the children and bread and butter. To see him then dash off to war with such eagerness is to her a sign he doesn't care for the home at all. This poor fellow was very lost. For these simple people, though they may have little companionship in marriage, it is unnatural even to them to divorce or be without a mate, and the hurt and scar remain for years and years.

Then when I was about to go off duty at 4:30, I went to the lounge to empty ashtrays and tidy things generally, and a man looked up at me from his wheelchair and said: "You look tired." With that I went over and sat down and talked to him. Some people spill their troubles right away but he was primarily concerned with *my* fatigue and said: "When you get home take a bath and go to bed with all the windows open."

"But I have two children to feed."

"Oh, let Papa do that tonight."

"Papa's in Germany."

"I'm sorry. Well, do you have a headache?"

"No, I'm fine."

So we chatted a while. He's worried because he and his wife separated before he went overseas and she can't make up her mind whether to come back to him. He gave a graphic description of their struggle through the war before he went over. "I don't know whose fault it was. I would get home three nights a week, at 2 A.M., and get up and leave at 6:00 for camp, and she was angry that I wasn't there more often. As soon as I'd get inside the door she'd start asking questions and one day I just blew up. Jeez, this war makes a guy tense!" He's waiting for her to decide. If she comes back to him it's for good, and if she doesn't it's for good too.

I could see how the whole thing preyed on him. No furlough in two and a half years. No time to live quietly and normally together and straighten matters out—all those matters which need so much time and so much peace and so much gentle talking. It makes one ache. I was glad to have been with him, because when I left he said: "I won't worry!"

BREMERHAVEN, 6 JULY 1945

Captain R. came home this evening to convalesce here—looks well, if frail, and we are glad to have him back. I don't believe he has an enemy hereabouts or many of them anywhere. I feel more warmly toward him than toward any man I know.

So I continue to run the company, which has meant a good deal of running lately, attending meetings, answering phones, signing and signing papers, and wishing for the good old rough-and-ready days of combat, when a soldier was a man and not a number or a gap filled in the ranks.

Today I prepared a list of decorations for combat awards— K Co. far surpasses any other in the division in this respect. Our totals run:

Medals of Honor	1
Distinguished Service Crosses	2
Silver Stars	48
Bronze Stars	91
Purple Hearts	506

These figures represent awards earned by members of the company from D-Day to V-E Day—eleven months—during which the names of more than 1100 men—the equivalent of more than five full-strength companies, Janie—appeared on our rolls. It's a grim measure of the casualties suffered.[16] I've left out one Croix de Guerre and two British Awards.

16. 29th Division casualties from D-Day in Normandy to V-E Day were over 20,000.

Thanks for the seventy-five dollars. Also for the underwear.
No, there was no Red Cross girl in Cannes. Or anywhere else,
green eyes!

I think your description of Joan is pretty sweet, playing with
the pots and pans you allowed her to take from the kitchen
cupboard and quoting my Mother's: "I think I'll go up State
Street and save gas!" Why do children pretend and so delight
themselves? What is their magic happiness in make-believe?

A big E.T.O.[17] sports program is underway which is taking
seven of our boys on a swimming team to Paris tomorrow. I was
entered in the tennis doubles and singles but couldn't attend—
and compete for the E.T.O. finals at the Riviera in late July—
because of affairs here. They include general supervision over the
guard in the docks area, seeing that my 200 men keep an eye on
from seven to ten recently arrived cargo ships (plus the *Europa*)
and nearly as many warehouses, that pilferers are arrested and
turned over to the M.P.'s etc. Just now the stevedores are largely
amateurs, volunteers or forced labor of all classes, procured in
Bremen by our military government. However, yesterday several
boatloads of ex-P.W.'s arrived from Norway and they may prove
better workers. The civilians have been a failure. They shirk on
the job or don't come to work, and when they do come spend
most of their time trying to steal food, of which they are very
short. We've arrested several score. One had a ham hidden in his
trouser leg.

Have I told you of Axis Sally, our puppy? France and I were
driving along in a jeep and met a German woman wheeling a
bicycle and carrying this puppy under her arm. I slowed down.
France held out his hands and the woman placed the dog in them.
France gave her a cigarette in return. She protested. So he gave
her the rest of the pack. And we drove off with Sally—black with
brown eyes, grayish underneath, probably some Airedale in her,
and much affection.

She sleeps on F.'s bed when he's in it and guards it sedulously
when he's not. Now and then she goes on mad sprees, scattering
bits of paper and general confusion through our quarters to the
dismay of Marta, our dour housekeeper. "Alles mennen schlecht!"
(All men no good!) Marta declares, including Sally in her disap-
proval. But Sally, who loves all men, at that very moment while

17. European Theater of Operations.

I was reading a picture book on Italy, jumped from the sofa into my lap and cuddled up there.

Marta is brightening too. She hates men because her husband deserted her. But she can't resist American tomfoolery and we keep her laughing most of the time. She cleans from 9 to 4 and does our laundry and sewing, and has begun to bring flowers which suddenly appear in vases. She thinks highly of the captain. Today, with great hush-hush, she shyly brought two bottles of schnapps in honor of his homecoming.

So there you have Marta and Sally, our two kept women.

SANTA BARBARA, JULY 26, 1945

Just having said I'm reconciled to a next phase of waiting, I feel overwhelmed with the desire to see you! Here I sit in this lonely bed and know you are out of danger, except from those frauleins you have devoted so many letters to, but I still want to see you. As a matter of fact, I am amazed at your long eulogies about those poor dumb German girls. I think you like a bovine type, hale and hearty and muscular. Well, I shall never be one of those. And the way you silly men act about them, one can see you are starved for females of any sort. Just keep your distance, young man, or I shall be over there, as you suggest, with all the other wives, to make their men happy again, and I shall give you a good whipping, my man. So you see that I'm as ready as ever to make a jealous scene.

The big news today: Churchill is out. Overwhelmingly defeated. I am sure it is right that he should go now. Like the bulldog he is, he would never have been ready to quit. Now he will live in history as a great man who did a superb job.

I know only too well the despair you feel about the United Nations peace plans. I feel it too and so does John. But when you say the premise is wrong, exactly what premise could you suggest? I don't wonder your boys are asking to volunteer for the C.B.I. I even wonder if you may want to go too. If you should, please do so! I don't want you back until you feel you've had enough of war! Certainly do not deprive yourself of it for my sake. Women and children have learned that they must be put aside to wait when a war claims their man. I am not able to say that I *wish* you to volunteer for the C.B.I., but I can say that I will not beg you

not to, or: "Now it's time you thought of ME, come home!" I
don't feel any of those things.

I want you to do what you wish and I shall be able to manage
as long as you are doing what you think you should. Please
remember that—for wartime and peacetime! I hope it doesn't
sound fishy and sentimental and altruistic. I'm not *any* of those
things and shall put up plenty of hot fights in years to come, don't
you worry! But I want you to feel *right* in your mind and soul.

Darling, what time of day or night will it be when I see you
again? I am longing to see you at any hour of course, but it's
maddening not to know just when it will be. I'm sure you are
more attractive at thirty than at any previous age. People tell me:
"Bob will be amazed at how much better looking you are now
than then." So maybe we'll both be rather divine when we meet.
I shall love you when I am 100 and you 102.

BREMERHAVEN, 26 JULY 1945

Well, let Churchill go—and let younger men and those who call
themselves the Labor Party come in. Let the concept of empire
go and those who fought in its cause head toward the rocking
chair. I see in all this the trend of the times—a groping for a new
order, a world where something better can happen.

I wonder how far mankind has progressed toward the concept
of world sovereignty? Not far, judging from the results of the
United Nations San Francisco Conference! And I don't suppose
the threat of total destruction of the human race in the next war
will be enough, either. Must we wait and see that destruction
and then begin to practice world sovereignty?

Communism or Russianism doesn't alarm me in the least. I
can't for the life of me understand being alarmed by somebody
else's form of government just because it differs from ours. People
aren't the same politically. What suits one will not suit others.
And just as we have red, black, and white peoples, and peoples
who wear purple clothes, and no clothes at all, so reasonably we
should expect to have different kinds of governments on the face
of the earth and still get along together.

Tonight I'm in my attic studio at my typewriter, the sturdy
German upright I traded my new portable for. Except for the
positions of two or three letters, its keyboard is the same as ours.
I've finished a draft of the 3rd part of The Commander Series,

titled "The River." It comes to about 30 pages and might be good
enough to sell on its own.

SANTA BARBARA, JULY 27, 1945
A letter came this morning with a little snap in it of you which
made me sing with joy. I can't tell you what even a snatch of
your life via a picture does for me. I see that you are as trim and
slim and flat in the stomach as ever. I could not abide a man out
of condition and if you are going to sit behind a typewriter many
hours a day you must also contrive to be active the other hours
or I shall forsake you soon.

July is almost over. August will pass too. Last summer seemed
so dark and ugly, so full of woe and anxiety. This one is so much
better. We must never cease thanking God that you and John
are safe and well. John is out of VII Corps and into the occupation
and heaven knows *when* he'll get home but at least he's all right.
When are YOU coming home? I simply must know at once, so
I can start counting days and months and weeks and so on.

I wish I had fallen in love with you when I was two years
old.

BREMERHAVEN, 27 JULY 1945
The lifting of the non-fraternization ban makes Bremerhaven's
parks and streets look like an Army camp back home on Sunday
evenings: every soldier with a girl. All to the good, I say. You
can't organize Americanism into a program and impose it. It must
be learned day by day as people casually intermingle. For instance,
we are trying to arrange a dance for enlisted men and German
girls. We'll make arrangements through churches and other community organizations, have the girls selected, and invite certain
families to attend—the burgomaster's and church elders', say—
as well as the priest, serve beer and cookies, let our boys show
these frauleins the swing and the old hoe-down rhythms of the
South.

Now here's news: in the next few days I'm being transferred
to the 69th Division at Kassel, down toward the Rhine, and
sometime between the 1st of November and the 1st of January
the 69th will sail for home—I with it if all goes well. What do
you think of that?

About 3000 of our high-point men have already been transferred in exchange for an equal number of low-point 69th men.
I'll be part of a similar swap. Whether I wait for the 69th to go
home as a unit or whether I go on a quota—as originally the high-
point men went from here—is still a question. What happens after
arrival in the States, nobody seems to know. They say high-point
enlisted men are being discharged and a few *very* high-point
officers are being discharged, while the majority of officers go to
training camps and other garrison duties or possibly to the Pacific.

I'll write more in the next few days—another phase ending
after eight momentous months—but regretful as I am at thought
of leaving friends and experiences shared, I do feel things here
are over, for me, and that my wife and girls are waiting.

Would you want me in combat in the Pacific?

Or do you feel we have done enough?

Please let me know.

As to your volunteering for Japan, I shall simply not cross that
bridge until the time comes and you've been home and we see
whether it's spring or summer when you arrive and how close
Japan is to defeat. Reports are that by next summer Japan will be
through.

For my own life, it matters not so much whether you get
back to stay this next spring or wait for another year and fight in
Japan. But I'm now beginning to have misgivings about the
children so long without a father. They need you always; but from
two on, they need you terribly badly. We have not given them
the home they should have had, with a mother and father, and
I do feel that when you see them you will realize your place may
be with them.

Katherine will be two when you see her, Joan three and a
half. You may want to do what is best for them—aside from your
own ideas on combat in comparison to garrison life. God knows
I have a pretty clear idea of what the garrison army is like and I
know even in Germany and the added interest of being abroad,
it is deadly beyond words.

In any event, there may be times when you want to go direct
to the C.B.I. and not come home until the war is over. Here is
my plea: *Please* don't go without getting back here first. I'm afraid

that if you were killed and had never seen Taffie I should have rather a large wound to heal in my heart, and it might never heal. I also think it is the children's due to have you back a while.

After you've seen them and realized you are so essential to them, you may decide that your place is with them. I do sincerely feel that for you and me any length of time apart can be managed, but when I think of them, their lives, their characters, it seems to me they do need you as soon as you can get here.

Even if you feel you want to see foreign places and have more experiences, even if battle is often man's greatest joy, even if you long for travel and the final victory in the Far East, do remember you and I are not alone. We are responsible for two other human beings.

Frankly I have an idea it might be rather selfish of you to go off again. It might be satisfying Bob and not the father. You have a lot to learn about your girls and a lot of work to do with them. I have done what I could. But there are vast and deeply important regions only you can fill for them. I do beg of you to give them your best as you have always given me.

Does this sound dramatic? I don't mean it that way. Thank you for not springing something on me in the dark. You used to do that and it was painful. I shall never like being excluded from any plans, even very nebulous ones.

FRIEDLOS, GERMANY 29 JULY '45

Several hundred of us—all 85 to 95 pointers—arrived late last night after 12 hours in trucks from Bremerhaven, joining many 29th Division men already hereabouts. Friedlos is a village near the town of Bebra which in turn is somewhat southeast of the city of Kassel in south-central Germany, and I'm now a member of Co. B, 272nd Infantry Regiment, 69th Division.

Our situation—that of the 69th—is odd. We have no duty but to wait. We're simply a holding unit for men waiting shipment home. Many high-pointers have already gone and more are scheduled to leave in quotas even before the 69th does. As for the 69th, it was originally scheduled to sail the first of the year. But dates have been revised and the best rumor now places ours at about Nov. 1st. Still other rumors I like to listen to move the date absurdly near, but whenever it is it promises good, far better than I ever hoped.

Leave-taking at K Co. was hard. Big party night before last. Liquor ration arrived opportunely just before supper—champagne and Scotch. The captain, France, Snipas, and I were there to consume it. Members of my old 2nd Platoon joined us—after I took them a bottle to be shared with me in their platoon C.P. Songs followed, then long stories about old days, then more songs, jokes on everybody, France was put to bed—which was itself very funny—then more songs; the 2nd Platoon boys left; and finally Captain R. and I were alone, walking beside the river under the stars arm-in-arm. We walked a long time, talking; then sat on a bench and watched the water flow by.

R. is not a man to use first names. I can count on my fingers the times he's called me "Bob." I never have addressed him as anything but "Captain." But there on the bench in the warm darkness I believe I came closer to him than to any other man. I told him about himself—all the things I've told you, and more. And he to me the same—what he held deepest in his thoughts about me, and you too—whom he feels a great person, having read some of your letters and listened to me talk. He said that once or twice in the Army he'd felt there were men who could do the job better than he and that I was one of those. Though it was the highest compliment I've ever received, I quickly disillusioned him.

I added what I believed: that there is a measure for each of us of happiness and sorrow, all things are never granted one man, I had the love of a woman as he did of many men. I dwelt upon this, told him how the men depended on him, loved him as a father, would follow him anywhere.

By then he was confessing to moments when he felt he'd let them down—the horrible night attack through a minefield on Hasenfeld Gut on the Roer, when the company was nearly wiped out—an entire platoon and an officer captured, 30 more killed, wounded or missing. He told me with sobs how he stood petrified among the mines in the dark, his men blowing up around him, heard Staff Sgt. Jordan who'd just had both legs blown off, calling from the darkness for the medics *not* to come to him. "Don't come to me! Leave me alone! There's mines all around me!"

"And I didn't have guts enough to go to him, Bob. I didn't have the guts—and he was only 20 feet from me, my own man calling to me!"

No need to tell you more about that night—two weeks before

I joined the company—but only that this man, whom I believe one of the great ones, after all he's done still feels himself lacking.

He wept when he spoke of his eight-year-old daughter. "I love her Bob. I love her. You know how I do."

Janie, I can give only a feeble outline of our conversation. We moved inside each other and spoke from the soul.

Afterwards he helped me pack, went to breakfast with me at five o'clock, and when I was on the truck with the others he shook my hand a last time—my captain. All my life I shall never have another. He's going to stay on here and make the Army his career.

I wait hungrily for the mail to be forwarded, which was misbehaving so before I left, and to see your red-and-blue envelopes and your stout scrawl reach me here as everywhere else on the earth's face except at home, where I should be.

SANTA BARBARA, AUGUST 5, 1945

I am SO, SO HAPPY! Today brings word you will sail for home between Nov. 1 and Jan. 1st.

When I opened your letter and read the wonderful words I felt a big lump of tears and laughter in my throat and couldn't quite make out what was happening to me! Then I called your mother and my mother and we all cried over the phone and Judy was the worst of the lot of us. She simply sobbed and sobbed. She is a great powerhouse of violent emotions: very sweet, very tender, very full of feeling. I really cannot know where to start to tell you what all this means.

It's wonderful, it's miraculous, it's heaven. Joan will be three years old in Nov. and Taffie not two yet, so you will see part of her young childhood. I'm already beginning to count the days. With this to look forward to, I shall not mind seeing the summer die.

I am so excited that nothing makes sense. I can't concentrate. I shouted to Joan that Daddy was coming soon and she said: "I'm going to hug him!"

Let's not have me try and rush to New York to meet you. I think it's better for the children's first meeting of you if we are here for your arrival. I suppose it will be dead of night! The trip East would be so awful in these bad traveling days and this other way you can get here as fast as possible and we would save the tremendous expense of my going. Let me know what you say to this. I suppose you will telephone when you land and we shall have a hard time saying anything at all!

You ask my opinion on your future movements in the Army. You probably will NOT be discharged until after Japan is done for, which most conservative people think will be by next sum-mer. That would give you only six months in this country in training camps and garrison life. Will you do that for me? I ask you from the heart and the head. I have thought out rather carefully the last months, since V-E Day, what I would say about your going into action again, unless the Army sends you there. I now think I can ask you not to volunteer for C.B.I. I do believe that you have done enough. I think you have given all you could and now the time is come to turn toward our two little ones. They need you terribly, as you will see. I need you, though my need is secondary and purely selfish. But I think that there is no need to risk your life again in this war.

I keep thinking of how Pop would beg you to stay out. Your parents are, naturally, ready to disown you if you venture into any more combat. I don't feel quite so violently. I want you to know, however, that I am asking you to stay in this country until you can come back to me as a civilian and be my husband in peace.

I cannot let you go again. I hope you do not feel bitterly disappointed. Naturally the final decision rests with you. I hope you will be able to honestly say that you have had enough of war, and not just for my sake. But haven't you done enough? If you were killed in the C.B.I. wouldn't it be worse for your little family?

I mean, there are men who have never risked anything sitting in this country, whose turn it is to strike off and fight a little too. The Army wants these men to go, and it is people like you they wish to have stay in this country and get ready to return to civilian life. I hope I am not crushing dreams of yours. You ask about a return to Germany. I hope you will not feel that is necessary either.

Now you know what I think about it all, please tell me your own ideas. I hope I do not appear a selfish woman fighting for her heart and her children. I AM fighting for the children, of course, and I am longing for you to be safe until the end. I was willing when you went over to give you to the war as far as I could, but now it would seem to be asking too much of our lucky star to tempt Fate any more.

It is seven o'clock on a heavenly August evening. The sun is warm in this golden valley between wooded hills. Contented sounds rise from the village below—most of them of the barnyard type—and come in my open window. Radios are playing and G.I.'s are out in the dirt street playing catch.

I've just walked over the hill behind the house, west, toward the sunset, as I've walked a good many times since being separated from you. This particular hill is striped gold and green with wheat and barley and clover and patches of potato plants and cabbages, cut by occasional grassy gullies lined with apple trees.

Part-way up I stopped and sat a while among some newly shocked-up oats, watching the sun go down and listening to the sound of the peasants at work not far away with scythes and wooden rakes and pitchforks. I hoped to see a deer venture out into the shadow at the edge of the woods that crown the hilltop. These woods are man-made, carefully cared for, of pine and fir and elm, and very dense along the crests of the hills. You see deer in them and the wrecks of the Wehrmacht's abandoned vehicles, propped up on logs, their wheels removed. And now and then along the valley roads, usually at a curve, you come upon a burned-out German tank, rolled over on its back like a big dead bug, and sometimes one of ours likewise. Not far from here, the spearheads of the First Army joined with those of the Third, last April.

My first few days have been pleasant enough, if somewhat tinged with homesickness for K Company. As you see, I've brought my German typewriter along—embarrassingly large as it made my bed-roll—and mean to bring it home. Can you really believe I might be home by Christmas? At least be in the States?

This division, though not this company, made the original link-up with the Russians on the Elbe, but you hear little about it. It's already ancient history.

Next Evening:

This afternoon we all went to a great gathering on an open hillside a few miles away—about 10,000 of us—to hear Jack Benny and some fellow entertainers crack jokes. Unfortunately Jack had a cold and couldn't appear but his second-in-command, Larry Adler, carried on. A blonder specimen called Martha Tilton sang—screeched, I should say—and joined with Adler in suggestive jokes. Then somebody appeared I really was glad to see. Ingrid Bergman. She's a beautiful lady and a hefty one, almost as tall as you. I inspected her through field glasses at two hundred yards and was quite smitten. She can't compete with Rita Hayworth or Betty Grable for the title of champion pin-up girl. But she has something else. Call it elegance and grace. She says she's going to appear on the stage soon in Maxwell Anderson's new play about Joan of Arc and told us some of Joan's story, enacting a scene or two as her narrative went along; and then, afterwards, felt obliged to show herself one of the girls by going through some clowning with Adler. Then good old Larry played the harmonica for us, which he should have been doing all along, for he's good at it—did the "Minuet in G," the "Hungarian Rhapsody," and finally the "St. Louis Blues."

On the hill behind us, scores of *fräuleins* and *fraus* with children, all in their Sunday best, were standing and I wondered what they thought of the St. Louis Blues.

Otherwise my days are uneventful. One hundred of our 143 men go to classes all morning: History, Business Arithmetic, Blueprint Reading, Business English, etc. The rest go through the motions of a drill schedule. My only duty at the moment is V.D. officer, which means I have charge of venereal disease control, investigate each new case, try and pick up the girl and send her to a hospital where she is examined—released if she has no V.D., cured if she has. And most of them have. As the boys say: "This is a clapped-up goddamn country"—among other things. Prostitution is the rule—the *fräuleins* having been so well indoctrinated on the subject by Hitler they don't seem able to get out of the habit. And with time hanging heavy on everybody's hands, the health of the men is a problem. So think of your modest husband careening around corners in a jeep after some elusive V.D. case.

Have I written about our 5th platoon, colored? Normally each infantry company has four platoons but in the 69th an experimental fifth platoon composed of Negroes who volunteered for combat has been added. Its noncoms, like all its enlisted men, are black; its officers white.[18] They are said to have performed very well in combat and for the most part are as fine a group of boys as I've ever seen. They keep their quarters clean, are not too bad about V.D., play on the company baseball team the same as anybody, and generally get along without friction. Maybe sharing combat has been a leveler here, too, eliminating racial prejudice as far as it ever can be.

SANTA BARBARA, AUGUST 6, 1945

I suddenly realize I haven't told you about my new college-girl helper, Carol. She is petite, brown haired, a little on the plump side but vivacious and attractive. She came day before yesterday. In return for board and room she gives me three hours of work a day, helps with breakfast and supper, washes dishes, helps with the children who adore her, which is a big plus. I can always leave them with her, and another grown-up in the house gives a sense of added security. It has been a bit lonely at times.

I hope you approve. There will be some slight extra cost, mainly for her meals, but I think she will be worth it. There's a good deal to do, managing a household with two small children as I think you will see when you come, and though I am strong as an ox this will allow me to be even stronger when you arrive.

Carol has the bedroom off the kitchen just through the bathroom from your study. She may still be here when you appear, but don't let that give you any ideas, young man, because I'll be watching your every move like a green-eyed hawk!

I love managing this house with its Victory Garden[19] full of vegetables and its fruit trees and flowers. I preside over them all for you, my darling, and that thought keeps my happiness renewed each day.

18. These platoons were among the Army's first moves toward racial integration, which became standard throughout the armed forces in 1948 when President Truman signed Executive Order 9981. The black volunteers of 1945 represent a remarkable and not entirely pleasant story. See Appendix.

19. Nearly every household had its wartime "victory garden" to increase food production and reduce food bills.

You can imagine the horror the news of the atomic bomb[20] gives me. Now I believe we may live to see the greatest event in history: the end of the world—unless humankind does far better than it has done. As I heard the news I thought how old-fashioned everything we are doing has become, our way of living, our sources of power, our transportation, our knowledge of other worlds besides this one; and how quaint this war we are fighting will soon seem. And if there is another war, it will very probably be the last one—because finally, after trying so long, mankind seems to have found the means of destroying itself.

This latter thought is continuously in the back of my mind, overshadowing the great news of Russia's entry against Japan— and the conviction the war will end within a month or sooner.

Now I believe we shall have to work harder, think clearer, live better than we ever dreamed we could, Prusse. Will you step with me over the threshold from one age into another?

The possibilities are as thrilling as they are frightening, aren't they? They might be used for tremendous good, mightn't they? What undreamed of things we shall see, shall we not? And what a far, far, different world—even a universe—our children will grow up in!

Interim of two hours to make an inspection of quarters. The 5th platoon (colored) was the best. They are an exceptionally fine lot of boys, intelligent, strong, all volunteers as I've mentioned, many of them taking a bust—that is, losing their ratings— to join the infantry and fight. Nothing but good is said of them in combat. One day near Leipzig when another platoon was pinned down at the base of a hill by enemy fire, the 5th attacked right over the white boys and took the hill in fifteen minutes.

One sergeant, who lives in Los Angeles, is trying to get a pass to England to marry an English girl. He's a fine, courteous person. He hopes to stay in England where prejudice against black skin is negligible.

I'm acting as company commander. Last night I talked three hours with a Catholic chaplain, a captain, 27, Brooklyn Irish, who comes from a large parish there and looks like anything but

---

20. Dropped on Hiroshima, Japan, on August 6.

a priest. He wears his helmet liner cocked on one side, comes slouching in and shoots the breeze with the boys, takes a drink and cigarette—and didn't impress me favorably at first. But after our talk I found his outward appearances were the disguises of his trade. He makes much sense, about how American history should be taught (with short 12-minute movies, the rest of the class discussion, as the Army has learned to do), about how political consciousness at home could be increased (by making the vote compulsory and by having short films, as above, drawn up by a committee composed from members of both sides in a controversial question, say the purchase of the local power company by the city—these films to *show* both sides and to be run in all theaters with the short subjects before the main feature), and so on.

Then we got onto religion—Protestants and Catholics, the dogma, Martin Luther, the Douay version of the Bible (the only one authorized for Catholics), St. Jerome's translation of the Vulgate. I have his address. Someday we might drop in on him in Brooklyn and see if he has a tree growing there.[21]

SANTA BARBARA, AUG. 11, 1945

My work at the hospital keeps me in touch with the reality which we must never forget. Today I talked for a long time with a man who'd been horribly burned in a blast of some sort. Almost his entire face was scar tissue. And from it his eyes looked out like the eyes of all the millions upon millions, Bobbie, who've seen and suffered the ravages of this war. Yet he was not bitter. Just subdued and so gallant! "Tell me about your husband," he said, and when I had waxed a little eloquent about you, he said: "Give him my regards!"

O, Bobbie, I wanted to cry. In those words were all the union, all the comradeship, all the pain and sorrow the world has been suffering through and we have had the privilege to know and share.

His name is Lindsay. He comes from near Des Moines, Iowa. I promised to talk to him again next week. He has two small children like ours and a farm which his parents look after. His wife died suddenly while he was overseas. When I think of such

21. Reference to a popular novel, *A Tree Grows in Brooklyn*, by Betty Smith.

Germany, 1945. "Fifth platoon" infantrymen, all volunteers, pose with their white officers after capturing twenty-four SS troops. (The Bettmann Archive)

things I can hardly bear them. But his spirit was so bright it gave me new courage and hope.

Keep my heart in yours, growing and strengthening and remembering always.

GERMANY, 12 AUG. 1945

I leave early tomorrow for Marseilles. The train trip promises to be tedious but every moment is tedious now progress homeward has begun. Still, if I do get to Marseilles, I'll be fortunate once more—to be in a region I like, perhaps with a chance to visit Avignon, Arles, and Nîmes, and sail home past Gibraltar—all something new and exciting.

You'll be wondering whether to meet me in New York and buying a train ticket already. Well, I'm not sure about

Jane's volunteer Red Cross work at Hoff Army General Hospital included much playing of cards or Ping-Pong and plenty of conversation with patients. (Santa Barbara Historical Society)

any of that but will let you know in plenty of time. What they'll probably do is whisk us off to some camp somewhere, and then some other camp, and then some other, till they decide what they want to do with first lieutenants of 89 points. But I daresay somewhere along that line there'll be time to stop and kiss my wife.

Boy-o-boy but I'm happy to be moving! Sitting still for five minutes is a terrible ordeal. Tomorrow can't come soon enough. And the thought of going south into the sun is a joy too. Goodbye to Germany—not that I dislike the country and people so greatly—but the war is over, the new day is here, and every step away from the military is just that much better. Perhaps the carbine I just turned in to the supply room is the last one I shall ever carry.

Know what I'm thinking? "There will soon be no war anywhere on the whole face of the earth!"

The last parade: Bielefeld, Germany, V-E Day, 1945. (Colonel Sidney V. Bingham)

SANTA BARBARA, VICTORY DAY,[22] AUGUST 14, 1945

How small words are tonight! The war is over—we can rejoice—soberly, gaily, madly, and still with thoughts of those who cannot come back. I keep thinking of Pop, but Mum seems fine and speaks only of the joy of victory. She has become a very gallant woman and makes people happy wherever she goes. I wonder where you are? If you were here tonight I think I'd be totally mad and sing and dance with you and drink too!

As it is, Renzo came by at 4 P.M. and brought me news of final victory and we drank Dubonnet and sherry together and talked of you and John coming back and of the new life ahead. It's all pretty incomprehensible still. Cars are going up and down State Street with horns blaring and the Mission bells are ringing. Carol, my college girl helper, and I are sitting in the study listening to the radio which is giving us news of peace being welcomed all over the world. I keep blinking my eyes trying to get used to a new meaning of life. War has threatened us ever since we met. Do you realize that? Can we love each other in peace? Oh, darling, can I give you my heart again? Can I give you my love and all my life anew? To live in peace with you! Our life is just beginning—do you realize that?

I get so excited when I think of all ahead that I'm good for nothing else. I've danced about with the children and done my best to explain the war is over. Joan keeps saying: "The war is over! Daddy's coming and he will sleep in Mumsie's bed!" Think of you meeting your daughters!

It's a lovely summer evening—and there is no war.

22. Also known as V-J Day for "Victory over Japan Day."

CHAPTER 10

They speak, I think, of perils past.
They speak, I think, of peace at last.
VACHEL LINDSAY

Epilogue

She's one of the new Victory Ships that are replacing the smaller slower Liberty Ships, workhorses for the Allies since early in the war. She's painted a dull military gray but to us boarding her the *Lewiston Victory* looks like a carnival ship ready to begin the most exciting cruise imaginable. Her captain, as if catching the spirit, announces he hopes to set a speed record by rushing us from Marseilles to New York in something under nine days. Instead his overdriven vessel breaks down in mid-Atlantic and we lose about twenty-four hours—which may be fortunate because it brings us into New York Harbor just as the rising sun strikes the Statue of Liberty. We crowd on deck with lumps in our throats and there are spontaneous cheers.

After being processed at Camp Shanks on the Hudson, I board a military DC-3 for Los Angeles. It's a paratroop plane with shallow buttock-shaped metal seats, hard as rock, extending along the interior on both sides. Its passengers range from private to colonel but distinctions of rank drop away as we fly back into a civilian world where all men are created equal. However, paratroop planes aren't designed for transcontinental flights and this one stops frequently for fuel or other reasons, taking twenty-three interminable hours to transport us from New Jersey to Southern California.

On November 8, 1945 as she finally wings in at six hundred feet over the San Bernardino orange groves toward March Field, her right-hand engine begins to cough, then suddenly goes dead. We look at each other and grin a bit apprehensively. After all that's happened, are we going to be made into orange crush on our home turf? As if in answer the engine roars back to life.

After a last night in barracks at Fort MacArthur at San Pedro where I was inducted into my military experience, I meet my mother and father at the gate. Like many of those moments anticipated for years, it suddenly takes on unexpected dimensions. My parents seem to have shrunk. They seem not to have changed their clothes. They seem almost like strangers. I love them. I know they love me. They've done everything they could for me—before I was married and afterward for Jane and me and the children. Yet I find myself resenting the fact they haven't undergone some marvelous transformation because of all that's happened to the world, to me.

As we drive north between hills and ocean, the route the Greyhound bus followed nearly four years ago taking me to basic training at Camp Roberts, we talk in what seem incredible banalities about the weather, about gasoline being plentiful again, about old friends and neighbors who sound like inhabitants of another world. Where are the words to express the horror, the glory, the destruction, the heroism, the suffering, the despair and hope, the miracle of survival, and the new world we should be talking about? They speak as if nothing has happened, as if everything will go on as before.

Deep inside I want to shout "No, no, it can't!"—to try and tell them all that has happened to me, to the world; but know that I cannot, that it is impossible and probably always will be. And deep down I know they're right. Nothing has changed. Life is made up of banalities and trivia, and the impossibility of uttering all that has happened.

Early rains have turned the hills as green as when I saw them last. There is the sea. There is the sky. People are going about their daily affairs. We pass a Greyhound bus. Nothing has changed. Yet it all seems to be saying so generously: "Here is another chance."

Tactfully my parents let me out on the corner and I walk alone the few steps to my front door.

Jane waits nervously. She knows I'm coming but not when—doesn't know H-hour. The girls are freshly dressed. The house is in order. But she feels strangely numb. The months, the years, have boiled down to this. The cliché greeting we've joked about crosses her mind: "Hello, how are you?" "Hello, how are you?" Suddenly Katherine has to go pee-pee. Just as she does, upstairs with Mum-Mum's help, the front door opens. Joan shouts from the top of the stairs: "It's Daddy!"

All three come pouring down into my arms. Then Jane and I cling to each other, just the two of us, laughing and crying, while our little girls gaze up in wonder. It is all over—and it's all beginning.

In Lampasas, Texas, our dream house materializes into a white cottage on a hill where the town ends and open range begins. We are looking for a place as far away as reasonably possible from loving but hovering parents as well as painful wartime associations, a new place deep in the American heartland where we can put down roots and rediscover each other, our children, our country, and our new identities as peacetime mates.

Lampasas has remained our dream place and as we come over the last rolling prairie and see the little town in its green hollow, we get the same thrill of homecoming we'd had during the war—that this is our place, the one we'd discovered and cherished, the one meant for us. But it almost didn't happen. We'd found the little house on the hill overlooking town by pure good fortune during an earlier reconnaissance. In 1946 housing was still virtually non-existent. There'd been almost no private residential construction during the war. But Uncle Charlie Wachendorfer, who knows everything and everybody in town, happens to remember that Roger Carpenter mentioned something about wanting to sell. We close with Roger for 6,500 for two bedrooms and bath, living room, kitchen with dining nook, garage attached, on 75 x 150 feet and a backyard that looks straight out into open range where horses and cattle graze.

On the July day we arrive with the children there are drawbacks. The thermometer is somewhere around a hundred and the humidity about the same, and the chiggers and cockleburs immediately manifest themselves on bare feet and ankles. Furthermore Bob has no job or prospects of one. We've simply cast our bread on the waters and hope luck will see us through, because we've chosen the place of our heart's desire. To tide us over financially are wartime savings plus rent from the Santa Barbara house. But things begin to look grim when the editor of the local weekly offers nothing in the way of jobs and the superintendent of schools does likewise. Bob has brought his saddle along thinking he may have to go back to cowboying. But before that happens he tries the oldtime country editor in the nearby hamlet of Lometa.

E. C. Lowe, grizzled, tobacco-chewing, inky-handed, has been publishing his weekly almost singlehandedly during wartime. Even now he needs help but can't afford it. Enter the G.I. Bill of Rights which we are to bless henceforward. Thanks to it

Bob gets a job with E. C. as apprentice printer-editor. It brings us $90 a month from the taxpayers of the United States, which we gratefully regard as part of their appreciation for Bob's wartime service. Commissions on advertising add another hundred. Before long Lowe's son Ward comes home from the Army and he and Bob and E. C. start a weekly in Lampasas, *The Dispatch*, with Bob as editor and Ward as business manager.

Meanwhile Jane is being introduced to the intricacies of local social life, including formal "coffees" at 10 A.M. where you arrive dressed as for afternoon tea, and evening occasions when women are expected to congregate on one side of the room and gossip while men talk business on the other side. Men rule the roost, often buying groceries and clothing with their wives in order to supervise the outlay of cash, their cash. Eyebrows are raised when Jane signs her own checks, almost the only woman in town to do so.

Our girls attend Mrs. Jackson's kindergarten, which she conducts warmly and ably in her home a few blocks down our unpaved street, and we all feel extremely happy, busy and fulfilled until the asthma strikes. Bob publishes stories in *Collier's*, *Holiday* and other magazines, and works on a historical novel about California. Jane housewifes, keeps her journal of family activities, and corresponds with friends and relatives in various parts of the world. We go partners with Jake Stiles in the cattle business, we buying two whitefaced cows and Jake and Allie keeping them at their place at Topsey in return for half the increase (half the calf crop), our share going to our frozen food locker as eventual table meat.

Asthma and allergies are the curses of Central Texas, at least they were for us. It's in the cedar—actually juniper—and ragweed belt and besides is the recipient of pollens that blow down across the Great Plains with every norther or up from the Gulf with every August-September rain or thunderstorm. Noses began to run, eyes to water, sinuses to ache, lungs to gasp for breath. When for the second time Rush McMillin, our doctor, makes a house call around 4:00 A.M. to give Joan a shot of adrenalin so she can breathe—she sitting up in bed between us and beginning to turn blue in the face as she gasps for air—we begin to think of changing our climate. Little was known of allergies in those days. Seventy miles east of us in Austin, the state capital, there were no allergists. The nearest was in San Angelo 150 miles away in West

Texas. Persistent sinus trouble nags at Jane's health, and when our 1947 baby Ellen finally becomes so debilitated by asthmatic croup that we take her to the hospital to be fed intravenously, we decide the time has come to think of leaving our beloved Lampasas, where life is making our dream house miserable.

In Tuscany that house becomes a golden brown *villino* on a farm in the Chianti region twenty minutes south of Florence. Bullet chips in the plaster near the front door testify that Allied troops passed this way not long ago en route to liberating Florence and Jane's old home at Villa Negli Ulivi from their German occupiers. Among U.S. forces involved was the 88th Infantry Division with which her father served and with which he'd hoped to free his beloved city and beloved home.

Jane drives our two older girls to town every weekday morning in our Fiat Jardinetta stationwagon, about as big as a large bug, drops Joan off at Miss Barry's American School where she herself once attended and Katherine at the English Kindergarten, then does errands or visits friends until noon when she picks up the girls and all come home for lunch at Villa Rosina. It has two stories, eight furnished rooms and costs us thirty dollars a month rent, plus the expense of coal for the furnace and wood for the hot water heater in the bathroom.

Bob spends mornings at his Royal Portable in the study off our dining room, while Maria, lovely daughter-in-law in the *contadini* family who live in the rooms below ours, takes charge of three-year-old Ellen, taking her along to feed chickens, cut grass for the rabbits, gather herbs to season the marvelous pastas she cooks us, or to watch her husband Metello plowing among the grapevines and olive trees behind a pair of huge white oxen. We participate in the *vendemmia* or grape harvest, and subsequent wine-making, and generally share the life of the *podere* with its wonderfully kindly and hardworking tenants. We swim in the pool at the Ugolino Country Club not far away and we two revisit the Villa Negli Ulivi which had been occupied by German SS troops, enjoy tea at Villa La Pietra across the lane with Arthur Acton and drinks at Doney's with John Horne Burns whose novel *The Gallery* remains near the top of World War II writing, in our view.

We seem to be fitting very agreeably into our new life when

asthma and allergies again raise their ugly heads. Joan and Ellen
are stricken and Joan hospitalized. The final blow is Jane's "unnatural pregnancy." We'd long wanted a fourth child. But not one
that was "upside down in the womb" as a leading Florentine
obstetrician informs us.

There are other adverse pressures. The Cold War is reaching
freezing temperature. The Korean War has broken out and there
is serious talk of the Russian Army advancing to the English
Channel, over a Western Europe where a rather thin line of U.S.
troops is the only significant barrier. General Eisenhower, not yet
president but very much a war hero and symbol of American
might, makes a highly publicized visit to London and Paris to
show we will resist any Russian advance in the west, such as the
Russian-backed North Koreans are making in the east.

Early in 1951 we arrive back in Santa Barbara where our
obstetrician pronounces Jane's baby quite normally positioned,
and Joan's and Ellen's asthmatic croup disappears as they breathe
mild sea-moist air.

Today our dream house is a little red farmhouse built in 1925 on
a hillside overlooking Santa Barbara, so nearly like the one we
dreamed of before we married—before we even met—as to be
almost uncanny. A horse stands most of the time under the oak
tree just west of the garage. Quail nest in the garden. Bob writes
every day. Jane keeps house and reads or listens to everything he
writes. She's a well-seasoned sounding board after nearly half a
century, and if it sounds good after bouncing off her, it is usually
right. We watch our diets, walk three to five miles daily, go to
bed early, subscribe to Thomas Mann's dictum: "Genius is ninety
percent a good night's sleep." Young people sometimes ask us
how we've managed to stay married so long. We say there's
no mystery about it. Chemistry helps. Shared interests help.
Commitment helps: if you go into it conditionally it probably
won't work; if you go in totally for better for worse, for richer for
poorer, in sickness or in health, it probably will work.

We're active in the environmental and other movements
and in working for peace as best we can, including support of a
strong military deterrent to war such as we lacked in '41. We've
gladly recanted our doubts about the United Nations and with
admiration support its diplomacy and peacekeeping. Bob from

With our four girls, 1972. Standing, right to left: Joan, Katherine, Ellen, Jane.

time to time has combined his writing with teaching, manual laboring, civil engineering and acting as writing consultant to the Port Hueneme Naval Civil Engineering Laboratory where engineers and scientists think more mathematically than grammatically. This is his fifteenth book, Jane's second.

We've had our blows. Katherine is dead, an early victim of the drugs that have plagued our country as, seemingly, a price of peace and affluence. But she left us two wonderful children. Jane's mother died in 1960, a victim of cancer. Bob's parents lived into their nineties, active and productive until almost the end. Jane's brother and sister too are gone. But Joan is alive and well, married, with two children and has just published her second book on birdwatching, having been fascinated by feathered creatures since she first identified them by name on the lawn at 317 Burlingame

Avenue in Los Angeles. Our postwar daughters Ellen and Jane
are thriving, Ellen with four children, Jane teaching in the Mon-
tessori School in Oakland. We have much to be thankful for.
But surrounding it all, embracing it all, is our gratitude for the
peace that has prevailed, however shakily, however incomplete,
for nearly half a century to this moment of 1990 and to the best
new hope in all our time that true worldwide harmony and
understanding can endure.

Hardly a day goes by that we don't think of the war. It killed
more people—about 50 million—caused more destruction, more
suffering, cost more money than any other event in human history. Its consequences for good and bad remain incalculable. But
we line up on the side of hope. Especially when we talk with our
daughters, our grandchildren or other young people, or when we
think of those—Jane's father and millions of others—who gave
their lives or maimed bodies. Thanks largely to them we have
what we have, are what we are, hope as we hope.

Consider this. Anyone who'd predicted on the day after
Pearl Harbor that the United States and Japan would someday be
friends and allies would have been thought a candidate for the
nuthouse or been reported to the F.B.I.; and anyone who'd predicted on V-E Day that Germany and France, Italy and England
would someday be military allies and trading partners in a common market and planning a federation of European states would
have been laughed at; as would anyone crazy enough to say
India would be a viable democracy and Africa a noncolonial
continent—or that from being among the most persecuted people
on earth Jews would become among the most respected, or that
a black would be elected governor of Virginia. And who would
have predicted just a few months ago that the U.S. and Russia
would be working together for reduced armaments and world
peace, and the restructuring of the Soviet Union along democratic and free-market lines? Or that Nicaragua would freely
and fairly elect a democratic government? Or that—making our
World War II V-for-victory signs with their upraised fingers—
Chinese students would demonstrate in Tian An Men Square to
all today's world that human freedom is as precious as life itself
and then pay for that belief with their blood and their lives?

Beyond today's Mideast confrontations caused by Iraq's sei-
zure of Kuwait and the U.S. and United Nations response to it,

lies a promised land of marvelous possibilities. The way there may be hard. But harder than where we've been?

Not when you remember that miracles can happen; dreams, even fabulous ones, can come true; and that we humans can make a positive difference if we will.

October 1990

Appendix
The Black Volunteers

The "integrated volunteers," as the pioneer black infantrymen serving with white divisions on the Western Front were called, began assembling at Noyon near Paris in early January 1945, for a refresher course in infantry tactics.

They'd come from noncombat rear-area units in response to an invitation issued by the Supreme Allied Commander in Europe, General Dwight D. Eisenhower. Eisenhower's statement read in part: "It is planned to assign you without regard to color or race to the units where assistance is most needed, and give you the opportunity of fighting shoulder to shoulder to bring about victory. Your comrades at the front are anxious to share the glory of victory with you."

Eisenhower's invitation was caused by a shortage of infantrymen in the fall of 1944 as result of mounting casualties and was accentuated by the Battle of the Bulge beginning in December. Not only black but white volunteers were called for and many of both races responded.

Thus the black volunteers exchanged the safety of noncombat assignments for the risks of frontline experience, many of them taking reduction in rank and pay to do so, since private first class was the highest rank offered them. Their motives were mixed. Some were moved by simple patriotism. Some were looking for excitement. Some wanted to escape current situations. Some heard about the "bad time Americans were having in the Battle of the Bulge and wanted to help out." Some hoped combat would offer an opportunity to prove themselves and their race in their own eyes and the world's and help reduce racial prejudice in their native land and elsewhere. Some were also motivated by Hitler's often declared belief that the "Aryan race" was superior to all others and by his hatred of blacks. In all nearly 5,000 volunteered, according to official figures (one independent source puts the figure nearer 30,000), but only 2,800 were accepted.

By early March they were joining eleven divisions in the 1st and 7th Armies and soon were in action, usually with rifle companies as "fifth" or additional platoons, invariably with a white platoon commander and usually a white platoon sergeant. Sometimes they were designated as "J" platoons, there being no "J" company in infantry tables of organization.

Though I didn't experience combat with them, white officers and enlisted men who did expressed admiration and respect to me for the way they performed. "They took no prisoners," Lynn Johnson, formerly of F Company, 272nd Regiment, 69th Infantry Division says. "They were tough." His comment is typical of what I heard in 1945 and hear today. But when whites and blacks first mingled there was some friction. "Some of our white boys made the mistake of picking on a black volunteer," Johnson says. "After he won both fights, there was no more trouble. And this was especially true after we got into combat and the boys of both colors fought and bled side by side."

There was considerable bleeding. The black platoon of Company K of the 69th's 271st Regiment suffered nearly one-third casualties in the battle for Leipzig, remembers Wilfred Strange, one of its sergeants and squad leaders, now a successful Washington, D.C., businessman. Other accounts confirm his. After the war was over in Europe a survey conducted by Eisenhower's headquarters of white officers and platoon sergeants of black platoons revealed that 80 percent of those interviewed thought blacks had performed very well in combat. Nearly as many saw no reason why black infantrymen should not perform as well as white if they had the same training and experience. Most reported getting along very well with black volunteers—the harder the fighting, the closer the bonding.

A number of white enlisted men were similarly queried and gave similar responses, most admitting they at first disliked the idea of soldiering with blacks, and most declaring their mistrust had turned to trust and friendship after shared combat experience.

But the official survey was discounted by high authority, including Generals Bradley and Marshall, as dealing with an atypical or elite sample composed entirely of volunteers who scored higher than average on the Army General Classification

Test and were in other ways more highly motivated than the average black soldier. Though both Marshall and Bradley thought the possibility of integrating black units into white units should be followed up, the survey was not made public. No blacks were interviewed during the survey.

For these and other reasons some bitterness developed among black volunteers. Some resented the fact that though Eisenhower's invitation indicated they would be integrated as individuals in the same units as whites, they were segregated into separate platoons. Some resented the fact that while much was made of the 69th Division being the first American unit to link up with the advancing Russians, no mention was made of its black members. Some volunteers felt discriminated against when some regimental and division histories made no mention of them and did not print photographs of them. Some felt discriminated against when, soon after the war was over, they were ordered to return to the rear-area units from which they'd come. They wanted to remain with the units they'd fought with and come home proudly as members of combat divisions. Protests and outright resistance to this order seem to have resulted in some cases.

Some white G.I.'s supported these protests. "If they were good enough to fight with us, they're good enough to come home with us." In some cases volunteers remained with their divisions and did come home with them. Yet even today some of their white comrades-in-arms are still indignant about the unfair way they were treated. The full story of what happened to the volunteers during and after the war remains to be told and needs telling. You can look in vain for mention of them in most books about World War II and most newspapers and magazines of the time.

On the whole I sense a feeling of pride among those I talk with today as I did in Germany in 1945—pride in having served themselves, their race and nation, and the cause of freedom well despite difficulties, unfairness, despite risk and cost—in a process, however incomplete, of liberty and justice for all. I find their general lack of bitterness as moving as the example they set by their wartime conduct.

Some like Robert Matthews made the army their career. Some like Wilfred Strange made their mark in civilian life. Some became lawyers, doctors, ministers. One is a judge. A number share membership in veterans organizations with white ex-G.I.'s.

The black volunteers were the army's second step toward

full integration. The first was the integration of officer candidate schools which I experienced in 1942 in the person of Mr. Daniels in our class at Camp Hood. Both steps contributed to the culminating third one of 1948, President Truman's integration of all the armed services.

For further information see Morris J. MacGregor, Jr., *Integration of the Armed Forces: 1940–1965*; *The Employment of Negro Troops* by Ulysses Lee in *The United States Army in World War II* series; and Professor Jerome H. Long's ongoing studies at Wesleyan University, Middletown, Connecticut, aimed at telling the full story of the black volunteers of 1944–45.

Acknowledgments

Our first acknowledgments go to the men and women of World War II, home front and war front, in uniform or out, in many lands, whose experience we directly or indirectly shared. We especially salute members of the 825th Tank Destroyer Battalion, 29th Infantry Division, and 69th Infantry Division with whom we were closely associated—likewise the "war widows" of Santa Barbara who with other friends helped sustain Jane through trying times with absent mates, and also the Red Cross volunteers, staff and patients at Hoff Army General Hospital, Santa Barbara. All of you helped make our book possible.

For help in writing and production we are especially indebted to Sandra Dijkstra, Anne and Shelly Lowenkopf, Mary Dresser, Alice and George Kladnik, Mariette Risley, Noel Young, Joe and Chuck Saveriano; also Dr. Christopher R. Gabel of the Combat Studies Institute, U.S. Army Command and General Staff College; Dr. Theodore A. Watson, U.S. Army Center of Military History, Washington, D.C.; Paul C. Winters, national adjutant of the 29th Division Association; Joseph H. Ewing, division historian; Col. Sidney V. Bingham, commander of the 116th Infantry Regiment 1944–45; former 69th Infantry Division members Crandon F. Clark, Carl Christol, Lynn C. Johnson, Robert C. Matthews, Wilfred Strange; Clarence Marshall, president, and Robert J. Kurtzman, Sr., treasurer of the Fighting 69th Infantry Association; also Walter Jones of the National Association for Black Veterans.

Also Morris J. MacGregor, Jr., chief historian of the U.S. Army Center of Military History; Professor Jerome H. Long of Wesleyan University, Middletown, Connecticut; David F. Myrick and Michael Redmon of the Santa Barbara Historical Society; Mark Hall-Patton, director, the San Luis Obispo County, California, Historical Museum; Msg. Albert E. Davis, Installation Historian, Camp Roberts, California; Toru Miyoshi, chair of the Santa Barbara County Board of Supervisors; Bill Richardson, Margot Collin, and the reference staff at the Santa Barbara Public Library.

Also J. H. Trimble of the National Archives Still Pictures Division; Marcia Lein of Wide World Photos; Reid Rossman of The Bettmann Archive; Debra Cohen of Life Picture Service; and Wayne McCall and Bill Dewey of Santa Barbara and Richard Gardner of The Battery Press, Nashville, for their help with photographs.

For help in refreshing our memories and for background material for footnotes and interpolations we are indebted to the files of the *Santa Barbara News-Press, Los Angeles Times, San Francisco Chronicle,* and *New York Times*; to Dwight D. Eisenhower's *Crusade in Europe*; Winston S. Churchill's six-volume history of the Second World War, especially *Closing the Ring* and *Triumph and Tragedy*; Peter Elstob's *Hitler's Last Offensive*; John S. D. Eisenhower's *The Bitter Woods*; David Eisenhower's *Eisenhower: At War, 1943–1945*; William Manchester's *American Caesar: Douglas MacArthur, 1880–1964*; Ronald H. Spector's *Eagle Against the Sun: The American War With Japan*; and *World War II* by the editors of Time-Life Books.

Also *The Simon and Schuster Encyclopedia of World War II* edited by Thomas Parrish; Joseph H. Ewing's history of the 29th Infantry Division, *29 Let's Go!*; *Conquer: The Story of the Ninth Army; Highway: A History of the 825th Tank Destroyer Battalion* edited by Michael J. Sheridan; *The Blue Devils in Italy: A History of the 88th Infantry Division in World War II* by John P. Delaney; Bert D. Webber's *Silent Siege—II: Japanese Attacks on North America in World War II*; Christopher R. Gabel's *Seek, Strike and Destroy: U.S. Army Tank Destroyer Doctrine in World War II*; Warren Olney III's *Law Enforcement in the Earl Warren Era* published by the Bancroft Library, University of California, Berkeley; Dr. Frederick G. Novy III's research into the sinking of the *Montebello* and other vessels off the Pacific Coast by Japanese submarines; and Jürgen Rohwer's *Die U-Boot-Erfolge Der Achsenmächte: 1939–1945* which lists such sinkings.

The quotation at the beginning of chapter 2 is from Franklin D. Roosevelt's Message to Congress, December 8, 1941. The quotation at the beginning of chapter 3 is from Marion Hargrove's popular wartime book, *See Here, Private Hargrove*. The quotation at the beginning of chapter 5 is from Nancy Shea's *The Army Wife*, 1942. The quotation at the beginning of chapter 6 is from George Washington's First Annual Address to Congress, January 8, 1790. The quotation at the beginning of chapter 8 is from Bill

Mauldin's book, *Up Front*, 1944. The quotation from Douglas
MacArthur at the beginning of chapter 9 is from his statement
to Secretary of War Henry L. Stimson quoted in William Manchester's *American Caesar: Douglas MacArthur 1880–1964*. The
quotation from Vachel Lindsay at the beginning of chapter 10 is
from *The Chinese Nightingale*, 1917.

To the unidentified U.S. Marine combat pilot whose diary
fragment appears on pages 146–147 we are deeply grateful. Please
let us hear from you if you read this.

Very special gratitude goes to Sandy and Jim McDonald
for their untiring support during seven years of work. Special
appreciation also goes to wartime friends Bob and Irene Darville,
Renzo Fenci, and Elmer C. Reagor.

Finally the help of John Drayton, Sarah Nestor, Suzanne
Harrell, Beverly Todd, and Patsy Willcox of the University of
Oklahoma Press has been invaluable.

To all these and all others who helped make our book
possible with their experiences, sacrifices, friendship, love, good
work, we say thank you.

—R. E. and J. E.

Index

Designations RE and JE refer to Robert O. Easton and Jane Faust Easton, respectively.